Interpersonal Foundations
of Psychopathology

Interpersonal Foundations of Psychopathology

Leonard M. Horowitz

American Psychological Association
Washington, DC

Published by
American Psychological Association
750 First Street, NE
Washington, DC 20002
www.apa.org

To order
APA Order Department
P.O. Box 92984
Washington, DC 20090-2984
Tel: (800) 374-2721; Direct: (202) 336-5510
Fax: (202) 336-5502; TDD/TTY: (202) 336-6123
On-line: www.apa.org/books/
E-mail: order@apa.org

In the U.K., Europe, Africa, and the Middle East, copies may be ordered from
American Psychological Association
3 Henrietta Street
Covent Garden, London
WC2E 8LU England

Typeset in Century Schoolbook by Stephen McDougal, Mechanicsville, MD

Printer: United Book Press, Inc., Baltimore, MD
Cover Designer: Aqueous Studio, Arlington, VA
Technical/Production Editor: Casey Ann Reever

The opinions and statements published are the responsibility of the authors, and such opinions and statements do not necessarily represent the policies of the American Psychological Association.

Library of Congress Cataloging-in-Publication Data

Horowitz, Leonard M.
Interpersonal foundations of psychopathology / Leonard M. Horowitz
    p. cm.
  Includes bibliographical references and index.
  ISBN 1-59147-081-1 (hardcover : alk. paper)
  1. Psychology, Pathological. 2. Interpersonal relations. I. Title.

RC454.H675 2003
616.89'071—dc22   2003021876

British Library Cataloguing-in-Publication Data
A CIP record is available from the British Library.

Printed in the United States of America
First Edition

For Sue, Jeremy, Jon, Suzy, Hailey, and Heidi—with love.

Contents

Acknowledgments

This book has evolved over a period of years with input from many sources. I am fortunate to have had so many talented friends and professional associates who have contributed to my thinking about psychopathology. Because of space limitations, I cannot thank everyone individually, but I would like to express my gratitude to all.

My current views of psychopathology were first shaped during my three-year postdoctoral clinical training at the Mt. Zion Psychiatric Clinic in San Francisco, an exemplary training program that was still in its golden age at the time of my training. The impressive staff at Mt. Zion possessed a wealth of experience, knowledge, intellectual acumen, interpersonal sensitivity, and, equally important, rich internal norms about indicators and consequences of psychological difficulties. I am particularly grateful to Harold Sampson, an outstanding clinical mentor whose intellectual astuteness, capacity for empathy, and remarkable clinical insight contributed greatly to my development as a clinical psychologist. I have also been privileged to work with many intelligent, deserving, and thoughtfully self-reflective patients, both at Mt. Zion and in my subsequent private practice, and I am beholden to them for all that I have gained from our mutual contact.

In addition, I have been blessed at Stanford University with a truly gifted group of graduate students and postdoctoral fellows. I would like to acknowledge just a few from the recent past whose contributions to my thinking have helped shape the contents of this book: Kim Bartholomew, Edward Bein, Emily Butler, Louis Castonguay, Michael Constantino, Christopher Dryer, Rita French, Mikkel Hansen, Kenneth Locke, Bertram Malle, Kristin Nelson, Eric Person, Nicole Shechtman, Donna Shestowsky, Deborah Tatar, Bulent Turan, John Vitkus, David Weckler, Kelly Wilson, and Pavel Zolotsev. I have treasured our many thought-provoking and gratifying discussions together. I am also grateful to other friends and colleagues who have enriched my thinking about interpersonal issues. I especially thank Lynne Henderson, Hans Kordy, Lester Luborsky, Albert Marston, Joel Meresman, Saul Rosenberg, Ellen Siegelman, Jan Smedslund, Bernhard Strauss, Hans Strupp, and Neil Young for their responsiveness to ideas over the years and their useful insights and critiques.

I would also like to acknowledge two professional societies that provided forums in which the views expressed in this book have found a critical, yet discerningly receptive audience. The Society for Interpersonal Theory and Research has been a wonderful catalyst to my thinking about interpersonal processes. I am especially grateful to Lynn Alden, Michael Gurtman, Kenneth Locke, Aaron Pincus, Stephen Strack, and Jerry Wiggins for their generous support, sharing of ideas and data, and constructive feedback. I am grateful to the many members of the Society for Psychotherapy Research (SPR), with whom I have had engaging and fruitful discussions over the years concerning interpersonal issues related to psychopathology. I have always been impressed by SPR's combination of tough-minded thoughtfulness and limitless humanity.

Finally, my single greatest debt is to my wife, Suzanne L. Horowitz, for her very wise and intelligent suggestions, insights, and solid contributions to this book. She has been lovingly supportive and infinitely patient in the face of endless repetition, revision, and rampant flights of fancy. She has been a consistently gentle but firm critic, with very impressive knowledge, clinical skills, and good sense. To her I convey my deepest gratitude with love, esteem, and admiration.

Interpersonal Foundations
of Psychopathology

1

Introduction to the Interpersonal Approach

Interpersonal communications can be very powerful. The message one person conveys to another, whether verbal or nonverbal, may gratify a salient motive, causing joy; it may frustrate that motive, causing distress. It may rouse a person to action, or it may de-energize that person. It may draw people closer, or it may alienate them from one another.

This book examines the proposition that psychopathology is often related to interpersonal processes. It applies principles of interpersonal psychology to the phenomena of psychopathology. An interpersonal approach poses characteristic questions. What do people seek when they interact with one another? How can these goals be systematized? How are interpersonal goals related to the person's self-image, and how does self-image affect interpersonal interactions? How do symptoms of psychopathology emerge from the interplay of self-image, interpersonal goals, and interpersonal interactions? Research on interpersonal processes has proliferated in recent years, and this book was written to systematize that knowledge in relation to psychopathology.

Of all the theoretical approaches to psychopathology, the interpersonal approach is probably the one that is most compatible with all of the others. First, like the biological approach, it assumes that innate differences in an infant's temperament can cause differences in interpersonal interactions. For example, infants who are temperamentally irritable are difficult to soothe, and, as we report later, parents treat hard-to-soothe infants differently from easy-to-soothe infants. As a result, innate differences in temperament are sometimes magnified by interpersonal processes.

Second, like the cognitive–behavioral approach, the interpersonal approach emphasizes the role of cognitions in interpersonal interactions. As we show, an aggressive schoolboy may perceive a peer's accidental act as intentional. Because of such cognitions, the child may strike back in situations that another child would ignore as accidental. As a result, the child may acquire a reputation for aggression, and this reputation may in turn have further interpersonal consequences.

Third, the interpersonal approach, like the humanistic approach, emphasizes the self, dyadic relationships, communication, empathy, and social support. All of these topics are prominent throughout this book.

Finally, the interpersonal, like the psychodynamic approach, emphasizes motivation and motivational conflict. Many questions that we pose are questions of motivation. What do people want from dyadic interactions? Are they trying to avoid isolation by connecting with other people? Are they seeking autonomy, trying to separate, display competence, or establish a clear identity? What motivates a person to have a temper tantrum, tell lies, or disagree for the sake of disagreeing? Is the person seeking autonomy or self-definition, or is the person seeking contact, connection, or caretaking? When a child is oppositional, is that child trying to separate from adults or trying to connect with them? Or both? These and many other questions of motivation are examined in this book.

Because it harmonizes with other theoretical approaches, the interpersonal approach is integrative: It draws from the wisdom of other approaches to systematize our understanding of psychopathology (Pincus & Ansell, 2003). Contemporary trends in clinical psychology tend to overemphasize the biological and the cognitive–behavioral, so the interpersonal approach may help restore a more balanced weighting of theoretical mechanisms.

The book is divided into six parts. Part I (chaps. 2–5) delineates the basic principles of an interpersonal approach. Chapter 2 considers the interpersonal motive as an explanatory concept and examines the role of interpersonal motives in an interpersonal approach. Interpersonal motives, broadly speaking, seem to fall into two abstract categories, *communion* and *agency*, which subsume narrower categories of motivation. Communion includes motives for intimacy, friendship, and group belonging (among others). Agency includes, among others, motives for autonomy, control, and self-definition. These narrower categories, in turn, subsume even narrower categories. In other words, motives are conceptualized hierarchically from the broad and abstract to the narrow and specific. As we show, the meaning of a symptom like self-starvation or suicidal behavior is often unclear until we can describe the higher order motive behind that behavior. In other words, the very same symptom may have a different meaning for two people in distress, and we may be unable to treat a disorder unless we understand its meaning to the person receiving treatment.

Communal and agentic motives make their first appearance in infancy with the phenomena of attachment and separation–individuation. In chapter 3 we systematically examine the relevant concepts, empirical findings, deviations from the norm, consequences for a child's "working models" of the self and others, and possible links to psychopathology.

Chapter 4 summarizes evidence that communal and agentic motives help clarify interpersonal behaviors during adulthood. It shows that interpersonal behaviors may be organized around two underlying dimensions (or themes) that correspond to communion and agency. The meaning of an interpersonal behavior can be represented graphically in two dimensions. Thus, the graphical representation tells what the person is trying to achieve. An interpersonal behavior may be largely communal, largely agentic, or a combination of the two. A behavior would be ambiguous if its graphical location were unclear. When the location is understood, however, we can describe what the person desires from others as well as reactions that would frustrate the person's motive and cause distress. Chapter 4 provides examples of the process from everyday life and from psychopathology.

A person's self-image helps explain why certain motives are so salient for that person, and chapter 5 examines the self-image as a construct. Dependent people, for example, regard themselves as helpless, so they are strongly motivated to seek a connection (communion) with potential caretakers. Narcissistic people seem to fear that they are ordinary, so they are strongly motivated to be admired in order to dispel that fear. People sometimes perform interpersonal tests to dispel negative hypotheses about themselves. In this way, the person's self-image helps clarify the motive behind some types of interpersonal interaction.

In part II (chaps. 6 and 7), we apply the principles of part I to four personality disorders. (Later we examine the other personality disorders.) Most personality disorders are associated with a salient interpersonal motive that is easily threatened or frustrated. Thus, the dependent personality disorder is attributed to the person's fear of being helplessly alone, hence the intense desire to be in a relationship with a caretaker. The paranoid personality disorder is attributed to the person's intense desire to avoid humiliation.

In the course of the book we examine all 10 personality disorders that are currently recognized in the *Diagnostic and Statistical Manual of Mental Disorders* (4th ed.; *DSM–IV–TR*; American Psychiatric Association, 2000). We develop the hypothesis that the diagnostic criteria of most personality disorders contain four kinds of information: (a) a motive that has become very salient; (b) typical strategies the person uses to satisfy that motive (e.g., being dramatic or theatrical to attract attention); (c) negative emotional reactions when the motive is frustrated (e.g., rage after feeling abandoned); and (d) ways in which the person copes with this negative affect (e.g., suicidal gestures).

In part III (chaps. 8 and 9), we consider the interpersonal foundations of syndromes. A syndrome is ambiguous if the interpersonal motive behind it is unclear. A woman with anorexia nervosa, for example, may starve herself because she desires nurturance (a communal motive) or because she wishes to affirm mastery, self-control, and self-discipline (an agentic motive). The syndromes highlighted in chapters 8 and 9 illustrate this kind of ambiguity.

The psychopathologies described in part III of the book have been selected because they illustrate the principles described in part I. Some disorders, like anorexia nervosa (chap. 9), primarily arise from interpersonal processes. Other disorders, like panic disorder with agoraphobia, seem to arise from either a biological (e.g., endocrine) or an interpersonal event; but once activated, the syndrome may have interpersonal consequences that further aggravate the disorder. The same is true for depressive disorders. A third group of disorders, like the obsessive–compulsive disorder, exhibit syndromes often considered to be purely biological events. As shown in chapter 9, however, interpersonal mechanisms can play an especially important role in certain forms of this disorder.

In part IV (chaps. 10–12) we consider disorders that involve an identity disturbance with interpersonal consequences. A particular type of identity disturbance seems to be relevant to certain personality disorders and to certain syndromes. For example, the diffuse identity associated with a histrionic personality disorder is evident among people with a conversion disorder. The two disorders need not co-occur—indeed, each has its own particular set of criteria—but without a diffuse identity, each disorder would seem unlikely. Chapters 10–12 all examine personality disorders and Axis I disorders that seem to involve a particular type of identity disturbance.

Finally, in part V (chap. 13) we summarize the major themes of the book. One theme, for example, suggests that psychopathology arises from an interaction of factors. Throughout the book, we assume that a child's temperament (biological predisposition) interacts with interpersonal experiences to produce a vulnerability to psychopathology. That is, vulnerabilities arise from a particular combination of nature and nurture. Adverse interpersonal experiences have an especially severe impact on a biologically sensitive child. In addition, we assume that the resulting vulnerability interacts with situational factors to produce psychopathology. For example, certain people, because of their unique combination of nature and nurture, are especially vulnerable to interpersonal loss; and under certain kinds of major stress (e.g., an impending death, a threatened divorce), they succumb to certain forms of psychopathology. These themes are developed throughout the book and brought together in the final chapter.

In brief, then, this book attempts to systematize an interpersonal approach to psychopathology. I hope that professional psychologists in clinical, abnormal, personality, and social psychology will find the conceptualization compelling, useful, and intellectually gratifying. I have also tried to organize and systematize the content with sufficient clarity that students who are being trained for careers in academic and clinical professions will find the approach helpful and rewarding.

Part I

Foundations of an Interpersonal Approach

2

Interpersonal Motive as an Explanatory Construct

This chapter concerns interpersonal motives, their hierarchical organization, and their relevance to psychopathology. First we consider the interpersonal motive as an explanatory construct. Then we examine anorexia nervosa and show how a syndrome remains ambiguous so long as we do not understand the person's motives. We also examine ontological insecurity and show how a conflict between communal and agentic motives can paralyze a person with severe psychopathology. After that, we consider the presenting complaint of a person who telephoned a suicide prevention center to help us understand the person's distress. We identify facets of the person's complaint and expose the interpersonal motive that apparently caused the problem. Finally, we show how the interpersonal approach supplements information provided by the diagnostic categories of the *Diagnostic and Statistical Manual of Mental Disorders* (4th ed.; *DSM–IV–TR*; American Psychiatric Association, 2000).

Interpersonal Motives as an Explanatory Construct

Motives comprise only one of several kinds of explanation for a behavior. Sometimes we prefer to ascribe a behavior to a physiological cause. For example, at times we would ascribe a panic attack to a thyroid malfunction. Aristotle systematically described four common types of causal explanation. In order to place the motivational explanation in a broader context, we first review Aristotle's classification.

Aristotle's Four Types of Causal Explanation

Aristotle identified four kinds of explanations that people commonly use to explain natural phenomena (Cameron & Rychlak, 1985). The first type is rarely used to explain psychological phenomena, but the other three are all familiar to psychologists, especially the fourth, which is the one that is most pertinent to an interpersonal approach. As Aristotle noted, one explanation does not preclude others; together, they enrich our understanding of the phenomenon.

Aristotle called the first type a *material* cause; it explains a phenomenon in terms of the substance out of which the phenomenon is made (Aristotle, 1952, pp. 267–277). For example, we say that water is "caused" by the chemical combination of two hydrogen atoms and one oxygen atom. Early in the history of psychology, structuralists like Wilhelm Wundt tried to explain complex mental experiences by analyzing them into basic sensations and other simple elements.

A second type of cause was Aristotle's *efficient* cause. (The word *efficient* is related to the word *effect* as in *cause and effect*.) Explanations of this type identify antecedent forces that produce the observed phenomenon, the "effect" of the antecedent forces. A visual sensation, for example, is caused by a photochemical reaction in the retina, which then sets off a chain of events in the nervous system. Behavioral theories of learning postulate that environmental stimuli (antecedent events) are the cause (efficient cause) of pathological behavior like phobic reactions.

A third type was Aristotle's *formal* cause, which explains a phenomenon in terms of an underlying form, pattern, plan, shape, or blueprint by which the phenomenon is organized. If we present a list of associated words for people to recall (*bed, rest, awake, tired, dream, night, deep, comfort, sound, slumber, snore, pillow*), many people, in recalling the words, incorrectly include the word *sleep*. Sleep is "recalled" only because it is part of the pattern or schema that the list had activated. Similarly, when an event activates depression in someone (e.g., a woman's husband dies), her depression may include characteristics (e.g., loss of self-esteem) that are not directly induced by her husband's death; these characteristics seem to occur as part of an underlying pattern of associated characteristics.

The fourth (and for us, the most important) type of cause was Aristotle's *final* cause. (The word *final* is related to the word *end*, as in *the means to an end*. A final cause explains a phenomenon in terms of the actor's intention, motive, or purpose. When we say that a histrionic woman wears dramatic clothing because she wants to draw attention to herself, we are ascribing the woman's behavior to her own motivation. Final-cause explanations are also called *teleological explanations*. (*Telos* in Greek means "end.")

These four types of causes are not mutually exclusive. In fact, Aristotle assumed that the more causes one could cite to explain a phenomenon, the richer the explanation. We, too, shall use different types of explanations on different occasions. However, a final-cause (motivational) explanation is very prominent in an interpersonal approach. Like the psychoanalytic theory, which draws heavily on final-cause explanations, the interpersonal approach often explains phenomena by emphasizing the interplay of motives within a given person. Biologists, in contrast, generally emphasize material-cause and efficient-cause explanations (Cameron & Rychlak, 1985; Rychlak, 1977). The major theories of learning, like those of J. B. Watson (1919) and B. F. Skinner (1938), also tend to de-emphasize motivation in their account of human nature. However, an interpersonal approach to psychopathology often asks what the person is trying to achieve or what frustrated motive the person is trying to satisfy.

Theories that rely on material-cause and efficient-cause explanations are said to adopt the perspective of a third-party observer: "Why did he do X? Because Stimulus S struck the actor, and Response X followed" (an efficient cause explanation). In contrast, theories that emphasize motivation adopt a first-person account of the actor: "Why did he do Y? Because the actor wanted to achieve goal G" (final-cause explanation). A typical cognitive–behavioral account does not describe a person's intentions or goals: "Automatic thoughts kept coming to mind, causing his depression (efficient cause); then, the techniques of cognitive therapy were used to replace those automatic thoughts with other thoughts."

Motivational approaches have a long tradition in the field of personality. Contemporary approaches date back to H. A. Murray (1938), F. Allport (1937), and G. W. Allport (1937). A number of writers, beginning with F. Allport (1937), suggested that to understand the individual's personality, we must understand the individual's motives—what the person is trying to do . The term *motive* refers to a broad cluster of goals, desires, or needs that affect the person's well-being. A motive may be conscious or unconscious. When the motive is satisfied, the person experiences positive affect; when it is frustrated, the person experiences negative affect (Emmons, 1989; McAdams, 1988; McClelland, 1985).

Hierarchical Organization of Motives

As already noted, motivational constructs vary in their breadth or level of abstraction. A broad desire, like a desire for intimacy or a desire to belong to a group, is more abstract than a narrow desire, like a desire to spend time with a romantic partner. The latter desire, in turn, is more abstract than a still narrower desire, like a desire to date a particular individual. These levels of abstraction may be conceptualized hierarchically (Emmons, 1989). That is, a desire for intimacy constitutes a superordinate (more abstract) category, which subsumes narrower categories; and those categories each subsume still narrower categories. The term *motive* usually designates a high level of abstraction (e.g., desire for autonomy), whereas the term *goal* usually designates a narrower, more specific category. This way of conceptualizing motivation is very common in contemporary psychology (Austin & Vancouver, 1996; Cropanzano, James, & Citera, 1992).

When interpersonal motives are conceptualized this way, we commonly assume that two very broad, abstract categories are at the top of the hierarchy, namely, communion and agency (Bakan, 1966). A *communal motive* is a motive for selfless connection with one or more others; it is a motive to participate in a larger union with other people. In contrast, an *agentic motive* emphasizes the self as a distinct unit, separate from other people; it focuses on the person's own performance as an individual. Bakan (1966) expressed the distinction this way:

> I have adopted the terms "agency" and "communion" to characterize two fundamental modalities in the existence of living forms, agency for the existence of an organism as an individual, and communion for the participation of the individual in some larger organism of which the individual is a part. Agency manifests itself in self-protection, self-assertion, and self-expansion; communion manifests itself in the sense of being at one with other organisms. Agency manifests itself in the formation of separations; communion in the lack of separations. . . . Agency manifests itself in the urge to master; communion in noncontractual cooperation. (pp. 14–15)

The earliest expression of the communal motive appears in the literature on infant attachment, which we examine in chapter 3. The infant's motive to attach to an adult caretaker keeps the child near the adult, thereby increasing the child's chances of surviving infancy. Later, when the child feels sufficiently secure in this attachment, the child separates from the caretaker and explores the environment, a first step toward autonomy. The motive to separate and explore is thus the earliest manifestation of an agentic motive. Whenever the child's safety is threatened, however, the communal motive is again activated. Over time each motive becomes differentiated into subordinate motives. Communion comes to include motives like intimacy, sociability, and belonging to groups. Agency comes to include motives like autonomy, individualism, achievement, control, and self-definition. Communion is always interpersonal, but agency may be interpersonal or intrapersonal. Agency includes a desire to influence other people, but a desire that is initially interpersonal (e.g., gaining approval, avoiding criticism) can become internalized and intrapersonal (e.g., striving for perfection).

Many behaviors stem from a combination of motives. A person who enjoys giving advice may find advice giving gratifying for more than one reason—displaying competence and knowledge (agentic), influencing others (agentic), connecting with others (communal). Similarly, a person who loves a particular sport may enjoy playing that sport for various reasons—belonging to the team (communal), displaying a skill (agentic), winning competitions (agentic), being like one's parent (communal), and so on. In chapter 4 we consider ways of assessing the strength of different motives.

Western culture emphasizes agency (initiative, individualism, accomplishment, productivity, uniqueness of the self), whereas other cultures emphasize communion (affiliation, group membership, cooperation). Nonetheless, we assume that communal and agentic motives are present, to some degree at least, in the behavior of every human being. Different cultures provide different outlets for satisfying these motives. If a culture discourages individualism, agentic motives may still be satisfied through one's contribution to the group. Even in Western culture, a woman who chooses to enter a marriage primarily for closeness and intimacy may be willing to relinquish some autonomy, control, and decision making to her partner, while still satisfying agentic motives through her domestic competence and career outside of the home.

The term *motive* is usually used to designate a very high level of abstraction (e.g., intimacy, autonomy). The term *personal striving* has been used to designate an intermediate level of abstraction, and the term *goal* (or *specific action unit*), to designate the narrowest, most specific category (Emmons, 1989). This way of conceptualizing motivation is very common in contemporary psychology (Austin & Vancouver, 1996; Cantor & Kihlstrom, 1987; Cropanzano, James, & Citera, 1992; Klinger, 1987; Little, 1983). A communal motive for sociability, then, would include personal strivings like "getting to know new people" and "doing nice things for people." An agentic motive for achievement would include personal strivings like "excelling academically" and "being competent at work." A personal striving, like excelling academically, would, in turn, subsume still narrower goals, like "preparing well for tomorrow's chemistry test." As shown in Figure 2.1, the hierarchy moves from the very broad category (communion or agency) to the very specific action units (goals). A simplified

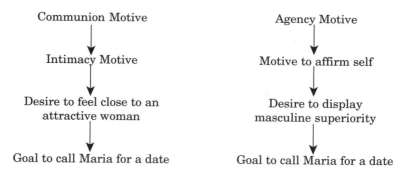

Figure 2.1. Two possible motive hierarchies for the same goal.

pathway through one person's hierarchy of motives might be as follows: communion motive → intimacy motive → desire to feel close to an attractive woman → goal to call Maria for a date.

Suppose we know a man's goal, namely, that he intends to call Maria for a date this weekend. Can we infer the higher order motive from which this goal stems? If two men both plan to call Maria for a date this weekend, are they both necessarily trying to satisfy an intimacy motive? Not necessarily. As shown in Figure 2.1, one may be seeking intimacy (a communal motive), whereas the other may be seeking respect, admiration, or envy of his friends (an agentic motive). Thus, the meaning of a goal, by itself, is often ambiguous. Only when we locate the behavior in the person's hierarchy of motives can we understand its meaning. If someone sitting next to us on an airplane started chatting amiably, we might assume a communal motive (to socialize). However, if the person then asked in all seriousness, "Have you heard the Word of the Lord today?," we might quickly perceive an agentic goal (to proselytize, to influence) and revise our interpretation of the person's chattiness.

Symptoms of psychopathology are frequently ambiguous in this way. An individual with anorexia nervosa might aspire to lose weight, but the meaning of the person's behavior (self-starvation) would not be clear until we could locate it in the hierarchy of motives. For one person, self-starvation might have an agentic meaning: agentic motive → motive to exercise autonomy → desire to display self-control → desire to lose weight → goal to eat nothing but lettuce this weekend. For another person, however, self-starvation might have a communal meaning: communal motive → motive to be nurtured by the family → desire to seem small, thin, and frail → desire to lose weight → goal to eat nothing but lettuce this weekend. (A blend of the two is also possible, as described more clearly in chapter 4.) Some theories of anorexia emphasize a communal motive to maintain family harmony (e.g., Minuchin, Rosman, & Baker, 1978), whereas other theories emphasize an agentic motive to exhibit self-control and strength (e.g., Bruch, 1973). The behavior itself (self-starvation) is ambiguous until we can describe the broader motive from which it arose. In the same way, a major depression or agoraphobia may result from a frustrated motive, and that motive may be communal or agentic (or both). Sometimes the disorder is precipitated by a frustrated communal motive, sometimes by a frustrated agentic motive, sometimes by a combination of motives. Similar views about the importance of motives in psychopathology have been expressed by Caspar (1995, 1997), Grawe (2003), and Grosse Holtforth and associates (Grosse Holtforth & Grawe, 2002; Grosse Holtforth, Grawe, & Egger, 2003).

Frustrated Motives and Psychopathology: Two Examples

In this section we examine two forms of psychopathology, the self-starvation behavior of individuals with anorexia nervosa and the ontological insecurity associated with some forms of schizophrenia. We show that frustrated communal or agentic motives are involved in each of these syndromes.

Example 1: Anorexia Nervosa

Consider the symptoms associated with anorexia nervosa. People with anorexia are typically young women who starve themselves to the point of reducing their bodily weight by 25% or more. No matter how thin they become, they continue to worry about being overweight, and they diet compulsively. The disorder is agonizing for the person, but it is interesting theoretically because hunger is usually considered a primary human drive, not one that people surrender voluntarily. Other things being equal, a person would generally satisfy a severe food deprivation before satisfying other desires. Yet the person with anorexia is driven by some other, very powerful motive that overrides the primacy of hunger. What is this motive?

Some therapists have concluded that many people with anorexia are motivated by a strong desire to affirm a sense of control over their own internal and external environments (e.g., Bruch, 1973). Research in recent decades by both behavioral psychologists (e.g., Bandura, 1977, 1982) and psychoanalytic investigators (e.g., J. Weiss & Sampson, 1986) has recognized the importance of an (agentic) motive to gain control over aspects of the self and the environment. Certain actions produce a clear sense of control, efficacy, or mastery that satisfies this higher order motive. When people with anorexia deprive themselves of food, they are sometimes exchanging the satisfaction of eating for an even greater satisfaction—that of displaying the strength of their will power. In those cases, their very thinness becomes a badge of honor by which they certify (to themselves and others) an impressive feat of self-discipline and self-control: By renouncing the need to eat, the person overrules the demands of the body, resisting pressures from the body's physiology and from well-meaning others. The person's will power thus overrides both internal and external demands, and the person's thinness declares to the world that he or she is autonomous and self-sufficient, dominated by neither physiological nor social pressures. The important motive, according to this interpretation, is agentic.

How might an agentic motive gain such strength? What is its origin? According to many behavioral scientists, human beings, starting early in life, progressively seek to separate from the control of others and are intrinsically motivated to achieve greater autonomy. This theme of increased autonomy, self-regulation, and self-determination recurs developmentally in interpersonal interactions. For example, the child says to the parent, "No, I do it by myself;" or the child shows pride and pleasure in mastering skills. The motive to be autonomous becomes increasingly apparent during the years of childhood. To some extent, the motive affects the child's self-image—aspirations, goals, self-expectations—and these in turn affect subsequent interactions with other people.

The course and vicissitudes of this sense of autonomy have not yet been charted in clear detail by developmental psychologists. Many subtle, sometimes idiosyncratic, factors determine who will breeze through successive developmental milestones and who will struggle with control and autonomy throughout life. Those who struggle must find ways to reassure themselves of their own autonomy. Many factors play a role in the process: In addition to the parent–child relationship patterns, one must consider the child's imaginal processes, fantasies, chance observations, interpretations of events, and so on.

Some version of an agentic motive (independence, autonomy, self-control) is often at the heart of an interpersonal account of psychopathology. People who crave a sense of autonomy, power, competence, self-respect, and independence but suspect that they are not really autonomous may discover specific behaviors that produce the desired feeling. For some individuals with anorexia, self-starvation may be one way. By displaying extraordinary self-control, the person dispels, at least for the moment, doubts about autonomy and self-determination. We should not underestimate the satisfaction that self-starvation can produce in some people. Nor should we underestimate the physical harm it can cause and its maladaptive potential.

Self-starvation can also be used to satisfy a frustrated communal motive. A number of theorists have emphasized ways in which communal motives can fuel anorexia nervosa—motives to preserve a cohesive family unit (e.g., Minuchin, Rosman, & Baker, 1978); to avoid feeling lonely and alienated (e.g., Fairburn, 1997; Fairburn, Welch, Doll, Davies, & O'Connor, 1997; Ratti, Humphrey, & Lyons, 1996); to feel loved, nurtured, and protected (Pike, 1998; Pike & Rodin, 1991). By becoming thin, frail, childlike, or sickly, the person with anorexia hopes to get other people to become more nurturant, caring, concerned, and solicitous. Who, after all, could reject or abandon a malnourished child? Thus, self-starvation can be used to satisfy either communal or agentic motives.

Example 2: Ontological Insecurity (a Fragile Sense of Self)

In some forms of psychopathology, the behavior that would satisfy one motive may simultaneously threaten another motive, causing a motivational conflict. The following example illustrates a severe conflict between communion and agency, as observed in individuals with some forms of schizophrenia.

Most people have a stable view of the self—the "me" that is housed within my body; it is separate from the body but contemporaneous with it. For most people the concept "me" or "myself" is an organized image that includes characteristic traits, beliefs, goals, knowledge, feelings, attitudes, expectancies, likes, dislikes, and so on—reasonably coherent, reasonably stable across time, and experienced as unique. Changes do occur over time in this conception of the self, but abrupt discontinuities are rare. The person generally feels that the person I am today ("myself") is the same as the person I was yesterday and the same as the person I shall be tomorrow.

Not everyone has such a consistent and coherent sense of self. For some people, the self is more fragile. They feel convinced that important aspects of the self (ideas, beliefs, feelings) might be replaced: that other strong-minded people can impose their own ideas, beliefs, or feelings with such force as to displace contents that originally defined the "self." In that case, the person would feel that his or her original self can be transformed by someone else, causing his or her original self to vanish or cease to exist. Anxiety about one's continued existence has been called *existential anxiety* or *ontological insecurity* (Laing, 1965).

Ontological insecurity implies a threat to the (agentic) motive to control or influence one's own thoughts and feelings. The person has to guard against the influence of other people, and to do so, the person might have to avoid getting too close to another person—avoid disclosing private thoughts and feelings, listening too attentively to another person's views, empathizing with another person's mood, or complying with another person's wishes. Closeness would threaten the person's existence such that the person's sense of autonomy may be profoundly impaired. Sometimes the fear may be so great that the person has to avoid other people altogether. In avoiding other people, however, the person may feel isolated, lonely, and disconnected from others. In other words, communal motives are frustrated by the person's attempt to preserve the self. The person wants to relate to others, but the act of relating arouses anxiety. To summarize, the person faces a dilemma: relate to others (causing anxiety) or isolate the self (causing severe loneliness).

The artist Edvard Munch suffered greatly from an impaired sense of autonomy, severe ontological insecurity, an avoidance of other people, and a profound sense of isolation (Horowitz, 1994; Steinberg & Weiss, 1954). According to Steinberg and Weiss, this preoccupation is reflected in much of Munch's work. Figure 2.2 shows one example: As in many works by Munch, the male figure is being enveloped by the female figure with whom he is close. The works seem to depict a preoccupation with closeness and the engulfment of one person by another. This existential anxiety is expressed in Munch's famous work, *The Scream*. Apparently, this level of anxiety affected Munch's interpersonal relationships: if he related to others, he felt very anxious; if he remained separate to protect himself from engulfment, he felt lonely and isolated. The two motives were linked for Munch, and attempts to satisfy one threatened the other. Such dilemmas may be observed in severe forms of psychopathology.

Manifestations of Distress and Frustrated Motives

People who seek help for psychological problems are often unable to articulate the cause of their problems. People with anorexia, in general, cannot describe the reason for their self-starvation: Is it an attempt to gain a greater sense of

Figure 2.2.   Work of Edvard Munch illustrating ontological insecurity. Copyright ©
2003 The Munch Museum/The Munch-Ellingsen Group/Artists Rights Society (ARS),
New York. Reprinted with permission.

control, or an attempt to be nurtured by the family, or something else? People
with severe existential anxiety do not have the vocabulary, standards of comparison, or distance from the problem to speak of "a fragile sense of self." Instead, when people talk frankly about their problems, they primarily describe
immediate feelings of distress—uncomfortable feelings, disturbing thoughts,
dysfunctional behaviors. A woman with anorexia, for example, might say that
she feels like "a totally out-of-control pig" when she eats or that she feels dis-
gusted with herself and tell us how she obsesses over her weight and body image, how she worries about her physical appearance, how she forces herself to
exercise regularly, how pressured she feels by these internal demands. If she
were happy with her extraordinary self-discipline, there would be no problem.
However, people with anorexia are usually not happy; they typically feel frustrated, depressed, and pressured. Self-starvation does not fully satisfy their
broader agentic or communal motive, and it complicates their lives. Likewise,
people with severe existential anxiety can readily describe feelings of panic,
fears of merging, and feelings of rage—for example, because someone tried to
get too close, someone wanted to touch or kiss them, someone tried to change
their thoughts, or someone threatened their security. They can readily describe
agonizing feelings and disturbing thoughts, but the notion of a fragile sense of
self or frustrated motives may not be part of their report.

We learn most about people's distress when they seek psychotherapy. They usually feel miserable and want help finding a way out of that misery. They typically describe three pressing types of distress: (a) uncomfortable feelings, which include anxiety, guilt, shame, depression, rage, worry, loneliness, and jealousy; (b) disturbing cognitions, which include expectancies and thoughts of impending disaster, personal shame, perceptions of one's own incompetence, thoughts of being exploited by others; and (c) dysfunctional behaviors, which include any performance that the person cannot regulate (e.g., inability to concentrate, to sleep at night, to get along with colleagues at work, to resist influence from other people, to be assertive). When people describe their reasons for seeking psychotherapy, they usually mention all three types of distress.

A task for a psychotherapist is to uncover these and other aspects of the person's problem and then integrate them into a coherent, comprehensive, and meaningful whole. Aspects of the problem often include frustrated motives that the person cannot articulate (e.g., a desire to feel more connected or more autonomous). They may also include unsuccessful attempts to satisfy those motives (e.g., "fighting too much with people who get in the way of the person's autonomy"). Still other aspects include consequences of frustrated motives (e.g., being depressed when one feels rejected) and strategies for reducing that distress (e.g., using cocaine to overcome the depression that results from feeling rejected). These various aspects of the problem may hang together coherently. Nonetheless, to understand the complaint fully, we have to identify the basic motive that has been frustrated and show how it organizes and integrates other facets of the overall complaint.

As an illustration, consider the distress of a woman who telephoned a Suicide Prevention Center for help. The woman, Ms. A, was 31 years old. The following text reports her complaint verbatim. Identifying information has been deleted.

> Everybody is being very nice and reminding me of all the wonderful things I have to live for. But I don't give a damn, I don't care about my life anymore. Everything is too much of a struggle, and I don't even care. Isn't that terrible? You know what I did? I can't forgive myself, I feel so guilty—I feel guilty about almost everything. I practically destroyed my own family and other people's. I took my entire savings, and I bought about $2,000 worth of cocaine. I've lost my car, my boyfriend, my clothes, and almost my profession. I cut my wrists. I've created an enormous hole for myself, and I might as well go completely under. I called a doctor at work who does research on cocaine, because I just wanted to get high. I think it's perverted, sick, obscene. I'm like a junkie, it's horrible.
>
> Telephone counselor: Are you working now?
>
> I'm a teacher. I don't have problems at work. But I almost lost my job because I flipped out—I was in the hospital for a week. If I had lost my job, I'd probably have killed myself. But I'm usually successful at making a living. Work is not an area that I go to a psychiatrist for. It's interesting, my mother decided that I owe her money. She wanted me to give her some money this month. I told her, yeah, maybe I'll give you the money instead of giving it to my psychiatrist. I broke off relations with my family this week. This time I'm not going back on my word. I thought of signing the little bit of money I

have over to my mother. She makes me feel like a complete loser. I wanted to kill myself and leave the little I have to her. Isn't that ridiculous? She nags at me constantly. She's also jealous of my doctor. Since I've been going to the doctor, I've started to talk back to her, and she can't stand it. When I tell her she's getting her ideas mixed up with mine, she screams at me. I tell her I don't want her to tell me how I feel or get *her* feelings mixed up with *mine*. I can't stand to be with her. I agree to go and see her sometimes—I cancel all my appointments so I can see her—and then I don't go. What happens is, she catches me at a bad time, and it's easier to say yes, I'll go to see her, so I say I'll go; but then I don't.

Ms. A's complaint certainly has many facets. To identify some of them, I asked a group of clinical psychologists to listen to the tape-recording and identify the facets that must be addressed in treatment. The facets that were mentioned most often were the following:

- feels depressed;
- uses cocaine excessively;
- has low self-esteem (e.g., thinks she is worthless, feels guilty);
- has trouble getting along with her mother;
- cannot separate psychologically from her mother; and
- lacks a clear identity.

The list contains uncomfortable feelings (she feels depressed), disturbing cognitions (she thinks she is worthless), and dysfunctional behaviors (she has trouble getting along with her mother). It captures important aspects of the larger problem, and no one entry is more accurate than any other. Furthermore, the list as a whole gives a clearer picture of Ms. A's problem than any single entry. Indeed, if Ms. A were asked periodically to characterize her main reason for seeking help, she herself would probably report a different aspect of the problem on different occasions (Sorenson, Gorsuch, & Mintz, 1985). On one occasion she might emphasize her drug abuse, on another occasion her difficult relationship with her mother.

What interpersonal motive (or motives) would organize the various facets of Ms. A's overall problem? The list that we generated suggests some possibilities. One is that Ms. A would like to separate psychologically from her mother, but she is unable to do so. That is, she cannot comfortably hold onto her own feelings, thoughts, and wishes in the face of her mother's opposition; her mother's wishes, feelings, and criticisms seem to upstage her own. A related motive is that Ms. A lacks a clear identity and would like a clearer self-definition. That is, she would like to have clearer and firmer opinions, goals, and plans and stronger convictions. Thus, two salient motives have more to do with Ms. A's self, individuality, and separateness (agency) than with her connections and relationships (communion). Her fighting with her mother may also reflect an agentic problem: She would like her mother to get off her back and allow her to be autonomous ("I don't want her to tell me how I feel or get her feelings mixed up with mine"), and she fights with her mother in hopes of making this change.

When a person has severe difficulty satisfying an important interpersonal motive, that person is said to have an interpersonal problem. An interpersonal problem always reflects a discrepancy between what the person wants and what the person is getting. Interpersonal problems have many different causes. The person may be miscommunicating his or her wishes, unintentionally sending signals that invite unwanted reactions. Or the person may have two competing motives: The person may want to be assertive (an agentic motive) but worries about losing friends (frustrating a communal motive). Or the person may simply be repeating interpersonal patterns learned earlier in life that frustrate the person's wishes. We shall examine these and other causes of interpersonal problems later in the book.

Several measures of interpersonal problems have been constructed, and we examine one of them in chapter 6. The Inventory of Interpersonal Problems (Horowitz, Alden, Wiggins, & Pincus, 2000) contains eight different subscales that are organized in terms of communion and agency. One subscale, for example, describes problems with intimacy—difficulties showing affection and feeling close. Another subscale describes problems with autonomy—difficulties behaving assertively and feeling self-confident. Individual items concern narrow goals and problems; each subscale score concerns a higer-order motive; and two broad composite scores concern the two overarching categories, communion and agency.

This measure might show that Ms. A's interpersonal problems are primarily agentic, that a major theme in her life is unfulfilled agency. If so, we would then assume that the facets of her presenting problem could be organized around a motive for greater autonomy and self-definition. For example, we might then infer that her fights with her mother were an attempt to differentiate herself from her mother. Her agentic problem would also explain her depression and low self-esteem ("She makes me feel like a complete loser"). We might then generate a tentative hypothesis that organizes different facets of the problem around her frustrated motives. As an example, the tentative hypothesis might be as follows:

> Ms. A's presenting complaint reveals two related agentic motives that have been frustrated over a period of years, namely, a difficulty in separating psychologically from her mother and a difficulty in establishing a clear identity of her own. She seems to feel thwarted by her mother and therefore keeps fighting with her. Because of these and other frustrations, she feels ineffective, experiences low self-esteem, and feels depressed. In an effort to overcome her distress, she has been using cocaine.

A tentative hypothesis like this is called an *interpersonal case formulation*—a succinct, case-specific set of hypotheses that organizes different aspects of the person's problem around frustrated interpersonal motives. As new information comes to light, the interviewer or therapist can revise the formulation. If a gaunt woman with anorexia were to declare during an interview, "I obviously need to lose more weight," the interviewer might ask: "What would you gain by losing more weight?" Her answer might shed light on the motive and clarify her self-starvation.

An interpersonal case formulation thus highlights the purpose of a treatment and clarifies the problem (Eells, 1997; Sperry, Gudeman, Blackwell, & Faulkner, 1992; Turkat & Maisto, 1983). An interpersonal case formulation of Ms. A's problem, of course, is not the same as Ms. A's own account. Her own account may emphasize her most pressing subjective distress and dysfunction; but an interpersonal case formulation would go beyond that complaint by stating the problems that the treatment ought to solve.

Even if three therapists agreed about an interpersonal case formulation, they might disagree about the best way to treat the problem. One might begin by treating Ms. A's drug problem behaviorally; another might begin by treating her depression with cognitive therapy; a third might begin by treating her relationship with her mother. All three therapists, however, whatever their approach, would need to consider all aspects of the problem because interpersonal factors affect the patient–therapist relationship. For example, a therapist might be inclined to offer practical advice to Ms. A—perhaps advice about budgeting her money or being thrifty. Such advice could be very unwelcome to a person like Ms. A, who (a) was already receiving unwanted advice from her mother, (b) was already too susceptible to influence, and (c) was trying to establish her own identity. As we show in chapter 4, the act of advice giving may seem supportive to one person but condescending to another.

What Does an Interpersonal Approach Add to a Diagnosis?

So far we have shown that interpersonal motives can help clarify the meaning of an otherwise ambiguous dysfunctional behavior. We have also shown that a salient interpersonal motive can integrate and organize different facets of a person's psychological problem. *DSM–IV–TR*, the diagnostic system most commonly used in this country, does not mention interpersonal motives, however. Therefore, we need to examine the relationship between a diagnostic approach and an interpersonal approach. Are they complementary or incompatible? We believe that each approach provides a specific kind of information that is useful in treatment. Therefore, as the final section of this chapter, we examine some specific shortcomings of the *DSM–IV–TR* that can be clarified by an interpersonal approach.

Diagnostic Categories of the DSM–IV–TR

The *DSM–IV–TR* (American Psychiatric Association, 2000) is a comprehensive work of descriptive psychiatry. The most commonly used diagnoses fall into two broad categories, Axis I disorders and Axis II disorders. The Axis I (clinical) disorders are defined in terms of symptoms and signs. A *symptom* is a self-reported change that reflects subjective distress or impaired functioning. It reflects a discontinuity with the person's past experience. A person might say, for example, "Six months ago I started feeling too anxious to leave my house." Apparently, the fear of leaving home came on recently and relatively abruptly. A *sign* is a similar change that is noted by someone else. An observer might say, "Just before Christmas last year, his speech became unintelligible; we understand his words, but the ideas often make no sense."

A *syndrome* is a cluster of symptoms and signs that tend to go together. Depression is a syndrome that often includes a feeling of sadness, a loss of energy, a lack of appetite, self-reproaches, feelings of guilt, and so on. The symptoms and signs of a syndrome typically include uncomfortable feelings, disturbing thoughts, and dysfunctional behaviors. Because the Axis I categories are defined in terms of syndromes, they reflect a discontinuity from the person's past behavior and experience.

The Axis II disorders (personality disorders) are defined in terms of enduring personality traits. Traits (e.g., "perfectionism," "dependence," and "introversion") are generally continuous; they do not have a sudden onset. They develop gradually over the years, and by late adolescence or early adulthood they seem to become well-established. A trait develops so gradually during the formative years that, in general, we cannot recall when it first appeared. Even if it grows more intense or salient with age, it does not seem like an abrupt departure from the person's past behavior. A personality disorder implies that, over time, certain traits come to be maladaptive. Consider a man who is an extreme perfectionist. Initially, the trait may even be adaptive; for example, his work may be admired as careful, thorough, and accurate. When we say that he has a personality disorder, however, we imply that the trait has come to cause problems. For example, he may be so afraid of making a mistake that he cannot make decisions or consider a job finished. As a result, his functioning might become impaired; he might even get fired from his job, causing subjective distress, like tension, anxiety, and depression. To summarize, the traits that define a personality disorder do not, by themselves, imply a personality disorder. Only when the person's behavior interferes with his or her functioning or causes subjective distress do we speak of a personality disorder.

When *DSM–IV–TR* was developed, experienced diagnosticians came together to define, systematize, and standardize the diagnostic categories. To make the system acceptable to a wide audience of mental health professionals, the authors tried to avoid theoretical speculation and controversy. For instance, they avoided older terms that are associated with any one theory. The term *neurosis*, for example, was historically linked to the psychoanalytic theory, so they replaced the earlier term *neurotic depression* with the modern term *dysthymic disorder*. For the same reason, the committee listed features but did not try to integrate them conceptually. As a result, the *DSM–IV–TR* is a thoughtful, systematic, and relatively nontheoretical description of psychopathology, but it has its limitations as a guide to treatment. In the following section, we examine one of the limitations, which we try to correct through the interpersonal approach.

Limitations of the DSM–IV–TR

OMISSION OF THE FRUSTRATED MOTIVE   The features that define a diagnostic category are stated as a list, and every feature receives equal weight. Furthermore, the motive that organizes these features may or may not be included in the list. As a result, the category may be interpreted in alternate ways. For example, consider a now-outmoded diagnostic category, the *school phobia*. This label was once used to describe children who become very anxious when they have to leave home to go to school (e.g., A. M. Johnson, Falstein, Szurek, & Svendsen, 1941). The label *school phobia* suggests an aversive situation at school (bullies, a critical teacher, being teased, being humiliated) that would seem to call for a desensitization to the feared school situation.

However, a number of studies have shown that this interpretation is not always correct. Many children who fit the category of school phobia are more afraid of leaving home than they are of going to school. For one thing, a feared situation usually produces a fear gradient; the degree of fear increases as the person approaches the feared situation. Therefore, a child who fears school should show increasing fear as the child approaches school. However, many children show their greatest fear when they leave home, not when they reach the school (Kennedy, 1965).

Furthermore, many of these children report disturbing cognitions that something dreadful might happen if they leave home. For example, A. M. Johnson et al. (1941) described parents who unwittingly and unintentionally suggested to their children that it was dangerous to leave home. A number of articles have described patterns of family interaction that induce such beliefs and make the child anxious about leaving home. In one common pattern, the child comes to believe that the mother needs the child at home, and the child feels obliged to stay with the mother or protect her from danger (Bowlby, 1973; Clyne, 1966; Hersov, 1960; Kennedy, 1965; E. Klein, 1945; A. A. Lazarus, 1960; Sperling, 1967; Talbot, 1957). Some children worry that their parents will be kidnapped, attacked by monsters, or killed in a car accident (B. Murray, 1997).

Thus, the two characteristics—"is afraid to go to school" and "is unable to separate comfortably from home"—may both be technically correct. However, to make sense of the disorder, we need to know which characteristic is psychologically primary. In many cases, the second is the more basic characteristic: The child is afraid to separate from home. As a consequence, the child is afraid to go to school—and afraid to go to summer camp and afraid to sleep at a friend's house. In this case, a communal motive (to maintain contact with the parents) is the salient motive behind the disorder.

However, cases also exist in which a genuine fear of the school situation is primary. Children may doubt their own intellectual competence, anticipate being humiliated when they fail a test, and feel inferior or ashamed of their lack of ability (B. Murray, 1997). In those cases, a school-related sense of incompetence and inefficacy—an agentic problem—causes anxiety, not a concern about losing contact with the parents. In that case, we would say that the basic characteristic is the child's fear of going to school. As a consequence, the child is afraid to leave home and afraid to leave for school from any other starting point. In this case, an agentic motive (to avoid feeling incompetent, inferior, or ashamed) is the salient motive behind the disorder.

The *DSM–IV–TR* now classifies the two cases separately. The communal disorder is called the *separation anxiety disorder*. A true school phobia, the agentic disorder, is now classified under *specific phobia, situational type*. The labels *school phobia* and *separation anxiety disorder* thus highlight the central issue for treatment: whether to help the child feel more competent at school or to help the child feel comfortable separating from the parents. As we show in later chapters, other Axis I categories are still ambiguous.

A DIFFERENCE BETWEEN SYNDROMES AND TRAITS   By definition, syndromes are salient in Axis I disorders, and traits are salient in Axis II disorders. What is the difference between syndromes and traits, aside from their type of onset (abrupt vs. gradual)? One difference is that a trait is enduring; it often reflects a salient and abiding motive. A sociable person wants company, an assertive person wants to be in charge, a theatrical person wants attention, a narcissistic person wants admiration, a dependent person wants to be cared for. Therefore, a personality disorder can often be organized around a salient motive. In contrast, a syndrome (e.g., depression) may reflect a recently frustrated motive, but that motive may not be unique to that syndrome. Depression may result from a frustrated communal motive for one person, from a frustrated agentic motive for someone else. Likewise, a person who becomes anorexic or hypochondriacal or agoraphobic or delusional may be struggling with either type of frustrated motive (or a combination of both).

Thus, interpersonal motives can help us refine our thinking about diagnostic categories. They appear as an organizing construct throughout this book. In the chapters that follow, we continue to lay the interpersonal foundations that help explain psychopathology. Because communion and agency first appear in infancy, we next examine the relevant literature about childhood.

3

Attachment and the Stress of Separation

Attachment marks the first appearance of communion in an infant's life, revealing a powerful motive for the child to connect with other people. Very early on, the infant is oriented toward other people and is ready to bond with available caretakers; the infant also exhibits distress when separated from significant figures in an unfamiliar setting. In this way, nature keeps the child close to adults, thereby protecting the child from danger. Attachment also marks the first appearance of an agentic motive because a child who feels secure and protected takes active steps to separate from the adult in order to explore, experiment with, and master the environment. The child's zest for exploring fosters a sense of efficacy and a desire to function autonomously.

Beginning in infancy, then, a child alternates between communal and agentic motives. The motive to connect eventually allows the child to become intimate with others, give and receive nurturance, form friendships, and be part of larger social units. The motive to become autonomous eventually allows the child to function independently, take initiative, and form a coherent identity. For these reasons, the infant's attachments constitute an important foundation for later development.

In this chapter, we examine the typical attachment pattern in early childhood as well as atypical patterns. Analogous patterns are also observed in adulthood. Two motives commonly expressed by people in psychotherapy are to feel attached—close to and accepted by others—and to be autonomous—able to assert oneself and function independently (Waldinger et al., 2003). Furthermore, attachment patterns are related to the person's cognitions (e.g., to the person's view of other people). In later chapters, we use these insights to interpret and organize the features of several personality disorders.

The chapter also raises a number of questions about the effect of early attachment patterns on interpersonal behavior later in life. Do early attachment patterns have long-term consequences? Are early patterns stable over time? How are they related to physical and psychological well-being and to psychopathology in adulthood? We begin the chapter by examining normal attachment in early childhood.

Background: The Nature of Attachment

In many animal species, the newborn infant forms a bond shortly after birth with an older organism (usually the mother). For animals as diverse as birds and primates, the mother can discriminate her own young from other newborns within hours of birth, and the infant quickly learns to discriminate its mother from other adults. The infant stays close to the mother, thereby increasing its chances for survival; and whenever the mother and infant are separated, each takes steps to re-unite with the other, using locomotion, attention-getting calls, and visual displays (Lorenz, 1957). The infant seems to be hard-wired to become attached to an available adult member of the species, even if the adult does not satisfy any other physiological need (Harlow, 1958).

The same phenomenon is evident in the three- to four-month-old human infant. Infants of that age respond in a characteristic way to the primary caretaker. They smile, vocalize, and visually follow that person more than anyone else (Bowlby, 1969; Stern, 1977). Whenever they are hungry, sense danger, or feel distressed, they try to attract the adult's attention. They seem to feel secure when that adult is around, and no other adult can be as effective in soothing or comforting them at times of distress. Usually the primary attachment figure is the mother, but infants also form attachments to other caretakers, including the father, older siblings, nannies, and other family members. When infants are greatly distressed, however, they usually prefer the mother (Cassidy, 1999).

John Bowlby, an English psychoanalyst, wrote extensively about social bonding in humans. He regarded this early relationship as crucial for the child's survival. In his account the infant is initially helpless and totally dependent on caretakers for food, water, and protection. The child's relationship to the adult has several characteristics (Bowlby, 1977). For one thing, it is specific to that adult, who is better able than anyone else to comfort the child. Second, the attachment, once formed, persists; new attachments do not keep replacing old ones. Third, the emotions displayed are specific to events in that relationship. When the child anticipates an unwanted separation, the child becomes anxious or angry; when the attachment figure is gone, the child becomes sad; when the attachment figure reappears, the child becomes joyful.

In his early works, Bowlby (1944) studied 44 children who had been incarcerated for stealing. He concluded that these young thieves had more often experienced prolonged separations from their parents than other children. In some cases, the child had been placed in foster care repeatedly because of a parent's illness. One subgroup seemed especially affectionless; Bowlby observed that those children had been separated from their parents more often than other children in the sample.

Bowlby (1951) also studied children who, for one reason or another, had been institutionalized (hence, deprived of maternal care); many of them developed the very same symptoms. In a much-quoted comment, Bowlby concluded that a mother's availability is as important to the child's development as proper diet and nutrition (Kobak, 1999). His report highlighted the potential emotional damage that can result from long-term separation. Even in an institution with a well-trained staff, strangers cannot readily step in for a child's accustomed caretakers (Karen, 1994; Kobak, 1999).

Isolation and Failure to Thrive

When human infants are deprived of parenting altogether, their development is profoundly affected. R. A. Spitz (1945) studied infants who were being raised in an orphanage. This particular institution had a head nurse and five assistant nurses to care for 45 infants; they were generally too busy to attend closely to any one child. For the most part, the children were left alone in their cots except when they were fed or cleaned. Bed sheets were hung over the railing of the cot, creating a kind of solitary confinement for the child. Although the institution had high standards of hygiene and nutrition, many of the children did not thrive. From the third month on, they were extremely susceptible to infection and illness of various kinds. Of the 88 children observed, 23 died by age 2 1/2. Spitz compared these orphanage children to infants born to women prisoners. Those babies had access to their mothers and to a staff of nurses. The babies in the two groups were comparable in background, diet, clothing, and medical attention. Yet the babies in the orphanage were slower to develop language and motor skills. Even by age 2 1/2, very few spoke more than a few words or were able to walk. Hardly any could eat alone, and none was toilet trained.

Is this damage reversible? The answer seems to be yes, provided the deprivation was not too severe or prolonged (Ordway, Leonard, & Ingles, 1969). During and after the political upheavals in Eastern Europe in the 1990s, orphanages were found in Romania in which many of the children had been deprived for months or years of the opportunity to form a close bond with a trusted adult caregiver (W. A. Collins, Maccoby, Steinberg, Hetherington, & Bornstein, 2000). Some were later adopted into middle-income families in England before two years of age, and they showed severe intellectual deficits. When the children were four years old, follow-up studies showed that they had made considerable gains in their cognitive and educational development (Rutter, 1998). However, later studies suggested that those who were severely deprived were still impaired (T. G. O'Connor et al., 2000). The degree of recovery seemed to depend on the duration and severity of the original deprivation.

The effect of social isolation has also been studied experimentally in lower primates. McKinney (1974) summarized a number of experiments showing that rhesus monkeys reared in isolation become very anxious and behaviorally aberrant. Typically in these studies, the infant was removed from its mother at birth and reared for 15 days in a laboratory nursery. When the monkey was able to feed itself, it was placed alone in a cage, where it could not see or touch other monkeys. Rhesus monkeys reared in total isolation for the first 6 to 12 months subsequently spent most of their time huddled in a corner, rocking, clasping themselves, and refusing to play or interact with peers. Sometimes they would become aggressive toward themselves or other animals. In addition, they failed to exhibit appropriate sexual behavior when they reached puberty and adulthood. When a female in this category became pregnant through artificial insemination and delivered her first infant, she was typically indifferent to the infant (McKinney, 1974).

Animals raised in isolation also showed a general deficiency in social communication skills. Mirsky (1968) conducted an experiment in which two monkeys had to work cooperatively in order to press a lever to avoid a shock. One was able to see a cue that indicated the correct lever but was unable to reach that lever. The other animal could not see the cue, but, if prompted by the partner, could press the correct lever and avoid the shock. Thus, the two animals had to communicate to solve the problem. Normal monkeys can perform this task without difficulty, usually communicating through facial expressions. Monkeys raised in isolation, however, did not make good partners; they were particularly poor at reading facial cues.

The Attachment System

We assume that attachment behavior is goal-directed—that a one-year-old who extends its arms toward the mother wants contact with the mother. The desired contact may be physical (e.g., being lifted) or symbolic (e.g., hearing the mother's voice). Contact could also be aversive (if the child did not want it). For example, a mother who stares at an infant as the infant keeps gazing away would seem to be frustrating, rather than satisfying the child's wishes.

Attachment behavior primarily occurs when the child feels internal discomfort or perceives danger (Bowlby, 1969/1982; Cassidy, 1999). If the child's distress is moderate, the mother's soothing sounds may suffice; if the distress is intense, the child may want physical contact. The attachment system is often likened to a thermostat that regulates the temperature of a room. When the child is in distress, it is activated; when the distress passes, the attachment system shuts down.

Attachment behavior has obvious survival value. By communicating needs to the adult, the child is more apt to be sheltered, protected, and nurtured. These interactions with an adult also help the child survive by learning about people, about the self, and about the environment. Thus, attachment behavior has evolutionary significance and is viewed as "a normal and healthy characteristic of humans throughout the lifespan, rather than a sign of immaturity that needs to be outgrown" (Cassidy, 1999, p. 5). Many psychologists (both behavioral and psychodynamic) once believed that attachments are acquired through secondary reinforcement. According to this theory, the adult satisfies the child's basic needs, so the child comes to associate need satisfaction with maternal contact; through this association maternal contact becomes desirable. However, Bowlby and other attachment theorists argued against this view, claiming that attachment is a biological given (see Bowlby, 1980; Cassidy, 1999; Karen, 1994). Even when the mother is abusive or neglectful, the child becomes attached to her. Indeed, almost every child attaches to one or more adults and is more readily comforted by attachment figures than by strangers (Cassidy, 1999).

Attachment behaviors are more complex than reflexes. When a puff of air is directed at a person's eye, it reflexively produces a blink—a predictable response to an easily described stimulus. However, attachment behaviors are more complex than reflexes. If a child wants contact with an adult, the child may first exhibit one attachment behavior, then another, and then a third until the goal is achieved. For example, the child may first extend its arms, then whimper, and finally cry until the adult responds in the desired manner.

Other Affectional Systems

The attachment system should be distinguished from two other affectional systems. The *caretaking system* refers to the adult's reactions to the child's bids for contact and comfort. Both are affectional systems, but they are different. In general, the child seeks comfort from the adult, not the reverse. If a mother, frightened by a thunderstorm, clings anxiously to her child for protection, she is displaying attachment behavior toward the child. According to Bowlby, this kind of role reversal is "not only a sign of pathology in the parent, but also a cause of it in the child" (1969/1982, p. 377; see also Cassidy, 1999).

Another affectional system is the *sociable system*, which refers to the behavior of playmates (usually peers) toward one another. Through these interactions, children also learn a lot about other people, about the self, and about the world.

The Fear System

Cues that signal danger to a child can be subtle. Sroufe, Waters, and Matas (1974) showed experimentally that a child may interpret the very same event differently in different contexts. Ten-month-old infants were tested at home and in the laboratory. In both settings the mother put on a mask in the child's presence. At home the mother's behavior produced pleasure and laughter; when the mother performed the same act in the laboratory, however, the children became wary, anxious, and tearful. Apparently, the children felt safe in one context but not in the other.

Furthermore, an older child may perceive danger that a younger child does not. Sleep researchers have observed that newborn babies generally settle down and sleep through the night by three months of age. Then, between 6 and 12 months (when attachment issues become salient), the frequency of night waking increases. At that time, one third to one half of all babies begin to awaken during the night (Anders, 1978; Emde & Walker, 1976; T. Moore & Ucko, 1957). Anna Freud (1966) remarked that falling asleep at that age is no longer just a physical matter. According to her explanation, the child now reacts to the mother's absence. By three years of age, however, most children have overcome this fear.

What conditions help a child feel safe? Initially, the caretaker's physical proximity is critical in comforting a child, but in time, symbolic signals may suffice—a comforting glance, smile, or vocalization. According to some attachment theorists (e.g., Bretherton & Munholland, 1999), a child is always monitoring cues to danger and signs that the caretaker is available. Several kinds of experiences reduce a child's confidence in a caretaker's availability.

1. A distracted, inattentive, or unresponsive adult would seem unavailable.
2. A child who had suffered a prior loss (e.g., the death of a parent) might think that the present caretaker is not permanent.
3. A caretaker who kept threatening to leave, to commit suicide, or to send the child away would seem unreliable. More than 20% of parents interviewed in the United States and England admitted that they use threats like these to discipline their children (Kobak, 1999).

The effect of the mother's availability has been studied experimentally in rats. Mother rats differ in their mothering styles. "Nurturant" mothers lick and groom their newborn more often than other mothers. They also actively arch their backs to help the youngster nurse. Compared with rats reared by nonnurturing mothers, rats reared by nurturant mothers are not as timid about leaving the home cage to obtain food or to explore a novel environment. As adults, they produce lower levels of stress-related hormones when they are stressed (Caldji et al., 1998; Liu et al., 1997).

How can a human infant tell whether a caretaker is attentionally engaged? Many subtle cues are probably used (e.g., the caretaker's bodily orientation, eye-to-eye contact, facial expressions, appropriate vocalizations). Tronick (1989; Tronick & Gianino, 1986; see also Stern, 1977) studied mothers interacting with their infants. The mothers experimentally alternated between (a) displaying normal, responsive facial and vocal behavior and (b) going deadpan and silent while gazing at the baby. Infants became very distressed when their mothers were nonresponsive and silent.

When a caretaker is inattentive or nonresponsive, the attachment system gets activated, and the child seeks a way to elicit greater attentiveness. Numerous clinical reports describe strategies that children frequently use: talking incessantly, acting cute, hitting, hurting, or shocking people, destroying property (e.g., L. S. Benjamin, 1996; Fitzgerald, 1948; Krohn, 1978; Millon & Davis, 2000). I once treated a man who, beginning in childhood, started fabricating experiences, adventures, and exotic illnesses as a way of engaging other people's attention.

To summarize, children can apparently detect subtle cues about the caretaker's internal state. If sustained over many years, these perceptions may have a lasting effect on the child. Wiseman et al. (2002) compared two groups of adults in Israel whose mothers had survived the Holocaust. The mothers of one group had never revealed details about their trauma to the child, whereas those of the second group had. Later, in adulthood, participants of the first group reported significantly greater difficulty connecting with other people.

Separation Anxiety

When children between the ages of 6 months and 4 years are separated from their primary caretakers for a long time, they become very distressed. Heinicke and Westheimer (1965) studied children who were separated from their mothers and placed in a residential nursery. The children were between 13 and 32 months, and the separation lasted 12 to 148 days. In some cases, the mother had to be hospitalized while giving birth to another child, and the father could not take time out from work to care for the child. When the parents left, the child typically protested, cried loudly, and kept calling for the mother. Members of the staff had little success in consoling the child. Crying was especially salient during the first 3 days, particularly at bedtime and during the night. Children who had had a prior experience at the same nursery were even more upset than first-timers.

Ainsworth (1982), a colleague of Bowlby, observed that the quality of a child's play declines when the child is distressed over separation. She hypothesized that the feeling of security in the presence of an attachment figure allows a child to relax, explore the environment, and become engrossed in play.

This sense of security enables a child to become increasingly autonomous over time (Maher, Pine, & Bergman, 1975). The mother seems to provide a secure base or a safe haven (Ainsworth, 1982; Cassidy, 1999). Even in unfamiliar surroundings, the child can become engrossed in play if the mother is present. If the mother makes a move to leave the playroom, however, the child feels threatened, stops playing, and focuses instead on re-uniting with the mother.

To study this process systematically, Ainsworth and her colleagues developed a standardized laboratory procedure, which they called the *Strange Situation* (Ainsworth & Bell, 1970; Blehar, Lieberman, & Ainsworth, 1977; Stayton & Ainsworth, 1973; Tracy & Ainsworth, 1981). The procedure is designed to study 12- to 20-month-old children. It elicits reactions from the child under standardized laboratory conditions as the mother briefly leaves the playroom. The test takes place in pleasant, but unfamiliar surroundings, where the child has an opportunity to explore toys, and, at times, interact with an adult stranger. First, the infant and mother are led into the playroom. A stranger then joins them and sits down, talking first to the mother and then to the infant. Then the mother leaves the room. Later she returns and the stranger leaves. Then the mother leaves again, so the infant is alone. Then the stranger returns, and finally, the mother returns. Each episode lasts three minutes (Ainsworth, 1982).

Usually, in the first episode, the child is willing to separate physically from the mother and explore the toys, and when the stranger appears, the child is friendly and continues playing. (The mother is still present.) Then, when the mother leaves, the child typically shows signs of distress, and the child's play becomes subdued; the stranger is not very effective in soothing the child. When the mother does return, the infant is pleased to see her, typically seeks contact with her, and calms down. Even if a child has not been particularly distressed during the mother's absence, the child usually greets the mother enthusiastically when she returns.

Children differ in their reactions to the Strange Situation. When the mother leaves, most children show some distress. Their facial expressions, head shaking, and gestures all reflect anxiety and protest. The child's concern with separation clearly overrides any earlier interest in the toys. Later, when the mother returns, the child's relief is also clear. Some children require more contact than others, but most children can be comforted.

Atypical Reactions

The above reactions are typical for young children. However, two kinds of atypical reactions are also observed. One is called avoidant ("A") behavior. Children who exhibit the A pattern seem to be relatively unconcerned about the mother's departure or return. When the mother leaves the room, the child seems cool, undistressed, and unconcerned; the child's play is relatively unaffected. Later, when the mother returns, the child scarcely greets or acknowledges her. Attachment theorists interpret an avoidant reaction as one way of coping with an unavailable attachment figure—namely, becoming prematurely self-reliant (Weinfield, Sroufe, Egeland, & Carlson, 1999).

Another atypical pattern is called resistant–ambivalent behavior or "C" (for "conflicted") behavior. Children who exhibit the C pattern protest greatly when the mother leaves and cling to her when she returns. But even after the mother has returned, the child seems to resist her efforts to comfort. Some push the mother away, some become petulant. They seem to crave contact with the mother, but they also seem angry with her for having left. All of these reactions have been observed in every culture in which attachment has been studied (van Ijzendoorn & Sagi, 1999).

After a prolonged separation, many young children show an atypical reaction when the mother returns. Heinicke and Westheimer (1965) reported that the children who were left in a residential nursery for 12 to 148 days generally showed an avoidant reaction when the mother returned. They turned around, backed away, or stared into space as though they did not recognize the mother. Avoidant behavior continued for 3 days after the reunion, and many mothers complained that their children treated them like strangers. In subsequent weeks, however, the children did eventually warm up to the mother again.

Internal Working Models

Why do some children show A and C reactions in the Strange Situation? Why are some children prematurely self-reliant and others extremely emotional but difficult to console? Bowlby (1973) hypothesized that young children form images of other people and of the self from attachment experiences. He suggested that these images (or *internal working models*; p. 204) shape the child's expectations about other people: "Is my caretaker someone I can count on?" Children who display a typical, normative reaction are thought to feel relatively secure; they expect the caretaker to return and can count on the person's availability. Internal working models are discussed further by Bretherton (1985) and Bretherton and Munholland (1999). The normal reaction is called the "B" pattern, falling alphabetically between the A and C patterns. In contrast, children who show A or C reactions are less sure of the caretaker's availability. Apparently they are less trusting and have adopted ways to cope with a relatively unreliable caretaker. Some cope by becoming self-reliant (Type A), others by creating a commotion (Type C). According to attachment theorists, both reflect insecurity about the caregiver's availability, and they are therefore called "insecure" (or "anxious") attachment patterns.

An insecure attachment is frequently observed among children who have been seriously maltreated. Egeland and Sroufe (1981a, 1981b) compared 18-month-old children whose mothers had been unavailable, neglectful, or abusive with a comparison group that had not been maltreated. In the Strange Situation those in the maltreated groups more often showed A and C reactions. A high incidence of A and C reactions has also been reported for children of mothers who were depressed (Radke-Yarrow, Cummings, Kuczynski, & Chapman, 1985) and for children of mothers with schizophrenia (Naslund, Persson-Blennow, McNeil, Kaij, & Malmquist-Larsson, 1984).

Two Important Distinctions

A distinction can be made between an "available" caretaker and an "over-involved" (or overprotective) caretaker. An available caretaker satisfies needs as they arise; an overinvolved caretaker offers care that is not needed or wanted, frustrating a child's intrinsic motive for autonomy. Over-involved caretaking can also convey doubt and anxiety about a child's competence.

The second distinction to be made concerns the correct interpretation of the "cool" behavior of an avoidant child. Is an avoidant child truly unconcerned about the adult's absence? Is the child genuinely nonanxious? We need to distinguish between two aspects of a stress reaction. Levine (1983; Levine, Coe, Smotherman, & Kaplan, 1978) separated infant monkeys from their mothers and placed them in an unfamiliar environment for 6 hours. The animals were clearly agitated at first. Samples of their blood showed elevated levels of cortisol, a secretion of the adrenal cortex that occurs under stress. After 6 hours, the animals seemed quite calm (behaviorally), but their blood samples showed increasingly elevated levels of cortisol; after 6 hours, the level of cortisol was as high as it had ever been. In other words, an organism's overt behavior might not agree with a biochemical index of stress.

Anxiety is sometimes disguised behaviorally. Anxiety is so unpleasant and disruptive that people learn ways to suppress its behavioral manifestations (Gross, 1999). Most of us have experienced circumstances in which we have suppressed anxiety. Driving along a freeway, we encounter an unexpected icy patch on the road and lose control of the car. We then become extremely vigilant, regain control of the car, and manage to avoid an accident. Later, recalling the experience, we realize that we felt tense but clear-headed, firm, decisive, and not truly anxious. After the crisis has passed, however, we relax slightly and then begin to feel the symptoms of anxiety, such as sweating palms, trembling, and an accelerated heart rate. Apparently, by concentrating hard on the crisis, we manage to distract ourselves and suppress the most debilitating behavioral components of anxiety.

We probably use the same method to avoid other forms of emotional distress. John Steinbeck (1939) provided a clear example of this phenomenon in his masterpiece, *The Grapes of Wrath*. In that story the Joad family, forced by the Great Depression to leave their home and farm in Oklahoma, traveled to California in search of a better life. Traveling in an overcrowded and unreliable jalopy, they endured numerous bitter hardships along the way and eventually found temporary housing in a government camp, a safe haven that provided more help, hope, and humanity than they had ever experienced along the way. At that happy moment, Ma Joad, the pillar of the family, observed, to her surprise, that she felt very sad. She commented:

> "Funny, ain't it? All the time we was a-movin' and shovin', I never thought none. An' now these here folks been nice to me, been awful nice; an' what's the first thing I do? I go right back over the sad things . . . Them things . . . now come a-flockin' back. Granma a pauper, an' buried a pauper . . . An' Noah walkin' away down the river . . . We ain't never gonna know if he's alive or dead. Never gonna know. An' Connie sneakin' away. I didn't give 'em brain room before, but now the're a-flockin' back. An' I oughta be glad 'cause we're in a nice place." (pp. 287–288)

Throughout the arduous journey, she managed to avoid her enormous sadness, but at a moment of safety and comfort, her grief returned. A child's avoidant reaction in the Strange Situation may resemble the first stage of this process. Behaviorally, the child appears nonanxious and self-sufficient; but at the biochemical level, there is reason to suspect substantial stress (Fox & Card, 1999).

The Disoriented–Disorganized Attachment Pattern

Main and Solomon (1986, 1990) identified another atypical reaction in the Strange Situation, which they called the *disoriented–disorganized (D) attachment pattern*. This reaction seems odd to an outside observer: When the mother returns to the Strange Situation after an absence, the child appears to be dazed, spaced out, or confused. Some children move slowly or unsteadily. Others seem odd in other ways—a child who has been screaming loudly might suddenly grow silent and freeze for several seconds when the mother appears. In contrast to an avoidant or resistant–ambivalent reaction, the disorganized reaction seems like a collapse under stress.

The disorganized reaction has been associated primarily with three groups of children: children who have been abused, children who are currently under stress, and children whose parent is psychologically disturbed (Cicchetti & Barnett, 1991; Crittenden 1988; Lyons-Ruth, Connell, Zoll, & Stahl, 1987; M. J. O'Connor, Sigman, & Brill, 1987; Spieker & Booth, 1988). Half an hour after leaving the Strange Situation, children classified as disorganized still show significantly higher levels of cortisol in their saliva than comparable children classified as secure (Hertsgaard, Gunnar, Erickson, & Nachmias, 1995; Spangler & Grossmann, 1993).

What produces a disorganized reaction? Some writers (e.g., Lyons-Ruth & Jacobvitz, 1999; Main, 1995) have argued that a child who exhibits disorganized behavior has previously been terrorized by an attachment figure. That is, the very person who comforts the child has also frightened the child, producing contradictory reactions. In the Strange Situation, should the child seek comfort or avoid further anxiety? Perhaps the clearest example is that of a physically abused child. Carlson, Cicchetti, Barnett, and Braunwald (1989) studied a sample of maltreated infants; 82% showed a disorganized reaction to the Strange Situation. A caretaker might also frighten a child unwittingly. One mother, intending to be playful, used to creep up behind her child, produce weird sounds, bare her teeth, and distort her face. In another case, the mother was herself severely phobic, and, when panicked, would cling to her 2-year-old child for protection.

Is the disorganized attachment pattern important theoretically? Children who have been abused are more likely than other children to have interpersonal difficulties when they get older (Cicchetti, Lynch, Schonk, & Todd-Manly, 1992; Lyons-Ruth & Jacobvitz, 1999; D. A. Wolfe, 1985). Maltreated children are more aggressive toward peers than other children. As a group, they are also more withdrawn and more depressed (Kazdin, Moser, Colbus, & Bell, 1985). When they later become parents, they are more likely to mistreat their own children. Still, one might ask whether the concept of attachment helps explain the relationship between parental abuse and the child's later aggressive behavior toward peers. Perhaps the relationship is explained more simply by a principle of modeling: The parent exhibits abusive behavior, and the child copies that behavior. Perhaps the Type D attachment is simply a sign of stress but not essential for explaining the relationship.

However, attachment may have a special mediating role that is important for understanding the abused child's later aggression. Consistent with attachment theorists, we assume that a child classified as D has experienced a significant dilemma. The adult who has comforted and protected the child has also scared the child. The two images of the caretaker are contradictory: a positive, comforting image and a negative, punishing image. These disparate images of the very same person are difficult for a small child to integrate. Unintegrated images of the same caretaker are sometimes called *split images*. Later in the book we use this concept to explain abrupt shifts and discontinuities that occur in a person's feelings, thoughts, and behaviors.

Stability and Predictive Value of Attachment Patterns

How stable is a child's attachment pattern from, for example, age 12 months to age 18 months? If the level of stress within a family is reasonably constant during this period, the attachment pattern would be reasonably stable. Lamb, Thompson, Gardner, and Charnov (1985) reviewed nine studies and showed an average concordance of 77% between the two testings. Children who were rated secure (or insecure) on one occasion tended to be rated the same way on the second occasion. Should we attribute the consistency to a stable mother–child relationship or to the child's (biologically-determined) temperament? Perhaps an avoidant child, for biological reasons, is relatively disinterested in people (including the mother) and therefore displays relatively little interest in the mother's coming and going on both occasions. According to this biological hypothesis, a child's avoidant behavior is due to an innate characteristic, not to a quality of the mother–child relationship.

However, the biological hypothesis also implies that the child's reaction in the Strange Situation should be the same, no matter who has brought the child for testing. If the child's reaction depends on the relationship, the child might react differently when tested with the mother than with the father. A number of studies have shown that the child's reactions can be very different with different parents (Patterson & Moran, 1988). Thus, the child's reaction would seem to depend upon the child's relationship to that parent. Clinicians have observed the same phenomenon in children who are sometimes brought to therapy by one parent and sometimes by the other. When the child leaves the parent to join the therapist, the separation may be considerably more difficult with one parent than the other.

A child's reaction in the Strange Situation also varies with the amount of stress in the child's life. When the family is under stress (e.g., the father loses his job), insecure patterns are more frequent (Egeland & Farber 1984; Egeland & Sroufe, 1981a, 1981b; Patterson & Moran, 1988; B. Vaughn, Egeland, Sroufe & Waters, 1979). This result also suggests that temperament alone does not determine the attachment pattern.

The Role of Temperament

Temperament refers to traits that are biologically determined (hence, relatively stable in the first two years) but modifiable over time through maturation and experience (M. K. Rothbart & Ahadi, 1994). One temperamental characteristic is a child's general responsiveness; some children are much more responsive to stimuli than others. Another temperamental characteristic is a child's susceptibility to distress. A distress-prone child is irritable and fussy early in life and cries more often than other children. According to A. H. Buss and Plomin (1984), early distress is the forerunner of fear and anger.

A child's temperament has two important effects on the child's later experience. First, the very same event (e.g., a stranger entering the room) would be more threatening to a distress-prone child than to a placid child. After many of these "threatening" experiences, the distress-prone child would come to expect threat while the placid child would not. Thus, a calm, stable, predictable environment might be very important for a distress-prone child but less important for a placid child. Second, caregivers react differently to distress-prone and placid children (Crockenberg & Acredolo, 1983; Linn & Horowitz, 1983). A placid child is more pleasant to raise than a difficult child, because a placid child in distress is easier to soothe, and the caretaker feels very competent.

Suppose that we identified temperamentally irritable babies shortly after birth and tested them in the Strange Situation at age 1. Suppose further that we observed at age 1 that those babies were often insecurely attached. Would we attribute their insecurity to their temperament or to their trust in the caretaker? Van den Boom (1989) assessed infants on the 10th and 15th days of life to identify 15 irritable and 15 nonirritable infants. All of the infants were healthy, first-born children from intact, lower income families. During the first six months of life, the mothers and infants were observed at home. When the infants were six months old, the mothers of irritable infants were asked to describe their babies; as expected, they described their infants as relatively difficult to raise. Behavioral observations at home showed that the mothers of irritable babies, over the first six months, had become less responsive to their babies than had mothers in the other group. For example, they more often ignored the child's crying. Then the infants were tested in the Strange Situation at 12 months of age. More than half of the irritable infants were insecurely attached (A and C reactions), whereas most of the other infants were securely attached (B reactions).

Van den Boom (1994, 1995) then conducted another study in which she tried to determine whether this effect could be altered by training the mothers of irritable infants. She assessed nearly 600 newborns to identify 100 irritable infants. When these infants were six to nine months of age, half of the mothers received special parent training, and half received no training. The training was designed to improve each mother's sensitivity to her child. The mothers learned to perceive and interpret signs of distress in the infant and to respond effectively. They were shown how to engage the child (e.g., imitating the child's own vocalization) and how to avoid overstimulating the child (e.g., becoming silent whenever the child averted its gaze). Training of this type not only increased the mother's know-how and sense of efficacy but also probably convinced the mother that the child's irritability was due to the child's temperament, not to her own failure as a mother.

Mothers who received the training were observed at home when the child was nine months old. They were more stimulating to the child than nontrained mothers and more in control of the infant's behavior. Their infants were judged to be more sociable; those infants also explored more and cried less. Then, when the infants reached 12 months of age, they were all tested in the Strange Situation. At 12 months, the infants of trained mothers behaved normally (they were indistinguishable from nonirritable infants); 68% were judged to be securely attached. In contrast, the untrained mothers (observed at home when the child was nine months old) seemed to be less sensitive to the child's needs. They responded primarily to negative behaviors in the child and often ignored positive and mildly negative behaviors. When their children were tested in the Strange Situation at 12 months, 72% were judged to be insecurely attached (mostly avoidant). Thus, a temperamentally irritable infant is harder to raise. Without training, those mothers were apt to give up and the child became insecurely attached. Parent training, however, can reverse the trend. Apparently, temperament can interact with child-rearing to produce a secure or insecure attachment. If a parent (in self-defense) comes to ignore a distress-prone child, the resulting neglect can affect a child's attachment style.

Experimental studies with rhesus monkeys also support this conclusion. Suomi (1987, 1999) and his colleagues selectively bred two strains of rhesus monkeys. One was highly emotional; the other was normally reactive. The investigators then identified two groups of mother monkeys that differed in the quality of their maternal behavior (as observed with prior offspring). Those in one group were highly nurturant, and those in the other group were normative (average). Shortly after the infant's birth, the investigators experimentally paired each type of infant with each type of foster mother, producing four experimental conditions—emotional versus normal infants paired with nurturant versus average foster mothers. When the youngsters reached 6 months, they were placed in a larger living group with other cross-fostered youngsters, and their behavior was observed. The type of mothering had a dramatic effect on the highly emotional youngsters, but not on the normally reactive ones. Emotional infants reared by average foster mothers reacted emotionally to minor environmental disturbances, explored less, and were often at the bottom of the dominance hierarchy. However, emotional infants reared by nurturant foster mothers coped very well: They left their mothers relatively early, explored the environment more readily, achieved a higher position in the dominance hierarchy, and showed less behavioral disturbance (Suomi, 1987; 2000).

Continuity Over Longer Periods

Should we expect an attachment classification in the first two years to persist over time? One reason to think so is that the young child forms images of other people that affect the child's later interactions. If the child expects other people to be unfriendly, the child might be relatively unfriendly. Other people would then respond to the child's unfriendliness with rejection or indifference, a self-fulfilling prophecy (R. A. Thompson, 1999).

However, there are reasons to expect a child's image of other people to change over time. New experiences can alter a person's expectancies, beliefs, and attitudes (R. A. Thompson, 1999). First, a child's reality may change. A parent who once felt burdened by a difficult infant now finds delight in a high-spirited preschooler; a parent who once enjoyed nurturing a needy infant now gets exasperated by endless battles of will. Second, new stressors may appear or old stressors may disappear. Marital tension between the parents may adversely affect a child's once secure attachments. Third, a maturing child may come to perceive a caretaker's behavior differently. A caretaker who once seemed powerful may now seem vulnerable and needy; a caretaker who once seemed scattered and unreliable may now seem earnest and well-meaning. Finally, as a child matures, new gifts (or defects) may emerge, making a child more (or less) appealing to others. A once-undistinguished child may become good-looking, intelligent, socially skillful, or athletic. A formerly promising child may turn out to be learning disabled, socially inept, or physically clumsy. Thus, a secure attachment at 12 or 24 months may launch a promising journey, but later reversals may occur. For reasons like these, we might argue against continuity across the years.

R. A. Thompson (1999) has summarized the literature on continuity. Many studies of infants have shown that securely attached children do display relatively more positive affect toward their mothers outside of the Strange Situation. They are less easily frustrated than insecurely attached children and less often aggressive. They are also more enthusiastic, and they comply more readily with their mothers' wishes. Furthermore, a child who is securely attached to the mother at age one is apt to be securely attached at age two. However, as the time interval between the two assessments increases, the size of the correlation decreases.

Evidence for long-term continuity is mixed. Some investigators have reported a significant relationship between a child's attachment classification at 12 months and the child's social behavior in school. For example, Main, Kaplan, and Cassidy (1985) studied children at age six who had been tested in the Strange Situation at 12 months. They created a test of separation anxiety involving pictures in which a child was being separated from the parents (e.g., the parents were leaving for a two-week trip); the examiner asked what the child in the picture was feeling. A response was considered good if it indicated an appropriate feeling (e.g., the child felt lonely, scared, angry, or sad). A response was considered poor if the respondent was unable or unwilling to talk about feelings. One child, for example, claimed that the child in the picture felt good and then began repeating "widididi" nonsensically. The six-year-olds were also asked what the child in the picture might do. A solution was considered good if it was constructive ("urge them not to leave"); it was considered poor if it was nonconstructive ("kill them," "run away"). Both kinds of scores (at age 6 years) were significantly correlated with the attachment style at age 12 months.

However, many other studies that R. A. Thompson (1999) reviewed did not reveal a long-term relationship between early and later attachment classifications. The discrepancy in the literature may be due, in part, to three methodological issues. First, many empirical studies classified children as secure, avoidant, or resistant-ambivalent, but they omitted the disorganized category; the disorganized category may be the most sensitive predictor of later psychopathology (M. T. Greenberg, 1999). Second, in many studies the child's attachment pattern was assessed just once (e.g., at 12 or 18 months), and that one-time classification was then correlated with the child's later behavior. A one-time classification, however, is not as stable or reliable as a composite of several testings. After all, stressors in a child's life come and go, so the child's behavior in the Strange Situation also fluctuates to some degree. However, a classification that is stable across three testings (e.g., avoidant at ages 12, 18, and 24 months) would be a better predictor than a one-time classification.

Third, many studies in R. A. Thompson's review involved children from intact, middle-income families in the United States. The parents were often volunteers who were only too happy to have their "pride and joy" tested. However, children selected in that way are generally not at great risk. They are not very likely to display an insecure attachment (or deviant social behavior later on). They constitute a low-risk population. Because insecure attachment and deviant social behavior are both very rare in a low-risk population, we would need to test a very large sample to demonstrate a statistically significant relationship between early attachment and later social behavior. When the sample is small and the behaviors of interest are rare, statistical tests are said to lack power (Fagot & Kavanaugh, 1990; M. T. Greenberg, 1999). Indeed, many studies have tested children from a low-risk population and have not detected a relationship between early attachment and later outcomes (Bates, Bayles, Bennett, Ridge, & Brown, 1991; Bates, Maslin, & Frankel, 1985; Fagot & Kavanaugh, 1990; Goldberg, Lojkasek, Minde, & Corter, 1990; M. T. Greenberg, 1999; M. Lewis, Feiring, McGuffog, & Jaskir, 1984).

However, some investigators have studied children from families at greater risk (e.g., poor families living in an unsafe neighborhood; father-absent families with a young, unemployed mother; families with an ill or psychologically impaired parent). Such families are consistently under stress, and the children show more cases of insecure attachment in infancy (and deviant social behavior later on). Thus, a statistical relationship would be easier to detect in a high-risk sample (M. T. Greenberg, 1999). In the following section we examine evidence for this relationship. Each study that we cite meets at least one of the three methodological criteria—the disorganized attachment category was included in the evaluation, the participants were assessed more than once, or the children were drawn from a disadvantaged (high-risk) population.

Insecure Attachment, Other Risk Factors, and Psychopathology

An insecure attachment that persists over many years seems to be one of several factors that put a child at risk for psychopathology. In this section we consider some of the other risk factors.

Exhibit 3.1.   Diagnostic Criteria for Oppositional Defiant Disorder

A. A pattern of negativistic, hostile, and defiant behavior lasting at least 6 months, during which four (or more) of the following are present:
    (1) often loses temper
    (2) often argues with adults
    (3) often actively defies or refuses to comply with adults' requests or rules
    (4) often deliberately annoys people
    (5) often blames others for his or her mistakes or misbehavior
    (6) is often touchy or easily annoyed by others
    (7) is often angry and resentful
    (8) is often spiteful or vindictive

    Note: Consider a criterion met only if the behavior occurs more frequently than is typically observed in individuals or comparable age and developmental level.

B. The disturbance in behavior causes clinically significant impairment in social, academic, or occcupational functioning.
C. The behaviors do not occur exclusively during the course of a Psychotic or Mood Disorder.
D. Criteria are not met for Conduct Disorder, and, if the individual is age 18 years or older, criteria are not met for Antisocial Personality Disorder.

Note. From *Diagnostic and Statistical Manual of Mental Disorders* (4th ed., text revision, p. 102) by the American Psychiatric Association, 2000, Washington, DC: Author. Reprinted with permission.

Multiple Pathways to Psychopathology

The signs and symptoms of psychopathology arise from many causes. Consider the oppositional defiant disorder as one example. The criteria of this disorder (see Exhibit 3.1) reflect "a pattern of negativistic, hostile, and defiant behavior." To qualify for the disorder, the child must show four of the eight behaviors in the table. These behaviors suggest that the child is angry (argumentative, defiant, deliberately annoying, touchy, resentful, spiteful) but we need additional information to understand why the child is angry (and at whom). Perhaps the child would like the parents to be more responsive, available, reliable, and comforting (an attachment issue). Or perhaps the child desperately wants greater freedom from over-controlling parents (an autonomy issue). In other words, the child's oppositional behavior might arise from a frustrated attachment motive or from some other frustrated motive. Alternate pathways exist, and we cannot understand the disorder (or treat the child) until we know why the child is angry.

Sources of Stress as Risk Factors

An insecure attachment is only one of several risk factors. M. T. Greenberg (1999) has added three additional categories. One includes personality traits that predispose a child to stress. For example, children who are temperamentally irritating, medically ill, or physically deviant, deformed, or disfigured are apt to be rejected by peers. Though not an issue of attachment per se, that kind of rejection adds stress to a child's daily experience.

A second category includes environmental stresses on a family that are not directly related to attachment. This category includes chronic stress from poverty and material deprivation, realistic dangers in the family's neighborhood, traumas that affect a family's security, and tension and psychopathology within the family.

The third category includes stress resulting from the parents' ineffectiveness in disciplining the children or managing the household. For example, some parents are overly harsh and punitive; others are excessively critical and controlling; still others provide too little guidance and structure. Even a child who feels securely attached—secure about the parents' availability, responsiveness, and goodwill—can experience stressful power struggles and thwarted attempts at independence.

These four sources of stress, then, are quite diverse—insecure attachments, traits that cause stress, environmental stresses on the family, and ineffective parenting. They constitute four important classes of risk factors. According to M. T. Greenberg (1999), the greater the number of risk factors, the greater the likelihood of psychopathology. These risk factors are not necessarily independent of one another. A physically abused child, for example, might well experience stress from several correlated sources: an insecure (disorganized) attachment, family violence, ineffective parenting, and parental psychopathology.

Risk Factors and Psychopathology

M. T. Greenberg (1999) has proposed a list of principles that relate risk factors to psychopathology. One principle states than an insecure attachment, by itself, does not cause psychopathology. A child who shows an avoidant reaction at 18 months (and no other risk factor) would not be a candidate. However, a physically abused child who was insecurely attached and witnessed other family violence and psychopathology would be a candidate.

A second principle is that a given form of psychopathology is not due to one specific cause. An oppositional defiant disorder can arise for different reasons. As we have seen, a child with an oppositional defiant disorder might be reacting to frustrated attachment wishes or to frustrated separation wishes.

A third principle is that a particular risk factor does not always produce the same disorder. Three children with a mother who is depressed, a physically abusive father, and an insecure attachment may differ in the syndromes that they display. One may become very anxious, another very depressed, and a third very aggressive. We are never surprised when two brothers—one temperamentally frail, frightened, and sensitive, the other temperamentally tough, callous, and thick-skinned—react differently to similar stresses.

Empirical Studies Relating Attachment and Psychopathology

An insecure attachment in combination with other risk factors does foreshadow later psychopathology. In one important longitudinal project, the Minnesota Parent–Child Project (Egeland & Sroufe, 1981a, 1981b; M. F. Erickson, Sroufe,

& Egeland, 1985; Sroufe, 1983), researchers studied 174 infants of young, single mothers. The infants were classified as avoidant, secure, or ambivalent in the Strange Situation at 12 months and at 18 months. By assessing each child twice, the investigators could identify children with a stable classification. Each child was later studied in preschool (M. F. Erickson et al., 1985; Sroufe, 1983; Troy & Sroufe, 1987), in elementary school (Renken, Egeland, Marvinney, Mangelsdorf, & Sroufe, 1989; Sroufe, 1990; Sroufe, Egeland, & Kreutzer, 1990), and in pre-adolescence (Urban, Carson, Egeland, & Sroufe, 1991). Children who were judged to be insecurely attached at 12 and 18 months showed poor peer relationships at later assessments; they were moodier, reacted more intensely to stress, and showed more signs of aggression and depression than children initially judged to be secure. At ages 10 to 11, 47 children of the original group were observed at a summer day camp (Urban et al., 1991). Those who had seemed securely attached as infants were judged to be more socially competent; they also seemed less dependent.

Lyons-Ruth, Zoll, Connell, and Grunebaum (1989) studied infants whose primary caretaker was depressed. According to subsequent ratings by their preschool teachers, the children who were judged to be most hostile in preschool had generally seemed insecurely attached as infants. Of the children with two early risk factors (disorganized attachment and depressed mothers), 55% were judged to be hostile in kindergarten. Of the children with neither risk factor, only 5% were judged that way. Shaw and Vondra (1995) studied a high-risk sample and found that the infant's attachment style at 12 months was correlated with behavior problems in preschool at age three. Children classified as disorganized at 12 months (a first risk factor) whose parents rated them as temperamentally "difficult" at age two (a second risk factor) were particularly high in aggression (Shaw, Owens, Vondra, Keenan, & Winslow, 1997).

Attachment in Adulthood

According to some theorists (Ainsworth, 1991; R. S. Weiss, 1982, 1991), adults also experience bonds of attachment toward romantic partners. That is, the bond is not only affectional but also comforting at times of stress. Therefore, when spouses divorce, they are sometimes surprised to discover feelings of loss, anxiety, and stress (R. S. Weiss, 1973, 1975).

One correlate of stress is an increased output of the pituitary-adrenal system. When the output is sustained over time, it tends to have a harmful biological effect. For one thing, it suppresses immune mechanisms so the organism becomes more vulnerable to disease (Levine, 1983). Blood samples drawn from people who recently lost a spouse show a reduced immunocompetence at the cellular level. As a result, bereaved people are less able to fight disease and are more susceptible to a wide variety of chronic diseases (Bartrop, Luckhurst, Lazaurs, Kiloh, & Penny, 1977). Likewise, people who describe themselves as lonely show a similar deficit and are more vulnerable to illness (e.g., Kiecolt-Glaser, Garner, et al., 1984; Kiecolt-Glaser & Glaser, 1987; Kiecolt-Glaser, Ricker, et al., 1984). Thus, across the life span, separation from significant others seems to have a biological cost. That separation and isolation are stressful and harmful has been demonstrated in five types of studies.

Experimental Studies of Isolation

Many older studies have shown that people become anxious when they are completely isolated from other people. In one experiment, male college students were paid to live in isolation for a week (Zubek, Bayer, & Shephard, 1969). Each student in the experimental condition stayed by himself in a small, brightly decorated, air-conditioned room, with reading material, crossword puzzles, travel slides, and instrumental music. Participants were not allowed to have visitors. Another group was treated the same way, but they were allowed to watch television and have visitors. A third group simply came to the laboratory periodically to be tested. Twenty percent of those in the isolated group found the isolation unbearable; they dropped out of the experiment by the second day, forfeiting their pay. Those who did remain described themselves as feeling lonely, anxious, restless, and worried. They also reported other symptoms of anxiety: Some felt that they were losing contact with reality, some experienced a temporal disorientation, and some reported novel or peculiar ideas.

Ways We Humanize a Lonely World

Polar explorers and solitary seafarers have reported similar reactions. They have reported that they reminisced and thought of people, sometimes even hallucinated people and anthropomorphized the inanimate world. For example, Joshua Slocum (1972), the first man to sail around the world alone, reported whimsically that he began talking to the moon after 4 months at sea. Later, as he became lonelier, he also hallucinated a benign companion. Nasby and Read (1997) studied a man who, at the age of 54, circumnavigated the earth nonstop in his sailboat; the trip took 150 days. By the third day, his log reported intense loneliness, depression, and anxiety. At first, he occasionally telephoned home, but those calls left him feeling even sadder and more lonely. He wrote, "It seems I cope better with the loneliness when I do not remind myself of the delicious alternative" (cited in Nasby & Read, 1997, p. 838). He allowed himself to read, but when he came across content describing "warmth and love shared by family and friends," he found himself crying uncontrollably. By Day 41, he worried about losing control of his melancholy.

    Ex-prisoners of war (POWs) in North Vietnam have also been interviewed about their strategies for coping with solitary confinement. Their favorite methods were ones that produced a feeling of interpersonal contact. For example, Deaton, Berg, Richlin, and Litrownik (1977) identified 27 different methods that were regularly mentioned. One helpful cluster included activities that, in the mind of the prisoner, produced a quasi-relationship with the captor. For example, some POWs spent time studying the captor's behavior in order to laugh at him (privately), thereby turning the enemy into a significant other. The strategy that was judged most useful of all was communicating with another captive through a secret code, like tapping on the wall. In contrast, impersonal methods (doing mental exercises, keeping a diary, performing ritualistic behaviors) were deemed substantially less useful.

Loss, Loneliness, and Illness

Isolated people are susceptible to a variety of physical disorders. In one early study, Kraus and Lilienfeld (1959), using data from the National Office of Vital Statistics, studied death rates in the United States over a two-year period. They showed that widowed men and women, at all ages, are much more vulnerable to premature death than married people. The death rate was higher for all of the leading causes of death, including heart disease and cancer. Similarly, Berkman and Syme (1979) interviewed 5,000 residents of California and assessed their longevity over a nine-year period. They found that married people as a group lived longer than unmarried people. The mortality rates of married men at ages 30 to 49, 50 to 59, 60 to 69 were, respectively, 3%, 12%, and 27%, whereas the corresponding rates for unmarried men were 9%, 26%, and 34%. Similar results were reported by House, Robbins, and Metzner (1982) and by Shye, Mullooly, Freeborn, and Pope (1995). Young, Benjamin, and Wallis (1963) studied nearly 4,500 bereaved men over the age of 55 and found that death rates increased approximately 40% during the first six months of bereavement. Widowed men who remarry apparently have lower mortality rates than men who do not remarry (Helsing, Szklo, & Comstock, 1981).

The same pattern holds for divorce and separation. Carter and Glick (1976) showed the negative impact of divorce on people's health. Although both genders were affected, the negative effect for men seems to be more severe than that for women (D. R. Brown, 1996; Helgeson, 2002; Schone & Weinick, 1998; Umberson, 1987; Waldron, Weiss, & Hughes, 1997). The gender difference, however, has not been entirely consistent across studies (Hope, Power, & Rodgers, 1999).

The most thoroughly studied cause of death has been heart disease. In one study, Moriyama, Krueger, and Stamler (1971) compared the death rate ascribed to heart disease for widowed, divorced, and single people with that of married people. The death rate of divorced men between the ages of 35 and 44 was divided by that of married men. A ratio of 1 indicates equal rates; a ratio above 1 indicated that divorced men had a higher death rate than the corresponding married men. At every age each category of single, divorced, and widowed people had a ratio greater than 1. In some categories the death rate was two to five times that of married people.

Everyday Stressors

Stressful events of everyday life also impair a person's health, and the most stressful events seem to involve separation and loss. T. H. Holmes and Rahe (1967) compiled a list of common life events and scaled the stressfulness of each event; hundreds of people were asked to judge how much adaptation that event would seem to require. The value "500" was assigned to the event "marriage," and every other event was rated relative to marriage. The ratings assigned to each event were then averaged and divided by 10 to yield the values shown in Table 3.1. (The list of stressful events has been updated in recent years. For an updated list of stressors and norms, see Hobson et al., 1998; M. A. Miller & Rahe, 1997; Moos, 1995; Moos & Moos, 1997. For a discussion of methodological issues, see Tausig, 1982.)

The life events in Table 3.1 are listed in order of their stressfulness. The three events judged to be most stressful (the death of a spouse, divorce, and marital separation) all involve the loss of one's spouse. The next most stressful event, jail term, also involves a separation from home and family, and that event was judged to be just as stressful as the death of a close family member. Thus, the five events that people consider the most stressful are events that involve a major interpersonal loss.

Effect of Social Support

Many researchers have examined the relationship between stress, social support, and susceptibility to illness. In one typical study, A. W. Williams, Ware, and Donald (1981) asked more than 2,000 people in Seattle to complete a questionnaire about recent stressful events. Participants were also asked about sources of social support and about physical and psychological symptoms. Both kinds of symptoms were reported most often by people with many stressors and little support, for example, by people who lose their jobs (Gore, 1978). Patients with schizophrenia have a substantially higher mortality rate if they lack social support (Christensen, Dornink, Ehlers, Schultz, 1999).

How can social support help reduce symptoms? Several mechanisms have been proposed. One is that a lack of social support itself is stressful. That is, the person wants contact with other people, but human contact is not available (see, e.g., G. C. Andrews, Tennant, Hewson, & Vaillant, 1978; Lin, Simeone, Ensel, & Kuo, 1979). A second mechanism is that social support proactively buffers negative events. That is, a negative event does not seem as stressful if the person has supportive others. According to this hypothesis, the mere availability of support buffers the experience of a negative event so that it seems less harsh (Dean & Lin, 1977). A third mechanism is that social support retroactively moderates the stress induced by a negative event. That is, a supportive person's words make the negative event more tolerable, thereby reducing stress and vulnerability to illness (e.g., Cobb, 1976; LaRocco, House, & French, 1980; Thoits, 1982). In the next chapter we examine this mechanism more closely.

Adult Attachment Styles

The concept of an attachment bond also helps clarify the behavior of adults in relationships. When we say that an adult is attached to a romantic partner, we mean that the person feels affection for that partner and the partner is able to comfort the person at times of stress. Therefore, we might ask whether different attachment styles exist among adults that are analogous to the styles observed among children. Hazan and Shaver (1987, 1990; Shaver & Hazan, 1988) postulated three adult attachment patterns, a secure pattern and two insecure

Table 3.1.   Social Readjustment Rating Scale

Rank	Life event	Mean value	Rank	Life event	Mean value
1	Death of spouse	100	22	Change in responsibilities at work	29
2	Divorce	73	23	Child leaving home	29
3	Marital separation	65	24	Trouble with in-laws	29
4	Jail term	63	25	Outstanding personal achievement	28
5	Death of close family member	63	26	Spouse begins or stops work	26
6	Personal injury or illness	53	27	Begin or end school	26
7	Marriage	50[a]	28	Change in living conditions	25
8	Fired from work	47	29	Revision of personal habits	24
9	Marital reconciliation	45	30	Trouble with boss	23
10	Retirement	45	31	Change in work hours or conditions	20
11	Change in health of family member	44	32	Change in residence	20
12	Pregnancy	40	33	Change in schools	20
13	Sex difficulties	39	34	Change in recreation	19
14	New family member	39	35	Change in church activities	19
15	Business readjustment	39	36	Change in social activities	18
16	Change in financial state	38	37	Mortgage or loan less than $10,000	17
17	Death of close friend	37	38	Change in sleeping habits	16
18	Change to different line of work	36	39	Change in number of family get-togethers	15
19	Change in number of arguments with spouse	35	40	Change in eating habits	15
20	Mortgage over $10,000	31	41	Vacation	13
21	Foreclosure of mortgage or loan	30	42	Christmas	12

Note. Marriage was arbitrarily assigned a stress value of 500; no event was judged to be more than twice as stressful. For convenience, the resulting values have been divided by 10. From "The Social Readjustment Rating Scale," by T. H. Holmes and R. H. Rahe, 1967, *Journal of Psychosomatic Research, 11,* p. 216. Copyright © 1967 by Elsevier Science, Inc. Reprinted with permission.

patterns. They wrote a brief description of each pattern and asked adults to select the pattern that best captured their feelings in a romantic relationship. The descriptions were as follows:

> Secure. "I find it relatively easy to get close to others and am comfortable depending on them. I don't often worry about being abandoned or about someone getting too close to me."
> Avoidant. "I am somewhat uncomfortable being close to others; I find it difficult to trust them completely, difficult to allow myself to depend on them. I am nervous when anyone gets too close, and often, love partners want me to be more intimate than I feel comfortable being."
> Anxious–Ambivalent. "I find that others are reluctant to get as close as I would like. I often worry that my partner doesn't really love me or won't want to stay with me. I want to get very close to my partner, and this sometimes scares people away." (Hazan & Shaver, 1987; p. 515)

The sample contained approximately 200 men and 400 women, who responded as follows: 56% selected the secure category, 25% the avoidant category, and 19% the anxious–ambivalent category. (The corresponding percentages for the infant categories are 62%, 23%, and 15%; Campos, Barrett, Lamb, Goldsmith, & Stenberg, 1983). Compared with those in the avoidant or anxious–ambivalent categories, people who described themselves as securely attached also described their romantic experiences as happier, friendlier, and more trusting. Their rate of divorce was lower, and their relationships, on average, lasted longer.

Since then, other personality inventories have been created for assessing a person's attachment style. One measure, the Experiences in Close Relationships Inventory (K. A. Brennan, Clark, & Shaver, 1998; Fraley, Waller, & Brennan, 2000), contains 36 statements on which people rate themselves. The items are organized into two different subscales. One subscale describes a person's preference for closeness—to be close or distant from the partner. A typical item is, "I feel comfortable sharing my private thoughts and feelings with my partner." The other subscale describes the person's anxiety about being left by a romantic partner. A typical item is, "I worry about being abandoned." A respondent receives a separate score for each subscale.

The two subscales are uncorrelated, so a person can obtain any combination of scores. Each subscale can be regarded as a dimension on a graph. In Figure 3.1, the X-axis represents the person's preferred degree of closeness (from *prefer distance* to *prefer closeness*). The Y-axis represents the person's anxiety about the partner's leaving (from *worried* to *self-confident*). Each quadrant of Figure 3.1 describes a different combination of the two dimensions. The upper right-hand quadrant describes people who like being close to their partner and are confident that they will not be abandoned. They are said to be "secure." The lower right-hand quadrant describes people who like to be close but worry that the partner will leave; they are said to be "preoccupied with relationships" (analogous to the resistant–ambivalent category of childhood). The other two quadrants describe people who prefer more distance in a relationship (analogous to the avoidant category of childhood). Those in the upper left-hand quadrant do

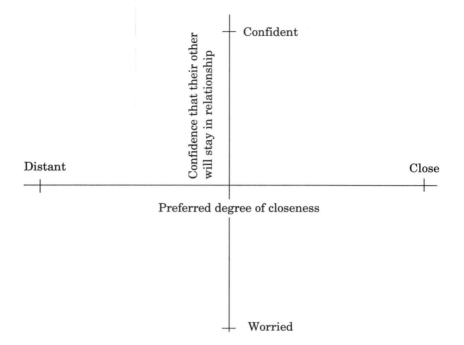

Figure 3.1. Two dimensions in attachment measure.

not worry about losing their partner ("dismissing–avoidant"), and those in the lower left-hand quadrant are very worried about losing their partner ("fearful–avoidant"). Thus, Figure 3.1 suggests four rather than three adult attachment patterns.

Bartholomew (1990) originally proposed this four-category classification. Using Bowlby's (1973) theory, she reasoned that children acquire two kinds of internal working models. One concerns the child's image of other people (positive vs. negative) corresponding to the X-axis in Figure 3.1. The other internal working model concerns the person's image of the self (positive vs. negative) corresponding to the Y-axis in Figure 3.1. Bartholomew showed that people with a negative self-image generally report more subjective distress of all kinds (e.g., less self-confidence and more anxiety, depression, and loneliness). In Figure 3.2, the image of others and the image of the self are each dichotomized to produce four combinations. Each combination represents one of the attachment styles described in Figure 3.1 (Bartholomew, 1990; Bartholomew & Horowitz, 1991).

Sometimes case examples illustrate how a profound experience early in life can shape a person's later views of relationships. Consider the work of René Magritte, a 20th-century surrealist artist. Magritte lost his mother when he was 13 years old. His mother had been depressed for years and attempted suicide several times during his childhood. Then one night she left her bedroom and drowned herself in a nearby river (Sylvester, 1992). Exact details about the incident are unclear, and Magritte almost never spoke about his mother's death to anyone, including his wife (E. H. Spitz, 1994; Sylvester, 1992). However, toward the end of his life, he told his biographer that his mother's face had been

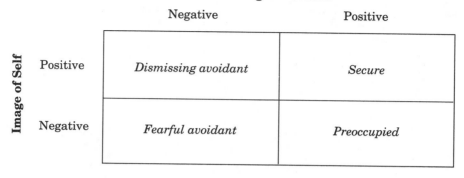

Figure 3.2. Four combinations of "Image of Self" and "Image of Others." From "Attachment Styles Among Young Adults: A Test of a Four-Category Model," *Journal of Abnormal Psychology, 61*, p. 227. Copyright © 1991 by the American Psychological Association. Reprinted with permission.

covered by her nightgown when she was found and that the only feeling he recalled (or perhaps imagined that he recalled) was a feeling of intense pride at being the pitiable center of attention.

One art historian (E. H. Spitz, 1994) has suggested that Magritte's depressed and suicidal mother was relatively unavailable to the child. Burdened with physical pain and fatigue, she had three sons in close succession. René was the oldest, and his experience of seeing his dead mother with her nightgown over her head (whether observed, fantasized, or dreamed) seems to have left him with images and feelings that had a lasting impact on his art. The death of his mother echoes the themes in his work—death by water, faces missing or concealed, human figures that defy human connection. Many of his paintings depict a person having severe difficulty connecting with another person: The other person is cold, lifeless, or mannequinlike.

One of Magritte's paintings, shown in Figure 3.3, artistically and creatively reflects his preoccupation with loss, separation, and longing. This disturbing image, *The Spirit of Geometry*, depicts a role reversal between mother and child, devoid of any emotional engagement. Other paintings by Magritte show figures that are unable to connect. In several cases, the figures do not make eye contact. In a painting called *The Lovers*, two figures kiss, but their faces are covered and concealed from each other. Another disturbing work, *The Month of the Grape-Harvest*, places the viewer in an empty room looking out the window. Outside, a crowd of men stare into the room. There is nothing in the room for them to look at except the viewer, but none of them makes eye contact with the viewer, as though the viewer does not exist. Apparently, Magritte's long-standing preoccupation with human connection was, in this way, put to creative use.

Summary

Attachment styles help clarify a person's motives in interpersonal relationships: Does the person want closeness, or does the person prefer distance? Does the

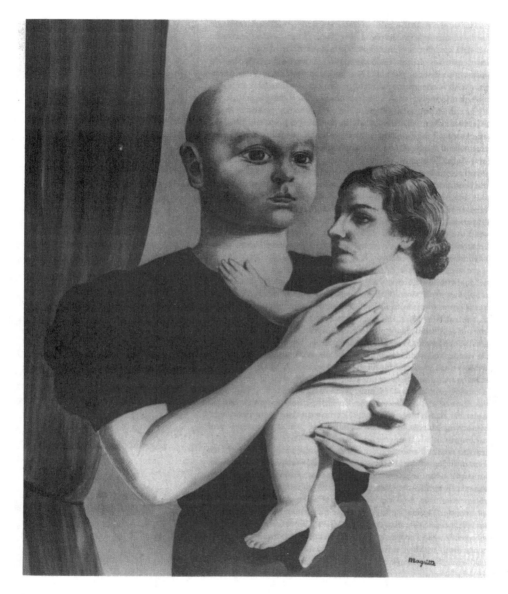

Figure 3.3 *The Spirit of Geometry* by René Magritte. Copyright © 2003 C. Herscovici, Brussels/Artists Rights Society (ARS), New York. Reprinted with permission.

person feel in control of relationships, or does the person feel helplessly vulnerable to rejection and abandonment? Some people routinely avoid closeness in order to protect themselves from rejection. Some yearn for closeness but desperately fear abandonment. These distinctions will help us understand personality disorders in later chapters.

Attachment patterns also clarify the person's image of the self and image of other people. These images (cognitions) affect the person's interpersonal interactions. A person who judges others to be friendly behaves differently from one who judges others to be unfriendly. In the next chapter we examine interpersonal interactions in everyday life. We summarize empirical evidence that highlights communion and agency as the organizing themes behind interpersonal behaviors. We show how a person systematically strives to satisfy goals through interpersonal interactions. We also show how interpersonal interactions may cause frustrated goals and negative affect.

4

Communion and Agency in Interpersonal Interactions

Interpersonal behaviors can be organized in terms of their meaning. Because interpersonal behaviors arise from underlying motives (or goals), it is no surprise that two organizing dimensions of meaning correspond to communion and agency. In this chapter we examine a contemporary version of an interpersonal model that has been evolving for years to explain certain forms of psychopathology. We emphasize (a) the motive behind the behavior and (b) the type of reaction from a partner that would satisfy (or frustrate) that motive. The principles that we describe are used in later chapters to explain personality disorders and other forms of psychopathology.

History of the Interpersonal Model

Interpersonal theories, like those of Horney (1945), Leary (1957), and Sullivan (1953), began to emerge in the 1940s and 1950s, typically as a reaction against prevailing theories of the time, particularly psychoanalysis and behavioral theories of learning. Behavioral theories had reduced interpersonal events to discrete stimuli and responses: One person's action was viewed as a stimulus that elicited the other person's reaction as a response. However, Leary (1957) argued that people do not merely "emit" actions in each other's presence. A person who boasts to another person "is doing something *to* the other person" (p. 91). Boasting communicates a variety of messages, including a desire to be acknowledged as superior. A boaster wants something from the listener, which the listener may or may not provide. Our model draws on Leary's thinking to clarify what a person wants from the interaction.

Early interpersonal theories also challenged classical psychoanalytic thinking. Originally, the psychoanalytic theory focused on the energy that an organism receives from the environment and the vicissitudes of energy expended through sex and aggression. It particularly emphasized processes within the person that were thought to impede the release of energy, thereby causing psychiatric symptoms. Later psychoanalytic writers (Horney, 1945; Sullivan, 1953), however, preferred to explain psychiatric symptoms in terms of people's social interactions. Karen Horney (1945), for example, identified three broad classes of interpersonal behaviors that she considered central to psychopathology—behaviors in which the person (a) moves away from other people, (b) moves toward other people, or (c) moves against other people. Whereas most people flexibly exhibit all three kinds of behavior in their everyday interactions, some people, trying to avoid anxiety, rigidly overuse one of the categories. In Horney's theory, a person with a compliant personality is one who has learned to avoid anxiety by being friendly and conciliatory—overly generous, self-sacrificing, caring, and agreeable. A person with an aggressive personality is one who has learned to avoid anxiety by being hostile and dominating—ungenerous, cold, suspicious, and critical. A person with a detached personality is one who has come to mistrust interpersonal involvements altogether and has learned to avoid both intimacy and aggression, preferring to be alone when working, sleeping, or eating. The interpersonal model presented in the next section also identifies clusters of behaviors. First, however, we must underscore two general assumptions.

1. *Interpersonal behavior is motivated.* When Person A initiates an interaction with Person B, we assume that A's behavior is purposeful (goal directed). The person may or may not be conscious of the goal, and goals may range in importance from trivial to vital. The importance of a particular goal to a given person may also vary in importance from time to time. On average, however, some goals are generally more important to one person than to another. Being admired may be vitally important to one person but unimportant to another. Finally, we assume that people feel happy when an important goal is satisfied and unhappy (sad, angry) when it is frustrated.

2. *Two people may have different perceptions of the same interpersonal interaction.* When we observe two people interacting, we sometimes forget that three (or more) different perspectives may be identified. Suppose we observe Jack dominating Jill and Jill yielding to Jack's influence. Jack's behavior and Jill's reaction might be described differently by Jack, by Jill, and by an outside observer. To say that Jack is dominating Jill might be accurate from Jill's perspective or from an observer's perspective, but not from Jack's perspective. Therefore, the terms used by one party to describe an interpersonal behavior might not be accurate from someone else's perspective. It is always important to specify the perspective when we analyze an interpersonal interaction. As we shall show, a difference in perspective often explains miscommunications, misunderstandings, and interpersonal problems.

The model that we present borrows heavily from other models—for example, those of Benjamin (1974, 1986, 1996); Birtchnell (1993); Carson (1969); Horowitz and Vitkus (1986); Kiesler (1983, 1996); Leary (1957); Orford (1986); and Wiggins (1982). The version described in this chapter is discussed in three sections. The first section concerns the organization of interpersonal behaviors on two dimensions of meaning. The second section explains why, theoretically, interpersonal behaviors are organized that way. The third section considers the complement of an interpersonal behavior—the reaction from the partner that would satisfy the instigator's goal or motive.

The model presented here should be regarded as a conceptual tool that helps us think systematically about interpersonal processes and psychopathology, not a precise theory (at this time) that yields specific predictions for every individual in every situation. After we have examined the model, we shall use it to clarify three issues in the research literature. First, we re-examine the concept of social support, showing how social support should match the goal (wishes) of the recipient if it is to be useful. Then we use the model to show how unwanted support can sustain or even exacerbate psychopathology. That is, a well-intentioned friend, trying to help a depressed person, may unwittingly sustain (or aggravate) the depressed person's distress. Finally, we examine miscommunications more generally.

The Organization of Interpersonal Behavior Along Two Primary Dimensions

To begin with, consider a domain that is interpersonal (e.g., interpersonal behaviors or interpersonal traits). The domain of interpersonal behaviors includes all behaviors that fit the frame "Person A [does this to] Person B": "A dominates B," "A pampers B," "A ignores B," "A gives advice to B," "A loves B," "A welcomes B," "A takes care of B," "A exploits B," "A attacks B," "A yields to B," "A walks away from B," "A leans on B," and so on. Our task is to determine the main dimensions of meaning that run through the different behaviors. Then we need to use those dimensions to display the semantic structure.

Interpersonal behaviors vary along many dimensions of meaning, but two dimensions are especially salient for much of the variation in meaning. If we could identify those dimensions, we could construct a graph, locate each behavior graphically to describe its approximate meaning and then compare different behaviors to one another. Two behaviors (e.g., "A welcomes B" and "A takes care of B") would be close to each other on the graph, whereas two other behaviors (e.g., "A avoids B" and "A welcomes B") would be far apart. Thus, their proximity on the graph would reflect their similarity of meaning.

Various statistical procedures have been used to expose the basic dimensions of meaning: factor analysis, principal components analysis, and multidimensional scaling. To apply these methods, the investigator first evaluates the similarity of each pair of interpersonal behaviors (e.g., the similarity of "dominates" and "gives advice to" or the similarity of "dominates" and "yields to." How can similarity be assessed? One possible procedure would be to have a representative group of participants judge how often they have exhibited each behavior during the past month. If two behaviors are similar in meaning, people who often express one behavior often express the other, and people who seldom express one seldom express the other. As a measure of similarity, the investigator would compute the degree of correlation between the participants' ratings for every pair of interpersonal behaviors. Two behaviors that are highly correlated are considered to be similar; and two behaviors that are negatively correlated are considered to be dissimilar.

Factor analysis or a similar statistical procedure would then be used to simplify the pattern of correlation coefficients. These procedures identify hypothetical dimensions that are suggested by the pattern of correlation coefficients. They show how much information in the original matrix of correlation coeffi-

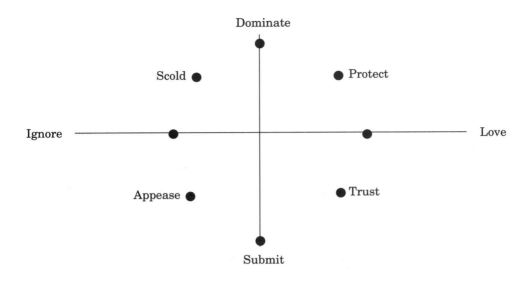

Figure 4.1.   Interpersonal behaviors placed in a two-dimensional space.

cients can be explained by 1 or 2 (or more) hypothetical dimensions. Usually, in the interest of parsimony, we want to identify the smallest number of hypothetical dimensions that adequately approximates information in the original matrix of correlation coefficients. Criteria exist by which we can determine the smallest number of dimensions that is considered adequate.

The procedure of factor analysis provides a coordinate for each interpersonal behavior along each hypothetical dimension. We can then plot a graph showing each behavior on each dimension. For example, Figure 4.1 shows interpersonal behaviors on a two-dimensional graph. The behavior "A loves B" falls at the positive end of the X-dimension, and "A ignores B" falls at the negative end. "A dominates B" falls at the positive end of the Y-dimension, and "A yields to B" falls at the negative end. Other behaviors in Figure 4.1 reflect other combinations of the X- and Y-dimensions.

If we wanted to describe the domain of interpersonal traits, we might identify many interpersonal traits, ask people to rate themselves on each, and then compute the Pearson correlation coefficient for each pair of traits. A factor analysis would then reveal the most salient hypothetical dimensions (Wiggins, 1979). Each trait could then be located on a graph like the one shown in Figure 4.2. Traits like *kind* and *compassionate* fall at the positive end of the X-dimension, and traits like *cold* and *miserly* at the negative end. Traits like *assertive* and *domineering* fall at the positive end of the Y-dimension, and traits like *compliant* and *unassertive* at the negative end.

Over the past 50 years many investigators have used variations of these methods to expose the most salient dimensions of meaning; the studies have yielded very similar results. LaForge and Suczek (1955) and Leary (1957) first characterized interpersonal traits in this way. Later, investigators applied the procedures to a variety of other interpersonal domains (e.g., Benjamin, 1974,

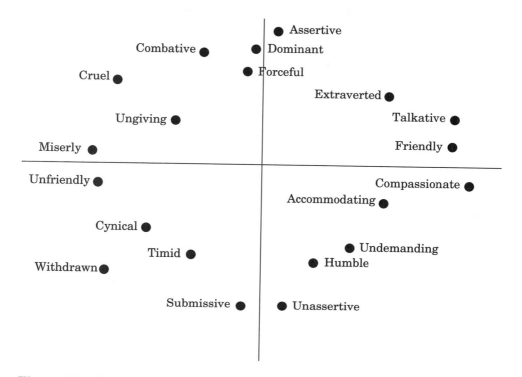

Figure 4.2. Interpersonal traits organized in two dimensions.

1977, 1986, 1996; Berzins, 1977; Bierman, 1969; Carson, 1969; DeVoge & Beck, 1978; Kiesler, 1983, 1996; Locke, 2000; Lorr & Strack, 1990; Moskowitz, 1994; Strack, 1987; Strack, Lorr, & Campbell, 1990; Trobst, 1999; Wiggins, 1979, 1982; Wiggins & Trobst, 1997). Most of these investigators have concluded that two dimensions adequately approximate the information contained in the original matrix of correlation coefficients. The exact amount of variance explained by the first two dimensions depends on the particular method, the items selected for study, and the context of the study. Dimensions beyond the second do add nuance to the meaning of the elements, but the first two dimensions seem to provide a good first-approximation. We can use these two dimensions, then, as a heuristic device to help us think abstractly about interpersonal behaviors.

Statistical procedures do not name the dimensions, however. Researchers have referred to the X-axis as *connectedness, affiliation, love, warmth,* and *nurturance,* and we use the superordinate term *communion* for this axis. The Y-axis has been called *influence, control, dominance, power,* or *status,* and we use the superordinate term *agency* for that axis. Thus, *communion,* as the horizontal dimension, ranges in meaning from "connected, loving, or close" to "disconnected, indifferent, or distant." *Agency,* as the vertical dimension, ranges in meaning from "influencing, controlling, or dominating" to "yielding, relinquishing control, or submitting." Many behaviors are described by a combination of the two dimensions. In Figure 4.1, "A protects B" is positive in communion and

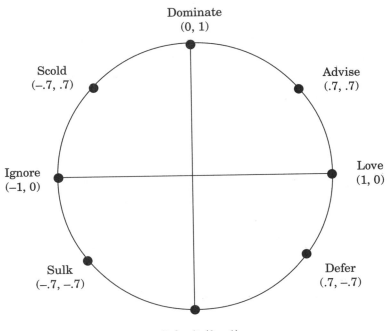

Figure 4.3.   Interpersonal behaviors with corresponding graphical coordinates.

positive in agency; "A criticizes B" is negative in communion but positive in agency. Behaviors occur at every location on the graph.

Notice that the elements in Figures 4.1 and 4.2 tend to fall around the circumference of a circle. The metric that is used to describe the "amount of X" and the "amount of Y" is arbitrary, so it is sometimes convenient to think of interpersonal behaviors or interpersonal traits on a unit-circle (a circle whose radius is 1). An illustration is shown in Figure 4.3. Each dimension ranges numerically from −1 (the negative extreme) through 0 (neutral) to +1 (the positive extreme). The behavior "A loves B" has the coordinates (1, 0)—it is maximal on communion and neutral on agency. "A dominates B" has the coordinates (0, 1)—neutral on communion and maximal on agency. The behavior "A advises B" is a composite of X and Y. In Figure 4.3, the coordinates of that behavior correspond to a point on the unit circle (.7, .7) that reflects equal amounts of X and Y.

If the elements fall along a circle, then the squared coordinates of every element must add up to a constant: $x^2 + y^2 = r^2$. If the radius of the circle is 1, then $x^2 + y^2 = 1$. In Figure 4.3, an element like *love*, which is extreme in communion (x = 1), has to be neutral in agency (y = 0). In other words, an element that is extreme along one dimension is neutral along the other dimension. Apparently, a behavior or trait that is extreme in communion (x = 1) is generally not extreme in agency. Likewise, a behavior like *dominate* that is extreme in agency (y = 1) is generally not extreme in communion. When the elements on the graph fall along a circle, they are said to form a *circumplex*.

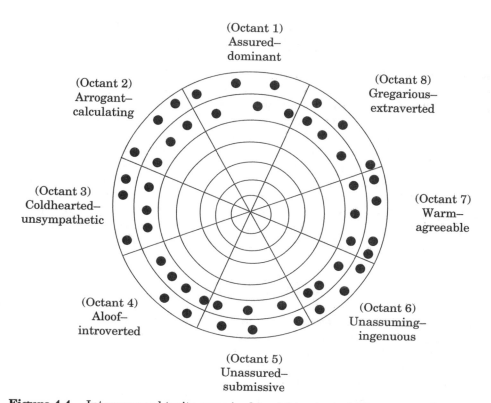

Figure 4.4. Interpersonal traits organized in eight octants (eight personality scales). From "The Prototype as a Construct in Abnormal Psychology," by L. M. Horowitz et al., 1981, *Journal of Abnormal Psychology, 90.* Copyright © 1981 by the American Psychological Association. Reprinted with permission of the authors.

Two elements that are close together in the circumplex (similar x- and y-coordinates) have similar meanings, and they are positively correlated. People who strongly exhibit one behavior or trait would tend to exhibit the other; people who rarely exhibit one would rarely exhibit the other. However, behaviors that are diametrically opposite each other have contrasting meanings; they are negatively correlated: People who often exhibit one rarely exhibit the other. Thus, the proximity of elements tells us about their degree of correlation.

Wiggins (1979) divided the graph into eight regions (octants) to create eight personality scales. To understand his procedure, consider the traits in Figure 4.2. The graph as a whole may be divided into eight octants, as shown in Figure 4.4. Octant 1 contains traits that are high in agency but neutral in communion (e.g., *assertive, dominant, self-confident, forceful,* and *persistent*). People are asked to rate themselves on 16 of these traits, and the self-ratings are summed. The score on that scale thus measures a higher order trait (which Wiggins called *assured–dominant*). Similarly Octant 7 contains traits that that are high in communion but neutral in agency (e.g., *kind, sympathetic, charitable, nurturant,* and *warm*). Each person's ratings on 16 of those traits are summed, and the score is said to measure the higher order trait *warm–agreeable*. Octant 8 contains traits that are high on both dimensions (e.g., *cheerful, jovial, enthusiastic, outgoing,* and *extraverted*). The resulting score for that octant is said to measure the higher order trait *gregarious–extraverted*. In that way, Wiggins created separate scales to assess each of the eight octants.

In general, scales that are near each other (e.g., Scale 7 and Scale 8) are positively correlated, whereas scales that are diametrically opposite each other are negative correlated. Scales that are 90° apart, like Scale 1 (reflecting agency) and Scale 7 (reflecting communion), are generally uncorrelated: A person might have any combination of scores on Scale 1 and Scale 7—high on both, high on one and low on the other, low on both—producing a correlation coefficient of 0.

As a heuristic device, then, we approximate the meaning of interpersonal elements in terms of the two most salient dimensions, communion and agency. When interpersonal behaviors or traits are plotted on the two-dimensional graph, they tend to fall around a circle. Elements that are near each other have similar meanings and they are positively correlated. Elements that are diametrically opposite each other have contrasting meanings and they are negatively correlated. Elements midway between the two extremes are uncorrelated.

Interpretation of the Two Dimensions as Motives

Why are communion and agency so salient as organizing dimensions? One possible reason is that communal and agentic motives give rise to the corresponding interpersonal behaviors. Behaviors that connect two people provide a comforting sense of security. Behaviors that influence others or display competence provide a sense of autonomy. As we have seen, the two dimensions reflect two developmental tasks that every child encounters: (a) to connect securely with other people to form a larger protective community and (b) to achieve a reasonably stable and realistic sense of competence, influence, and effectiveness (Angyal, 1941; Erikson, 1963).

An interpersonal behavior may be ambiguous until we understand the motivation behind it. When a wife says to her husband, "Let's straighten the apartment before we go out," her goal may be largely communal; but her husband may interpret it to be agentic. That is, she may desire closeness through teamwork, whereas he may perceive her intent as controlling. We cannot locate the behavior graphically until we understand the motive behind it.

Basic Motives and Personality Development

Blatt (1990) has written that personality develops as an interplay between two developmental lines, one that leads ideally to satisfying intimacy with others (communion) and one that leads ideally to a stable, realistic, autonomous, and essentially competent self-image (agency). Development along one line requires development along the other line. As described in chapter 3, children initially need a sense of trust in other people. Given that, they can take risks and separate from the adult to explore, trusting that the adults will rescue them if necessary. Acquiring competence thus requires a backlog of positive interpersonal experiences. The converse is also true: To become intimate with someone requires self-confidence. A person who feels grossly inadequate may not freely exchange intimate self-disclosures because shameful secrets might be revealed and the person might get rejected. According to Blatt, interpersonal difficulties can arise either because of problems with connectedness, problems with individuation, or problems with both.

Blatt and Schichman (1983) postulated two primary configurations of psychopathology that correspond to these developmental lines. Some psychopathologies, like the histrionic personality disorder, reflect distorted and exaggerated attempts to maintain interpersonal connections. Other forms of psychopathology, like the obsessive–compulsive personality disorder, reflect distorted and exaggerated attempts to exercise control and present the self in an acceptable light. Whereas one reflects a preoccupation with closeness, intimacy, and love, the other reflects a preoccupation with control, autonomy, and self-definition.

Even among people who function very well, there are those who greatly exaggerate one motive at the expense of the other. The award-winning play *Wit* (Edson, 1999) concerns a woman whose prominent agentic motives obscured her need for communion. The play is about Vivian Bearing, a professor of English, who had spent years studying the brilliant but complex *Holy Sonnets* of John Donne, poems concerning issues of life, death, and God. Although some people consider teaching to be a nurturing profession, Professor Bearing's approach was exclusively work- and achievement-oriented. In the play she describes herself as tough, demanding, and uncompromising, "never one to turn from a challenge." "After 20 years," she reports, "I can say with confidence, no one is quite as good (a scholar) as I." Then, at age 50, she is diagnosed with terminal ovarian cancer. The hospital physician who is assigned to treat her is a research fellow in oncology, once a student in her notoriously difficult undergraduate class. Like her, he has little concern for bedside manner and views her primarily through the lens of science (and his own future career). As the story unfolds, her case breaks new medical ground: She survives eight excruciating rounds of chemotherapy (though her cancer is not controlled), and she wryly notes that she has broken the record and become something of a celebrity. As her stay in the hospital lengthens, however, she is stripped of every symbol of her former achievement. In time she finds herself agonizingly alone, terrified and agitated, and discovers an intense yearning for human contact. In a rare display of vulnerability, she poignantly concludes, "Now is a time for simplicity. Now is a time for, dare I say it, kindness." Thus, in time, her need for communion catches up with her.

Conflict of Motives

Agentic motives and communal motives sometimes conflict with one another in everyday life. Suppose a woman competed with a good friend for an elective office and won. In the process of satisfying her own agentic striving, she may have disappointed and alienated her friend, thereby jeopardizing the friendship. Exline and Lobel (1999) discuss this type of conflict, showing how strivings for personal mastery and self-definition can clash with strivings for communion. For this reason, people often conceal their success or downplay its significance. In one experiment (Brigham, Kelso, Jackson, & Smith, 1997), college students were told that they had outperformed other students, whom they then met for a face-to-face discussion. The results demonstrated the participants' reluctance to divulge their own score to their partners. For similar reasons, academically gifted students frequently conceal their superior abilities from peers through a variety of "camouflaging" strategies (Arroyo & Zigler, 1995; Cross, Coleman, & Terhaar-Yonkers, 1991). The conflict is especially salient among people with strong communal needs. Santor and Zuroff (1997) told female college students that they had outperformed a friend on a test. The students were then asked to work together with their outperformed friend and redo the test. Participants with strong communal needs more frequently changed their answers to match those of their outperformed friend.

To summarize, interpersonal behaviors seem to be organized around the two broad classes of motives, communion and agency. A communal motive and an agentic motive do sometimes conflict with one another, but normal development requires some reasonable satisfaction of both. In psychopathology, individuals exaggerate one type of motive at the expense of the other. Much research concerning interpersonal forms of psychotherapy examines motives that conflict. For example, a person may want to be both close to someone and at the same time free to pursue his or her own interests. Sometimes a conflict becomes apparent in the relationship with the therapist. A huge body of literature has examined ways of identifying these conflicts and evaluating change in conflicts in the course of treatment (e.g., Beutler, 1979; Crits-Christoph & Connolly, 2001; Horvath & Luborsky, 1993; Luborsky & Crits-Christoph, 1998; Perry, 2001; Piper, Joyce, McCallum, & Azim, 1993; Safran & Muran, 1996; Stiles, Shapiro, & Elliott, 1986; Strauss, Eckert, & Ott, 1993; Winston, Winston, Samstag, & Muran, 1994).

Interpersonal Complementarity

If a person's interpersonal behavior arises from a motive, then the partner's reaction could satisfy or frustrate that motive. When Person A dominates Person B, we assume that A wants B to yield. When A self-discloses to B, we assume that A wants B to reciprocate closeness. In other words, an interpersonal behavior seems to invite a particular class of reactions from the partner. The invited reaction is called the behavior's *complement* (Carson, 1969; Kiesler, 1996; Leary, 1957); it is the behavior that we assume will satisfy the person's goal, motive, or desire. When we say that one person invites a particular reaction, we are implying that the person's behavior communicates a desire for the complement. When A brags to B, for example, A is not merely reciting achievements; A is inviting B to "admire me, look up to me, respect me." If the communication is unambiguous, both parties understand it the same way. The important point is that A's action invites a specific reaction from B, and B may grant that wish or not. Neither party needs to be fully aware of A's desire.

What is the formal relationship between an interpersonal behavior and its complement? How can we describe it on the two-dimensional graph? According to the interpersonal model, an interpersonal behavior and its complement are similar with respect to communion (connection invites connection, detachment invites detachment) and reciprocal with respect to agency (control invites deference, deference invites control). Warm control (e.g., giving friendly advice) and warm deference (e.g., seeking advice) are complements; each invites the other. The same holds for detached control and detached deference. When A scolds B (detached control), A invites B to apologize or justify himself (detached deference). When A helplessly discloses a personal problem to B (warm deference), A is inviting B to help, advise, or encourage (warm control).

What if one person invites a particular reaction but the partner's reaction is noncomplementary? If two people keep trying to influence each other, for example, they might become stuck in a power struggle in which neither satisfies the goal of the other. A similar frustration would occur if each tries to defer to the other. For example, one person might say, "What do you want to do this evening?" And the other might reply, "I don't know; I'll leave it up to you." Then the first might reply, "No, you decide;" to which the other replies, "No, you decide." Neither would accept the invitation to take charge, and both parties would become frustrated.

Kiesler (1996) and his colleagues (e.g., Kiesler, Schmidt, & Wagner, 1997; Wagner, Kiesler, & Schmidt, 1995) divided the action–reaction sequence into four steps: (a) Covert processes in Person A (goals and other subjective events) lead to (b) Person A's overt action, which in turn leads to (c) covert processes in Person B (emotional reactions, perceptions, and other subjective events), which lead to (d) Person B's overt reaction. This description emphasizes the many subjective events that contribute to the communication between partners. As a result, two partners may perceive the same behavior differently. As we have noted, Person A's intention and Person B's perception of that intention may be very different. Person A may wish to influence Person B, but B may not recognize that wish. Or B may recognize A's wish and try to comply, but A may not perceive B's reaction that way. Systematic miscommunications like these are discussed in the section "Three Applications."

Empirical Studies of Complementarity

A number of studies have been summarized by Bluhm, Widiger, and Miele (1990), Dryer and Horowitz (1997), Horowitz and Vitkus (1986), Kiesler (1983, 1996), and Orford (1986). Some of these studies have interpreted complementarity in strictly behavioral terms, as though an interpersonal behavior (the stimulus) elicits the complement as an automatic reflex. According to this interpretation, an action and its complement would constitute a fixed action pattern: The stimulus mechanically and automatically elicits the response. The literature does not support this interpretation of complementarity. That is why we stress the communication between the two parties. An interpersonal action invites the partner to react in a particular way, but an invitation does not guarantee the desired reaction.

The clearest study of complementarity was conducted by Strong et al. (1988). These authors divided the interpersonal space into eight octants. As shown in Figure 4.5, they labeled the behaviors in these octants *leading, self-enhancing, critical, distrustful, self-effacing, docile, cooperative,* and *nurturant.* Eighty female students (the participants) each interacted with a female confederate–actress, who was trained to enact behavior corresponding to one of the eight octants. (Confederates in the "leading" condition, for example, behaved in ways

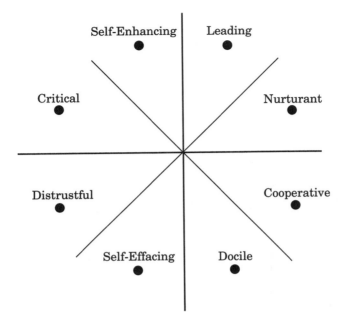

Figure 4.5. Behaviors enacted in eight experimental conditions. From "The Dynamic Relations Among Interpersonal Behaviors: A Test of Complementarity and Anticomplementarity," by S. R. Strong et al., 1988, *Journal of Personality and Social Psychology, 54,* p. 799. Copyright © 1988 by the American Psychological Association. Adapted with permission.

that observers could recognize as leading.) Each participant was paired with a confederate, and the partners were told to create a story together using pictures from the Thematic Apperception Test (TAT; Murray, 1943). During the interaction each confederate enacted her pre-assigned role. Every interaction was videotaped, and the partner's reactions were transcribed verbatim.

For every category of confederate behaviors, the investigators examined the participants' reactions. Consider those occasions when the confederate was "leading" (i.e., her behavior was friendly–dominant): The complement to "leading" in the authors' system (Strong & Hills, 1986) is "docile" (leading behavior invites docile behavior), so the investigators expected a high frequency of docile reactions. The single most frequent reactions were indeed docile behaviors; they comprised 31.2% of the responses. Other frequent reactions were other forms of friendly–yielding behavior (see Table 4.1 [column a]). Therefore, for the leading category, the participants often accepted the invitation and responded with the complement. Some participants did not, but the majority did. Likewise, when the confederate's behavior was docile (Table 4.1 [column d]), the participant's reaction was most often leading. Similar results occurred for every category on the right-hand (connected) side of the graph.

The participants' reactions to detached behaviors, however, were less often complementary. As shown in Table 4.1 [column h], "self-enhancing" (bragging) behavior, for example, rarely led to the complement, "self-effacing" behavior. Instead, the participants often reacted to the partner's bragging with coopera-

Table 4.1. Relative Frequency of Different Participant Responses to Various Confederate (Stimulus) Behaviors

Participant's response	Confederate's (stimulus) behavior							
	[a] Leading	[b] Nurturant	[c] Cooperative	[d] Docile	[e] Self-Effacing	[f] Distrustful	[g] Critical	[h] Self-Enhancing
Leading	19.6	27.8	49.4	42.2	9.8	16.4	18.2	10.5
Self-Enhancing	4.0	4.6	2.6	7.0	5.4	14.6	5.0	4.4
Critical	1.6	2.0	3.9	10.6	6.2	17.2	14.6	8.2
Distrustful	2.4	1.6	2.8	0.6	4.2	3.8	14.3	6.0
Self-Effacing	5.2	11.8	7.9	4.1	20.7	16.2	9.0	7.1
Docile	31.2	7.4	4.9	2.4	12.4	2.1	19.2	11.9
Cooperative	29.5	30.6	12.1	1.2	15.5	10.6	8.6	32.0
Nurturant	6.5	14.1	16.2	32.0	25.7	19.3	11.2	20.1

Note. From "The Dynamic Relations Among Interpersonal Behaviors: A Test of Complementarity and Anticomplementarity," by S. R. Strong, H. I. Hills, C. T. Kilmartin, H. DeVries, K. Lanier, B. N. Nelson, et al., 1988, *Journal of Personality and Social Psychology, 54,* p. 806. Copyright © 1988 by the American Psychological Association. Adapted with permission from the authors.

tive behavior—as though the participant were trying to transform a cool disengagement into a warmer interaction. Clearly, people do not react automatically to disengaged control with disengaged compliance. They may refuse the invitation and then try to influence the partner. One person might criticize, blame, or scold the other, and the partner might criticize, blame, or scold back. Or the partner might try to steer the invitation for cool behavior into a warmer direction. Tracey (1994) noted that, in U.S. culture, people generally exhibit friendly behavior more often than cool behavior, even when the initiating behavior is cool. That is, friendly behavior has a higher base rate than cool behavior, and that is one reason for noncomplementarity.

Tiedens and Fragale (2003) showed experimentally that people display complementarity in nonverbal ways as well. In their experiment, each participant worked with a partner–confederate, who adopted one of three physical postures during the task: an "expansive" (domineering) posture, a neutral posture, or a "constricted" (yielding) posture. Expansive confederates draped one arm over the back of an adjacent chair and rested their right foot on their left thigh, making their right knee protrude. Constricted confederates sat slightly slouched, with their legs together and their hands in their lap. Ech participant's "expansiveness" was then measured from the videotape. Participants working with an expansive confederate became increasingly constricted during the session, whereas those with a constricted confederate became increasingly expansive. In a second experiment, participants believed that their skin conductance was being measured; the apparatus required them to assume a particular posture, which was manipulated experimentally to be expansive or constricted. The confederate's posture was also varied systematically. Participants indicated that they liked the confederate better and felt more comfortable when the confederate's posture complemented their own.

Similarly, Sadler and Woody (2003) used an elegant statistical model to demonstrate complementarity in interacting partners. They showed that one person's dominanting behavior tends to be followed by the other partner's yielding behavior, and vice versa. They also showed that the behavior of one tends to be followed by behavior in the other that matches the level of friendliness.

Frustrated Goals and Negative Emotions

If Person A were to invite a communal behavior from Person B but B's reaction did not satisfy A's goal, then A's goal would be frustrated. If that goal really mattered to A, then A would experience negative affect. Suppose A invited communion ("How about having dinner together tonight?") but B refused ("No, I don't think so."). By frustrating A's goal, B's reaction would induce negative affect in A (sadness, anger). Person A might then walk away, or try to negotiate further, or retaliate by finding a way to frustrate some goal of B's.

Writers of drama deliberately frustrate the goals of characters to arouse our curiosity about ensuing consequences. As one example, consider the play *A Streetcar Named Desire* by Tennessee Williams (1947). A number of scenes in this play exhibit struggle, negotiation, and eventual resolution. The play involves a young married couple, Stella and Stanley, who receive a visit from

Stella's sister, Blanche. From their earliest encounters, Stanley and Blanche do not get along. Blanche, a lively, flirtatious, and somewhat flamboyant Southern belle, keeps trying to manipulate Stanley with her feminine charms; and Stanley, a tough, macho truck-driver, refuses to be dominated by his sister-in-law. The two get into repeated power struggles.

Exhibit 4.1 shows a fragment of an early scene in which Stanley and Blanche confront each other. Students were asked to examine each utterance of the script and to rate it along each interpersonal dimension. Every student rated either Stanley's behavior or Blanche's behavior, first along a dimension of communion from −1 (detached) through 0 (neutral) to +1 (friendly) and then along a dimension of control from −1 (yielding) through 0 (neutral) to +1 (controlling). The mean rating of each utterance was then computed. In the first quarter of the utterances, the behaviors were not complementary. According to the mean ratings, Blanche's behavior was friendly–controlling (.4, .6) and Stanley's was detached (−.3, 0). For example, Blanche said to Stanley "I'm going to ask a favor of you in a moment," and he replied, "What could that be, I wonder?" The dramatic tension begins with this early noncomplementarity. In successive blocks of utterances, the interactions continued to be noncomplementary. By the last quarter of the utterances, a power struggle was clear as both partners exhibited disconnected–dominance: for Blanche (−.3, .7), for Stanley (−.2, .7). Then, in the next to last line, Stanley boomed out his disengaged–dominating remark (−1, 1), "Now let's cut the re-bop!," which Blanche then complemented with her disengaged–submissiveness (−.3, −.9), "Ouuuuu!" Her reaction reduces the dramatic tension, producing a momentary feeling of closure, and the curtain can fall. Scenes of this type occur throughout the play, building up to a final crescendo later in the play when Stanley rapes Blanche—as though she were an object to be manipulated—and Blanche surrenders with a "nervous breakdown"—overpowered, helpless, unable to fight back. The tension of noncomplementarity is resolved, and the audience feels the pathos of Blanche's plight.

Some interpersonal theorists have described the X-dimension as ranging from hostile behavior to affectionate behavior (e.g., Leary, 1957). In fact, Leary called it a *love–hate dimension* (p. 64). In our view, however, "hostile" behavior reflects anger related to the frustration of an important goal. That is why we label the negative end of the dimension *detached* or *unconnected*, rather than *hostile*. In our view, the contrast to love is indifference, not hostility. Detached behavior invites detached behavior. A person who wants to be left alone might feel frustrated (irritated, angry) if a partner keeps offering love or intimacy (Moskowitz & Coté, 1995). However, hostile behavior does not invite hostile behavior; it simply indicates that some motive or goal has been frustrated.

Experimental Demonstration

The self-descriptive traits of assertive people (e.g., *dominant, forceful, firm, controlling*; see Octant 1, Figure 4.4) suggest a strong agentic motive. If an assertive person is motivated to influence (and not be influenced), that motive would be frustrated by a dominating co-worker. When an assertive person interacts with a co-worker who dominates, the frustration might even induce anger.

Exhibit 4.1.   Fragment of a Scene From *A Streetcar Named Desire* (T. Williams, 1947)

Blanche:
  I'm going to ask a favor of you in a moment.
Stanley:
  What could that be, I wonder?
Blanche:
  Some buttons in back! You may enter!
  [He crosses through drapes with a smoldering look.]
  How do I look?
Stanley:
  You look all right.
Blanche:
  Many thanks! Now the button!
Stanley:
  I can't do nothing with them.
Blanche:
  You men with your big clumsy fingers. May I have a drag of your cig?
Stanley:
  Have one for yourself.
Blanche:
  Why, thanks! . . . It looks like my trunk has exploded.
Stanley:
  Me an' Stella were helping you unpack.
Blanche:
  Well, you certainly did a fast and thorough job of it!
Stanley:
  It looks like you raided some stylish shops in Paris.
Blanche:
  Ha-ha! Yes—clothes are my passion!
Stanley:
  What does it cost for a string of fur-pieces like that?
Blanche:
  Why, those were a tribute from an admirer of mine!
Stanley:
  He must have had a lot of—admiration!
Blanche:
  Oh, in my youth I excited some admiration. But look at me now! *[She smiles at him radiantly]* Would you think it possible that I was once considered to be—attractive?
Stanley:
  Your looks are okay.
Blanche:
  I was fishing for a compliment, Stanley.
Stanley:
  I don't go in for that stuff.
Blanche:
  What—stuff?
Stanley:
  Compliments to women about their looks. I never met a woman that didn't know if she was good-looking or not without being told, and some of them give themselves

continues

credit for more than they've got. I once went out with a doll who said to me, "I am the glamorous type, I am the glamorous type!" I said, "So what?"

Blanche:

And what did she say then?

Stanley:

She didn't say nothing. That shut her up like a clam.

Blanche:

Did it end the romance?

Stanley:

It ended the conversation—that was all. Some men are took in by this Hollywood glamour stuff and some men are not.

Blanche:

I'm sure you belong in the second category.

Stanley:

That's right.

Blanche:

I cannot imagine any witch of a woman casting a spell over you.

Stanley:

That's—right.

Blanche:

You're simple, straightforward and honest, a little bit on the primitive side I should think. To interest you a woman would have to—[*She pauses with an indefinite gesture.*]

Stanley [*slowly*]:

Lay . . . her cards on the table.

Blanche [*smiling*]:

Well, I never cared for wishy-washy people. That was why, when you walked in here last night, I said to myself—"My sister has married a man!" —Of course, that was all that I could tell about you.

Stanley [*booming*]:

Now let's cut the re-bop!

Blanche [*pressing hands to ears*]:

Ouuuuuu!

Note. By Tennessee Williams, from *A Streetcar Named Desire*, copyright © 1947 by the University of the South. Used with permission of New Directions Publishing Corporation.

Shechtman (2002; Shechtman & Horowitz, 2003) tested this hypothesis experimentally. Unacquainted participants were divided into pairs, introduced, and told that they would be working together on a problem-solving task. They sat in adjacent rooms, each at a computer, and they were to communicate by computer. Their task, the Desert Survival Problem, required them to imagine themselves as co-pilots of an airplane that had crash-landed in the desert; they were to rank-order 12 objects for survival value in the desert. The 12 objects included a flashlight, a book entitled *Edible Animals of the Desert*, and a quart of water. Each participant was to exchange initial rankings with the partner and discuss each object. Half of the participants were assertive people (they had high scores on a test of assertiveness); the others were nonassertive people (they had lower scores).

In actual fact, however, the communications that each participant received were not from each other but from a computerized script that only seemed to be from the partner. These communications recommended changes in the participant's rankings—for example, that the participant's fourth-ranked object be moved to rank 1. The preprogrammed script also provided reasons for recommending these changes. The language of the message was manipulated experimentally to make the partner seem either dominating or not. In one condition, the partner's words were dominating (e.g., "The flashlight is the only reliable night-signaling device. Put it higher."). In the other condition, the partner did not seem dominating (e.g., "Do you think the flashlight should maybe be rated higher? It may be a reliable night-signaling device."). Thus, the experiment paired an assertive or nonassertive participant with a dominating or nondominating partner, for a total of four experimental conditions.

From the transcript of each participant's statements during the session, every hostile (angry) comment was identified. Here are two examples: "I have NO idea what you're thinking, so just fill me in." "It's a frickin' book!" On average, assertive participants working with a dominating partner produced about three hostile comments per interaction. The mean of every other condition was .5 or fewer hostile comments.

Would assertive participants make hostile comments if they believed that their partner was inanimate? In the four conditions described above, the participants believed that they were interacting with a person. Therefore, the same four experimental conditions were repeated with one simple change of detail: The participants were told that they were interacting with a computer that was continually updating its internal norms in search of an optimal solution to the problem. Here, hostile comments rarely occurred, even when an assertive person was working with a "dominating" partner. Apparently, an interpersonal motive is aroused primarily when the partner is thought to be a person. Thus, hostile comments occurred primarily when an assertive participant believed that the dominating partner was a person (frustrating his or her interpersonal motive to influence).

To summarize, interpersonal behaviors seem to invite reactions that satisfy a corresponding motive. When that motive is frustrated, negative affect results. When we examine personality disorders later in the book, we shall often identify a salient interpersonal motive that is easily frustrated, producing negative affect.

We now turn to three applications of the interpersonal model. One clarifies the mechanism of social support. The second describes a dilemma that depressed people face when they receive unwanted forms of social support. The third examines miscommunications in everyday life.

Three Applications

Social Support

In everyday interactions people tell their problems to other people, inviting social support, and the responses are generally words of comfort. As described in chapter 3, social support seems to enhance the receiver's well-being (e.g., Burleson, 1994; Burleson, Albrecht, & Sarason, 1994; DeLongis, Coyne, Dakof, Folkman, & Lazarus, 1982; Sarason, Sarason, & Pierce, 1990). However, we still need to understand how the process works. What are the active ingredients in social support? What kind of social support is apt to be effective in reducing stress? And why?

We assume that a person who tells a problem to someone is doing so for a reason: The problem-teller wants something from the listener. A truly supportive reaction may be regarded as one that satisfies the person's desire. Therefore, a listener has to determine what the problem-teller wants and react in a way that satisfies that want. Does the person want advice? Does the person want compassion? Does the person want help in solving a problem? Does the person want help in regulating an emotion? A listener has to judge the kind of reaction that would satisfy the want.

What cues might a listener use? One type of cue resides in the problem itself. Some problems are solvable (fixable), and the person may want help in solving the problem. Useful advice might enable the person to solve the problem, thereby empowering the person to act effectively (increased agency). Other problems highlight subjective distress, and the person may want a connection that helps reduce distress. Different kinds of problems may call for different kinds of support.

TWO CATEGORIES OF STRESSORS   Problems that people tell others about may be classified broadly into two categories that correspond to communion and agency. Some situations leave people feeling rejected, abandoned, isolated, alone, or lonely, and they may want to feel securely reconnected, understood, or loved. Other situations leave people feeling like failures (inept, powerless, inferior, unable to act), and they may want to feel more empowered (able to perform, achieve, or do). When a person's sense of competence, mastery, or self-esteem is at stake, he or she may want tactful advice to help restore a sense of control or efficacy (Brown & Levinson, 1987; Goldsmith, 1994). O'Brien and DeLongis (1996) examined the various kinds of problematic situations that produce stress. In their terms, communal problems involve "strivings for love, intimacy, friendship, affiliation, emotional relatedness, belongingness, mutuality, group cohesion, communality, and relationship maintenance" (p. 80), whereas agentic problems involve "strivings for mastery, power, achievement, work performance, and instrumental task completion" (p. 80). In other words, communal problems, which focus on isolation and alienation, imply a wish for community, whereas agentic problems, which focus on action, imply a wish for a greater sense of agency. Some problems reflect a combination of both.

TWO CATEGORIES OF SOCIAL SUPPORT   Typical reactions to the problem also fall into two broad categories. Cobb (1976), in writing about social support, differentiated between "emotional support," on the one hand, which provides connection, affiliation, or warmth, and "esteem support," on the other hand, which provides greater efficacy, agency, or status. His distinction again highlights the two interpersonal dimensions. Support along one dimension grants the person acceptance, empathy, and a sense of belonging; support along the other dimension enhances the person's sense of competence. Trobst (1999; Wiggins & Trobst, 1997) scaled a sample of different forms of social support and empirically derived the two-dimensional structure. Figure 4.6 shows how different forms of social support vary along the two dimensions. Cutrona and Suhr (1992, 1994)

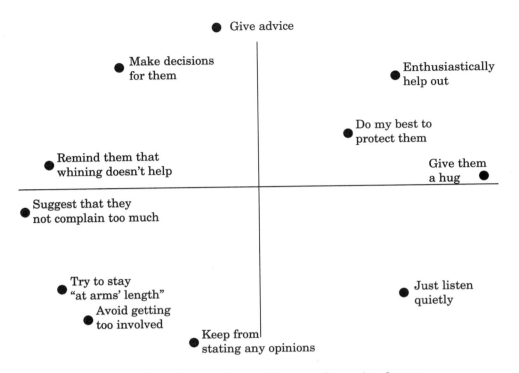

Figure 4.6.   Forms of social support located in a two-dimensional space.

also classified different forms of social support into categories that correspond to communion and agency (see Exhibit 4.2). "Emotionally supportive" (communal) forms of support seem directed at helping the person feel connected, whereas "action-facilitating" (agentic) forms seem directed at helping the person act.

A MATCHING HYPOTHESIS   Communal problems suggest communal support, whereas agentic problems suggest agentic support (Horowitz et al., 2001). To help a person feel connected, a listener might empathize, show compassion, or display understanding. The listener might accurately paraphrase the person's thoughts and feelings or elaborate correctly on the person's experience. These communal reactions should attenuate feelings of isolation.

To help a person feel more competent and effective, a listener might find a way to reduce the person's feeling of helplessness. Sometimes a listener may suggest or demonstrate an effective solution or help the person discover an effective solution. Sometimes relevant information can help a person realize the difficulty of the task, thereby reducing the feeling of failure. The comment "All of my friends failed that midterm exam, too, but by the end of the term, they all did very well" can be helpful (Nowinski, 1999).

Sociolinguists Jefferson and Lee (1992) tape-recorded dyadic conversations that occurred between co-workers in the workplace. They identified two types of conversations, which they called *service encounters* and *troubles-telling*. Their distinction corresponds to the distinction between agentic and communal prob-

Exhibit 4.2.   Common "Supportive" Reactions

Emotionally supportive reactions

- Express empathy and understanding
- Tell P that L cares about P
- Just be there
- Tell P it's not P's fault
- Reassure P that things will get better
- Express concern
- Express physical affection
- Emphasize P's positive qualities and strengths
- Agree with P's point of view
- Promise not to tell others

Action-facilitating reactions

- Offer to introduce P to somebody who might be able to help P
- Offer to introduce P to somebody who has gone through the same experience
- Give some information
- Give advice
- Offer to help
- Reassess the situation
- Tell P about a similar experience of L's own
- Pray with P

Note. P = person with problem; L = listener. From "Social Support Communication in the Context of Marriage," by C. Cutrona and J. A. Suhr, in B. R. Burleson, T. L. Albrecht, & I. G. Sarason (Eds.), *Communication of social support*, 1994, p. 122, Copyright © 1994. Reprinted with permission of Sage Publications, Inc.

lems. In a service encounter, a speaker describes an agentic problem; for example, "I've been using the new equipment, and I can't get the lever to stay down; it keeps popping up." The speaker is apparently receptive to advice (e.g., "Try holding the lever down for 3 seconds; then it will stay in place"). In a troubles-telling, a speaker describes a communal problem; for example, "I behaved like a drunken idiot at the party last night; people must think I'm weird." Apparently, in this case, the speaker would be receptive to compassion that neutralizes a sense of rejection or abandonment.

The Dilemma of a Depressed Person

Depression (a syndrome) is a complex experience. It usually includes feelings of sadness, plus many other mental states: characteristic bodily sensations, thoughts, feelings, expectancies, and so on. As discussed in chapter 7, one person's depression may highlight feelings of isolation, aloneness, loneliness, and emptiness, whereas another person's depression may highlight feelings of failure, incompetence, shame, and humiliation. On the surface, however, both depressed people may seem sad, passive, and helpless.

Suppose a person has just suffered a communal loss (e.g., an ended romance) and now feels alone, isolated, and empty, in need of communal support. An outside observer might notice that the person seems sad, passive, and helpless. Perceiving the person's helplessness, the observer might interpret the behavior as a tacit invitation for agentic support—a request for advice, influence, and control: "You should take time off, take a trip, have some fun." Such advice, of course, completely misses the person's loss and feeling of aloneness. Furthermore, in giving advice, the observer invites the depressed person to yield to influence ("I'll have to try that; thanks for the advice"), which might serve no useful purpose at all. We examine one common sequence more closely that might even sustain a depressed person's depression.

1. The depressed person approaches others for help. Coyne, Aldwin, and Lazarus (1981) interviewed depressed and nondepressed people seven times at 4-week intervals to determine how depressed and nondepressed people typically cope with stress. The participants were asked about the most stressful events that had occurred during the previous month—what happened and how they had coped. Depressed and nondepressed people reported a similar number of stressful events, but depressed people more often reported that they had sought help from others. Joiner, Katz, and Lew (1999) showed that negative life events seem to produce a drop in self-esteem that leads a person to seek reassurance from others.

2. In approaching others, depressed people often seem passive and helpless. A depressed person's apparent helplessness has been well documented and much discussed (e.g., Seligman, 1975). In addition, numerous investigators (e.g., Altman & Wittenborn, 1980; Beck, 1967; Blumberg & Hokanson, 1983; Cofer & Wittenborn, 1980; Gotlib & Robinson, 1982; Hokanson, Sacco, Blumberg, & Landrum, 1980; Salzman, 1975) have observed that depressed people often self-derogate, and their self-derogations often convey passivity, helplessness, and incompetence (Horowitz et al., 1991).

3. Partners react to the depressed person's apparent helplessness with advice and other forms of influence and control. Horowitz et al. (1991, Study 3) studied the effect of self-derogations experimentally. Participants interacted with a confederate of the same sex. Both partners received a list of topics (e.g., "the kind of people I find it easy or hard to talk to"), and they selected a topic to talk about. They took turns talking. The confederate always followed a prepared script, which was varied to form three experimental conditions (self-derogating, other-derogating, or nonderogating). Participants were assigned to one of the conditions at random. Each participant reacted to the confederate's monologues, and their reactions were classified into two broad categories: (a) reactions that advised the person to think, feel, or behave differently and (b) reactions that simply acknowledged the partner's remarks. As expected, controlling reactions occurred significantly more often toward a self-derogating confederate. Initially people apparently react to comments from a person who seems depressed with concern and a desire to help (Coates & Wortman, 1980; Lowenstein, 1984). Over time, however, their behavior becomes increasingly controlling (Burgess, 1969; Coyne, 1976b; Hinchcliffe, Hooper, &

Roberts, 1978). For example, people reported that they try to distract a depressed person, offer advice, or tell the person to cheer up (Blumberg & Hokanson, 1983; Coyne, 1976b; Grinker, 1964). Watzlawick, Weakland, and Fisch (1974) commented that the other person's attempt to cheer the depressed person is really a "demand that the depressed have certain feelings (joy, optimism) but not others (sadness, pessimism)" (p. 34). To summarize, the depressed person frequently approaches others for help, and others usually give advice and take control.

4.   When the depressed person's depression does not subside, the partner reports negative affect. Many researchers have studied the impact of a person's chronic depression on a partner who is not depressed. Coyne (1976a) studied 20-minute telephone conversations between a patient with depression and a female college student whom the patient had never met. Each student was assigned to one of three partners: (a) a patient in treatment for depression, (b) a patient in treatment not for depression, or (c) a nonpatient. Conversations were tape-recorded, and afterwards the students completed a questionnaire describing their reactions. After the conversation, those who had spoken to a partner with depression reported negative affect; they felt more hostile, more anxious, and more depressed than those who had spoken to another type of partner. They were also reluctant to have future contact with that person.

Other research has confirmed this finding. In one study (Howes & Hokanson, 1979) students worked on a task with an actor–confederate, who enacted one of three roles—that of a person with depression, a physically ill person, or a control. The participants gave more advice and reassurance to the confederate with depression, but they also expressed more rejection, insults, and disapproval. When they were asked later whether they would be willing to work with the same partner in a later phase of the project, most participants in the control and physically ill conditions were willing to do so (95% and 88%, respectively), but not in the depressed condition (only 56%). These results are consistent with many other findings (e.g., Boswell & Murray, 1981; Gotlib & Beatty, 1985; Gotlib & Robinson, 1982; Hammen & Peters, 1978; Hinchcliffe et al., 1978; King & Heller, 1984; Lowenstein, 1984; Robbins, Strack, & Coyne, 1979; Stephens, Hokanson, & Welker, 1987; Strack & Coyne, 1983; Winer, Bonner, Blaney, & Murray, 1981). People seem to find interactions with a depressed person aversive, and their responses, though initially well-intentioned, may then be rejecting. It should be noted, though, that depressed partners seem to find an interaction with each other more satisfying than with a non-depressed partner (Locke & Horowitz, 1990).

Interpersonal Misunderstandings

According to Jefferson and Lee (1992), difficulties can arise whenever a speaker and listener do not understand each other's wishes. A speaker may want one kind of support, but the listener may interpret the message differently. If a listener offers unwanted advice, the speaker may even reject that advice (e.g., "Yes, I already tried that, but nothing helps"). People report dissatisfaction when a listener's reaction does not match their wish (Horowitz et al., 2001, Study 3).

A provocative example of miscommunication appears in the book, *Games People Play* (Berne, 1964, p. 116). In this book, the author described an interpersonal "game" that he calls "Why Don't You—Yes But." In this game, one player (Mrs. White) describes a problem to the other players—for example, "My husband always insists on doing our own repairs, and he never builds anything right"—to which the other players (Mrs. Red, Mrs. Green, Mrs. Blue) offer various pieces of advice—for example, "Why don't you buy him some good tools?" or "Why don't you hire a carpenter?" Mrs. White responds to each suggestion with an objection that begins "Yes, but . . . " (". . . my husband is too clumsy" or ". . . a carpenter is too expensive"). Eventually the other players run out of suggestions, and, according to Berne, Mrs. White is then declared the winner of the game.

We differ from Berne in our interpretation, however. According to Berne (1964, p. 118), Mrs. White is motivated by a desire to defeat the other players—soliciting their advice in order to reject it. According to our interpretation, however, Mrs. White's goal may be communal, not agentic. She may want to receive compassion (not advice), so advice-givers keep frustrating her communal goal. It is interesting that Berne suggested the following antidote for people who do not wish to play Mrs. White's game—namely, to reply "That *is* a difficult problem" (p. 121). According to our interpretation, this antidote provides compassion and in that way satisfies Mrs. White's communal goal.

Mismatched communications often occur among couples in distress (e.g., Jacobson & Margolin, 1979, p. 201). A wife, for example, may want compassion, but her husband may offer advice. Bereaved people and people with chronic illnesses frequently receive unwanted advice from well-meaning friends (Lehman, Ellard, & Wortman, 1986; Lehman & Hemphill, 1990). When a person's child has died, for example, the advice "Consider yourself lucky that you can still have other children" is offensive; it completely ignores the person's major loss.

Some miscommunications arise because people confuse communion and agency. In her book *You Just Don't Understand,* Tannen (1990) argued that "connection" (communion) and "status" (agency) are gender-linked in our culture. In Tannen's view, women tend to be connection-oriented, and men tend to be status-oriented. In her view, women worry about whether other people care about them. Women want to feel intimate and close to others and they want to avoid feelings of isolation. Men, according to Tannen, worry about whether other people respect them. Men want to feel competent and self-respecting and they want to avoid feelings of failure. Whereas a woman readily perceives an opportunity for community, rapport, and support, a man readily perceives an opportunity for competition, self-promotion, and prestige. Where a woman offers empathy, a man offers advice.

In our view, all people, men and women alike, have multiple interpersonal motives that vary from time to time across different situations. Everyone at times has a desire to connect with others; everyone at times has a desire to disconnect from others. Everyone at times has a desire to influence others; everyone at times has a desire to be guided by others. A motive that is intense on one occasion may be minor or absent on other occasions. Furthermore, people vary in the salience of any particular motive over many different occasions. For some people the motive to influence others is often salient; for others that motive is rarely salient. When we describe a person as domineering, we mean that, relative to others, the person is often motivated to influence others. When we describe a person as affiliative, we mean that, relative to others, the person is often motivated to connect with others. These personality differences, although modestly correlated with gender, seem more useful than gender in explaining a person's behavior. When a partner says, "You must be feeling very sad," some people (regardless of gender) experience compassionate support; others perceive patronizing condescension.

As a result, the very same message may be interpreted differently by two people. An empathic remark may seem supportive to a person seeking connection, but condescending to a person seeking status. Therefore, opportunities abound for misinterpretation and misunderstanding. Mrs. A might say to Mrs. B, "Tell me, my dear, have you always had a weight problem?" Mrs. A may think she is forging a connection with Mrs. B by initiating an intimate exchange, but Mrs. B may interpret the question as a hostile criticism. Some people show a systematic bias in interpreting other people's remarks. Paranoid people, for example, have a systematic bias (described in chapter 7) toward perceiving hostile control (criticism, derision, manipulation, exploitation).

We have applied the interpersonal model to three different areas: social support, the depressed person's dilemma, and everyday miscommunications. In all three applications, we have considered the motive behind the behavior, the person's reaction, and the consequence of a frustrated motive (negative affect). As shown in later chapters, biased interpretations are common in psychopathology.

Interpersonal Patterns as Learned Scripts

In an effort to satisfy one's own motives and those of other people, children learn common interpersonal patterns that become familiar scripts. When a persistently repetitive pattern fails to satisfy a person's own motives, it is said to be *maladaptive* (e.g., Kiesler, 1996; Strupp & Binder, 1984). Furthermore, a script acquired during childhood may generalize to patterns observed in adulthood. Consider the ways in which an interpersonal sequence learned in childhood can manifest itself in adulthood. Imagine a frequently scolded child who typically reacts to scolding by sulking and self-justifying. The child (B) has learned the entire interpersonal script: "A scolds B; then B sulks and self-justifies." By internalizing this script, B acquires the capacity to perform either role—as scolder or scoldee. The script can then manifest itself in three different ways, as described by L. S. Benjamin (1996).

Three Manifestations of a Script

The script can be manifested as *recapitulation* (L. S. Benjamin, 1996). The scoldee (B), having overlearned the sequence, may find others with whom to reproduce the pattern. We might call these other people A*. The script "A scolds B" then appears as "A* scolds B." For example, a woman (B), who has often been scolded by her mother (A), now finds herself scolded by her husband, by her friends, and by her boss (A*). Amitay, Mongrain, & Fazaa (2001) has shown that female college students who felt criticized by their mothers tend to have boyfriends who criticize them.

A second way a script can manifest itself is called *identification* or *modeling*. The scoldee (B), having learned a sequence, may now take on the role of scolder by finding substitute-scoldees (call them B*). The script "A scolds B" then appears as "B scolds B*." Amitay, Mongrain, & Fazaa (2001) have shown that mothers who criticize their daughters tend to have been criticized by their own mothers. This mechanism shows why a person who has been verbally, physically, or sexually abused may now become a victimizer. People may conceal or inhibit tendencies to victimize because of social censure, but when it is safe to express that behavior, the inhibition may be lifted (e.g., toward a helpless animal or toward a child), exposing an otherwise latent capacity.

A third way a script can manifest itself is called *introjection* (L. S. Benjamin, 1996). The scoldee (B), having learned a sequence, may now adopt both roles—scolding the self and then sulking and self-justifying. That is, the script "A scolds B" then appears as "B scolds B." In this way B comes to blame or downrate himself or herself and then reacts with feelings of depression, guilt, or shame. Thus, a depressed person first self-derogates and then feels ashamed or guilty. Amitay, Mongrain, & Fazaa (2001) have demonstrated that female college students whose mothers had criticized them tend to be self-critical.

Latent Capacity to Enact a Role

Sometimes a person possesses a capacity that is not evident from the person's everyday behavior. For example, a person might say, "I am unable to be assertive; other people tell me what to do, and I always do as I am told." To an outsider, the person may seem altogether acquiescent and compliant. However, the person may also be surprisingly assertive with pets, children, and nonthreatening others.

Should we say that this person lacks the skill to behave assertively? Or should we say, instead, that the person has trouble exercising an existing skill (because of some inhibition or interference)? If the person truly lacks a skill, we might think of correcting that deficit by training the person, step by step, to be assertive. However, if the person primarily has trouble accessing an existing skill, we might think, instead, of helping the person overcome the inhibition or interference.

Schwartz and Gottman (1976) compared nonassertive, moderately assertive, and highly assertive people in their ability to produce assertive responses under three experimental conditions. In each condition, the participants were asked to produce assertive responses to a set of unreasonable demands. In the first (least threatening) condition, they were to write possible responses (a benign, impersonal task). In the second condition, they were asked to imagine that a friend was being confronted with unreasonable demands and they were to respond orally on behalf of their friend. In the third (most threatening) condition, they were asked to imagine themselves actually being confronted with unreasonable demands. The results showed that nonassertive participants were just as competent as assertive people in the two less threatening conditions, but they had great difficulty producing responses in the third condition. Apparently, these people had the assertive skill as a latent capacity but they needed help overcoming anxiety and other kinds of interference.

As another example, people who describe themselves as lonely seem to perform poorly on tests of social skill (e.g., T. Brennan, 1982; French, 1981; Hansson & Jones, 1981; Horowitz, French & Anderson, 1982; W. H. Jones, Hobbs, & Hockenbury, 1982; Solano, Batten & Parish, 1982). Behavioral writers have sometimes ascribed this deficiency to a deficit in social skills—according to Bellack and Morrison (1982), to a limited response repertoire. However, in some cases lonely people do seem to possess the capacity, but, they are not able to display their skill because of anxiety, expectations of failure, and other sources of interference. When they feel safer, however, they seem to do very well (Arkowitz, Lichtenstein, McGovern, & Hines, 1975; Glasgow & Arkowitz, 1975; Vitkus & Horowitz, 1987).

Summary

This chapter has examined the interpersonal model. According to this model, an interpersonal behavior invites a class of reactions that satisfy the corresponding goal or motive. When that goal or motive is frustrated, negative affect follows. These principles help describe different forms of psychopathology. Once an action-reaction sequence has been learned (i.e., an interpersonal script), the person may later replay the same script using other people (recapitulation); the person may also assume the other role (identification or modeling); or the person may use the self to assume both roles (introjection). These principles are important in treatment, where interventions need to address the person's goal or motives (Piper, Joyce, McCallum, Azim, & Ogrodniczuk, 2001).

As described in the next chapter, the self is very important in understanding interpersonal interactions. Sometimes an interpersonal motive arises as a way of protecing a vulnerable self-image. Sometimes an interpersonal action or reaction makes sense only when we understand the person's self-image.

5

The Self-Image and Interpersonal Processes

Interpersonal motives are often related to a person's self-image. People who think they are helpless when alone have to find helpmates who stick by them. People who feel in danger of being abused have to find ways to avoid being abused. Personality disorders that are examined in later chapters can often be organized around a motive derived from the person's self-image. Therefore, this chapter examines the self-image. The self-image is related to interpersonal processes in two broad ways: (a) Interpersonal processes shape a person's self-image, and (b) a person's self-image prompts particular interpersonal behaviors.

Consider how interpersonal processes affect the self-image. In G. B. Shaw's (1916) play *Pygmalion*, Eliza Doolittle wisely comments that the difference between a lady and a flower girl is not in how she talks, but in the way she is treated. When Jack interacts with Jill, Jack's behavior communicates important messages to Jill—what Jack thinks of Jill, what Jack wants from Jill, whether Jack likes Jill. These messages have emotional consequences for Jill (R. S. Lazarus, 1991). If they satisfy Jill's goals, Jill will feel good; if they frustrate Jill's goals, Jill will feel bad. If Jack's behavior expresses disdain, Jill will feel inadequate. If Jack's behavior expresses respect, Jill will feel esteemed. When people are consistently belittled, they tend to feel unworthy. When they are consistently blamed, they tend to feel guilty. When they are deceived, they need to be on guard. When they are warned about dangers, they feel vulnerable and insecure. When they are chronically without friends, they feel disliked and alone.

Conversely, self-image affects interpersonal interactions. If people feel vulnerable to harm from others, they find ways to avoid being harmed. Consider the case of schoolboys who are overly aggressive. Some of them feel vulnerable to abuse. To protect themselves, they are vigilant for signs of ill-will and then swiftly fight back. Even when observers agree that the other's behavior was purely accidental, these boys tend to detect hostile intent (Dodge, 1993; Dodge & Coie, 1987). Examples of the ways in which a vulnerable self-image has specific maladaptive interpersonal consequences are presented in this chapter.

We begin with the concept of self and consider how a child's view of the self evolves during childhood. In some ways, self-image is like a theory of the self: The person seeks to confirm certain features and refute others. The schoolyard bully, for example, exhibits bullying behaviors in part to confirm hypotheses that he is strong, influential, or high in status. Similar mechanisms are described throughout the chapter to help deepen our interpersonal approach to psychopathology.

Self and the Self-Image

William James (1892) distinguished between two broad meanings of the term *self*. One refers to a person's role as executive in charge of the body, where the self controls and makes decisions about the body's actions. James used the word "I" to designate this agentic meaning of self. The feeling associated with a successful "I" is a sense of confidence (e.g., "I can execute acts that will satisfy my goals."). We call this feeling a sense of *agency* or *efficacy* (Bandura, 1977, 1986, 1997). When we speak of a person with anorexia as having an impaired sense of control, self-determination, or power, we are referring to a deficit in James's "I."

James reserved the word "me" for his other meaning of self. To Person P, "me" refers to P's conception of P—as though P were an outsider observing P. When people observe themselves from the outside, the corresponding image constitutes James's "me." We use the term *self-image* for this second meaning of self. When a person with anorexia exercises firm self-discipline ("I"), this observation (of "me") produces satisfaction and a feeling of pride. Such feelings spur the person on to new heights of dieting. The gratifying self-image ("a thin *me* that can really exercise self-control") further motivates the executive ("I") to keep up the good work.

Thus, James's two concepts, "I" and "me," interact to affect the person's performance. When people expect to perform poorly on a task, their motivation wanes and their performance declines. Expressed in the language of social learning theory, a person with expectations of low efficacy does not perform as well as a person with higher efficacy expectations (Bandura, 1977, 1986, 1997).

Smedslund (1988, 1997) described James's "me" this way: Consider a person (P) who is engaged in some action (A) toward an object (O). Perhaps P, A, and O denote, respectively, an infant (P) who is reaching for (A) a toy (O) or a dog (P) biting into (A) a dog biscuit (O). The action is directed toward the object. In each example, P is an agent operating on the environment to achieve a desired goal. Those behaviors are called *operant behaviors* because they operate on the environment for some purpose; they are intentional, motivated, and goal-directed.

Does a P–A–O sequence necessarily imply a self-image, that is, a sense of "me" or "my self"? Definitely not. The person P is certainly aware of the desired object O. However, an awareness of an object does not necessarily imply a concept of the self. Infants and lower animals show purposive (intentional) behavior that implies an awareness of objects. That kind of awareness might be referred to as "an awareness of an external object." A hungry dog that intentionally and enthusiastically pounces upon a dog biscuit is aware of the dog biscuit, but nothing about the experience implies a concept of "me" or "my self." Likewise, an infant who intentionally reaches for a toy is aware of the toy; and a 2-year-old who intentionally hits its mother is aware of the mother. However, none of these examples, by itself, necessarily reflects a concept of "me" or "my self."

A concept of "me" implies that a cognitive representation of the actor is embedded in a larger cognition of the actor's. Suppose the child Peter (P) performs an action (A) on an object (O), and exclaims, "Peter is reaching for the toy" or "Peter is eating a dog biscuit." Because Peter's comment now includes a reference to Peter, we would say that P's larger cognition includes P as one of its elements. In this case, we speak of Peter's self-awareness (Smedslund, 1988, 1997). In other words, Person P is said to be self-aware when P has a cognition that contains P as one of its elements.

P's self-awareness may entail an overt behavior ("P is pulling Rover's tail"), or it may describe an internal state ("P likes to pull Rover's tail"). A self-awareness of internal states eventually leads to concepts like "my feelings," "my wishes," "my needs," "my intentions," and "my perceptions." When these concepts do emerge, they allow the person to cite common self-awarenesses that describe the self.

It is important to distinguish between a person's simple awareness of an external object and a person's self-awareness. In the simpler case, the person is participating in a drama without simultaneously being a member of the audience; the person is exclusively a participant. In that case, we speak of a "participant-only" perspective. In a self-awareness, the person is simultaneously an actor and a member of the audience, simultaneously a participant and an observer. In that case, we speak of a "participant–observer" perspective (or "observing ego"). Every normal adult has both kinds of experience: We sometimes lose ourselves in an absorbing activity (participant-only) but later regain self-awareness when the fire alarm signals danger (participant–observer).

Self-Image as a Tool in Cognitive Development

To be able to explain an illusion, a person needs to be able to distinguish between an object independently of the self and that object as perceived. The person has to realize that "the way the object appears to me" (my perception) is not necessarily "the way the object really is." An object that looks black may in fact be red. By ages 6–7, most children are able to make this distinction. At that age, they can tell us that a red toy car behind a black filter is not really black and that it looks black only because of the viewing conditions. In that way the child is implicitly acknowledging a participant–observer perspective: "I (Person P) am perceiving (A) an object (O) that is red; but I perceive it as black because I am viewing it through a black filter."

Many techniques have been used to study illusions in children. Different kinds of filters and lenses have been used to change the apparent color, size, or shape of objects (Flavell, Flavell, & Green, 1983). An object that is really red, small, or straight can be made to look black, big, or bent. A child is then asked how the object "really is" and how it "seems to be." The studies show a marked improvement with age in a child's ability to answer the questions correctly. Very few 3-year-olds answer correctly, but almost all 6- and 7-year-olds do (Flavell, 1986; Flavell, Green, & Flavell, 1986). Special training designed to speed the process does not seem to help much (Flavell et al., 1986; M. Taylor & Hort, 1990).

It is noteworthy that by age 3 children do possess impressive abilities that are relevant to understanding illusions. A 3-year-old understands the concept of "pretend"; for example, that a toy block is a "pretend" car, not a real car, that a fake rock may look like a rock but is not a real rock (Bretherton, 1984; Rubin, Fein, & Vandenberg, 1983). Also, by age 3, children can predict correctly, after a few demonstrations, that the red car will look black when it is moved behind the black filter and that it will look red again when it re-emerges. Nonetheless, the child would still be unable to differentiate between "the way it appears to me" and "the way it really is." To the child, a car that looks red is red, a filter notwithstanding; a car that looks black is "really" black. Such changes do not seem to pose a problem for the child because the child viewing the car is having a participant-only experience. The 7-year-old, in contrast, can comfortably assume a participant–observer perspective that facilitates a new understanding. The older child can ascribe the perceptual change (from red to black) to his or her own mind, not to a magical change in O, the object.

In coming to understand illusions, the 7-year-old would have acquired a cognitive subtlety. Now the child can generalize the discovery to others—reporting that someone directly viewing the toy car might experience it differently from someone viewing it through a black filter. Thus, the child can now perform an advanced form of perspective taking. Flavell et al. (1983) showed children a bent straw that looked straight when it was seen through a bottle of liquid which distorted its shape. They asked each child how the straw would look to the examiner who viewed it directly. The child's ability to answer correctly was highly correlated with the child's success on the appearance–reality task.

These two abilities—the ability to differentiate appearance from reality and to describe the contrasting perspective of someone else—are achievements that build on the child's capacity for self-awareness. In time, every normal child acquires these capacities, but special training does not seem to speed the process very much. A 4-year-old boy who complains of a scary monster in the shadowy curtains of his bedroom actually sees a monster. He would probably not understand an adult's claim that it "only looks like" a monster. The child might well be comforted by an adult's reassuring and self-confident tone of voice, but the conceptual distinction is beyond the grasp of most 4-year-olds.

Social Interaction and the Self-Image

Now we turn to the self-image itself. A person's image of the self comes from countless experiences in which the person has been participant–observer—numerous self-observations of the most common feelings, desires, attributes, likes, dislikes, hopes, disappointments, aptitudes, shortcomings, and so on. A number of psychologists have tried to describe systematic changes that occur throughout childhood in a person's self-description (e.g., Harter, 1999). The earliest descriptors tend to be observables, such as physical attributes ("I have blond hair"), possessions ("I have a bicycle"), and category memberships ("I am a boy"). As the child gets older, self-descriptions come to include dispositions, aptitudes, and feelings, such as "I am smart," "I am good at baseball," "I like to draw pictures." Still later, they include interpersonal dispositions (e.g., "I am shy," "I am friendly," "I am competitive").

Early writers (e.g., J. Baldwin, 1897; Cooley, 1902; Mead, 1934) suggested that many important characteristics of the self are discovered through social interaction. Cooley (1902, chap. 12) proposed that people serve as a looking-glass to each other. Each reflects to the other what he or she thinks of the other's appearance, manners, deeds, aims, character, and so on.

From the first year of a child's life, adults encourage dyadic exchange, reciprocating sounds, smiles, and facial expressions that the child happens to generate. An adult's responsiveness draws the child into a state of joint attention (on objects, behavior, and internal states), helping the child learn labels. When an adult exclaims, "No wonder you're crying; you're hungry, you want food," the adult is helping the child identify and label states that eventually contribute to the child's conception of the self. Kohut (1984) suggested that the adult provides *empathic mirroring*, a term that reminds us of Cooley's "looking-glass self."

At times, an adult has to frustrate a child's wishes (e.g., when the child's safety is at stake). Therefore, from time to time, the child's desires, goals, and intentions inevitably get highlighted as they conflict with those of the adult. The child may want to play, but the adult wants the child to sleep; the child may want to be carried, but the adult would like the child to walk. Frustrations expose and highlight desires, goals, and feelings that may also contribute to the child's eventual self-image.

A child who has little social contact (e.g., a child whose caretakers are depressed, withdrawn, or absent) is at a disadvantage. Without much empathic mirroring, the child receives less help in labeling and identifying internal states (Raver & Leadbeater, 1995), possibly delaying a clear and detailed self-image. Social isolation in childhood is one risk factor for later psychopathology (e.g., Weinfield et al., 1999), although the exact mechanism is still unclear.

Experiments on nonhuman primates have been conducted to determine the effect of social isolation on self-recognition. One early study examined the chimpanzee's ability to recognize itself in a mirror. When normal chimpanzees first see themselves in a mirror, they treat the reflection as though it were another chimpanzee; they vocalize and make threatening gestures. After a few days, however, they catch on and use the mirror to groom themselves. Gallup (1970, 1991) devised a procedure to test an animal's capacity to use a mirror for self-recognition. The animals had never encountered a mirror before. First, the animals were anesthetized, and the experimenter dyed each animal's eyebrow and ear using a red, odorless, nonirritating dye. Then a mirror was placed in the animal's cage, and the experimenter observed how long it took for the animal to begin using the mirror to examine and groom the marked eyebrow and ear. Chimpanzees reared in isolation never came to use the mirror to groom themselves; those reared with normal social contact, however, did so within a few days. This result suggests that social interaction helps promote a concept of the self.

Social Interaction and Inferences About Intention

If social interaction contributes to an image of the self, it also contributes to an image of other people. Early on children perceive intentions or motives in other people, and that capacity allows them to form working models of other people as kindly disposed or not. Since children want to preserve their ties to attachment figures, it is important that they be able to decipher the caretaker's wishes so as to please the caretaker and preserve the relationship. Also, as noted previously, some aggressive children erroneously impute hostile intentions to other people, ascribing accidental acts to hostile motives. The following section examines the infant's ability to decipher an adult's intention.

The Infant's Ability to "Read" Another Person's Intention

When infants are approximately 9–12 months of age, they make a major breakthrough in understanding people: They infer people's intention from their behavior. Before that age (e.g., at 6 months), the infant can interact with an adult only in rather minimal ways (e.g., taking turns at vocalizing). By 12 months, however, the infant and adult can interact over a common focus of attention (Tomasello, 1999). The adult might gaze at a bird, and the infant will follow the adult's gaze and join the adult in attending to the bird.

Joint attention seems to play a major role in a child's psychological development (C. Moore & Dunham, 1995). One salient feature of joint attention is each party's ability to read the other's intention. When an adult says, "Look at the birdie," and the child does so, it means that the child understands the adult's intentions. Likewise, when the infant hands the adult a cup, the child's action is intentional (purposive). The child does not usually behave that way toward inanimate objects. To this extent, a 1-year-old child has the capacity to read another person's intentions (Tomasello, 1995).

The capacity to infer simple intentions is especially important when the child begins to imitate adults. Children observe an adult's behavior, interpret what the adult is trying to achieve, and later reproduce that behavior to satisfy goals of their own. By 18 months of age, children can even perform an act that the adult intended to do but did not complete. For example, Meltzoff (1995) devised some simple tasks that children could imitate. In one task, for example, the child was supposed to use a stick to press a button that activated a buzzer. The adult demonstrated the procedure to the child and then said, "It's your turn." In one experimental condition, the adult demonstrated the procedure perfectly. In another condition, the adult acted the same way, but at the last moment his hand "accidentally" slipped, so the stick "accidentally" fell. Nonetheless, most children got the picture and performed equally well in both conditions. Thus, 18-month-old infants understood the experimenter's intent and successfully completed the task. Similar results have been reported by Carpenter, Akhtar, and Tomasello (1998) with 16-month-old infants.

When children learn new words, they also seem to recognize cues that enable them to judge which object the adult is intending to label (D. A. Baldwin, 1995). Tomasello and Barton (1994, Experiment 4) devised a clever procedure for illustrating this point. An adult experimenter taught 2-year-old infants a newly coined word (e.g., *toma*). The children first observed five unfamiliar toys; then the experimenter hid each toy in a different bucket. Then the experimenter pointed to the buckets and said, "Hey, Annie! Where's the toma? Let's find the toma." The experimenter then searched in each bucket. In one condition, the experimenter found the toma on the first try; looking at the toy, she smiled and said "Ah!" In the other condition, the experimenter had to look into several buckets before she found the toma. In the first buckets that she examined, she held up the (nontoma) toy, frowned, and looked at the toy disapprovingly. Then on her third try, she smiled and said "Ah!" Afterward she tested the child to see whether the child could identify the toma correctly. More than half of the children in each condition learned to name the toy correctly, and the two conditions did not differ. Thus, the 2-year-old children were able to use smiles and frowns to interpret which object the adult called a toma.

I once treated a woman with depression who unexpectedly brought her 20-month-old daughter along to her psychotherapy session. The child played happily with her toys until she noticed that her mother was crying. She immediately stopped playing, went to her mother, patted her, and said, "Don't cry, baby!" The child's behavior would seem to be more than a parrotlike repetition of earlier observations; it seemed to reflect a relatively simple form of perspective taking. The child understood the adult's distress and displayed behavior learned by imitation. This kind of perspective taking clearly is much simpler than a 7-year-old's sophisticated ability to understand illusions under different viewing conditions. However, the 2-year-old's ability to interpret an adult's intention and smile (or frown) is also a form of perspective taking.

Sometimes a person's intention helps explain why that person appears to be different on different occasions. Suppose fun-loving Uncle Harry takes his 3-year-old nephew to a play in which Harry is performing. After the nephew is seated with other members of the family, Harry says goodbye, goes backstage, and then appears on the stage dressed as a monster. The figure is Uncle Harry, yet he looks like a monster. Has Uncle Harry magically turned into a monster in the same way a red car behind a filter turned black? Probably not. For unlike the toy car, Harry has intentions; he intended to dress up like a monster in order to have fun pretending, and this intention explains the change from the real Uncle Harry to a pretend monster. From the entire social interaction, Harry's message is apparently clear to his nephew: Harry likes his nephew and intentionally became a monster to enhance the fun.

Unexplainable Shifts in Intention

Suppose Uncle Harry gains custody of his 3-year-old nephew. And suppose Harry is known to be unpredictably temperamental: He is sometimes loving, warm, and kind, but other times, out of the blue, he becomes hostile, rejecting, and cold. His very intentions, as well as his appearance, seem to change magically from loving and warm to hostile and cold. Furthermore, these changes send contradictory messages to the child about the child: Sometimes the child feels welcomed and loved, whereas at other times the child feels rejected and forsaken. What if Uncle Harry were to take over as the child's primary caretaker? When Harry is nice, the child would feel loved, wanted, and protected; when Harry is nasty, the child would feel disliked, unwanted, and unsafe. How does a child understand this kind of unpredictable and uncontrollable change? It is more complex than the toy car's change from red to black because the adult has changed in intentions, feelings, and attitudes. An older, more sophisticated child might be able to integrate Harry's two sides: He is "really" nice, but sometimes he appears to be nasty (or vice versa). Younger children, however, cannot integrate the contradictions: There are two Uncle Harry's, and one can magically turn into the other.

This kind of process may help explain the disorganized (Type D) attachment style described in chapter 3. When the very caretaker who nurtures and comforts a young child also frequently terrorizes that child, the child seems to acquire contradictory images of the caretaker. In chapter 11 we examine consequences of these "split images" in certain forms of psychopathology.

Self-Esteem: Global Evaluation of the Self-Image

Many characteristics of the self-image are evaluative, evoking an attitude of approval or disapproval toward the self. Together, they provide a global evaluation of the self, which is usually called *self-esteem*. Considerable evidence indicates that children who have been neglected, mistreated, or abused evaluate themselves more negatively than other children (e.g., Beeghly & Cicchetti, 1994; Briere, 1992; Harter, 1999; Kaufman & Cicchetti, 1989; Kendall-Tackett, Williams, & Finkelhor, 1993; Vondra, Barnett, & Cicchetti, 1989).

One of the earliest measures of self-esteem (Butler & Haigh, 1954) contained 100 self-descriptive statements taken from psychotherapy transcripts, such as "I despise myself" and "I often feel humiliated." Since then, many other measures have been created. Blascovich and Tomaka (1991) summarized 19 self-esteem measures cited in journal articles and dissertations since 1967; the 3 most frequently cited were those by Rosenberg (1965), Coopersmith (1967, 1975), and Roid and Fitts (1988). Measures of self-esteem correlate negatively with measures of depression, loneliness, anxiety, and shyness (see, e.g., J. D. Brown, 1998; Peplau, Miceli, & Morasch, 1982; Peplau & Perlman, 1982).

Using methods of factor analysis, Tafarodi and his colleagues (Tafarodi & Milne, 2002; Tafarodi & Swann, 1995) have identified two dimensions of self-esteem. One corresponds to communal self-esteem ("my likeability, acceptability"), the other to agentic self-esteem ("my competence, efficacy"). The authors called the first *self-liking*, the second *self-competence*. J. D. Brown (1998, pp. 196–197) proposed a similar distinction. Items that assess self-liking include "I feel good about who I am" (positive) and "I tend to devalue myself" (negative). Items that assess self-competence include "I am a capable person" (positive) and "I don't succeed at much" (negative).

Following a negative life event, people typically report a drop in self-esteem; the more negative the event, the greater the drop in self-esteem (Joiner, Katz, & Lew, 1999). Tafarodi and Milne (2002) showed that the relationship becomes more precise if one distinguishes between the type of negative event (communal vs. agentic) and the type of self-esteem (self-liking vs. self-competence). If the negative events are communal (e.g., a romantic rejection), self-liking drops; if the negative events are agentic (e.g., a failed performance), self-competence drops.

Fuzzy Concepts and the Self-Image

Early concepts used to describe the self are well-defined, but later concepts are not. For example, *boy* has a clear objective referent, but later concepts like *sissy*, *wimp*, *stud*, and *whiz-kid* do not. When we say that a concept is well-defined, we mean that all examples of that concept meet specific criteria. A boy is defined as a male human child. Every boy meets these criteria, and every person who meets these criteria is a boy. The criteria are both necessary and sufficient for being a boy.

However, many self-descriptive concepts cannot be defined so precisely. Consider the term *sissy*, which has a fuzzy definition because we cannot state the necessary and sufficient criteria. Many possible criteria come to mind— effeminate, unaggressive, frail, timid, eager to please, cowardly—but none is absolutely essential. Some sissies have one subset of characteristics, others have a different subset of characteristics. The best we can do in defining *sissy* is to list the most common characteristics that people think of when they describe a sissy and regard the list as an idealized prototype. Then we judge how well a given person's characteristics approximate this prototype (Horowitz, Post, French, Wallis, & Siegelman, 1981; Horowitz, Wright, Lowenstein, & Parad, 1981). The more a person's characteristics overlap with those of the prototype, the greater the likelihood that we would call that person a sissy. Very few children called sissy would have all characteristics in the list, and very few characteristics in the list would apply to all sissies.

Some writers have suggested that the self-image can be viewed as a theory about the self, a set of hypotheses that get revised, to some extent, from time to time (Brim, 1976; Epstein, 1973). If a boy compared himself to the prototype of a sissy and observed many of its characteristics in himself, he would have to classify himself as a sissy. Of course, characteristics do vary to some extent from day to day. By performing a very aggressive or bold act, a boy with marginal characteristics could show everyone that the "sissy hypothesis" had been refuted. Later, however, if an authority figure publicly described him as "a very good boy who never causes trouble," the sissy hypothesis might get revived. Therefore, a child who marginally fit the category might have to protect his self-esteem by behaving in ways that refute the undesirable hypothesis (e.g., by being aggressive or oppositional).

Concept of an Interpersonal Test

In order to enhance their self-esteem, people sometimes create interpersonal interactions that confirm (or disconfirm) a particular hypothesis. Interpersonal behaviors that serve this purpose constitute an interpersonal test (J. Weiss & Sampson, 1986; see also Swann, 1996). For example, bullies challenge people who are easy marks, thereby "proving" that they are tough and strong. Narcissists solicit admiration, thereby "proving" that they are admirable. Obsessive– compulsive people are perfectionists, thereby "proving" that they are beyond reproach. Many more examples of interpersonal tests appear in later chapters.

Dissatisfaction With the Self: Discrepancies and Subjective Distress

When a person feels dissatisfied with his or her self-image, the distress is often due to a discrepancy between an image of the self as it is and an image of the self that is desired. The most sophisticated theory about discrepancies has been proposed by Higgins (1987, 1996). Higgins's theory used the term *actual self* to describe a person's image of "me as I usually am." People can also imagine other possible selves, and two important standards are called the *ideal self* and the *ought self*. The ideal self contains qualities that the person admires, and the ought self contains qualities that match other people's standards (e.g., duties, obligations, and responsibilities). A woman might value professional success (her ideal self), but, out of a sense of duty, she might devote herself to being a mother and housewife (following her ought self).

Types of Discrepancies

To describe a person's actual self, ideal self, and ought self, Higgins asked participants to list up to 10 traits that describe each. For example, a person might be asked to list traits describing "the type of person you think you actually are," "the type of person you ideally would like to be," and "the type of person your mother believes you ought to be." Then discrepancies could be identified. A man might describe his actual self as temperamental and his ideal self as even-tempered. Higgins's theory focuses on these discrepancies. Two sets of descriptors are discrepant if the words in one contradict words in the other.

Types of Resulting Distress

According to the theory, distress occurs when the actual self diverges from either standard. When the actual self differs from the ideal self, the person experiences deficiencies ("desirable qualities that I lack"); for example, "I would like to be even-tempered, but I am temperamental." When the actual self differs from the ought self, the person might engage in a self-criticism about violating a duty; for example, "I am lazy, but I ought to be industrious." The first reflects an absence of desired (admired) qualities, the second reflects the presence of duty-violating qualities.

Higgins (1987) argued that a lack of desired qualities leads to dejection, disappointment, sadness, and other emotions associated with depression, whereas duty-violating qualities lead to agitation, fear, threat, and other emotions associated with anxiety. Thus, shame reflects an absence of desired qualities, whereas guilt reflects a shirking of duties, responsibilities, and obligations. To summarize, a discrepancy between the actual self and the ideal self produces a feeling of loss, lack, or deprivation that may result in depression. A discrepancy between the actual self and the ought self might produce a sense of wrongdoing that results in anxiety. This anxiety reflects a motivational conflict between "what I do do" and "what I ought to do." The anxiety disorders (e.g., agoraphobia and certain forms of the obsessive–compulsive disorder) provide many examples of motivational conflict and guilt. In contrast, the depressive disorders seem to stem from feelings of loss, failure, shame, and deficiencies, rather than motivational conflict.

Two Experimental Implications

As a test of the theory, participants first provided self-descriptions, and two groups were selected and compared. Group I (for "ideal") contained people with a discrepancy between their actual and ideal selves. Group O (for "ought") contained people with a discrepancy between their actual and ought selves. The investigators hypothesized that Group I would be vulnerable to depression and Group O would be vulnerable to anxiety. The participants engaged in a guided imagery task in which they imagined an event that induced negative affect. Each person's mood was then assessed using an adjective checklist. Higgins (1987) reported that a negative mood induction produced depression among the participants of Group I and anxiety among the participants of Group O.

In another experiment (Higgins, 1987), participants were identified who exhibited both types of discrepancy (Both I and O) or neither type of discrepancy (Neither I nor O). The authors hypothesized that the first group would be vulnerable to both depression and anxiety, whereas the latter would be vulnerable to neither. As a priming task, the participants were asked to describe one or the other standard. In one condition their ideal self was primed as they described the kind of person that they would ideally like to be. In the other condition their ought self was primed as they described the kind of persons that they and their parents believed they ought to be. The participants also rated their mood before and after the priming task. Table 5.1 shows the results. When researchers primed the ideal self of Both I and O group members, they were reminded of their deficiencies, and they became 3.2 points more dejected. When their ought self was primed, they were reminded of their duty-violations, and they became 5.1 points more anxious. No other change in the table was statistically significant. In other words, people with both kinds of discrepancy were vulnerable to both kinds of distress. People with neither type of discrepancy were not vulnerable to either kind of distress.

Self-Esteem, Explanatory Styles, and Interpretations of the World

Chronic dissatisfaction with the self is part of a broad network of attitudes, beliefs, expectancies, and feelings that we call *low self-esteem*. In this section we examine one manifestion of low self-esteem, namely, the person's characteristic way of explaining failures and successes: People with low self-esteem tend to blame the self for failures but not credit the self for successes. A person's explanatory style also has consequences for interpersonal interactions, as described below.

Attributional Theory and Self-Esteem

Human beings often wonder about causes, especially the cause of events that have personal significance (Malle & Knobe, 1997). We ask ourselves questions

Table 5.1.   Mean Increase in Dejection (Depression) or Agitation (Anxiety) for Participants in Each Condition

	Ideal-self primed		Ought-self primed	
Condition	Dejection	Agitation	Dejection	Agitation
Both I and O	3.2	−0.8	0.9	5.1
Neither I nor O	1.2	0.9	0.3	−2.6

Note. I = image; O = ought.

like these: Why did my colleague seem unfriendly at the meeting this afternoon? Why did that good-looking woman brush her arm against mine? Why is my best friend's son on drugs? Why did I not get a better grade on my physics exam? Why do I feel so sleepy today? Social psychologists have studied the kinds of questions that people ask themselves and the kinds of answers that they commonly give (see, e.g., the review by Weiner & Graham, 1999).

Our answers (i.e., our "causal attributions") reveal characteristic ways in which we explain events to ourselves. In some cases, characteristic explanations are correlated with self-esteem. By understanding a person's typical explanations, we can better empathize with the person's subjective experience. Here we begin with one class of questions that people ask about the self.

ATTRIBUTIONS ABOUT OUR OWN PERFORMANCE   One class of questions concerns our own performance: Why did I do well on this task? Why did I do poorly on that task? In general, we tend to enhance our self-esteem by taking credit for our successes and attributing our failures to factors beyond our control. "I performed well on this examination because I am smart and I worked hard." "I performed poorly on that examination because my instructor was a poor teacher and the test was a poor test." This tendency has been called a *hedonic bias;* it helps the person maximize the pleasure (of success) and minimize the pain (of failure). It is also called a *self-serving attributional bias* (Weiner & Graham, 1999).

A vast literature has documented this bias (see reviews by Bradley, 1978; Mullen & Riordan, 1988; Weiner & Graham, 1999; Zuckerman, 1979). In some studies success or failure occurred naturally; in other studies, the outcome was manipulated experimentally. In one study, for example, teachers were asked to explain the good or poor performance of their pupils. When the students did well, the teachers attributed the success to their own superior teaching; when the students did poorly, they attributed the failure to the students' lack of ability or effort (e.g., McAllister, 1996; Weiner & Graham, 1999). A practical consequence of the hedonic bias is that it helps us maintain a favorable self-image. We avoid sadness, despair, and pessimism, keep ourselves motivated, and persevere in the face of failure (S. E. Taylor & Brown, 1988). We can also reverse the attributions to explain why our rival succeeded. He won the competition, not because of his superior ability, but because he was lucky (or had some other temporary advantage).

We use a similar strategy to explain success and failure of people with whom we identify. "Why did my child receive a low IQ score? He certainly is bright, so the score does not reflect his ability. Perhaps the examiner was incompetent." I once provided consultation to a researcher who, having taught sign language to a gorilla, had the gorilla tested on the Stanford–Binet Intelligence Test. Disappointed by the gorilla's poor performance, the researcher explained the outcome by saying, "That stinker knows better; she always gets stubborn when she's tested and refuses to cooperate."

Another way to enhance our self-image is to adopt a self-defeating (or "self-handicapping") behavior that could explain a subsequent failure. For example, a student might go out drinking the night before a test, then perform poorly on the test, and explain that "I failed, not because I lack ability, but because I spent the night before the test partying" (Arkin & Oleson, 1998; E. E. Jones & Berglas, 1978; Midgley, Arunkumar, & Urdan, 1996; Urdan, Midgely, & Anderman, 1998). According to Covington (1992), a student's worst indictment is to be labeled *stupid*, and a good way to avoid that label is to provide an obvious explanation for performing poorly.

ATTRIBUTIONAL STYLES OF PEOPLE WITH LOW SELF-ESTEEM   Not all people exhibit a hedonic bias, however. Some people do not take credit for their success. Instead, they ascribe success (as well as failure) to factors beyond their control. Rotter (1966) created a personality measure for assessing a person's "locus of control": Does the person feel in control of his or her own destiny (an "internal" locus of control), or does the person feel that outcomes depend on luck, chance, and other external factors? A voluminous literature using this measure has shown that people with an internal locus (i.e., people who feel in control) display better physical and mental health than people with an external locus of control (Lefcourt, 1992; Weiner & Graham, 1999). Many disorders that we discuss in later chapters, from anorexia nervosa to the dependent personality disorder, are organized around a deficit in the person's sense of control and its interpersonal origins.

Abramson, Seligman, and Teasdale (1978) proposed another attributional theory that is relevant to self-esteem. Seligman's earlier helplessness theory of depression (1975) had claimed that depression stems from a history of uncontrollable negative events: Generalizing from prior failures, the person does not expect a contingency between behavior and outcome (success or failure). According to the theory, the resulting "learned helplessness" reduces a person's motivation to persevere and causes maladaptive emotional reactions like depression.

To clarify the experience of helplessness, Abramson et al. (1978) then examined the helpless person's way of explaining failure. They wrote: "when a person finds that he is helpless, he asks why he is helpless. The causal attribution he makes then determines the generality and chronicity of helplessness deficits" (p. 50). The authors then described three dimensions along which an explanation of failure may vary.

1. The first dimension was an internal–external dimension: Was my failure due to a factor within myself (e.g., "I lack ability" or "I didn't

try hard enough"), or was it due to a factor outside of myself (e.g., "Some obstacle got in my way," "I had bad luck")?

2. The second dimension was a stable–unstable dimension: Was my failure due to a quality that is not apt to change ("I lack the ability to perform well"), or was it due to a quality that might change next time (e.g., "I didn't try hard enough")?
3. The third dimension was a global-specific dimension: Was the failure due to a global quality ("I am not intelligent"), or was it due to a more specific quality ("Under time pressure, I find it hard to solve math problems quickly")?

According to the theory, a thoroughly pessimistic way of explaining failure (e.g., "I failed because I am stupid"—internal, stable, and global) puts the person at greatest risk for depression. It leaves the person feeling hopeless, hence unmotivated to try again. An explanation that allows hope for the future (e.g., "I didn't try hard enough") leaves the person feeling more optimistic.

To assess a person's explanatory style, the investigators created a questionnaire containing hypothetical situations (e.g., "You go to a party and do not meet new friends"). The respondents were asked to state a reason for the outcome (in this case, for not meeting new friends). They then rated their reason on each of the three dimensions. The resulting score was said to characterize the person's "explanatory style" (Peterson, 1991). Many empirical studies have shown that people with an internal, stable, and global style of explaining failures (e.g., "I failed because I am stupid") are generally pessimistic; they have problems in school, are less productive at work, and have a poor prognosis for long-term physical and mental health (Peterson, Maier, & Seligman, 1993). For a critique of this research and the measure, see C. A. Anderson, Jennings, and Arnoult (1988); Carver (1989); and Cutrona, Russell, and Jones (1985).

A second theory concerns people's beliefs as to whether aptitudes and traits can be modified (Dweck, Chiu, & Hong, 1995; Dweck & Leggett, 1988). Some people, for example, consider intelligence a fixed "quantity", and others consider it "mutable" (modifiable with training and practice). In other words, some people consider aptitudes and traits to be permanently fixed by the person's native endowment ("you either have it or you don't"), and other people consider aptitudes and traits to be trainable ("with training, effort, and practice, you can improve"). If people believe that their biological endowment has already determined their intelligence, athletic ability, or social skills, then a few failures would automatically indicate an unchangeable handicap. Dweck and her colleagues have shown that people who subscribe to the first view are more likely to give up; they think that a future challenge would expose their deficit yet again. On the other hand, people who subscribe to the second view are more apt to accept a challenge, hoping to learn from errors and master the task.

Finally, a third theory has been proposed, relating attributions to self-esteem. This theory concerns people's confidence (or lack of confidence) in their ability to understand and explain events and other people's behavior: "Am I capable of understanding the causes of my trouble?" Weary and Edwards (1994) called the construct "causal uncertainty." They created a scale that contains items like "I do not know what it takes to get along well with others" (Edwards, Weary, & Reich, 1998). High-scoring people feel unable to explain outcomes; as a result, they are less motivated to work at solving personal problems. Scores on this measure also correlate significantly with low self-esteem, depression, anxiety, and uncontrollability (Edwards et al., 1998).

All of these theories help describe the subjective experience of a person suffering from low self-esteem. Depressed people, shy people, and lonely people all seem to experience this sense of helplessness and hopelessness. They ascribe their frustrations to internal, stable, and global shortcomings; therefore, their deficits are fixed and unchangeable. For all of these reasons, they tend to give up (C. A. Anderson et al., 1988).

A pessimistic explanatory style is undoubtedly part of being depressed, shy, or lonely. However, one might still ask whether it is possible to devise an exercise to retrain a person to use a different explanatory style, thereby reducing the person's depression, shyness, or loneliness (see Foersterling, 1985). Could "attributional re-training" alone repair a person's self-esteem, replace pessimism with optimism, and help the person overcome depression? The procedures of cognitive therapy do alter a person's explanatory style, but they may do so largely because of the client–therapist relationship. In cognitive therapy, the therapist conveys many subtle interpersonal communications. To illustrate: When a client comments, "I really am incompetent," and the therapist replies, "I don't get it; what evidence indicates that you are incompetent?", the reply is respectfully indicating that the therapist does not share the client's view. It does not openly disagree with the client or dismiss the client's statement as invalid. It simply questions the internal, stable, and global attribution. If the relationship and the interpersonal communications were unimportant, the procedure might as well be carried out by a new therapist for each session, or by an impersonal computer program.

The view that attributional retraining is nothing but rote practice is easily caricatured. The television comedian Al Franken created a character on *Saturday Night Live* named Stuart Smalley, a depression-prone man with low self-esteem. In the skit, Smalley, the host of a television interview show, often found himself magnifying his own minor mishaps and blaming himself without mercy. Then, using a mechanical formula that he had learned in his therapy, he would respond to each failure with a well-practiced mantra designed to alter his attributional style. It always ended with "because I'm good enough, and I'm smart enough, and, doggone it, people like me." Nonetheless, by the end of each episode, Mr. Smalley was usually steeped in depression. The humor exposes the inadequacy of a rote formula to help a person gripped by esteem-lowering circumstances. For the person to evaluate the self more benignly, he or she has to revise images of self and others. And that step probably requires an interpersonal relationship. Sometimes it also requires an acceptance of a genuine limitation that cannot be changed. Such limitations may be easier to face and accept in collaboration with a trusted, supportive, and nonjudgmental therapist.

Attributions and Interpersonal Interactions

A person's explanation for an interpersonal event can help clarify the person's feelings. It can also help explain the person's overt reaction to a partner (Weiner & Graham, 1999).

EFFECT OF EXPLANATIONS OF BEHAVIOR ON EMOTIONS   The way we explain our behavior determines the emotion we feel. Consider the difference between guilt and shame. Guilt implies that the person's behavior has violated some internal ethical norm (Lindsay-Hartz, de Rivera, & Mascolo, 1995); it conveys a feeling of personal responsibility: "I should have treated her differently." Shame, in contrast, implies that the person had no control or responsibility: "Some defect of mine (stupidity, incompetence, clumsiness) has just been exposed for others to see." Shame thus implies an audience, but guilt does not. Sometimes, people do not know whether they are feeling guilty or ashamed because they are unclear about their personal responsibility: "Am I overweight because I do not exercise self-control or because of biological factors beyond my control?" Some disorders highlight shame, some highlight guilt. A person with a paranoid personality disorder is particularly vulnerable to shame; the person is afraid of being humiliated and exposed (Shapiro, 1965, p. 81). In contrast, other disorders are organized around guilt (e.g., guilt over a desire to perform a socially forbidden act). By understanding the difference between guilt and shame, we can better describe the person's struggle.

EFFECT OF INTERPRETATIONS OF INTENT ON REACTIONS   The way we interpret another person's intent affects our reaction. Many everyday questions that we ask ourselves concern other people's intentions. "Why did he hang up my jacket; is he being helpful or critical?" "Why is my hyperactive son not doing his homework: Is he unable to focus attention, or is he being lazy?" The answers frequently have interpersonal consequences. If the son is literally unable to do his homework, the father feels compassion; but if the son is willfully fooling around, the father blames him and gets angry.

When we observe people in a predicament, we ask: Are they hapless victims of circumstance, or have they brought the problem on themselves? In one case, we feel compassion and offer help; in the other case, we feel annoyed and withhold help (Weiner & Graham, 1999). A man who falls down because he is ill arouses more compassion than one who falls down because he is drunk. Sick people are not held responsible, but drunk people are (Piliavin, Rodin, & Piliavin, 1969). Likewise, people with AIDS receive more help and sympathy if their disease is attributed to a blood transfusion than to sexual promiscuity (Dooley, 1995).

Thus, the way we answer our questions affects our reactions. Consider the subjective experience of aggressive schoolboys. Aggressiveness in elementary school predicts poor school performance, juvenile delinquency, school dropout during adolescence, and later criminality and psychopathology (Hudley & Graham, 1993). How do we explain the aggressive child's behavior? As noted earlier, certain aggressive boys tend to perceive hostile intent in other children, so they feel vulnerable to other children's ill-will (Crick & Dodge, 1994).

To study this phenomenon more closely, Dodge and Coie (1987) differentiated between two types of aggressive boys: boys who initiate aggressive interactions (e.g., schoolyard bullies) and boys who react aggressively to other people's actions. Reactively aggressive boys were expected to show an attributional bias. Teachers identified boys who were high in reactive aggression, and those boys were compared with others. A test was constructed, using videotaped vignettes; each vignette showed one child provoking another. One vignette, for example, showed a provocateur taking away the other child's toy. The vignettes contained enough cues that a viewer could judge the provocateur's intent (hostile, helpful, or ambiguous). After each boy watched a vignette, he was asked about the provocateur's intent ("Was he being mean?" "Was he trying to help?"). The boy was also asked about his own likely reaction in situations of that kind. Children classified as reactively aggressive, more often than other children, judged the provocateur to be intentionally hostile. In addition, they often reported that they themselves would react aggressively. The researchers also studied the same children in actual play, noting that they displayed a lot of reactive aggression on the playground (e.g., kicking a peer who seemed to have criticized them).

Adults who physically abuse their children also show this bias. They are ready to ascribe hostile intent to their child's misbehavior, and they overreact (Milner, 1993). The same is true of husbands who abuse their spouses. They, too, are more likely than nonviolent husbands to ascribe hostile intent to their wives' behavior (Holtzworth-Munroe & Hutchinson, 1993). Thus, a salient characteristic of reactively aggressive boys, abusive parents, and abusive spouses is their attributional bias and aggressive overreaction.

Can educators, parents, and therapists modify aggressiveness by retraining a person's attributional style? For some adults, the attributional bias is woven into the fabric of their self-images. Over many years, the person may have learned to avoid humiliation by anticipating other people's hostile motives. In paranoid adults, for example, the bias is so firmly entrenched that they might even ascribe hostile intentions to an interviewer who inquired about possible misperception or overreaction. Because the bias is so ingrained, the person may not be readily able to adopt the participant–observer perspective that is needed to discuss it. For such people, the attributional bias would be hard to modify.

In children, however, the bias may be more malleable. Hudley and Graham (1993) developed an attributional retraining program for aggressive boys. Their program, which was administered through the schools, was designed for boys between the ages of 10 and 12. It tried to sensitize the boys to the difference between intentional provocation and unintentional acts. It lasted 12 sessions (twice a week for 6 weeks); every session was 40–60 minutes long. The boys met with an experienced teacher in groups of 6 (4 aggressive boys and 2 nonaggressive boys per group). The first block of sessions got the boys to think about intentionality. By playing games, role playing, constructing a videotape, and discussing personal experiences together, the boys came to identify cues that helped them discriminate intentional from accidental acts and hostile from prosocial and ambiguous intentions. Later the boys focused on ways that they might react (e.g., when one child spills milk on another). The treated group was compared with children in two other conditions. Children in one comparison group, an "attention-training" group, received exactly the same number of sessions, but their program focused on nonsocial skills, like classifying information and following directions. Children in the other comparison group, a no-treatment control group, were simply tested twice, once before and once after the program.

The group that received attributional retraining showed definite improvement on specially devised laboratory tests; they clearly had learned proper answers to the test items. After the program ended, their teachers also reported a small but significant reduction in aggressiveness. However, in the 3-month period after the intervention, there was no change in the number of times that they were sent to the school office for disciplinary action. Thus, attributional retraining produced only a modest gain. As the authors noted, however, some of these aggressive children had had very harsh experiences that could not be easily undone. One 10-year-old boy, for example, who did not improve at all through the program, described frequent experiences in a local park, where, he said, "gangbangers smoke crack, act wild, and take our balls if they catch us." He felt that aggressive retaliation was usually justified because "if somebody does something to you, then you got to show them that they can't get away with it" (Hudley & Graham, 1993, p. 136). Thus, the researchers' program was up against strongly integrated attitudes, beliefs, expectancies, and feelings that were part of the child's images of self and others. The resulting behaviors are not so easy to change.

Differentiation and Integration of Elements in the Self-Image

Some disorders described later involve an identity disturbance. The term *identity disturbance* is used in two different ways. Sometimes it refers to a vague, diffuse, or undifferentiated self-image; other times it refers to an unstable, incoherent, or unintegrated self-image. As our last topic, we consider the meaning of these terms.

The self-image is sometimes called a *knowledge structure*. As with any knowledge structure (about one's automobile, neighborhood, or self), people differ in the richness of available details and in the degree to which those details are integrated. Early in life, the self-image is simple; later on, the person comes to know the self more deeply, discovering new, finer aspects of the self. By adulthood, some people would have acquired a very fine ability to describe diverse aspects of the self, whereas others may have not; their self-image remains relatively vague, diffuse, or amorphous. Psychological difficulties associated with a vague self-image are examined in chapter 10.

People also differ in the degree to which characteristics of the self are integrated. Even if two people use identical descriptors to define the self, one may integrate them in some meaningful way, whereas the other may not. For example, suppose two people used the same pair of contrasting descriptors. One might say, "Sometimes I am friendly and sometimes I am unfriendly." The two characteristics (friendly and unfriendly) are listed but not integrated. The other might say, "Sometimes I am friendly and sometimes I am unfriendly; usually I am friendly, but after a hard day at work, when I have to prepare a meal for my family and no one is willing to help, I can become very unfriendly." This description seems to integrate the contradictory traits. Psychological difficulties associated with an unintegrated (inconsistent, unstable) self-image are examined in chapter 11.

Procedures have been devised to assess the degree to which a person's self-image is differentiated, ranging from "vague or diffuse" to "richly detailed." Other procedures have been devised to assess the degree to which differentiated aspects are integrated, ranging from "poorly integrated" to "coherent or consistent" (Campbell, Assanand, & Di Paula, 2000, 2003). The sections that follow describe a procedure of each type.

An Empirical Measure of Differentiation

To assess the amount of detail in a person's self-image, we might simply ask people to describe themselves. However, it is easy for people to rattle off traits mindlessly. Anyone might say, "I am friendly, intelligent, hard-working, and honest." A subtler task is needed that requires a more thoughtful reflection about the self. Linville (1985) devised one such procedure. The participant is shown 33 traits, each on a separate index card. The traits include *competitive, quiet, relaxed, rude, organized, unfriendly, affectionate, studious,* and *playful.* The participant is asked to examine the cards and find subsets of traits that describe some meaningful aspect of the self. For example, a young man, thinking of himself at school (one aspect), might select the traits *organized, studious,* and *competitive.* Then, thinking of himself with his roommate (another aspect), he might select the traits *affectionate, relaxed, competitive,* and *playful;* and so on. Participants form as many sets as they can, each describing a different aspect of the self. Linville's measure is somewhat complex (Locke, 2003), but it correlates highly with the number of aspects that the person has generated (Rafaeli-Mor, Gotlib, & Revelle, 1999).

A person with a well-differentiated self-image is thought to have a more detailed knowledge structure. The person is believed to be able to think about the self in more diverse ways, situations, or roles. As shown in chapter 10, people with a diffuse identity sometimes describe themselves as lacking a "core me."

An Empirical Measure of Integration

Everyone behaves somewhat differently in different situations, but some people show unintegrated inconsistencies. How might we determine whether a person's self-image has such contradictions? Donahue, Robins, Roberts, and John (1993) presented students with a list of 60 traits (e.g., *talkative, considerate, responsible, emotional*) and asked them to rate themselves on each trait in each of 5 different situations—with other students, with friends, with a romantic partner, with parents, and with co-workers. Suppose one person's self-ratings looked like this:

			Situations		
	a	b	c	d	e
Talkative	4	2	6	5	1
Considerate	2	6	6	7	2
Responsible	2	5	7	2	6

This person's ratings are very inconsistent; the same trait receives very different ratings from situation to situation. The degree of consistency in a person's self-ratings can be measured and people vary considerably in the degree of consistency. Some are highly consistent across situations, whereas others are remarkably inconsistent. The researchers showed that people whose ratings are inconsistent tend, on average, to be more depressed, more neurotic, and lower in self-esteem than those whose ratings are more consistent across situations. Apparently, a person with an unintegrated self-image is more apt to experience subjective distress. One cause of inconsistency is examined in chapter 11.

Summary

This chapter has examined the self-image and its development over time. To a large extent, interpersonal interactions throughout childhood (and beyond) shape the person's view of the self and others. As the self-image becomes more sophisticated, it can be used as a knowledge structure that might help the person satisfy interpersonal motives. By knowing one's self well, for example, a person can discerningly choose long-term friends and a partner who will satisfy important interpersonal motives.

When a significant discrepancy exists between characteristics of one's self and characteristics of some more desirable self, the person experiences negative affect. Frequent dissatisfaction is usually part of a broader network of attitudes, beliefs, expectancies, and feelings that we commonly call *low self-esteem*. One manifestation of low self-esteem is the person's style of explaining failure and success: The self is blamed for failure but not credited for success.

Some interpersonal motives arise from an insecurity about one's self. For example, some people feel uncertain about their appeal to others and desperately seek evidence confirming their appeal. Therefore, they routinely seek attention from others. Similarly, some people suspect that others wish to humiliate them and desperately try to protect themselves from humiliation; like reactively aggressive boys, they vigilantly seek (and routinely find) hints of ill-will in others.

In part II we apply the principles that have been presented thus far to the personality disorders. We shall argue that a personality disorder can often be described to a motive that has come to be salient. For most personality disorders, one or more diagnostic criteria describe (or imply) a salient interpersonal motive. Other diagnostic criteria of a personality disorder describe (a) behaviors commonly used to satisfy that motive and (b) reactions observed when the motive is frustrated. These themes are developed in chapters 6 and 7.

Part II

Representative Personality Disorders

6

Dependent and Avoidant Personality Disorders

This chapter focuses on the dependent and avoidant personality disorders. Like most personality disorders, each of these is organized around a salient interpersonal motive that becomes vital to the person's well-being. Apparently the motive becomes salient throughout the person's life as the person acquires a need to protect the self-image. People who have the disorder try to satisfy the motive in characteristic ways. However, complications arise in the person's life when the motive gets frustrated.

Dependent people are agentically vulnerable; they feel helplessly incompetent and unable to manage alone. They need help from others and strive to avoid isolation. Their neediness, however, can complicate their lives without resolving their sense of inadequacy. Avoidant people also view the self as inadequate, that is, inferior and vulnerable to shame and rejection by others. They are therefore wary of social contact and steer clear of people they do not trust. This strategy, however, complicates their lives and compounds their distress.

The organizing motive (and strategies for satisfying the motive) are often described by personality traits (e.g., "dependent," "avoidant"). The concept of a personality trait, however, has been controversial for years, and so it is useful to summarize some of the controversies and resolve them in ways that justify using traits as a construct. Accordingly, this chapter includes a discussion of personality traits.

We begin the chapter by defining a personality disorder. The discussion highlights the association between traits and motives to show the importance of motives in conceptualizing a personality disorder. Then we describe the dependent and avoidant personality disorders and examine a way to assess motives and frustrated motives.

Defining a Personality Disorder

Personality disorders were first described by Wilhelm Reich in his book *Character Analysis* (1949). Reich, an associate of Freud, observed that many psychiatric patients who consulted him did not actually exhibit the kind of syndromes that classical psychoanalytic writings had explored—phobias, obsessions, compulsions, hysterical paralyses. Nonetheless, Reich's patients were experiencing real distress and significant problems of everyday life, frequently interpersonal problems. Reich used the term *character* as we now use the term *personality*. His concept of *character armor* implies that people come to adopt particular patterns of behaving, thinking, and perceiving to reduce anxiety. As a result, according to Reich, certain learned patterns become increasingly rigid; in Reich's terms, they "harden into a kind of armor" that protects the person from feeling anxious. Rigid patterns, of course, cut two ways. People who shut themselves off from experiencing trust and intimacy, for example, may avoid unwanted feelings of disappointment, rejection, or shame (in that sense, the patterns are adaptive), but their behavior may frustrate other motives, causing them to feel lonely, alienated, bored, or depressed; in that sense, the patterns are maladaptive.

Today we define a personality disorder in terms of maladaptive personality traits. According to the *Diagnostic and Statistical Manual of Mental Disorders* (4th ed., text revision; *DSM–IV–TR*; American Psychiatric Association, 2000), a personality trait is a pervasive pattern of "perceiving, relating to, and thinking about the environment and oneself" (p. 686). That is, each personality disorder reflects a characteristic pattern of behavior and experience—ways of relating to other people, ways of perceiving and thinking, ways of relating to oneself. The *DSM–IV–TR* highlights five properties that these characteristics should possess. First, they should be so prominent, intense, or frequent that they deviate markedly from the expectations of the person's culture. The person might be so shy, for example, that the shyness seems extreme to the person's peers. Second, the traits should be evident across a broad range of situations. A person with an antisocial personality disorder, for example, should exhibit antisocial behavior in a variety of contexts: with family members, with acquaintances, with strangers. Third, the traits should be stable over time. Fourth, they should date back at least to the person's adolescence or early adulthood. Finally, the traits should be maladaptive: They should cause significant distress to the person or impair the person's ability to function socially or occupationally. For example, a man might be such a perfectionist or so indecisive that he cannot complete tasks assigned to him at work. Or a woman might be so suspicious of others that she drives friends away and now feels lonely, alone, and unloved. The *DSM–IV–TR* provides the following definition: "A personality disorder is an enduring pattern of inner experience and behavior that deviates markedly from the expectations of the individual's culture, is pervasive and inflexible, has an onset in adolescence or early adulthood, is stable over time, and leads to distress or impairment" (p. 685).

Notice that personality traits, by themselves, are not necessarily "bad," "wrong," or "pathological;" they may even be admirable, adaptive, or endearing. A man who is rigidly devoted to work may find his work very satisfying. His devotion to work and his time away from his family might not be a problem for him unless his wife, dissatisfied with their marriage, threatens to leave. A woman with an eye for critical details may take pride in her ability to detect subtle flaws in a film or journal article; her sharp, critical eye might even be a great asset to her in her job as a movie critic or journal editor. Her critical abilities might not be a problem unless they begin to drive away her friends. The traits would not be considered maladaptive unless they caused subjective distress or impaired the person's functioning.

The concept of a personality trait has been discussed at length in recent decades. In the following section, we review some of the issues and describe some of the lessons we have learned. These insights also highlight the importance of motives in explaining personality disorders.

Personality Traits and Related Issues

A personality trait is more complex than a physical characteristic. A trait like *sociable, assertive,* or *conscientious* is often regarded as a label for an aggregate of co-occurring behaviors and internal experience (e.g., Alston, 1975; Buss & Craik, 1983). Whereas behavior is often observable, internal experience is not. An internal experience must be self-reported or inferred from behavior. When a trait is judged from overt action (e.g., aggressive), two observers would agree fairly well; when a trait reflects an inference about internal experiences (e.g., guilt-ridden), observers may not agree as well.

What is the relationship between the overt manifestations of a trait and the internal states (experiences) of the person? The American psychologist G. W. Allport (1937) regarded a trait as a predisposition to act in a particular way. He wrote that "behind the disagreement of judges and apart from errors and failures of empirical observation, there are . . .*bona fide* mental structures in each personality that account for the consistency of . . . (the person's) behavior" (1937, p. 289). In today's language, *mental structures* would include motives, goals, and desires, as well as other kinds of internal experience. We do not call a person "friendly" simply because we have observed a particular class of behaviors; we also need evidence of a communal motive and feelings of good-will.

At the time that Allport wrote, American psychology was dominated by two theories: (a) psychoanalytic theory (with its emphasis on unconscious motivation, conflict, and defense) and (b) behaviorism (with its emphasis on methodological rigor, the experimental method, and the conditioned reflex). Allport objected to both of these approaches. In contrast to the psychoanalytic approach, he emphasized conscious, rather than unconscious, determinants of behavior (e.g., conscious goals). In contrast to the behavioral approach, he emphasized the person's future plans (again, conscious goals) rather than the person's reinforcement history.

He therefore argued, first, that traits reflect a person's conscious internal experience—values, wishes, likes, interests, satisfactions, and so on. Friendly people have different wishes from avoidant people; assertive people have different wishes from compliant people. These internal states affect the person's behavior. Second, Allport argued that a trait always implies at least some cross-situational consistency. A person who is described as friendly exhibits friendly behavior broadly—toward coworkers, peers, friends, even toward strangers. Third, Allport argued that trait-relevant behaviors, though diversely expressed, are coherent in meaning. A friendly person is interested in other people, attentive to them, responsive to what they do and say, helpful, encouraging, and supportive. Friendliness is not simply a narrow behavior elicited by a narrow class of stimuli; rather , it implies an entire cluster of related behaviors that manifest themselves in many situations. Fourth, Allport argued that a person who possesses a trait expresses those behaviors toward novel as well as familiar stimuli. A person who is friendly exhibits friendly behavior even toward strangers in novel situations.

Finally, and perhaps most important for us, Allport explicitly stated that a trait like friendliness often implies a motivation to express that behavior. That is, the behavior satisfies some particular motive. The friendly person is not simply a passive reactor to stimuli; the person wants to connect in a friendly way with others. If the person cannot find someone to be friendly with, he or she continues to search for one. If necessary, the person will even create a situation in which friendly behavior can be expressed. According to Allport's formulation, a sociable person wants company, an assertive person wants to have influence, a theatrical person wants attention, a dependent person wants to be cared for, a timid person wants safety, and a narcissistic person wants admiration.

Allport's description has raised a number of questions about traits that have been discussed in recent decades. We consider some of these issues and the insights that they have yielded.

Does a Trait "Explain" Behavior?

In everyday discourse people often use a trait to explain a person's behavior. For example, we ask, "Why did she smile at me?" and answer, "She smiled because she is friendly." However, if we use "friendly" as a descriptive summary of prior behavior, we are committing a logical fallacy (e.g., Addis, 1981; Hampshire, 1953; O'Shaughnessy, 1970; Squires, 1968, 1970). When we then say that she smiled because she is friendly, we are going beyond the description and are now using *friendly* as a motivational construct. Our reasoning is therefore circular: First we observe that the person has often displayed friendly behavior in the past, so we call the person *friendly*. Then we infer that the person has a motive for friendliness and use that postulated motive to "explain" the friendly behavior. What have we gained by postulating the motive? We could state, simply, that past behavior is a predictor of future behavior so we expect a person who has been friendly in the past to be friendly again in the future. Using a descriptive trait as a motive to explain behavior seems to add nothing to our understanding of the mechanism; it is a tautology.

Still, without falling into this trap, we might ask about a (nontautological) motive that explains a trait. For example, we might ask why an avoidant person is avoiding social contact. Does the person have a biologically weak communal motive? Is the person trying to avoid criticism, shame, and humiliation? Is the person worried about being engulfed by others, trying to preserve the self? As we have noted before, behavior is often ambiguous, and a trait, as a summary of behavior and experience, can be ambiguous. When we understand the person's reasons for behaving that way, we better understand the cause of the person's avoidant behavior. In many cases, a trait, like a behavior, may arise from alternate motives.

As shown below, a personality disorder is defined in terms of a set of traits, and, in general, those traits collectively zero in on a particular motive or class of motives. For example, *DSM–IV–TR* indicates that a person with an avoidant personality disorder has the following characteristics (among others): views the self as inadequate; is preoccupied with being criticized; avoids interpersonal contact because of a fear of criticism, disapproval, shame, or rejection; and becomes involved with others only if he or she is certain of being liked. This larger set of traits provides a more precise fix on the person's motive than we could achieve with a single trait. As described later, a person with an avoidant personality disorder who seems to desire communion may sacrifice communion in order to protect the self from shame and rejection. Therefore, whenever we describe a personality disorder, we shall try to formulate the motive that drives the disorder.

Why Do Observers Often Disagree About a Person's Traits?

When we rate ourselves on sociability, we ask, not only about our displays of sociable behavior; we also examine our internal experience (Alston, 1975), including our motives and interests: "Do I desire, value, and enjoy social contact?" However, strangers have no access to our internal experience. Gifford (1994) had 60 students complete Wiggins's Interpersonal Adjective Scales (IAS; 1979); they rated themselves on various trait dimensions like "extraversion" and "warmth." Then each student interacted with two others of the same gender (all strangers to each other). Each group's conversation lasted 15 minutes and was videotaped. A separate group of observers watched the videotapes and rated every participant on the various trait dimensions.

Would we expect an observer who was rating a participant's "extraversion" to agree with that participant's own self-rating? The degree of correlation was not very high. For extraversion, the correlation was only .45. To clarify this result, Gifford identified overt behaviors associated with extraversion—nods, gestures, manipulating objects, and so on. He showed that observers (who did not know the person) relied heavily on overt behaviors to judge extraversion. If a student displayed many overt behaviors associated with extraversion, observers judged that student to be extraverted; the correlation between the frequency of extraversion behaviors and the observers' ratings of extraversion was .80. However, the students themselves did not use their own behavior to the same degree in rating themselves. The correlation between their self-ratings of extraversion and the frequency of their extraversion behaviors was only .41. They apparently knew themselves more intimately, so they could use knowledge of their internal desires, goals, and satisfactions to rate their own extraversion.

Similar results were obtained for every trait that was studied. The observers' ratings of "warmth" had a correlation of .79 with the frequency of warm behaviors; but the students' own self-ratings of warmth had a correlation of only .30 with the behavioral measure. Apparently, we judge our own warmth mainly from our own private, internal states, whereas observers have to rely on behavioral cues. For this reason, people are more accurate than peers who know them well in predicting their own emotional responses and behavior in the laboratory (Spain, Eaton, & Funder, 2000).

Traits vary in their visibility to an observer, and highly visible traits are easier to evaluate. Examples of highly visible traits are *talkative*, *assertive*, and *rebellious*; they are manifested in overt behavior. Examples of less visible traits (emphasizing internal experience) are *shy*, *suspicious*, and *thin-skinned*. Because it is relatively easy to rate a visible trait, raters agree with each other more often than not (Funder & Dobroth, 1987; M. K. Rothbart & Park, 1986; R. N. Wolfe, 1993). Funder and Dobroth (1987) had students rate themselves on each of 100 traits. In addition, two peers (roommates, friends) also rated every student. The peers agreed reasonably well with each other and with the student about the more visible traits, but they did not agree well about the less visible traits.

Shy people are particularly easy to misinterpret. Participants in a group at the Stanford Shyness Clinic were asked to select traits from a list that best described themselves. They were then asked to tell the group which traits they had selected, and the group discussed their self-disclosures. One participant, for example, regarded herself as warm, but the other group members had interpreted her shy reserve as coldness; her desire for social contact had not been recognized. Another participant described himself as anxious, but other group members had observed no behavioral evidence of anxiety; in fact, they regarded him as the calmest member of the group.

According to *DSM–IV–TR*, histrionic people are initially judged to be warm, open, and charming, but as people come to know them better, these qualities "wear thin. . .as [the histrionic person] continually demands to be the center of attention" (American Psychiatric Association, 2000, p. 711). In other words, we initially judge histrionic people by their overt behavior. Later, however, we revise our interpretation as we come to know them better and as we infer motives (e.g., seeking attention).

In *DSM–IV–TR*, some traits that define a personality disorder are highly visible, whereas others emphasize internal states. Here are some examples of highly visible traits in *DSM–IV–TR*: "is irritable and aggressive" (antisocial personality disorder); "is arrogant or haughty" (narcissistic personality disorder); "displays inappropriate, intense anger" (borderline personality disorder); "is sexually seductive or provocative" (histrionic personality disorder); "is excessively devoted to work or productivity" (obsessive–compulsive personality disorder). These traits would be relatively easy to judge, and judges would agree reasonably well with one another. In contrast, here are some traits that are less visible: "lacks remorse" (antisocial personality disorder); "chronic feelings of emptiness" (borderline personality disorder); "is preoccupied with unjustified doubts about the loyalty of others" (paranoid personality disorder); "is preoccupied with being criticized" (avoidant personality disorder). Judging these traits requires a deeper knowledge of the person's private experience, so casual acquaintances are apt to disagree (with the target and with each other). By asking about a person's internal states, we can sometimes shed light on less visible traits.

How Stable Are the Behaviors Associated With a Trait?

If a salient trait (e.g., sociable, theatrical, narcissistic, timid, assertive, dependent) generally reflects a salient motive (for company, for attention, for admiration, for security, for influence, for nurturance), we should observe behaviors across many situations that would satisfy that motive. That is, a person with the trait should show stability across occasions. Consider a relatively visible trait like *honest*. An honest person should consistently resist lying, stealing, and cheating to uphold personal standards. Are the behaviors associated with honesty reasonably stable across occasions? If we observed someone behaving honestly in one test situation, would that person behave honestly in another test situation? Can we predict behavior on a test of honesty by observing the person's prior behavior? Two very different issues are embedded in these questions, and we need to differentiate between them.

To begin with, consider a classic study by Hartshorne and May (1928), who studied honesty in a sample of schoolchildren. The investigators devised more than a dozen test situations that provided opportunities for the child to cheat, steal, or lie. Some assessed stealing in the classroom, at a party, or in play situations; others assessed lying and cheating. Here are some examples of typical test situations. In the Duplicating Technique, the children were first given an achievement test (e.g., of spelling or arithmetic). Their papers were then collected and duplicated. The next day the papers were returned to the children (apparently unscored), and the children were told to score their own papers. The self-scored papers were then collected and compared with a duplicate copy of the originals. In another situation, the Planted Dime Test, each child was given a box containing a dime plus pieces to several puzzles; the dime was ostensibly part of one of the puzzles. After working on a puzzle that did not involve the dime, the children were asked to return the puzzle pieces to the box and to place their box in a large receptacle. Each box had been numbered, so the investigators could determine whether or not the child had returned the dime.

Table 6.1 contains hypothetical data resembling those of Hartshorne and May. For simplicity, the table lists 10 different test situations (referred to as Situations a–j). It also shows hypothetical responses made by each child. In this example, "1" means that the child behaved honestly in that test situation, and "0" means that the child behaved dishonestly. Suppose we were to compute a correlation coefficient (r) between the responses to "Situation a" and the responses to "Situation b;" and suppose $r = .18$. In the same way, we could compute a correlation coefficient for every pair of situations. Then we might average these correlations to yield a "mean correlation coefficient" across all pairs of situations. Suppose that value were .23; it would tell, for the average pair of situations, the degree of correlation between behaving honestly in one situation and behaving honestly in the other situation. Here we refer to this value as "mean-r" ($\bar{r}$; $\bar{r} = .23$). In fact, the value that Hartshorne and May reported is $\bar{r} = $ ".23" (1928, Table LXXII, p. 383). Not a very strong relationship, but significantly greater than 0. Since the report of the study, numerous writers have expressed alarm that the figure is so low—that behaving honestly in one situation is not very strongly related to behaving honestly in a second situation. They concluded that "honest behavior" is not all that stable—behavior on one occasion does not accurately predict behavior on a second occasion.

Does this result mean that honesty is an unstable trait? Should we conclude that an honest man is not necessarily honest when the situation changes or that a broad motive does not exist across occasions? No, it does not. A trait like honesty is judged, not from a single behavior, but from many behavioral

Table 6.1. Hypothetical Data Showing How Children Responded to Test Situations

Child	a	b	c	d	e	f	g	h	i	j	Aggregate (A)
					Test situation for assessing honesty						
1	1	0	1	1	0	0	1	1	0	1	6
2	1	1	1	1	1	1	1	1	1	1	10
3	0	1	0	0	0	1	1	0	0	0	3
4	0	0	0	0	0	0	0	0	0	0	0
5	0	0	1	1	0	1	0	0	1	1	5
6	1	0	1	1	1	0	1	1	0	1	7
—											
—											
—											
100											

observations. When we say that a person is honest, we mean that we have observed the person across a variety of situations and, in the aggregate, that person behaved honestly. We reserve the trait for people whose behavior is consistent across situations; they are the ones with the abiding motive. It is true that most children vary considerably from occasion to occasion (hence, the low $\bar{r}$), but "most children" are not usually described as either honest or dishonest.

To be more specific, consider the 10 situations in Table 6.1. The last column of the table tells, for each child, how often the child behaved honestly. Let us call a child's total number of honest behaviors "A" (for "aggregate"). The value of A can range from 0 (never behaved honestly) to 10 (always behaved honestly). If a child's A equals 9 or 10, that child is unusual in that he or she demonstrates honest behavior in almost every situation; we call that child "honest." Similarly, if a child's aggregate equals 0 or 1, that child is also unusual in that he or she demonstrates dishonest behavior in almost every situation; we call that child "dishonest." Most children would have a value of A between the two extremes, and we would not call them honest or dishonest. Therefore, an aggregate of observations across many situations (A) is the real basis for the trait, not a one-time behavior.

We could ask whether "A," the 10-situation aggregate, is stable. If a child has a high A in one set of situations (a, b, c, . . j), would that child have a high A when observed in a second set of 10 situations (e.g., situations q, r, s, . . . z)? What would be the correlation between one 10-situation aggregate and the other 10-situation aggregate (same children)? As shown below, it is a rather high correlation, namely, .75.

One version of the formula for this correlation requires just two values—m, the number of situations that are being aggregated (in this example, $m = 10$), and $\bar{r}$ (in this example, $\bar{r} = .23$). The estimated value of this correlation coefficient is called *alpha*. Alpha estimates the stability of the aggregates, that is, the degree of correlation between them (Cronbach, Gleser, Nanda, & Rajaratnam, 1972). The formula for alpha is:

$$\text{alpha} = \frac{m\,(\bar{r})}{1 + (m - 1)\,(\bar{r})}$$

When 10 situations are aggregated ($m = 10$), alpha becomes

$$\frac{10\,(.23)}{1 + 9\,(.23)} = .75$$

Thus, we estimate the correlation coefficient between corresponding 10-situation aggregates to be .75.

Suppose we observed children in 20 situations, obtained a value of A for each child (now ranging from 0 to 20), and then tested the same children in 20 other situations? What would be the degree of correlation between the first 20-situation aggregate and the second 20-situation aggregate? The results show that $\bar{r}$ is still .23, but $m = 20$. Applying the formula, $\alpha = .86$. Thus, an aggregate of 20 observations is very stable; a child with a high A in the first set of situations would probably attain a high A in the second set of situations.

Finally, suppose we evaluate each child's behavior in 100 situations, determining the value of A (now ranging from 0 to 100), and then test each child in another 100 situations. In that case, $\bar{r}$ would still be .23, but now $m = 100$. Alpha would be .97, an extremely high correlation. We could now expect each child's A to be nearly identical for the two aggregates. In other words, the larger the aggregate, the more stable it is. When alpha is very high, we can almost certainly expect a high-scoring child (i.e., an "honest" child) to be high scoring when observed again in the same way.

To summarize, we need to differentiate between a person's behavior on a single occasion (a one-time observation) and behaviors aggregated across many occasions. A trait can be discerned from an aggregate of observations. It should be used only to describe a person who has behaved consistently across situations. That person is the one with a strong set of motives and goals that are consistent with the trait.

Traits like *impulsive, anxious, perfectionist,* and *avoidant* often appear among the criteria for personality disorders, so they imply cross-situational consistency. For example, *DSM–IV–TR* (American Psychiatric Association, 2000) describes the "antisocial personality disorder" this way: "There is a *pervasive* pattern of disregard for and violation of the rights of others . . . as indicated by *three (or more) of the following situations*" (pp. 706). The terms *pervasive* and *three or more* indicate cross-situational consistency. The specific criteria also emphasize consistency: (a) *repeatedly* performing illegal acts that are grounds for arrest; (b) deceitfulness, as indicated by *repeated* lying; (c) irritability and aggressiveness, as indicated by *repeated* physical fights or assaults; and (d) *consistent* irresponsibility, as indicated by *repeated* failure to honor financial obligations. In this way *DSM–IV–TR* requires that the behavior be consistent, not a one-time observation. We should never cite a one-time observation as justification for calling a person dependent, avoidant, antisocial, or impulsive.

Should We Regard a Trait as Global or Situation-Specific?

When we say that a person is "aggressive," should we consider the trait to be a global characteristic, ready to manifest itself in any provocative situation, or should we consider it to be situation-specific? Certainly a given person is provoked more easily by some situations than others, but the situation that is most galvanizing for one aggressive person might not affect another aggressive person at all. Consider three highly aggressive schoolboys. Perhaps one becomes especially aggressive whenever he feels ignored, a second whenever he feels criticized, a third whenever he feels controlled. The difference is easy to explain. Each boy has an idiosyncratic history and, therefore, a unique combination of goals, values, beliefs, and expectancies that lend idiosyncratic meaning to a given situation (Mischel & Shoda, 1998). As a result, one situation might threaten an important motive for one child but not for another child.

To illustrate this point empirically, Shoda, Mischel, and Wright (1994) observed the behavior of children attending a 6-week residential summer camp. First, the investigators identified five interpersonal situations that frequently occurred during a woodworking session. The five situations were labeled as follows: (a) "peer approach," in which a peer initiated positive contact with the child; (b) "peer tease," in which a peer teased, provoked, or threatened the child; (c) "adult praise," in which an adult praised the child; (d) "adult warn," in which an adult warned the child; and (e) "adult punish," in which an adult punished the child.

The investigators studied each child's reactions to each of the five situations. The amount of verbal aggression that a given child expressed to situations a, b, . . , e constituted a profile for that child. One child's profile, for example, showed high verbal aggression to situation e (adult punish) and low verbal aggression to situation b (peer tease). Another child showed high verbal aggression to situation b (peer tease) and low verbal aggression to situation e (adult punish).

How stable is a child's profile for verbal aggression? If the same five situations were observed in another setting (e.g., during cabin meetings), would each child's profile resemble the profile observed during woodworking? The investigators therefore replicated the entire procedure during cabin meetings. Each child's verbal aggression was assessed in each of the same five situations. Then the investigators computed the degree of correlation between each child's pair of profiles. On average, the correlation was .47, so the profile for verbal aggression seemed reasonably stable.

Even if a profile is stable, however, some children become aggressive in multiple situations, whereas others become aggressive in very few situations. One child's profile (Shoda et al., 1994, Figure 1) showed conspicuously high verbal aggression in three of the five situations: in situation d ("adult warn"), situation c ("adult praise"), and situation e ("adult punish"). When we use a trait to describe a person (e.g., calling a child "aggressive"), we usually mean that the child shows the characteristic in multiple situations, not in a single situation.

Consider the trait "sensitive to rejection." If a person were sensitive in just one narrow situation, we would not call the person "sensitive to rejection." We might say that she is "sensitive to rejection from her father whenever she hears him bragging about her brother's intelligence." However, we would not say that she is "sensitive to rejection" without qualification unless we were implying a degree of cross-situational generality.

A characteristic that appears in multiple situations can be used to predict behavior in a novel situation. Downey and Feldman (1996) created a measure of "sensitivity to rejection" that asks people about their sensitivity in 18 hypothetical situations. To obtain a high score, a person has to report sensitivity to rejection in several situations. High- and low-scoring people were tested in a novel laboratory situation. Each participant was first introduced to a partner (a confederate) and told that they would have two brief conversations to help them get acquainted. After the first conversation, they were seated in separate rooms to complete questionnaires. Then the experimenter told each participant that the second conversation would not take place. Participants in one condition (the experimental condition) were told that the partner did not want to continue; those in the other condition were told that time had run out. Then the participants completed a final questionnaire describing their current mood. As hypothesized, high-scoring participants in the experimental condition indicated that they had felt rejected by their partner; low-scoring participants did not feel that way. It is important that a characteristic manifest itself in multiple situations before the person is described as having the trait.

In some personality disorders, the *DSM–IV–TR* specifically requires cross-situational generality. For example, a person with an antisocial personality disorder is supposed to show antisocial behavior in at least three (of seven) situations listed in the manual (2000, p. 706). In other words, two people with the same diagnosis may have different profiles, but they must exhibit antisocial behavior in more than just occasional situations.

To summarize, a trait is more than a summary of frequent behaviors; it describes internal experience as well. Internal experience cannot be observed directly, so observers who know the person only casually are especially apt to disagree in judging those traits. However, visible or not, a trait should not be said to exist unless the characteristic has been observed in multiple situations. Furthermore, people who possess a trait may exhibit different profiles for expressing that trait.

The Dependent and Avoidant Personality Disorders

People with a dependent personality disorder seem to consider themselves incompetent (negative agency). They seek help from people who can be relied on to take charge. People with an avoidant personality disorder seem to expect hostile behavior from others and feel vulnerable to criticism and shame. To protect themselves, they avoid social contact (negative communion). In the sections that follow, each disorder is explored more fully.

Dependent Personality Disorder

Exhibit 6.1 lists the defining features of the dependent personality disorder. These features seem to fall in the lower right-hand quadrant of the interper-

---

Exhibit 6.1.   Diagnostic Criteria for Dependent Personality Disorder

---

A pervasive and excessive need to be taken care of that leads to submissive and clinging behavior and fears of separation, beginning by early adulthood and present in a variety of contexts, as indicated by five (or more) of the following:

(1) has difficulty making everyday decisions without an excessive amount of advise and reassurance from others

(2) needs others to assume responsibility for most major areas of his or her life

(3) has difficulty expressing disagreement with others because of fear of loss of support or approval. *Note:* Do not include realistic fears of retribution.

(4) has difficulty initiating projects or doing things on his or her own (because of a lack of self-confidence in judgment or abilities rather than a lack of motivation or energy)

(5) goes to excessive lengths to obtain nurturance and support from others, to the point of volunteering to do things that are unpleasant

(6) feels uncomfortable or helpless when alone because of exaggerated fears of being unable to care for himself or herself

(7) urgently seeks another relationship as a source of care and support when a close relationship ends

(8) is unrealistically preoccupied with fears of being left to take care of himself or herself

---

Note. From *Diagnostic and Statistical Manual of Mental Disorders* (4th ed., Text Revision, p. 725) by the American Psychiatric Association, 2000, Washington, DC: Author. Reprinted with permission.

sonal space described in chapter 4. Features 1, 2, 4, 6, and 8 depict an agentic deficit; they reflect a sense of incompetence, lack of efficacy, or lack of autonomy. People with the disorder leave decisions and responsibility to others (features 1 and 2), lack self-confidence (feature 4), feel helpless when alone (feature 6), and fear being left alone to care for themselves (feature 8). On the other hand, features 3, 5, and 7 reflect the use of communion to solve the agentic problem: The person agrees with others (feature 3), seeks nurturance and support (feature 5), and urgently seeks another relationship when an earlier one has ended (feature 7).

Some writers suggest that dependent people have experienced a secure attachment in infancy (e.g., L. S. Benjamin, 1996; Millon & Davis, 2000), so they do have a reasonably positive view of others as friendly, potentially helpful, and willing to take charge. Later childhood experiences, however, apparently stunt their autonomy. They may not feel free to explore, experiment, and take initiative; as a result, they come to feel inept and unable to function alone.

CASE EXAMPLE   Millon and Davis (2000, p. 206) described a 32-year-old woman, Sharon, who was the younger of two sisters in a traditional family. Her father was the strong, reliable head of the family, her mother a homemaker. Throughout her childhood Sharon was treated like a little doll. Her older sister became her guardian in school, protecting her from bullies and helping with her schoolwork. Teachers liked her because she was sweet and well-behaved. She never learned to drive a car. Instead, she relied on her sister to take her wherever she wanted to go. After graduating from high school, she married an appliance mechanic, Tom, who resembled her father; he was her first and only boyfriend. At first, Tom liked the idea of a stay-at-home wife who would keep house for him, and Sharon was happy in that role. In the morning he would drive her to be with her mother and sister, then he would pick her up again in the evening. In time, however, Tom came to see her as needy and suffocating. He urged her to enroll in a junior college, but she doubted that she could succeed. For 9 years she worked as a teacher's aide. In this position, she received guidance and direction from the teacher she was assisting. More recently, her sister was killed in a car accident, and she found the loss devastating. She became depressed and began clinging even more tightly to Tom, who then began to think about a divorce. Apparently, her situation was tolerable as long as her sister and her husband were both available. When her sister died, however, and her husband began thinking of divorce, her anxiety increased.

Did Sharon have a personality disorder before her sister died and her husband threatened to leave? Her communal needs were apparently met through her sister and husband. As they took charge of her affairs, perhaps she also experienced an indirect, vicarious sense of competence. As the "sweet little sister" or "good little wife," she simply had to ask for help, and help arrived. If she was content with this arrangement—that is, if she felt no subjective distress or impaired functioning—a diagnosis would not be appropriate. When the two relationships changed, however, she obviously suffered distress, and then she clearly qualified for the diagnosis.

CHARACTERISTIC COGNITIONS   A negative self-image implies a set of cognitions that reflect self-doubt (e.g., beliefs about one's own fundamental incompetence). One example is the belief that "I am helpless when I am alone." These beliefs, in turn, produce performance anxiety and impair a person's functioning (Beck & Freeman, 1990). Other beliefs are best described as conditionals: "If I am abandoned, I will not survive;" "I can function only if I have access to someone competent." From these, the person generates rules (imperatives) to live by (e.g., "I must not offend the caretaker"). Fleming (1990) also noted a rigid explanatory style that attributes past and future failure to a defect in the self. These attributions then fortify the maladaptive conclusion that "I cannot manage without someone to take care of me."

FAMILY BACKGROUND   What kinds of experiences might produce such self-doubt? Many writers (e.g., Millon & Davis, 2000) have attributed this to a caretaker who was overprotective. A caretaker who routinely takes charge casts doubt on the child's competence and discourages autonomy and free exploration. The overprotected child receives anxiety-laden messages about hidden dangers and future catastrophes: "Hold my hand, or you won't be safe." "I'll do that for you; you might break it." The warnings are not unkind (they express a sincere concern for the child's welfare), but they convey a message that undermines the child's self-confidence and feeling of efficacy. They also establish the speaker's authority, superior ability, and wish to take charge.

Some people, by temperament, are probably more susceptible to these messages than others. As we have seen, some children at birth are relatively more prone to distress than others (e.g., Kagan, 1994; M. K. Rothbart & Ahadi, 1994), giving rise to problems like timidity. Furthermore, problem behaviors can be very persistent into adulthood (e.g., Donovan, Jessor, & Costa, 1988; Hays & Ellickson, 1996; McGee & Newcomb, 1992). Thus, we assume that timid, fearful children are more apt to perceive danger than nonanxious children and that they are more apt to believe messages about hidden dangers. In addition, a traumatic life experience would especially undermine an anxious child's self-confidence. For example, an actual loss (e.g., death of a parent) or repeated threats (e.g., parent's threats to leave home) would particularly undermine an anxious child's self-confidence.

FORMULATION   To summarize, the dependent personality disorder describes a person whose autonomy has been constrained. Perhaps the person was, from the beginning, biologically vulnerable to anxiety. Over the years the person may have come to experience a deficit in efficacy, initiative, and confidence. The dependent person, however, does seem to trust the good will of (at least some) others and connect with them. As a result, a competent partner may satisfy communal as well as agentic needs. The person is therefore highly motivated to maintain such relationships. If the partner dies, abandons the dependent person, threatens to leave, or tires of the relationship, however, the harmony is disturbed, and the person becomes very distressed.

Avoidant Personality Disorder

Exhibit 6.2 lists the defining features of the avoidant personality disorder. These features occupy the lower left-hand quadrant of the interpersonal space described in chapter 4. Some are negative in communion, others are negative in agency. Features 5, 6, and 7 are negative in agency. They reflect feelings of inadequacy (feature 5), views of the self as inept and inferior (feature 6), and a reluctance to take personal risks that might be embarrassing (feature 7). Features 1, 3, and 4 are negative in communion—the person expects other people to be hostile. These features include a preoccupation with disapproval, rejection, and criticism (features 1 and 4). They also include a fear of being shamed or ridiculed (feature 3). One other feature (feature 2) is a blend of mistrust and inadequacy, an unwillingness to become involved with others without a guarantee of being liked. In attachment terms, the person has a negative image of the self and a negative image of others, that is, a fearful avoidant attachment style.

Some of these characteristics are visible (behavioral), especially the person's avoidance of other people. However, most of the characteristics are not visible because they concern internal states—fears of criticism, disapproval, or rejection; fear of being shamed or ridiculed; feeling of inadequacy; view of the self as socially inept, unappealing, or inferior. Because these traits are not visible, the person is frequently misunderstood. Thus, for example, a shy person might be judged cold and aloof.

People with an avoidant personality disorder are generally shy, quiet, and withdrawn. They deprecate their social competence, expect to be criticized and rejected, and are hypersensitive to negative evaluation. Disinclined to take personal risks, they keep a low profile by avoiding activities that might be embar-

Exhibit 6.2.   Diagnostic Criteria for Avoidant Personality Disorder

A pervasive pattern of social inhibition, feelings of inadequacy, and hypersensitivity to negative evaluation, beginning by early adulthood and present in a variety of contexts, as indicated by four (or more) of the following:

(1) avoids occupational activities that involve significant interpersonal contact, because of fears of criticism, disapproval, or rejection
(2) is unwilling to get involved with people unless certain of being liked
(3) shows restraint within intimate relationships because of the fear of being shamed or ridiculed
(4) is preoccupied with being criticized or rejected in social situations
(5) is inhibited in new interpersonal situations because of feelings of inadequacy
(6) views self as socially inept, personally unappealing, or inferior to others
(7) is unusually reluctant to take personal risks or to engage in any new activities because they may prove embarrassing

Note. From *Diagnostic and Statistical Manual of Mental Disorders* (4th ed. Text Revision, p. 721) by the American Psychiatric Association, 2000, Washington, DC: Author. Reprinted with permission.

rassing or lead to criticism, mockery, or derision. According to *DSM–IV–TR* (p. 718), they long for social contact but can only get close to someone if unconditional acceptance is guaranteed.

CHARACTERISTIC COGNITIONS   Beck and Freeman (1990) have described maladaptive cognitions that accompany the avoidant personality disorder. Cognitions about the self include core beliefs like "I am inferior" and "I am incompetent." Cognitions about other people include beliefs like "Others are always evaluating me" and "Others are apt to reject, ridicule, or shame me." Conditional beliefs follow, such as "If I attempt something, I am likely to fail." Imperatives then follow; for example, "I should never try anything new." According to Millon and Davis (2000, p. 151), a person with these beliefs expects to be shamed or criticized and therefore over-interprets neutral cues. Anticipating evaluation, the person is often anxious; "detecting" signs of rejection, the person is often depressed. By withdrawing, the person can at least hope to reduce anxiety and depression.

CASE EXAMPLE   To illustrate the avoidant personality disorder, Millon and Davis (2000) have described a 22-year-old undergraduate student, Leslie, who often isolated herself as a shield against anxiety. She was particularly anxious about attending classes. Sitting in class, she suspected that others might be making fun of her. Whenever she tried to attend class, her heart rate would rise and she would begin to perspire. In the past she occasionally worked as a volunteer at a botanical garden, but she could not hold a regular job because of her anxiety. When asked about friends, she had difficulty naming any. She did have a boyfriend when she was a senior in high school, but even then, she was afraid to voice opinions lest she lose that relationship. She has dreamt of marrying someone who would accept her unconditionally, but she does not expect that dream to come true. She now prefers to be left alone, where "no one can see your faults or criticize you" and "you are not apt to embarrass yourself."

As a child, Leslie experienced a lot of subtle rejection from her parents. Her parents were successful people who had high expectations of her, but they were excessively critical. She had been told that her birth was unintended and she came to view herself as a burden to her parents. Furthermore, life at home was without warmth; she used to spend a lot of time alone fantasizing in her room. She was extremely shy and got teased mercilessly by other children, probably adding to her crippling sense of inadequacy. In time, she learned to withdraw socially as a way of protecting herself.

FORMULATION   Children who are shy and inhibited seem to have a biological predisposition for experiencing fear and anxiety; they are also ready to anticipate and perceive danger (Siever & Davis, 1991, p. 1655). Kagan, Reznick, and Snidman (1988) compared a group of 2-year-olds who were cautious and restrained in an unfamiliar situation with a comparable group who were more spontaneous. By age 7, most children in the first group continued to be quiet, shy, and socially avoidant, whereas those in the second group were more talkative and sociable.

A temperamentally anxious child would be especially affected by criticism, derogation, and rejection. Nonanxious children can ignore criticism and rejection; they can even fight back. However, anxious children seem to accept the criticism and come to doubt their own competence. If other people tease the child for being shy, anxious, or hypersensitive, that teasing might further aggravate the child's sense of inadequacy.

According to L. S. Benjamin (1996), a person with an avoidant personality disorder may have experienced at one time a positive attachment and is therefore able to experience closeness as an adult. However, in later years (according to her analysis), the person may have been unrelentingly criticized, degraded, and mocked. As a result, the person has become hypersensitive to criticism, shame, and rejection. The person is therefore highly motivated to avoid social contact as a way of preventing aversive consequences. As an adult, the person desires communion but does not trust most people. Therefore, the person experiences a conflict between a desire for contact and a desire for the safety of isolation.

Assessing Interpersonal Motives and Problems

The self-image of dependent people and that of avoidant people reflect different kinds of inadequacy. A dependent person feels inept; an avoidant person feels vulnerable to shame. They protect themselves in different ways, too: The dependent person trusts others to be helpful and strives to connect; the avoidant person mistrusts others and strives to minimize shame-inducing social contact. Thus, both try to protect the self, but in different ways. What empirical procedures might be used to expose the difference in their goals? The sections that follow describe a measure designed to serve that purpose.

The Domain of Interpersonal Motives

Locke (2000) constructed a test of interpersonal goals. Every item in the test describes a different goal that people frequently report having. The 64 items

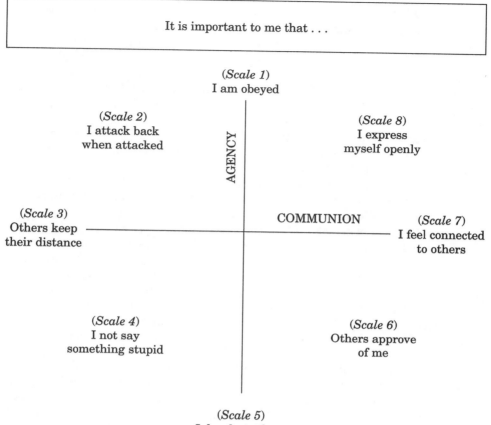

It is important to me that . . .

(Scale 1)
I am obeyed

(Scale 2)
I attack back
when attacked

(Scale 8)
I express
myself openly

AGENCY

(Scale 3)
Others keep
their distance

COMMUNION

(Scale 7)
I feel connected
to others

(Scale 4)
I not say
something stupid

(Scale 6)
Others approve
of me

(Scale 5)
I do what others
want me to do

Figure 6.1.   Illustrative items: Locke's (2000) measures of motives.

are organized into eight scales that form a circumplex. Every scale contains 8 items, corresponding to an octant of the two-dimensional space; the two organizing axes correspond to communion and agency. Illustrative items are shown in Figure 6.1. The item (goal) "It is important to me that I am obeyed when I am in authority" (Octant 1) is high in agency and neutral in communion. The item "It is important to me that others approve of me" (Octant 6) is high in communion and low in agency.

Each item describes a relatively narrow goal. People are asked to rate the importance of each item on a scale from 0 ("not important to me") to 4 ("extremely important to me"). Responses to the 8 items of a scale are summed to yield a score for that scale, and norms are available for each scale. Here we refer to the scales as *Scale 1* to *Scale 8*. A scale measures a broader motivational category than a single item. Individual items of Scale 1, for example, assess goals like "appearing self-confident," "being obeyed," and "not being told what to do." Scale 1 as a whole is designed to assess a motive for autonomy or self-definition. People with high scores on Scale 1 are strongly motivated to be in charge, to be seen as independent, correct, and confident; they have a strong agentic motive. Scale 2 and Scale 8 are also high in agency. In contrast, Scales 4, 5, and 6 are low in agency; they describe motives that are particularly salient among people with an agentic deficit. Scale 4, for example, describes a motive to avoid embarrassment by keeping a distance from other people. Scale 6 describes an approval motive, a motive to win acceptance by yielding to other people's wishes.

The scales also differ in communion. Scales 6, 7, and 8 are high in communion. People with high scores on Scale 7, for example, have a strong motive to connect with others in order to feel cared about and supported. Scales 2, 3, and 4 reflect an absence of the communal motive. People with high scores on Scale 3, for example, have a strong motive to detach themselves from other people, to conceal their private thoughts and feelings.

To assess the net strength of the communal motive, we could combine scores on all scales that are relevant to communion. That is, we would sum the scores on scales that are positive in communion (Scales 6, 7, 8), sum the scores on scales that are negative in communion (Scales 2, 3, 4), and then compute the difference between the two. To assess the net strength of the agentic motive, we would sum the scores on scales that are positive in agency (Scales 8, 1, 2), sum the scores on scales that are negative in agency (Scales 4, 5, 6), and then compute the difference between those two. The exact procedure is described in the Appendix.

To summarize, Locke's measure (for more details, see Appendix, this volume) allows us to assess motives at three levels. First, we can assess individual goals (single items). Second, we can assess broader motives using each of the eight scales. Third, we can assess the strength of the two broad, abstract motives, communion and agency, by combining scores on each of the relevant scales.

The Domain of Interpersonal Problems

When we can describe a person's interpersonal motives, we better understand the person's behavior. A person who strongly values communion would be especially bothered if friends did not reciprocate bids for a friendly exchange. In most personality disorders, a very salient interpersonal motive has been severely frustrated, leading to intense emotional distress. When an important interpersonal motive is chronically threatened or frustrated, we speak of an interpersonal problem. The following sections examine frustrated motives and corresponding interpersonal problems.

FRUSTRATED MOTIVES In general, most people are reasonably successful at satisfying their most salient interpersonal motives. They find ways to attain their desired levels of intimacy, friendship, influence, sense of efficacy, autonomy, and so on. Some people, however, are not as successful. A person may yearn for intimacy but find it hard to attain. Fearing rejection, for example, an avoidant person may avoid social contact and unwittingly invite others to keep their distance. Or a dependent person's overbearing desire for support may drive others away. In either case, the person's efforts to protect the self may backfire.

Why do people engage in behaviors that ultimately frustrate an important motive? Take unassertive behavior as an example. There are three broad reasons for unassertive behavior.

1. Sometimes a person lacks the capacity to be assertive. As described in chapter 10, some people have an extremely vague sense of self—they lack clear convictions, beliefs, wishes, and goals—and therefore find it difficult to assert themselves. Killingmo (1989) used the term "deficit" to describe this case.
2. Sometimes motives conflict. A person may therefore sacrifice one motive in order to satisfy another. For example, people with a dependent personality disorder may be unassertive in order to preserve harmony in relationships.
3. Sometimes people slip unwittingly into old interpersonal patterns (habits) that are no longer adaptive. An unassertive person may "recapitulate" an earlier script (see chap. 4, this volume). That is, the person may repeat earlier patterns automatically, never trying out other possible behaviors.

Thus, when a dependent or avoidant person says, "I find it hard to be assertive," the problem may be due to a lack of capacity, a conflict, or a habitual maladaptive pattern.

MEASURING INTERPERSONAL PROBLEMS   When people begin psychotherapy, they frequently describe their distress in three ways: uncomfortable feelings ("I feel very anxious"), disturbing thoughts ("I am thinking about killing myself"), and interpersonal problems ("It is hard for me to say 'no' to other people"). Usually interpersonal problems are expressed as a characteristic deficiency ("I find it hard to do X") or a characteristic excess ("I do that too much").

From statements made by patients, a 64-item test was formed, the Inventory of Interpersonal Problems (IIP-64; Alden, Wiggins, & Pincus, 1990; Horowitz, Alden, Wiggins, & Pincus, 2000; Horowitz, Rosenberg, Baer, Ureño, & Villaseñor, 1988). Illustrative items organized around communion and agency are shown in Figure 6.2. When people take the test, they read each statement and circle a number from 0 to 4 to indicate how much distress they have experienced from that problem. Norms are available that describe the responses of American adults (Horowitz et al., 2000).

Eight 8-item scales have been formed that correspond to each of the eight octants. The labels are Domineering/Controlling; Vindictive/Self-Centered; Cold/Distant; Socially Inhibited; Nonassertive; Overly Accommodating; Self-Sacrificing; Intrusive/Needy. It is convenient to number the scales, from Scale 1 (Domineering/Controlling) to Scale 8 (Intrusive/Needy).

Problems that are close together on the graph are positively correlated; they reflect similar amounts of problematic communion and problematic agency. A person who reports, "It is hard for me to tell a person to stop bothering me" is very likely to report, "It is hard for me to let other people know what I want." Because the two problems are very close to each other on the graph, their mean-

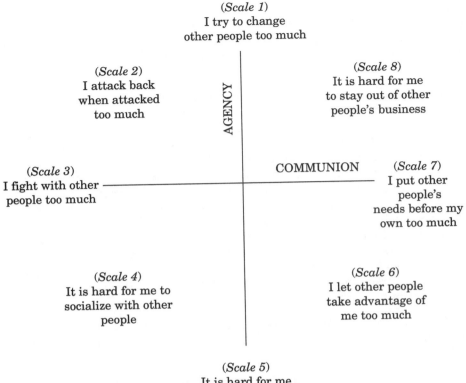

Figure 6.2.   Illustrative items: Inventory of interpersonal problems.

ings are similar, so a person who endorses one is likely to endorse the other. Similarly, Scale 6 is relatively close to Scale 5, so the items of these two scales also correlate positively with one another. On the other hand, problems of Scale 5 correlate negatively with problems of Scale 1. People who say they are too unassertive rarely complain that they are too domineering. The theory and expected pattern of correlations are discussed more fully in the Appendix.

Two Illustrative Patients and Their Interpersonal Problems

The IIP-64 allows us to describe the amount of distress a person experiences from each type of interpersonal problem. Using the norms of each scale, the person's scores can be standardized. They are usually expressed as standardized T-scores, which have a mean of 50 and a standard deviation of 10. A standardized T-score of 60 would be $(60 - 50)/10 = 1$ standard deviation above the mean of the normative sample. Standardized T-scores are usually presented graphically, as shown in Figures 6.4 and 6.6.

Case of a Dependent Personality Disorder: Ms. D

When Ms. D sought treatment, she was a married, 25-year-old homemaker whose husband was threatening to divorce her. She worried about being left alone, unable to care for herself. She sought treatment expecting the therapist to give her advice about being a better wife so that her husband would not leave her. She indicated that she was not able to disagree with her husband or tell him when she felt angry. She wanted to feel more competent, but feeling competent made her feel anxious. Thus, she seemed to be in conflict between autonomy and dependency.

Ms. D was the older of two sisters born 15 months apart. She believed that her mother favored her younger sister. She often found herself yearning to be cared for and nurtured by a mothering figure. She recalled a time during her elementary school years when her family moved to a new city, and for years she felt anxious if she strayed from home; she never did learn to drive a car or find her way around the city. She reported that she had always felt close to her father, whom she described as loving and nurturant, someone who could understand her without words. Her husband, like her father, seemed to enjoy being a caretaker, and she described him as an "excellent father" to their 3-year-old son. She described herself as an inadequate mother and felt that she could not manage the caretaking role by herself. She was also convinced that she could not get a job outside of the home because of her lack of competence, low self-esteem, and sense of inferiority.

Ms. D completed the IIP-64 just before she began psychotherapy. Using a table of norms for American women, her raw scores on each of the eight scales were transformed to standardized T-scores. Figure 6.3 shows the standardized T-score on each scale. Ms. D's greatest distress was reported on Scale 6 (Overly Accommodating); her standardized T-score on that scale was 77, which is 2.7 standard deviations above average, placing her at the 99th percentile for distress of this type. She also reported considerable distress on Scale 5 (Too Nonassertive); her standardized T-score was 71, corresponding to the 97th percentile. Ms. D reported her greatest distress over the following interpersonal problems: "It is hard for me to: 'take charge of my own affairs without help from other people;' 'be firm when I need to be;' 'confront people with problems that come up;' 'let other people know when I am angry.'" Ms. D's profile (Figure 6.3) shows at a glance that her distress on six scales resembled that of the general population but that she was deviant on two scales, namely, Scale 5 and Scale 6. This profile is typical for people with a dependent personality disorder, who generally describe themselves as nonassertive and overly accommodating.

Another way to present the same test results is to use a circular graph (see Figure 6.4). For each scale, a line extends from the origin to the perimeter of the outermost circle. Each line represents one of the 8 forms of distress. A dot is placed on the line to tell the standardized T-score on that scale. Again, a score above 60 is considered high, and one above 70 reflects considerable distress. The circular graph as a whole shows at a glance that Ms. D's distress was greatest on Scales 5 and 6.

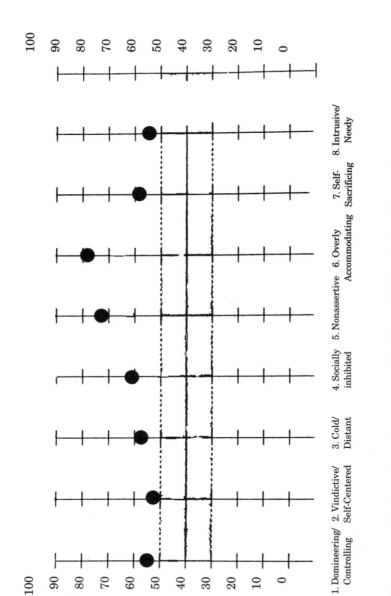

Figure 6.3. Ms. D's scores on the Inventory of Interpersonal Problems–64 (standardized T-scores).

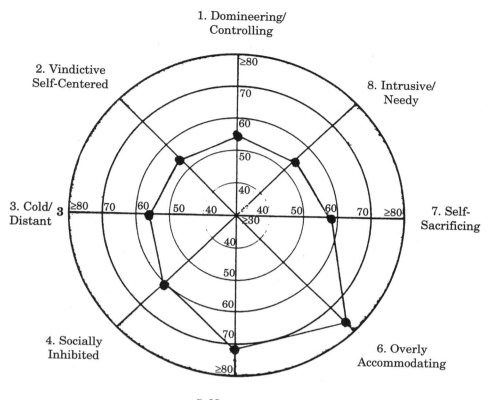

1. Domineering/
Controlling

2. Vindictive
Self-Centered

8. Intrusive/
Needy

3. Cold/
Distant

7. Self-
Sacrificing

4. Socially
Inhibited

6. Overly
Accommodating

5. Nonassertive

Figure 6.4.   Circular graph of Ms. D's standardized T-scores.

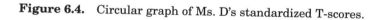

Case of an Avoidant Personality Disorder: Ms. A

When Ms. A sought treatment, she was a depressed, 23-year-old woman who had been in a relationship with her boyfriend for 3 years and felt uncertain that he loved her. She often needled him about his love and said that she found herself provoking him to the point where he would hit her. She was afraid that her provocative behavior was going to cost her the relationship. She described herself as shy and very concerned about other people's disapproval, criticisms, and rejections. She indicated that she would like to have more social contact, but she did not trust other people to treat her nicely. Therefore, she isolated herself from others.

Ms. A was the youngest of four siblings (one brother and two sisters). Although she believed that she was her mother's favorite child, she described her mother as cold, critical, and hard to please. She tried to please her mother by being a very good girl. Her parents divorced when she was 13 years old, and, in her view, this disruption led to intense rivalry between herself and her three siblings. She noted that she typically felt like an outcast during her teenage

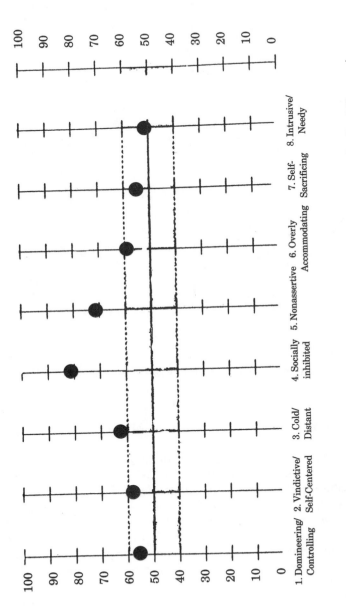

Figure 6.5. Ms. A's scores on the Inventory of Interpersonal Problems–64 (raw scores and standardized T-scores).

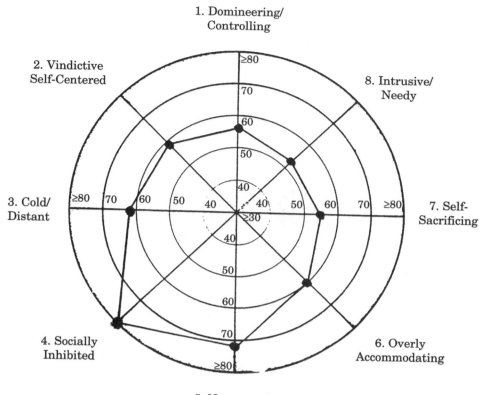

Figure 6.6.   Circular graph of Ms. A's standardized T-scores.

years, and even now felt in danger of being excluded by her siblings. She felt especially vulnerable with women (e.g., with her sisters, her boyfriend's sister, or her brother's wife). She described these other women as ready to betray, mock, or victimize her. For this reason she felt safest when she was alone.

Ms. A completed the IIP-64 before she began psychotherapy. Her raw scores on each scale are shown in Figure 6.5. Using the norms described earlier, her score on each scale was transformed to a standardized T-score. Her highest standardized T-score (82) occurred on Scale 4 (Too Socially Inhibited), placing her distress at the 99.9th percentile of the normative sample. Ms. A also reported considerable distress on Scale 5 (Too Nonassertive), for which her standardized T-score was 71, corresponding to the 98.5th percentile. Ms. A's profile of scores is shown in Figure 6.5. Figure 6.6 shows the same test results on a circular graph. This pattern is typical for people with an avoidant personality disorder.

Here are some of the problems that Ms. A rated as most distressing: "It is hard for me to: 'join in on groups;' 'introduce myself to new people;' 'socialize with other people;' 'believe that I am loveable to other people;' 'ignore criticism

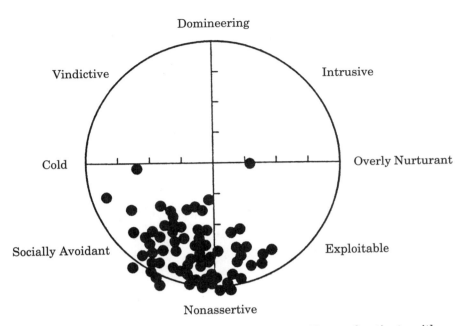

Figure 6.7.   Mean graphical location of interpersonal problems of patients with an avoidant personality disorder. As discussed in "Avoidant Personality Disorder: Interpersonal Problems as Predictors of Treatment Response," by L. E. Alden and M. J. Capreol, *Behavior Therapy*, 1993, from Alden and Capreol (1991; 1993). Copyright © 1993 by Association for Advancement of Behavior Therapy. Adapted with permission.

from other people;' 'be assertive with another person.'" She also reported great distress from the following problems: "I am too afraid of other people;" "I feel embarrassed in front of other people too much;" "I am too sensitive to criticism;" and "I am too sensitive to rejection."

Alden and Capreol (1992; 1993) studied 76 young adults with an avoidant personality disorder. Each dot in Figure 6.7 shows the average location of one patient's interpersonal problems. Almost every avoidant patient's problems were in Octants 4 and 5. The patients were randomly assigned to a brief group treatment or to a waiting list control condition. Those receiving treatment attended 10 weekly group sessions. The three types of treatment were (a) a behavioral treatment involving progressive relaxation and counter-conditioning, (b) social skills training, or (c) skill training that emphasized the development of intimacy and close relationships. Avoidant patients with the most negative scores on communion benefited only from the behavioral treatment. The other patients benefited from all three types of treatment, particularly from the intimacy-focused treatment. Apparently, a behavioral treatment is more tolerable to a person who has severe problems with closeness.

Summary

In this chapter we have examined the concept of a personality disorder and two disorders that are easy to understand. In each case, the features of the personality disorder describe the person's motive and strategy for protecting a vulnerable self. Dependent people strive to connect with competent caretakers; avoidant people strive to protect the self from shame and criticism. We have also examined methods to measure interpersonal goals (and frustrated interpersonal goals, or interpersonal problems). In the next chapter we examine two more personality disorders, obsessive–compulsive and paranoid personality disorders, that also reflect a motive to protect a vulnerable self-image using another strategy.

7

Obsessive–Compulsive and Paranoid Personality Disorders

The features of most personality disorders provide information of three kinds: (a) a salient interpersonal motive, (b) strategies used to satisfy that motive, and (c) consequences observed when the motive is frustrated. The *DSM–IV–TR* criteria of many personality disorders explicitly state the motive; for example, for the dependent personality disorder, it is "an excessive need to be taken care of" (p. 725). In some disorders, however, the criteria do not explicitly state the motive, yet the motive is implied. One example is the obsessive–compulsive personality disorder, which we examine in this chapter. Like the dependent and avoidant personality disorders, it concerns a particular strategy for protecting the self-image.

People with an obsessive–compulsive personality disorder are concerned about losing control, making mistakes, being criticized, and losing face. They therefore strive to affirm (to themselves and others) a sense of control, competence, and achievement, and they use a variety of agentic strategies. Their behavior, however, can complicate their lives in a way that leads to subjective distress or impaired functioning. Then we call it a *personality disorder*.

In addition to the obsessive–compulsive personality disorder, this chapter examines the paranoid personality disorder, which also emphasizes an agentic strategy for protecting a threatened self-image. The obsessive–compulsive and paranoid personality disorders differ in important ways (e.g., in the basic motive that organizes the disorder and in the strategies used to protect the self), but the two disorders also have much in common, such as a keenly focused attention that helps the person cope with threat.

Obsessive–Compulsive Personality Disorder

First we describe the obsessive–compulsive personality disorder, including the person's focused attentional style, and illustrate the disorder with a case example. Then we formulate the disorder and show how the formulation may be used in treatment. Finally, we show that the obsessive–compulsive personality disorder, like all personality disorders, is a fuzzy concept, and this fact has important consequences.

Description

According to *DSM–IV–TR*, people with an obsessive–compulsive personality disorder are preoccupied with "orderliness, perfectionism, and mental and in-

Exhibit 7.1.   Diagnostic Criteria for Obsessive–Compulsive Personality Disorder

A pervasive pattern of preoccupation with orderliness, perfectionism, and mental and interpersonal control, at the expense of flexibility, openness, and efficiency, beginning by early adulthood and present in a variety of contexts, as indicated by four (or more) of the following:

(1) is preoccupied with details, rules, lists, order, organization, or schedules to the extent that the major point of the activity is lost

(2) shows perfectionism that interferes with task completion (e.g., is unable to complete a project because his or her own overly strict standards are not met)

(3) is excessively devoted to work and productivity to the exclusion of leisure activities and friendships (not accounted for by obvious economic necessity)

(4) is overconscientious, scrupulous, and inflexible about matters of morality, ethics, or values (not accounted for by cultural or religious identification)

(5) is unable to discard worn-out or worthless objects even when they have no sentimental value

(6) is reluctant to delegate tasks or to work with others unless they submit to exactly his or her way of doing things

(7) adopts a miserly spending style toward both self and others: money is viewed as something to be hoarded for future catastrophes

(8) shows rigidity and stubbornness

Note. From *Diagnostic and Statistical Manual of Mental Disorders* (4th ed., Text Revision, p. 729) by the American Psychiatric Association, 2000, Washington, DC: Author. Reprinted with permission.

terpersonal control, at the expense of flexibility, openness, and efficiency" (American Psychiatric Association, 2000, p. 729). The term *mental control* refers to a person's control over his or her attentional processes, feelings, thoughts, and other mental processes. People who are obsessive–compulsive are rigidly attentive to detail; they like perfection and order. Exhibit 7.1 shows the eight diagnostic criteria. To be diagnosed with the disorder, a person must exhibit at least four of the eight characteristics. The diagnosis occurs in 3–10% of people who seek treatment; it is approximately twice as common among male as among female individuals.

SALIENCE OF AGENCY   People with an obsessive–compulsive personality disorder are preoccupied with matters of agency: achieving, accomplishing, having control, being right, being respected. Communal motives, such as affiliation, affection, intimacy, and empathy, are de-emphasized. Agentic motives, however, appear in the person's (a) devotion to work and productivity, (b) emphasis on correctness and perfection, (c) intense self-control, and (d) sensitivity to dominance and submission.

Consider the person's devotion to work. As described in *DSM–IV–TR*, people with the disorder rarely allow themselves an evening off from work. Even hobbies and play are approached as serious tasks requiring concentrated effort. The person seems to be driven to complete work, perform well, and be in charge. We might view the person's dedication as a test of the self: Through work, the person can keep displaying competence on manageable tasks that have reasonably objective outcomes.

Perfection, of course, is a very high standard, and people who are obsessive–compulsive seem to be on guard against possible errors. By concentrating on details, they can minimize slips, oversights, and errors. Striving for perfection, however, can cause other problems. If the criteria for perfection are not clear, the person may feel uncertain that the highest standards have been met. Then the person might have difficulty letting go of the job and meeting deadlines.

Perfectionism can express itself in morality as well. The person may be conscientious, scrupulous, even rigid, about ethical issues and insist that other people follow just as strict a moral code. The *DSM–IV–TR* describes a person who would not lend a quarter to a friend to make a telephone call, justifying his refusal by the rule, "Neither a borrower nor a lender be." Perfectionism may also be expressed in self-criticism. People who are obsessive–compulsive can be mercilessly intolerant of their own mistakes. As a result, they may find it hard to make decisions (lest it be the wrong decision), discard worn-out clothing (lest the clothing be needed one day), or spend money (lest the money be needed someday). After all, "you never know . . . "

Control is vitally important to the person, and certain kinds of activities help the person feel in control: double-checking details, tidying up messes, placing things in order, organizing, making and following lists of tasks to do, obeying rules, following schedules. The *DSM–IV–TR* describes a person who misplaced a list of tasks to be done and, instead of reconstructing the list from memory, spent a huge amount of time looking for the list. Control is also salient in interpersonal interactions. Individuals who are obsessive–compulsive are sensitive to rules about status—who may dominate, who must submit. When they themselves are in charge, they seem to demand compliance from subordinates.

ATTENTIONAL STYLE   A perfectionist needs to be able to concentrate on detail. In his book *Neurotic Styles*, David Shapiro (1965) described the way different people attend to environmental events. Like earlier writers, Shapiro first differentiated between two parts of the attentional field, the *figure* and the *background*. The figure (the center of the attentional field) is relatively distinct, detailed, and clear; the background (the periphery of the attentional field), is relatively fuzzy, vague, and impressionistic.

Figure and background have often been compared through a "dichotic listening" task (e.g., Cherry, 1953; Matlin, 2002; Wood & Cowan, 1995). In a typical study, the participant is asked to attend to a message delivered to one ear (the figure) and to ignore a message delivered to the other ear (the background). Later the participant is asked to recall the two messages. Details about the figure (the attended message) are well-remembered, whereas details about the background are not. Participants usually recall only global aspects of the unattended message—the gender of the speaker, qualities of the voice, impressions of the person.

People seem to differ in the degree to which they divide attention between the figure and the background. Shapiro noted that people with an obsessive–compulsive personality disorder seem to direct far more attention to the figure than to the background. That is, they seem to have a higher than average capacity to concentrate on the figure and ignore peripheral distractors. For Shapiro, the behavior of the person with obsessive–compulsive personality disorder is like an arrow being shot on a windy day: There is apparently so much tension on the bow and force on the arrow that the arrow is not diverted by incidental winds.

CASE EXAMPLE   Millon and Davis (2000, p. 172) described a young man who had been married for 2 years at the time of the interview; his wife was 8 years older than he. He was very focused on his career, and at the time of the interview, he had advanced quickly to a middle-management position. He was seeking treatment because of unexplained stomach pains and nightmares. He reported many details about his sensitivity to different foods, to smog, and to stuffy interiors. His stomach pains recently began to interfere with his sleep, and he was having nightmares involving a loss of control. When asked about his average day, he provided a lengthy description, with apparent pride in his detail, accuracy, and predictability. He would typically arrive early to work so that he could "smooth things out" before the workday officially began. He would also remain at work after the others had left in order to anticipate problems they might face in the morning. He was often reluctant to entrust a job to other people because they might "screw it up." He supervised the work of his subordinates scrupulously and was quick to discipline them for mistakes. He had never taken a vacation from work. His wife described him as a perfectionist. She said that once he made up his mind about something, he kept it made up. She also complained that he did not spend enough time with her. When asked about his childhood, he described his parents as distant and stern. Horseplay was punished, and he did as he was told. He liked to spend time in solitary activities, such as reading and coloring; but he remembered feeling that a stray mark would ruin a picture he was coloring.

Etiology

Why is the person who is obsessive–compulsive so bent on achievement, accuracy, and control? Why is work so important? Why is the person so committed to detail and perfection? Psychodynamic and behavioral writers have explained the etiology in terms of long-term patterns of parent–child interaction, and Pollak (1979, 1987) reviewed the relevant literature. According to his review, theorists and clinicians seem to agree that obsessive–compulsive individuals usually have a history of authoritarian parenting. That is, the child was pressured to follow the rules and conform to the parents' rigid values and expectations (e.g., L. S. Benjamin, 1996; Millon, 1981; Millon & Davis, 2000; Pollak, 1979, 1987). These pressures also discouraged autonomy, spontaneity, and initiative. Many case examples have described parents who relentlessly corrected the child's errors. L. S. Benjamin (1996, p. 243) described a woman who would typically correct a 9-month-old infant during play. The infant would place colored rings of different sizes on an upright plastic spindle. When the child managed to get the rings on the spindle, the woman would immediately re-arrange them in "proper" order by size.

From countless experiences of this type, a criticized child might find it hard to please the adult and, as a result, might not expect much pleasure from interactions per se. The child would learn that errors, imperfections, and oversights are apt to lead to criticism. Feelings of effortless mastery and control could not be taken for granted. Instead, effort, concentration, and vigilance would be needed. The child might come to believe that mastery, competence, and approval are at odds with spontaneity. Taking risks and deviating from the norm would pose a threat. To alleviate this anxiety, the person would have to find ways to be "beyond reproach." As people mature, they find areas (often work-related) that bring self-affirming approval.

The learning that takes place in a child's formative years generalizes to later behavior through three paradigms that we described in chapter 4.

1. Through recapitulation, the person expects others to judge and criticize. Thus, the much criticized child becomes an adult who is ready to be criticized.
2. Through identification, the person comes to judge and criticize others. That is, the much criticized child becomes a judgmental adult.
3. Through introjection, the person comes to assume both roles towards the self—criticizing the self and then reacting like a criticized child. In this way, the (now self-critical) person would have internalized the parents' standards. Just as the parents had once criticized the child, so the person now criticizes the self. Just as the parents had once controlled the child, so the person now controls the self.

In this way, self-control and self-criticism become salient features of the personality. The obsessive–compulsive individual is thus both critic and criticized, with a spotlight focused on the self: "Am I competent? Am I adequate? Am I in charge? Am I above reproach? Am I acceptable?" Unrelentingly, the person seeks affirmation.

Pollak's review suggests that the parents themselves also exhibit obsessive–compulsive traits (e.g., orderly, perfectionistic, conscientious). The transmission from parent to child may be partly genetic (perhaps some people innately find order pleasing; perhaps some are innately hypersensitive to disapproval). The transmission, however, is also partly learned. A sensitive child, for example, discovers early that criticism hurts and finds ways to please a demanding parent. Future research may show how biological factors interact with social processes to promote the development of the obsessive–compulsive personality disorder.

Formulation

The obsessive–compulsive personality disorder is organized around agentic themes, such as control, achievement, competence, and efficacy. We assume that these themes become salient during the person's childhood, when the person is routinely criticized, coerced, controlled, and corrected. The person learns to exhibit sanctioned behaviors and avoid risky, spontaneous behaviors. In this way, the person learns to be rule-abiding, attentive to details, hard-working, orderly, tidy, conscientious, and perfectionistic. By introjecting parental standards, the person also becomes self-critical and self-controlled.

Sometimes, however, the person's high standards and rigid behavior interfere with other aspects of the person's life. Psychiatric problems arise for reasons like these:

1. The person has difficulty making decisions (lest the unchosen option be the right one). Then the person might find it hard to complete tasks, causing problems at work.
2. The person's tireless pursuit of agentic goals comes to antagonize other people. For example, the person's intense drive, inflexibility, or stubbornness may offend or exasperate other people.
3. Frustrated communal goals may cause distress. For example, the person may come to discover a yearning for intimacy, and then complain of feeling lonely and depressed.

A valid formulation is useful in treatment. It helps explain the person's current problem, and it identifies salient goals, helps clarify their origin, and shows how the person's goal-directed efforts have backfired. The formulation thus exposes central issues that must be addressed. Suppose a man, plagued with indecisiveness, is unable to meet deadlines at work. The formulation would suggest one obstacle to his decision-making, namely, a severe concern about making mistakes, a connection that he may not have previously recognized. A formulation thus alerts a therapist to pertinent issues in the treatment.

Second, a formulation highlights sensitivities that are relevant to the therapeutic relationship. When a therapist knows that a person is sensitive to any loss of control, that knowledge can help avert an unproductive power struggle. For example, a therapist might avoid making statements that could be taken as the therapist's wish to take charge. Instead of offering advice (e.g., "You should get your own apartment"), a therapist might pose the idea as a question: "What would it be like for you if you had an apartment of your own?"

Third, a formulation is a fruitful source of hypotheses that might be investigated further. If a person met the criteria for a disorder, the formulation could suggest hypotheses about undisclosed details—other aspects of the problem, its origin, its interpersonal consequences, dilemmas that the person faces, and so on. By inquiring further, a therapist can often confirm or disconfirm those hypotheses and thereby achieve a fuller understanding of the case.

Relationship to Avoidant and Dependent Personality Disorders

People with an obsessive–compulsive personality disorder, like people with an avoidant personality disorder, seem to describe their parents as critical. Yet the traits associated with each disorder differ greatly: perfectionistic and achievement-oriented versus withdrawn and socially avoidant. Why the difference? To begin with, obsessive–compulsive people describe their parents as strict and authoritarian (Pollak, 1987). However, a strict parent's criticism might still convey hope for the future: "If you try hard enough, you will get it right." Future control is attainable.

The criticism described by avoidant people, however, seems more global and pessimistic. If a child were told what a disappointment he was because of an unchangeable global defect ("you are unintelligent like your grandfather"), that defect would seem internal, stable, and global, not controllable or changeable. The person might well feel hopelessly stuck with the trait and therefore withdraw in self-defense.

The obsessive–compulsive personality disorder might also be compared to the dependent personality disorder. For the dependent person, the parenting style can be described as overprotective, rather than critical. But overprotectiveness, no matter how kind, also conveys an implicit criticism. Instead of an encouraging "Try harder, aim for a higher standard," the overprotective message seems to discourage action: "Don't even attempt it by yourself; you lack the ability, and I will do it for you." Such messages might well contribute to a helpless dependency.

The Obsessive–Compulsive Personality Disorder as a Fuzzy Set

To qualify for an obsessive–compulsive personality disorder, a person must exhibit any four of the eight features. No single feature is absolutely necessary for the diagnosis, and two people with the diagnosis might not have a single feature in common. As described in this volume (see chap. 5), a construct that is defined this way is called a *fuzzy concept*.

Like every personality disorder, the obsessive–compulsive personality disorder is a fuzzy concept. The *DSM–IV–TR* lists n characteristics, and the person has to satisfy a subset of m characteristics. However, no single characteristic is necessary for membership in the category. Why are personality disorders defined this way? According to our formulation of the obsessive–compulsive personality disorder, the person tries to satisfy an agentic motive that can manifest itself in terms of specific goals (e.g., to achieve at work, to feel competent, to avoid mistakes, to seem above reproach). There are various ways to satisfy these goals: establishing meticulous order and organization, accomplishing prodigious amounts of work, being perfectionistic, displaying inflexible moral scruples, and so on. The diagnostic features of Exhibit 7.1 list some of the more common goal-directed agentic behaviors. No one of these behaviors is essential, however, and any subset of them could be used to satisfy the person's motive.

Let us call the various features a, b, c, .. h. In this disorder, the features are all specific goal-directed behaviors (or traits) for satisfying the motive. The formulation (call it "F") implies the features F => a, b, c, .. h. Thus, the features provide evidence in support of the formulation F. If a person displays enough of them, then F seems plausible. Therefore, when we observe perfectionism, a devotion to work, overconscientiousness, and a miserly spending style (or any other set of four), we tentatively hypothesize that F is valid: that the person is striving to satisfy an agentic motive.

Are the traits in Exhibit 7.1 correlated with one another? Pollak (1979, 1987) reviewed the studies that had examined the intercorrelation among traits,

Table 7.1.   Hypothetical Data Showing Distribution of Eight Traits

Participant	a	b	c	d	e	f	g	h	Score (# traits present)
1	1	0	1	1	0	0	0	0	3
2	1	1	0	0	1	1	0	0	4
3	0	0	0	0	0	0	0	0	0
4	0	1	0	1	0	1	0	0	3
5	0	0	1	1	1	1	1	1	6
6	0	0	0	0	0	0	0	0	0
7	1	1	1	1	1	1	1	1	8
8	0	1	0	0	0	0	0	0	1
9	1	0	0	0	1	0	1	0	3
1,000	0	0	0	0	0	0	0	0	0

like *orderly*, *perfectionist*, and *conscientious*. He concluded that these traits are indeed positively correlated; the correlations typically range between .30 and .40. As a concrete example, consider the hypothetical data in Table 7.1. Imagine that we had collected data for 1,000 people randomly sampled from the population and determined whether each person possessed each of the traits. In successive columns of the table, the traits are labeled a, b, c, . . .h. An entry of "1" (or "0") indicates the presence (or absence) of that trait for that person. The last column in Table 7.1 shows each person's total number of features. A person with a score of 4 or more would meet the 4-or-more criterion.

Scores in the last column of Table 7.1 range from 0 to 8. Because the various features (a, b, . . .h) have a mean Pearson correlation of approximately .35, we could compute the value of alpha to describe the stability of scores in the last column, using the formula from chapter 6 (see p. 111). With $n = 8$ and mean $r = .35$, alpha is approximately .81. In other words, the aggregated scores are considerably more stable ($\alpha = .81$) than the individual characteristics. If everyone could be retested, scores from the two testings would have a correlation of about .81.

Together, the eight characteristics describe an ideal case, and people approximate that ideal (or prototype) to varying degrees. Very few people would match the ideal perfectly. Some would possess 0 traits, some one trait, some two traits, and so on. Occasionally a person would possess all eight traits. Using the cutoff set by *DSM–IV–TR*, people with "4 or more" traits would qualify for the obsessive–compulsive personality disorder. Among people who do meet this criterion, those with higher scores are better exemplars of the category. Those who exhibit all eight characteristics are textbook examples. Bearing in mind that the cutoff is arbitrary, the difference between a three-trait person (who does not meet the criteria) and a four-trait person (who does) is probably not nearly as great a difference as that between a four-trait person and an eight-trait person. That is why we regard the eight features as a prototype that people resemble to different degrees. In this way, a dicotomous category is transformed into a continuous variable, as is generally preferred (e.g., Livesley, Schroeder, Jackson, & Jang, 1994; Widiger, 1989; Widiger, Sanderson, & Warner, 1986)

Methodological Implications

HETEROGENEITY OF PATIENTS WITHIN A CATEGORY   People who exhibit four of the eight obsessive–compulsive characteristics constitute a very diverse group. There are 70 possible combinations of four features out of the eight. Moreover, one person might show features a through d, another might show features e through h. Those two people would not have any features in common. For this reason, heterogeneity is the rule when we study people diagnosed with any personality disorder. However, heterogeneity in a research sample is generally undesirable, so researchers usually prefer to compare reasonably homogeneous groups. As the following study shows, results are usually clearer if we select one feature of a disorder and compare two homogeneous groups that differ with respect to that feature. The following section illustrates this procedure.

ATTENTIONALLY VIGILANT AND ATTENTIONALLY AVOIDANT PEOPLE FOLLOWING SURGERY   An interesting study by F. Cohen and Lazarus (1973) yielded a conclusion that has been confirmed by later investigators (see Carver et al., 1993; Mischel, Cantor, & Feldman, 1996; S. E. Taylor, Lichtman, & Wood, 1984). The study concerned 61 patients between the ages of 21 and 60 who were about to undergo elective surgery for a hernia, gall bladder, or thyroid condition. The patients were interviewed the night before surgery to determine what they knew about the surgical procedure, what else they wanted to know, how they felt about the surgery, and so on. From the interviews, the investigators evaluated the degree to which each patient had been thinking about details of the impending surgery, its risks, and its procedures. People at one end of the continuum were said to be attentionally avoidant (deniers) because they seemed to avoid thinking about the surgery. People at the other end of the continuum were said to be attentionally vigilant because they seemed to focus on surgery-related details. The two groups thus differed in this one respect.

One attentionally avoidant patient, for example, said, "All I know is that I have a hernia. I just take it for granted that the doctors know what they're doing. . . . I have no thoughts about it at all." In contrast, a vigilant patient first described the medical problem and surgical procedure in detail and then added, "I have all the facts, my will is prepared. . . it is major surgery . . . you're put out, you could be put out too deep, your heart could quit, you can go into shock." After the surgery, the two groups were compared on their speed of recovering: the number of days they were in the hospital, the number of minor complications (fever, infection, headaches, nausea), and the amount of pain medication that they had received.

The results showed that the avoidant patients seemed to recover faster than the vigilant patients. They left the hospital sooner and showed fewer postoperative complications. The investigators concluded that surgery may be one form of stress that responds better to an avoidant-denial form of coping. Similar results have been reported by other investigators. Apparently, patients adapt better to surgery and illness if they do not focus on stressful details (Carver et al., 1993; Mischel et al., 1996; S. E. Taylor et al., 1984). However, this result must be interpreted cautiously because avoidant people may simply be better able to distract themselves from pain, bodily discomfort, and other complications of surgery. In that case, they would complain less about postoperative complications and get discharged sooner only because they had distracted themselves from pain and other postoperative complications.

The avoidant style is sometimes called *blunting* because the person is passively distracted from threatening information. In contrast, the vigilant style is sometimes calling *monitoring* or *sensitization* because the person actively seeks information that could arouse further anxiety (Aspinwall & Taylor, 1997; S. M. Miller, 1987; Mischel et al., 1996; S. E. Ward, Leventhal, & Love, 1988). Generally speaking, blunting seems to be more adaptive if the stress cannot be controlled, whereas monitoring seems to be more adaptive if the stress can be controlled (Carver & Scheier, 1994; Compas, Malcarne, & Fondacaro, 1988; S. M. Miller, 1979; Mischel et al., 1996; S. E. Taylor & Aspinwall, 1996).

S. M. Miller and Mangan (1983) compared female blunters and monitors when they were undergoing a gynecological colposcopy examination. Before the procedure, patients in each group received much or little information about the procedure. According to the patients' later self-reports, blunters were more comfortable when they received little information, whereas monitors were more comfortable when they received extensive information. Apparently, some people benefit from information in a stressful situation, whereas others do not (Brouwers & Sorrentino, 1993; Scheier, Weintraub, & Carver, 1986).

Paranoid Personality Disorder

People with the paranoid personality disorder, like those with the obsessive–compulsive personality disorder, exhibit a vigilant attentional style and a strong need for control. Such people have a vulnerable self-image and chronic suspicions about the motives of other people. They are therefore on the lookout for hints of ill-will in others in an effort to protect the self from abuse.

Description

The paranoid personality disorder is characterized by a pervasive mistrust of other people that is based on little or no evidence. Other people are viewed as ill-intentioned plotters who have an intent to exploit, harm, betray, or deceive. The paranoid person expects hostile behavior from others and as a result, the person identifies many "false positives." The person erroneously reads hidden meanings into benign acts, innocent mistakes, and casual remarks. Compliments, humorous remarks, and other simple communal acts are frequently interpreted agentically, as though the other person intended to manipulate, coerce, or criticize.

Exhibit 7.2 shows the seven diagnostic features of the paranoid personality disorder. To meet the criteria for the diagnosis, a person must meet at least four of these criteria (plus subjective distress or impaired functioning). Though not stated explicitly in the criteria, the paranoid person usually tries to detect early signs that other people are out to expose humiliating defects. When suspicions

Exhibit 7.2.   Diagnostic Criteria for Paranoid Personality Disorder

A. A pervasive distrust and suspiciousness of others such that their motives are interpreted as malevolent, beginning by early adulthood and present in a variety of contexts, as indicated by four (or more) of the following:

   (1) suspects, without sufficient basis, that others are exploiting, harming, or deceiving him or her
   (2) is preoccupied with unjustified doubts about the loyalty or trustworthiness of friends or associates
   (3) is reluctant to confide in others because of unwarranted fear that the information will be used maliciously against him or her
   (4) reads hidden demeaning or threatening meanings into benign remarks or events
   (5) persistently bears grudges, i.e., is unforgiving of insults, injuries, or slights
   (6) perceives attacks on his or her character or reputation that are not apparent to others and is quick to react angrily or to counterattack
   (7) has recurrent suspicions, without justification, regarding fidelity of spouse or sexual partner

B. Does not occur exclusively during the course of schizophrenia, a mood disorder with psychotic features, or another psychotic disorder and is not due to the direct physiological effects of a general medical condition.

Note. From *Diagnostic and Statistical Manual of Mental Disorders* (4th ed., Text Revision, p. 694) by the American Psychiatric Association, 2000, Washington, DC: Author. Reprinted with permission.

seem to be confirmed, the person typically counterattacks or reacts with anger (criterion 6). Most of the criteria describe the person's vigilance. The person suspects hostile intentions in other people without much evidence (criterion 1); suspects infidelity in a spouse or partner without justification (criterion 7); obsessively questions the loyalty of friends or associates without justification (criterion 2); is alert to hidden hostile meanings (criterion 4); perceives attacks on his or her character that are not apparent to others (criterion 6); remembers prior insults, injuries, and slights very well (criterion 5); guards against self-disclosures that might give the enemy an advantage (criterion 3).

According to *DSM–IV–TR*, the paranoid personality disorder occurs in approximately 0.5 to 2.5% of the population and in 2–10% of people in treatment at an outpatient mental health clinic. The disorder is more often diagnosed among male individuals. It seems to originate in childhood and adolescence; early precursors include poor peer relationships, hypersensitivity, social anxiety, and solitariness (American Psychiatric Association, 2000, p. 692).

People with a paranoid personality disorder are generally hard to get along with for several reasons.

1. When they suspect malice, they often become angry—argumentative, fault-finding, sarcastic. They are critical of others and often become involved in legal disputes.
2. Because they mistrust others, they also strive to feel autonomous, free from the control of others. They therefore have difficulty collaborating. Not surprisingly, they also have difficulty relating to authority figures and co-workers.

3. Because paranoid people are so guarded and secretive, they seem cold to others, reject communal invitations, and elicit hostile reactions (which then confirm their own original expectations).

Cognitive Style

People with a paranoid personality disorder are "keen observers, with an outstanding attention to detail" (Millon & Davis, 2000, p. 391), especially the kind of detail that threatens the self. According to Shapiro (1965), the person "looks at the world with fixed and preoccupying expectation, and . . . searches repetitively, and only, for confirmation of it" (p. 56). Shapiro added that "suspicious attention . . . has an aim;" it is "purposeful, searching *for* something" (p. 59).

The paranoid person has a mission: to detect evidence of cheating, deceiving, exploiting, betraying, persecuting, and other forms of hostility. It is a biased search. Rational evidence to the contrary is simply ignored. When paranoid people do detect a bit of evidence, they quickly become convinced that their suspicion was confirmed: "He *wanted* to cheat me." That discovery then reinforces the original need for vigilance.

The paranoid person's attentional style may be described in terms of signal detection theory (Millon & Davis, 2000). The person evaluates interpersonal evidence as though it were a blip on a radar screen: Does it signify malice or not? Some indicators genuinely reflect malice, others do not. If the person correctly detects evidence of malice, it is a *hit* (or a *true positive*). However, if the person judges the evidence erroneously, it is a *false alarm* (or a *false positive*). Once in a while, a paranoid person makes a brilliant hit, but far more often, the person produces false alarms. The relatively high rate of false alarms reveals the person's bias or prejudice. According to Millon and Davis (2000), this tactic might be useful in warfare, where false alarms are tolerated in order to maximize the number of hits in detecting the enemy. In everyday interactions, however, the paranoid person seems to be distorting reality (Shapiro, 1965, p. 64) and acquires a reputation for distorting and over-reacting.

Case Examples

EXAMPLE 1   Millon and Davis (2000, p. 374) described a man who was required to seek counseling by the court because he had refused to pay child support to his former wife. During the interview, he appeared angry. He folded his arms across his chest and glared at the interviewer, challenging the relevance of the interviewer's questions. When he was asked why he was so evasive, he said, "Because you never know when something might come back to haunt you." He believed that his wife had been unfaithful to him and suspected that their children, ages 7 and 12, were fathered by his former best friend, who, like the children, had brown hair. (His wife also had brown hair, but he seemed to overlook that fact.) At the time of the interview, he was also having trouble at work; he suspected that co-workers had been manipulating the time clock in order to cheat him out of pay, using some of his money to pad their own pay checks. He felt that co-workers were trying to humiliate him by making it difficult for him to support his family. When the therapist asked him why he believed these things, he interpreted the question as skepticism, felt insulted, and became angry. He recalled injustices done to him over the years that he would not forget, and he was determined to avenge those wrongs.

EXAMPLE 2   A psychiatrist once conducted experimental research on alcoholism using cats as subjects. One of the experiments, which made alcohol available to cats, was publicized widely, and the psychiatrist received a letter of complaint objecting to this use of cats as research subjects. The letter stated that the researcher was torturing cats in the pursuit of a cure for alcoholics. It then asserted that a drunkard is a weak-minded idiot who belongs in the gutter and should be left there; it also urged the psychiatrist to use his influence to get a bill passed to exterminate drunks. The writer then expressed relief over being an ordinary human being who did not hurt any living creature and could sleep at night without seeing frightened, terrified dying cats—for he was sure that the animals must die after the researcher had finished with them. Finally, he added that no punishment is too great for the researcher, and he hoped to read one day about the researcher's mangled body and long suffering, stating that he (the writer) would then laugh long and loud.

From the tone of the letter, the writer seems to have had murderous impulses toward the researcher. How should we explain or interpret such an intense reaction? In the following section, we examine some explanations.

Mechanisms

Biological mechanisms probably play a role in every personality disorder. People who are susceptible to a paranoid personality disorder may begin life with a biological readiness to experience distress. In addition to biological factors, we also assume that negative childhood experiences play an important role. Psychodynamic and interpersonal theorists have suggested that a paranoid person's image of others arises from a history of humiliation and sadistic abuse (e.g., Cameron, 1963; McWilliams, 1994; Millon & Davis, 2000; Searles, 1956; Shapiro, 1965; Stone, 1993; Sullivan, 1956). Repeated humiliation affects a child's image of the self and of other people. Sullivan (1956) wrote that "the paranoid dynamism is rooted in (1) an awareness of inferiority (in oneself) . . . and (2) a transfer of blame onto others" (p. 156). Apparently, the person becomes hypersensitive to signs of hostility in others in hopes of deflecting humiliation that is expected because of defects in oneself.

Figure 7.1 shows how the interpersonal model describes the process. During the childhood years, other people (O) have humiliated Person P. In the top part of Figure 7.1, O's behavior lies in Quadrant II (disconnected dominance), and P's reaction lies in Quadrant III (disconnected submissiveness). The pattern is overlearned and leads to two forms of adult behavior: (a) Through *recapitulation*, P anticipates abuse from others; and (b) through *identification*, P finds a way to escape humiliation, namely, adopting the role of victimizer. In this way, P comes to berate others. Thus, the once-humiliated child comes to protect the self from abuse by humiliating others.

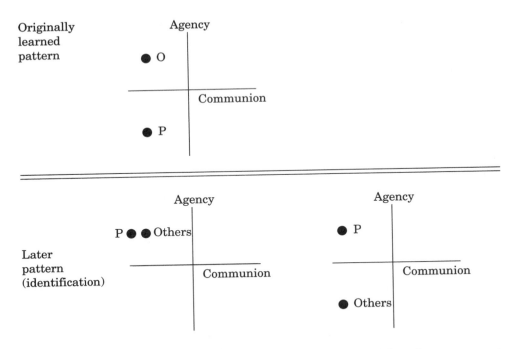

Figure 7.1.   Interpersonal mechanism for paranoid personality disorder.

Identification can be played out in two different ways, shown graphically in the bottom part of Figure 7.1. On the left, Person P fights potential humiliators—berating, criticizing, litigating. On the right, Person P finds anonymous others to berate without actually fighting (e.g., denouncing alcoholic individuals as "weak-minded idiots who belong in the gutter"). Thus, through recapitulation, the paranoid person (P) anticipates ill-will; through identification, the person attempts to gain the upper hand.

The psychoanalytic literature emphasizes the use of projection in the paranoid personality disorder, described as an immature way to reduce anxiety (see, e.g., Cramer, 1991, 1999, 2000; Cramer & Block, 1998). According to the theory, projection occurs when a person denies unacceptable motives, impulses, or traits in the self and ascribes them instead to someone else. For example, the letter writer in Example 2 may be ascribing his or her own hostility to the experimenter. According to the psychoanalytic theory, the paranoid person can now feel blameless by perceiving the other person as blame-worthy.

The exact meaning of projection has varied considerably across writers, and the large body of experimental studies is complex and somewhat inconclusive (see reviews by D. S. Holmes, 1968, 1978; Holmes & McCane, 1989). More recently, investigators have examined simpler component processes, like a person's readiness to blame other people (e.g., a spouse) for his or her misfortunes. Tennen and Affleck (1990) reviewed 25 studies involving people who had suffered an accident, a heart attack, a fire, or some other misfortune. Participants in the studies were all asked how they had coped with the trauma (e.g., blaming others, blaming the self). In most studies, people who blamed others took longer to recover; they remained in the hospital longer, had more complications, and complained of more physical symptoms. The authors inferred that blaming others is an immature, childlike strategy that is not very effective in reducing stress. A man who blames his wife for his heart attack, for example, would probably increase rather than reduce the stress he is under.

Paranoid people seem to work hard to feel free—free of other people's malice, free to do as they wish, free to be masters over themselves. Because of threats to their easily-humiliated self-image, however, they are not free at all; they have to be continually on guard to protect themselves (Shapiro, 1981).

Formulation

To conclude this section, we now formulate the paranoid personality disorder and use the formulation to identify some implications for treatment. We also compare the paranoid personality disorder to other personality disorders. To begin with, we assume that the paranoid person has had humiliating experiences over the childhood years. As a result, the person has acquired images of the self as defective and of other people as hostile. By adulthood, the paranoid person has become strongly motivated to block other people's hostile intentions; therefore, the person is generally suspicious and hyperalert to signs of potential abuse. The person acquires a reputation for being hypersensitive, contentious, and secretive. Because the person is unable to protect the self from humiliation, he or she feels depressed or anxious (or both).

IMPLICATIONS FOR TREATMENT   The formulation of paranoid personality disorder suggests some principles of treatment (which can be difficult). First, a paranoid person is not apt to trust a therapist initially. Therefore, a therapist must be patient and tolerant, willing to earn the person's trust slowly. Second, wherever ambiguity exists in a person's language or behavior, a paranoid person is apt to detect trickery, deceit, or manipulation. Therefore, a therapist's comments must be brief, crisp, and unambiguous. Long-winded or complex statements invite misinterpretation. Excessive friendliness or supportiveness may be misperceived as manipulative. For example, a therapist who addresses a middle-aged person by first name as a way of being friendly may come across as disrespectful.

Third, paranoid people feel very vulnerable; they fear that their own defects will be exposed and possibly used to their disadvantage. A therapist therefore should tolerate the person's guardedness. In time, if the person comes to feel safer, the person may relax his or her guard. Fourth, a paranoid person whose suspicious beliefs are challenged is apt to feel criticized, accused, or misunderstood. A therapist should be very careful in questioning the person's beliefs. If a therapist bluntly contradicted a particular belief, the paranoid person might interpret the message as manipulative (Shapiro, 1965). From the paranoid person's perspective, the belief is self-evident and a therapist's counterargument would not be convincing. Finally, at some time in treatment, a paranoid person is apt to blame, scold, or ridicule the therapist. A formulation helps a therapist maintain distance and avoid strong emotional reactions. By listening respectfully and responding nondefensively, the therapist has an opportunity to display self-confidence, a businesslike attitude toward the treatment, and goodwill toward the person.

COMPARISON WITH OTHER PERSONALITY DISORDERS   The paranoid and avoidant personality disorders have much in common. Both reflect a negative self-image and a motive to protect the self. In both disorders, the person is wary of being shamed or humiliated. However, the avoidant person seems readier to blame the self ("I might embarrass myself if I attend the party"), whereas the paranoid person is apt to blame others ("He wants to embarrass me by having me attend the party"). The avoidant person reacts to threat by passively withdrawing, whereas the paranoid person is apt to complain, argue, or fight back. Thus, the avoidant person seems to shrink from conflict, whereas the paranoid person seems to feel strengthened by fighting, confronting, and expressing anger.

We might also compare the paranoid personality disorder with the obsessive–compulsive personality disorder. In both cases, agentic motives (maintaining control, saving face) are particularly important. In both cases, the person strives to be rational—attentive to and focused on details. However, the two disorders reflect different preoccupations. Obsessive–compulsive people seem preoccupied with the quality of their own performance (keeping it beyond reproach), whereas paranoid people seem preoccupied with internal states: hostile intentions in others, humiliating thoughts and feelings in the self. Both groups are hypervigilant: Obsessive–compulsive people try to avoid mistakes, and paranoid people try to avoid humiliation.

Summary

Part II examined four personality disorders that reflect an agentic deficit or vulnerability. In an effort to protect the self from distressing feelings and thoughts, the person suffering from one of these disorders displays a particular set of goal-directed behaviors. Notice that the four disorders are not mutually exclusive. A person might meet the criteria for more than one personality disorder because the corresponding themes of each are relevant to different situations in the person's life. That is, the same person may be dependent with respect to some situations and avoidant with respect to others; or the same person may be avoidant with respect to some situations and paranoid with respect to others. The salient motive and strategies associated with one disorder can co-occur with the motive and strategies associated with another disorder.

In part III, we examine the interpersonal approach to syndromes and Axis I disorders. Then in part IV we return to the remaining six personality disorders, which are organized around themes other than those we have discussed thus far. The kinds of vulnerability observed in these personality disorders are also relevant to certain syndromes, so we examine those syndromes in part IV as well.

Common Syndromes

8

Syndromes and Axis I Disorders: Depressive and Panic Disorders

We now turn from personality disorders to syndromes. According to *DSM–IV–TR*, a *syndrome* is "a subjective manifestation of a pathological condition" (American Psychiatric Association, 2000, p. 828). It is a collection of symptoms (and objective signs) that often go together. The most common syndromes are organized around negative affect (e.g., sadness, fear, anger) that may result from a frustrated interpersonal motive. In this chapter we assume that the very same syndrome may develop for different reasons in different people; for example, in one person it may arise from a frustrated communal motive and in another, from a frustrated agentic motive. As a result, two people who are equally depressed may have become depressed for different reasons.

In this chapter we examine two typical syndromes. Then we describe four puzzling observations about syndromes and propose a way to conceptualize a syndrome that helps explain these puzzling observations. Finally, we examine two Axis I disorders and show how the same syndrome may arise in different people for quite different reasons.

The Nature of a Syndrome

A syndrome typically includes co-occurring mental states—internal experiences that are subjectively unpleasant or impair the person's functioning. They might include uncomfortable feelings (e.g., sadness), uncomfortable bodily sensations (e.g., fatigue), and unwanted cognitions (e.g., disturbing thoughts). Here are two examples.

Example 1. Panic attack. A panic attack is described in *DSM–IV–TR* as follows:

> a discrete period of intense fear . . . in the absence of real danger that is accompanied by at least 4 of 13 somatic or cognitive symptoms. The 13 symptoms are: palpitations, sweating, trembling or shaking, sensations of shortness of breath or smothering, feeling of choking, chest pain or discomfort, nausea or abdominal distress, dizziness or lightheadedness, derealization or depersonalization, fear of losing control or "going crazy," fear of dying, paresthesias, and chills or hot flushes. The attack has a sudden onset and builds to a peak rapidly (usually in 10 minutes or less) and is often accompanied by a sense of imminent danger or impending doom and an urge to escape. (American Psychiatric Association, 2000, p. 430)

This description includes feelings (e.g., a fear of dying) plus many bodily sensations (e.g., nausea) and disturbing thoughts (e.g., "I am going crazy").

Example 2. Major depressive episode. A major depressive episode includes a depressed mood (or a loss of interest or pleasure in nearly all activities) that lasts two or more weeks. According to *DSM–IV–TR*, individuals with this condition also exhibit

> at least four additional symptoms drawn from a list that includes changes in appetite or weight, sleep, and psychomotor activity; decreased energy; feelings of worthlessness or guilt; difficulty thinking, concentrating, or making decisions; or recurrent thoughts of death or suicidal ideation, plans, or attempts. (American Psychiatric Association, 2000, p. 349)

The basic requirement, a depressed mood, usually manifests itself in the person's self-report ("I am depressed," "sad," "hopeless,'" "discouraged," "down in the dumps"), but other signs are also accepted as evidence of a depressed mood (p. 349). For example, the person might complain of feeling "blah" or of having no feelings at all. Some people primarily report somatic discomforts (bodily aches and pains), others emphasize irritability or have angry outbursts in which they blame other people. In brief, very different complaints are taken as evidence of a depressed mood.

Thus, a syndrome is a fuzzy concept; it manifests itself differently in different people. One man's panic attack might emphasize (a) palpitations, (b) a shortness of breath, (c) chest pains, and (d) a fear of dying; another man's might emphasize (a) feelings of depersonalization, (b) a *paresthesia* (an unexplainable itching), (c) dizziness, and (d) a fear of losing control. One may suspect he is having a heart attack, whereas the other may believe he is going crazy. The symptoms of one do not necessarily overlap with those of the other, but both sets would constitute a panic attack.

Likewise, a major depressive episode varies from person to person. One woman might feel sad and report (a) overeating, (b) excessive sleeping, (c) decreased energy, and (d) feelings of worthlessness. Another might have bodily aches and pains and report (a) a loss of appetite, (b) insomnia, (c) difficulty making decisions, and (d) recurrent thoughts of death. One puzzling observation, then, is that a syndrome is a fuzzy concept. Why does it comprise different experiences in different people?

Another puzzling observation is that a syndrome may be triggered by a relatively minor event. It is not unusual for the reaction to be disproportionate to the instigating event. After the episode is over, the person may wonder why he or she reacted so strongly—why a relatively minor setback at work, a criticism, a rejection, or a loss evoked such a strong reaction.

A third puzzling observation is that a syndrome may include symptoms that seem unrelated (or indirectly related) to the precipitating event. When women become widowed, for example, they understandably feel alone, lonely, and sad. However, some widows also report a drop in self-esteem (e.g., Lopata, 1969); others report feeling abandoned by their late husbands. We are never surprised to learn that a widow feels sad, alone, or lonely (those feelings follow directly from the woman's loss), but why should she feel a drop in self-esteem?

Or why should she feel abandoned? These phenomena also require an explanation.

A fourth puzzling observation is that a syndrome seems to get activated more and more easily over time. After a first depressive episode, the probability of a second is .50–.60. After two episodes, the probability of a third is .70. After three episodes, the probability of a fourth is approximately .90. Furthermore, the first episode is apt to be precipitated by a stressful event—a woman's friend dies, a man's fiancée decides not to marry him, a long-time employee loses his job, a couple gets divorced. After the first or second episode, the precipitating event may not always be so evident (American Psychiatric Association, 2000, p. 349). This phenomenon also requires an explanation.

The Template as a Way to Conceptualize a Syndrome

The following sections describe a way to conceptualize a syndrome and apply it to explain the four observations. We develop the concept of a "template," a mental structure that evolves over many years out of the person's unique set of experiences. In particular, the template helps explain why the same syndrome (e.g., depression) can arise from frustrated communal motives, frustrated agentic motives, or a combination of both.

The Concept of a Template

To explain the four phenomena, we draw on associationist ideas and propose the concept of a template. A syndrome may be viewed as a pattern of reactions that include certain feelings, bodily sensations, thoughts, expectancies, and so on. We assume that a given reaction (e.g., a sad feeling) does not occur in isolation. A sad feeling is accompanied by other feelings, thoughts, and bodily sensations. For any one person, the set of reactions that occurs after one sad event differs somewhat from those that occur after another sad event. After one sad event, a person may feel humiliated; after another sad event, the person may feel angry. Across many sad events, however, some pairs of reactions co-occur very often. Because each person's experiences are unique, pairs of reactions that are most frequent for one person may not be most frequent for another person. Each reaction (a feeling, cognition, or bodily sensation) is stored in the nervous system, and co-occurring representations become associated. Over a period of years, a network of associated representations develops, and that network functions as a template or blueprint for future expressions of the syndrome.

Imagine an insecurely attached boy whose life is filled with unwanted separation. With every unwanted separation, he might experience other mental states, too, that differ somewhat from occasion to occasion. Typically, he would probably feel sad with each unwanted separation (a communal frustration). He might often feel abandoned and alone. Sometimes he might feel anxious, sometimes angry. Sometimes he might think "I am unwanted." Over a period of years, these various reactions would become associated with one another; some associations would be stronger than others. Over time, they would form a network of associated elements derived from a frustrated communal motive. In our view, that network constitutes a template for the boy's future reactions to separation.

Now imagine another boy with a different set of experiences, a child who often gets criticized for his performance (agentic frustrations). With each criticism, he, too, would react in characteristic ways that might differ somewhat from occasion to occasion. Typically, he would probably feel sad over the loss of esteem. Often he might feel humiliated and ashamed. Sometimes he might feel angry. Sometimes he might think that he is incompetent or inadequate. Over a period of years, each of his reactions would become associated with one another (again, some associations would be stronger than others). Over time, he, too, would acquire a template (derived from a frustrated agentic motive). Thus, both boys would have acquired a template in which sadness is prominent, but their templates would not have identical ingredients.

A *syndrome* may be viewed as a strongly activated template. According to this view, a major depressive episode would include feelings of sadness plus many associated elements, such as feelings of abandonment and helplessness for one person and feelings of shame and incompetence for another person. Similarly, a panic attack would include fear plus associated elements that vary from person to person. Furthermore, a person's templates for depression and panic may have many elements in common; for example, both may contain feelings of helplessness, abandonment, and aloneness. That overlap would explain why a major depressive disorder occurs quite often among people with a panic disorder (American Psychiatric Association, 2000, p. 435).

Resolving the Puzzles

Consider the four puzzling observations mentioned above. First, why does a syndrome manifest itself differently in different people? The question is now easy to answer: Syndrome manifestations differ because each person has a unique history, and hence, a unique set of associated elements.

Why does a man's death cause a drop in his widow's self-esteem? We assume that the widow's template for depression is a network of strongly associated elements from her past. Psychologists working in the associationist tradition (e.g., Bower, 1981; A. M. Collins & Loftus, 1975) have sometimes suggested that activation spreads across associated elements: The activation of one element induces activation in an associated element. Thus, a feeling of sadness (however it is induced) would tend to activate strongly associated elements (e.g., a feeling of abandonment or a feeling of shame). The stronger the association between elements, the more intense the activation.

If a widow has a template for depression, her template might contain elements that we call "low self-esteem." Because of the woman's particular history, low self-esteem may have been associated with many other elements in her template for depression. When elements of her template get activated, her low self-esteem is also activated. A different widow (with a different history and a different template) might not experience a drop in self-esteem when she feels very sad.

How does a relatively minor event precipitate the full syndrome? Suppose a person's template for anxiety contained many tightly inter-associated elements: a fear of abandonment; anticipated aloneness and helplessness; feelings of isolation; a sense of dread; and bodily sensations like heart palpitations, nausea, shortness of breath, and so on. Now suppose a relatively minor event activated just a few elements of the template. Perhaps a highly dependent woman, angry with her husband, begins to fantasize leaving her marriage. As she contemplates the separation, she feels a bit anxious, and activation spreads to other associated elements of the network (her isolation, helplessness, and so on). All of these reactions intensify one another, including bodily sensations (e.g., heart palpitations, shortness of breath). Eventually, with the spread and summation of activation, her anxiety snowballs.

Goleman (1995) coined the term *emotional hijacking* to dramatize the loss of control that can occur when a syndrome is activated. Lower structures of the brain—including the amygdala and the hippocampus—play an important role in emotional processes. They enable us to form associations, remember them, store and retrieve emotional memories, gauge the emotional significance of an event, and experience that emotion. Higher parts of the brain (including the left prefrontal cortex) enable us to modulate emotion by thinking about the event and re-appraising it. However, that process is comparatively slow. A signal from a sense organ travels first to the thalamus and then directly to the amygdala. By contrast, the brain circuitry to the cortex is more complex. Therefore, the amygdala can respond faster to a stimulus than the prefrontal cortex can. As a result, emotion and emotional meaning are registered before we have time to think about (or re-appraise) the event. Furthermore, nerve impulses travel from the amygdala to the adrenal glands, releasing hormones that prime the body for an emergency. As a result, a relatively minor event can, through emotional associations, produce a commotion in the endocrine system that upstages rational thought processes and prevents a re-appraisal of the event. Goleman (1995) has suggested that the lower (subcortical) brain structures

> proclaim an emergency, recruiting the rest of the brain to its urgent agenda. The hijacking occurs in an instant, triggering this reaction crucial moments before the neocortex . . . has had a chance to glimpse fully what is happening . . . The hallmark of such a hijack is that once the moment passes, those so possessed have the sense of not knowing what came over them. (p. 14)

Thus, when a panic attack, temper tantrum, or major depressive episode is set in motion, it may pass the point of no return and go out of control. Although the instigating event may have been relatively mild, the person may no longer be able to regulate his or her emotional reaction.

The fourth puzzling question is this: Why does a syndrome seem to arise more easily if it has been intensely activated before? We assume that the first time a syndrome is activated, a stressful event has directly activated elements of the template. For example, the premature death of a spouse might produce very intense feelings of loss, sadness, loneliness, disappointment, helplessness, and so on. This intense activation would further strengthen the association between each pair of elements. As a result, every element would acquire an even greater capacity to spread activation to other elements. After many major depressive episodes, relatively minor elements (feeling tired, feeling achy, feeling irritable) might activate other elements. The syndrome as a whole would be easily activated, and a major depressive episode might seem to arise "out of the blue."

This view of a syndrome helps explain experimental findings like the following. Miranda and Persons (1988; Miranda, Persons, & Byers, 1990) compared two groups of women: (a) women who had never been depressed and (b) women who, though not currently depressed, were vulnerable to depression because they had been seriously depressed in the past (they apparently had a template for depression). First, the women in the two groups completed the Dysfunctional Attitudes Scale (DAS; Weissman, 2000). This measure assesses negative beliefs related to low self-esteem like "People will probably think less of me if I make a mistake." Because the vulnerable participants were not depressed at the time of testing, their templates for depression were theoretically not activated. Therefore, the two groups were not expected to differ on the DAS at that time. As expected, the two groups had similar scores. Then the investigators induced a sad mood in each participant, using a standard mood induction procedure. Activating a sad mood should now activate other elements in the templates of the vulnerable women, so their scores on the DAS should now be higher. Indeed, they were. When the DAS was re-administered after the mood induction, the vulnerable women endorsed more dysfunctional beliefs than the women who had never been depressed. For further details about a person's vulnerability to depression, see Ingram (2003) and Ingram, Miranda, and Segal (1998).

Communal Versus Agentic Vulnerabilities: Different Templates

Thus, two people, each vulnerable to depression, may have different templates. For one, interpersonal loss, loneliness, and sadness may be central; for the other, failure, self-criticism, and sadness may be central. As a result, two people could differ in the type of event that precipitates a depressive episode. The first would be particularly sensitive to an interpersonal loss, the second to a criticism or failure. Furthermore, the two people are apt to experience depression differently—the experience of one would include feelings of isolation and separateness, that of the other, feelings of incompetence and shame. We refer to the first as a *communal template for depression* and the second as an *agentic template for depression*.

Psychodynamic and cognitive–behavioral writers have distinguished between communal and agentic subtypes of depression (e.g., Arieti & Bemporad, 1980; Beck, 1983; Blatt & Schichman, 1983; Pilkonis, 1988; Pilkonis & Frank, 1988; Robins, Block, & Peselow, 1989; Strauss, Buchheim & Kaechele, 2002). One emphasized frustrated communal goals; the other, frustrated agentic goals. Blatt and his associates (e.g., Blatt, 1974; Blatt & Schichman, 1983; Blatt & Zuroff, 1992) have referred to a *dependent* and a *self-critical* vulnerability to depression. We might say that a dependent vulnerability arises from a personal history that resulted in a communal template, whereas a self-critical vulnerability arises from a personal history that resulted in an agentic template.

Empirical Research

To assess each type of vulnerability, Blatt and his colleagues devised a measure, the Depressive Experiences Questionnaire (Blatt, D'Afflitti, & Quinlan, 1976), which contains two scales, one for assessing dependency and one for assessing self-criticism. Various studies have shown that dependent people are friendlier than self-critical people. Mongrain, Vettese, Shuster, and Kendal (1998) identified three groups of women: (a) those who were high on dependency, (b) those who were high on self-criticism, and (c) those who were high on neither (a control group). Each woman was observed together with her boyfriend as they discussed an issue about which they disagreed, and their interaction was videotaped. Later each woman rated her own behavior along a variety of trait dimensions (see Moskowitz, 1996). The woman's boyfriend and three objective observers also rated her behavior. The dependent women considered themselves especially loving; their boyfriends and the objective observers confirmed these ratings. By contrast, the self-critical women considered themselves less loving and more hostile; their boyfriends and the objective raters confirmed those ratings. In a similar study of dating couples, Zuroff and Duncan (1999) showed that self-critical women have negative views of relationships, which promote negative thoughts and negative affect during their interactions. The self-critical women often displayed overt hostile behavior toward their boyfriends.

Mongrain (1998) showed that dependent people are more apt to request and receive social support than self-critical people. Students kept a diary for 21 consecutive days, noting times when they requested or received social support. They also named five people who knew them well and could corroborate their reports. The dependent participants reported that others thought well of them and were available as a source of support; they felt that they belonged to a social network and could go to others for help. Their acquaintances corroborated this view. On the other hand, the self-critical participants indicated that they rarely asked for social support. They did not feel esteemed and did not believe that they could count on others for help. Their acquaintances also noted that they rarely asked for social support.

Is the experience of depression the same for dependent and self-critical people? Apparently not. Zuroff and Mongrain (1987) compared three groups of women on a laboratory task: a dependent group, a self-critical group, and a control group. Each participant imagined herself in one of two hypothetical situations: (a) a "rejection" experience (her boyfriend had decided to end their relationship) or (b) a "failure" experience (she had not been admitted to the school of her choice). After imagining the situation, each participant was asked to rate her affect on a list of possible feelings. After a rejection, the dependent participants reported uncomfortable feelings that reflected disconnectedness, such as feeling neglected, unwanted, unloved, lonely, uncared for, and abandoned (reactions to a communal frustration). Their ratings on these words were significantly higher than those of the other two groups (which did not differ from each other). After a failure, the self-critical participants reported uncomfortable feelings that reflected a loss of face, such as feeling inferior, guilty, self-critical, like a failure, and worthless (reactions to an agentic frustration). Their ratings were significantly higher than those of the control group, but not significantly higher than those of the dependent group. Words probably exist that describe clearer agentic feelings than those used in this study (e.g., *stupid, incompetent, a dummy, ashamed of myself, a loser*). Nonetheless, the three groups were distinctive. The dependent participants reported more communal frustration than the other two groups, and the self-critical participants reported more agentic frustration than the control group.

Origin of Self-Criticism

A voluminous literature describes the childhood experiences of people who later became depressed. The parents are described most often as "rejecting," "uncaring," "overprotective," and "abusive" (e.g., B. Andrews, 1995; J. Brown, Cohen, Johnson, & Smailes, 1999; Lewinsohn & Rosenbaum, 1987; Lizardi et al., 1995; Rodriguez et al., 1996; Segrin, 2001). These descriptions have also been confirmed by interviewing nondepressed siblings (Oliver, Handal, Finn, & Herdy, 1987).

Many fewer studies have tried to relate the parent's treatment to the child's type of vulnerability. However, the childhood origin of self-criticism has been studied more thoroughly than that of dependency. Several investigators have shown that self-critical participants describe their parents as critical, rejecting, and demanding of high achievement (Koestner, Zuroff, & Powers, 1991; McCranie & Bass, 1984; Thompson & Zuroff, 1999; Whiffen & Sasseville, 1991). Then, as we noted before, we might expect a young woman who has been criticized to display any of the following consequences.

1. Through recapitulation, she might later select a boyfriend who criticizes her.
2. Through identification or modeling, she might find others whom she can criticize (e.g., becoming a critical mother).
3. Through introjection, she might internalize both roles, scolding herself and then feeling incompetent and inadequate.

All three patterns were evident in a study of self-critical women, their mothers, and their boyfriends (Amitay, Mongrain, & Fazaa, 2001).

Templates for Other Syndromes

A similar distinction between communal and agentic vulnerabilities may exist for other syndromes (e.g., for anxiety and rage). However, no research has systematically examined those vulnerabilities. We assume that some people become anxious or enraged when they are communally frustrated (e.g., feel that they have been or might be abandoned), whereas other people become anxious or enraged when they feel that their performance has been or might be evaluated negatively, causing a loss of face.

Recent studies have distinguished among subgroups of people with the same syndrome. For example, consider social phobia, an Axis I anxiety disorder. Individuals with social phobia are said to exhibit "clinically significant anxiety [when they are exposed to] certain types of social or performance situations, often leading to avoidance behavior" (American Psychiatric Association, 2000, p. 429). Kachin, Newman, and Pincus (2001) studied the interpersonal problems reported by these individuals. The participants as a group seemed to fall into two broad groups. Those in one group described themselves as excessively friendly and yielding. They seemed to worry about displeasing others and spoiling relationships. Some worried for days or weeks about having to attend a social event, fearing that they might be ignored or disliked. Those in the other group described themselves as excessively hostile and controlling. They seemed to worry that they might be humiliated. Some were afraid of public speaking, lest other people notice their trembling hands or voices and judge them to be weak, stupid, or crazy. Thus, one subgroup seemed to exhibit a communal sensitivity, whereas the other subgroup seemed to exhibit an agentic sensitivity.

Major Depressive Disorder

In this section and the next, we examine a common mood disorder, major depressive disorder, and an anxiety disorder, panic attack with agoraphobia. Both are Axis I disorders defined in terms of a syndrome that seems to manifest itself when the corresponding template gets activated. To understand the disorder, it is necessary to understand (a) how the template got formed and (b) why it gets activated.

Description of a Major Depressive Disorder

To meet the criteria for a major depressive disorder: (a) the person must meet the criteria for a major depressive episode; and (b) that episode should not be explained by some more severe disorder like schizophrenia or bipolar disorder. A major depressive disorder is very debilitating and frequently accompanies other Axis I disorders, like panic disorder, obsessive–compulsive disorder, and anorexia nervosa. Up to 15% of people with this disorder commit suicide. Its lifetime incidence is estimated to be 10–25% for women and 5–12% for men. The incidence seems to be unrelated to ethnicity, education, income, or marital status. One year after the diagnosis of a major depressive episode, about 40% of the people still meet the diagnostic criteria.

Some people are probably biologically vulnerable to depression, but we do not yet understand the precise biological mechanisms that predispose a person to depression later in life. In addition to biological factors, an interpersonal loss (broadly defined) frequently precipitates the first major depressive episode. The term *loss* may be used in either a communal or an agentic sense; for example, the loss of a loved one (communal) or the loss of face that occurs when a person is humiliated (agentic). The theorist who first emphasized loss in activating a depressive disorder was Sigmund Freud. In his famous essay, "Mourning and Melancholia" (1917/1963), he highlighted loss and discussed the role of loss in both depression and mourning.

GRIEF   In "Mourning and Melancholia," Freud argued that depression resembles grief in some ways; both, for example, reflect a significant loss. A grieving person is one who has suffered a loss through death, whereas a depressed person has suffered some other kind of loss (e.g., an esteemed person has moved away, married someone else, or caused a loss of face by an insult, humiliation, or betrayal). In the process of mourning, the survivor needs to sever the tie with that person and adapt to the loss. Human beings do not easily disconnect from an attachment figure. According to Freud, the process of detaching is slow and gradual, eventually freeing energy so that the person can redirect that energy toward a new object of love. In some cases, the person in mourning has had ambivalent feelings toward the deceased, such that the object of love is also an object of anger. In that case, we hear the survivor expressing anger as well as longing. "Darn it; why didn't he take better care of himself?" or "That is so like her to spoil our Christmas season together by dying!"

When adults mourn the death of a loved one, they find ways to hold onto the deceased a bit longer: They imagine conversations with the person, recall hundreds of memories, revisit old haunts, re-examine old photographs, and sometimes adopt mannerisms of the deceased. Apparently, the custom of a funeral repast is very common across cultures—people gather together over food to talk about the deceased and ease each other's feelings of loss. Adults oscillate between moments when they distract each other from the death and moments when they jointly mourn the death. In time, survivors accept the loss and eventually form new attachments.

The process of mourning may be far more difficult for a young child. Children often blame themselves for a parent's behavior. "She died (or left) because she was mad at me," or "She was angry because of something I did" (e.g., Harter, 1986). Furthermore, a child does not have the cognitive and emotional ability to titrate stark reality with comforting fantasy. Unless a kindly, trusted adult takes the initiative, talks about the deceased, emphasizes the deceased person's love for the child, and reassures the child that he or she will be taken care of, the child's sadness, anxiety, or anger may be overwhelming. In that case, the child's preoccupation with loss may persist for life.

DEPRESSION   Freud's theory (1917/1963) acknowledged the role of biological factors in depression, but it emphasized the role of early experience. According to the theory, depression, like grief, is a reaction to loss. Some people are particularly sensitive to loss because of early experiences with separation and loss. For them, the corresponding feelings may be reactivated in adulthood by an actual separation or by a symbolic loss that leaves the person again feeling abandoned, abused, criticized, ignored, or rejected. Like a person in mourning, the person with depression, at that time, has little interest in new attachments. According to Freud's theory, bonds eventually get severed, energy is freed, and new attachments get formed.

According to Freud, depressed people have ambivalent feelings (perhaps without awareness) toward the lost or disappointing object. That is, a frustration has just occurred (producing negative affect) by the loss of a once-esteemed other (positive affect). In depression, according to the theory, these mixed feelings get directed at the self. As a result, the depressed person displays ambivalent feelings toward the self. Positive feelings toward the self may be observed in the person's attempts to comfort the self (by eating, sleeping, and using alcohol or drugs excessively). Negative feelings toward the self may be observed in the person's anger toward the self (self-criticism, self-blame, and self-mutilation). We now turn to two implications of the theory and empirical evidence.

Empirical Data

An interpersonal approach ascribes depression to communal and agentic frustrations that arise from loss, particularly from the loss of a relationship (a partner's infidelity, a marital separation) or from some loss of face (the loss of a job, news that a son is addicted to drugs). The proposition has two implications. First, events that precede a depression often reflect a loss that frustrates an interpersonal motive. Second, like a person in mourning, the depressed person is preoccupied with that loss and therefore exhibits less interest in other people. The following sections examine evidence for each proposition.

EVENTS THAT PRECIPITATE A DEPRESSION   Considerable data show that a depressive episode is initially precipitated by an "exit event," the loss of a relationship or some loss of face (e.g., G. W. Brown, Bifulco, & Harris, 1987; Paykel et al., 1969; Paykel & Tanner, 1976). Paykel and his associates tested this hypothesis empirically. They interviewed 185 depressed patients and 185 other individuals matched for age, sex, marital status, race, and social class. The investigators recorded every major life event that had occurred during the 6 months before the onset of depression (or during the corresponding period for the comparison group). Exit events were significantly more frequent among the depressed patients. The events that showed largest differences were: (a) increased arguments with one's spouse, (b) a marital separation, (c) the death of an immediate family member, (d) a serious illness of a family member, (e) a family member's leaving home, (f) a serious personal illness, and (g) a change in work conditions. Most of these events reflect a loss: a communal frustration (like the loss of a significant relationship) or an agentic frustration (like the loss of self-esteem in being fired from a job). People who are vulnerable to either kind of loss (because of the corresponding template) would seem to be at risk for a depressive disorder. The role of vulnerability is discussed further by G. W. Brown et al. (1987).

BEHAVIORAL CORRELATES OF DEPRESSION   People with depression frequently exhibit behaviors that suggest a focus on the self and an apparent disinterest in others. For example, compared to others, people with depression make less eye contact with a conversation partner and hold their heads downward (e.g., Dow

& Craighead, 1987; Fossi, Faravelli, & Paoli, 1984; Kazdin, Sherick, Esveldt-Dawson, & Rancurello, 1985; Troisi & Moles, 1999; Waxer, 1974; Youngren & Lewinsohn, 1980). They are facially less animated (except for sadness), and they smile less (e.g., Ellring, 1986; Fossi et al., 1984; Gaebel & Wolwer; 1992; Rubinow & Post, 1992). They use fewer gestures and head nods (Ekman & Friesen, 1972, 1974; Fossi et al., 1984; Kazdin et al., 1985; Troisi & Moles, 1999). They also engage more in self-touching, rubbing, and scratching (I. H. Jones & Pansa, 1979; Ranelli & Miller, 1981). We might ascribe these behaviors to the person's intense concentration on a significant problem (the frustrated motive) that needs to be resolved.

In addition, and compared to nondepressed people, depressed people talk less, are less responsive, and speak more slowly, more quietly, and with longer pauses (e.g., Ellring & Scherer, 1996; Hale, Jansen, Bouhuys, Jenner, & van der Hoofdakker, 1997; Segrin, 2001; Talavera, Saiz-Ruiz, & Garcia-Toro, 1994; Vanger, Summerfield, Rosen, & Watson, 1992). Those reactions also reflect little apparent interest in connecting; they seem to invite others not to connect. To other people, then, the person seems to be withdrawn (Troisi & Moles, 1999) and lacking in social skill (see review by Segrin, 2001).

The content of the person's speech also reflects a focus on the self—unsolicited self-disclosures that convey dysphoric feelings and self-devaluations (e.g., Blumberg & Hokanson, 1983; Breznitz, 1992; Gotlib & Robinson, 1982; Gurtman, 1987; Segrin & Flora, 1998; Wenzlaff & Beevers, 1998). Other people who mean well may offer social support, but, as described in chapter 4, the process may backfire, frustrating the depressed person as well as the partner.

Thus, a depressed person's dilemma is quite complex. A frustrated motive activates a template and poses a major problem that needs to be resolved. As the person turns inward, trying to solve the problem, overt behaviors invite other people to stay away. Some do, and others offer social support. Either way, as described in chapter 4, the process may further frustrate an interpersonal motive, sustaining the depression of the affected person.

Panic Disorder With Agoraphobia

Just as an interpersonal loss can lead to depression, the threat of a loss can lead to anxiety. In this section we examine an example of that phenomenon.

Description

SOME DEFINITIONS   We begin by distinguishing between a cued and an uncued panic attack. A cued panic attack is evoked by a particular situation (e.g., by a small, enclosed space like an elevator). In contrast, an uncued panic attack is one that seems to occur out of the blue; it does not seem to be activated by any circumscribed situation. In panic disorder with agoraphobia, the initial panic attack is uncued. The person does not know what triggered it. Typically, the person is taken by surprise and feels very upset. Many people fear that they are dying, having a heart attack, or losing control of their bodies. Such interpretations add to the person's anxiety.

A panic attack is so dramatic and unpleasant that the person immediately seeks relief. For some, the solution is to go home. Home provides a safe, secure haven associated with comfort, care, and protection. If the world outside seems chaotic, the world at home is familiar, benign, and controllable. Once calm has been restored, the person tries to understand and explain the earlier panic. Typical explanations ascribe the panic to situations like being in a crowd, traveling in an automobile, bus, or airplane, driving on the freeway, over a bridge, or through a tunnel, waiting in line at the supermarket, or being trapped in a hairdresser's chair. Some people then become uncomfortable about leaving home, fearing that they might encounter one of those situations again and have another panic attack. By remaining at home, the person feels better and seems to control the anxiety.

The *DSM–IV–TR* defines *agoraphobia* as "anxiety about, or avoidance of, places or situations from which escape might be difficult (or embarrassing) or in which help may not be available in the event of having a panic attack" (American Psychiatric Association, 2000, p. 429). No matter how the anxiety begins, whether physiologically or psychologically, psychological consequences follow: The person now anticipates another panic attack and avoids it by staying home (Barlow, 2002; Craske & Barlow, 1993). To qualify for a panic disorder with agoraphobia, the person needs to have had two or more uncued panic attacks and then to have developed agoraphobia.

Panic disorder with agoraphobia is the most common phobia of people seeking psychotherapy (Burns & Thorpe, 1977; Chambless, 1982; Marks, 1970). It occurs in approximately 0.6% of the population, three times more often in women than in men (American Psychiatric Association, 2000, p. 436). It usually begins between late adolescence and the mid-30s and rarely occurs for the first time after age 45 (Burns & Thorpe, 1977). The initial panic attack lasts from a few minutes to several hours. The person then becomes vigilant to internal signs of anxiety and avoids the place where the attack originally occurred. Despite the person's effort, however, the anxiety spirals (Foa, Steketee, Grayson, Turner, & Latimer, 1984), and within a year panic attacks become more frequent and agoraphobia develops.

Because the templates for anxiety and depression often have elements in common (e.g., feeling helpless, feeling alone), people who are vulnerable to one are often vulnerable to the other. Major depressive disorder, for example, occurs in approximately half to two-thirds of individuals with agoraphobia. Other anxiety disorders, like social phobia and generalized anxiety disorder, may also co-occur. Separation anxiety disorder in childhood is also associated with the disorder. Agoraphobia is not easy to treat. Among those who are treated, about 30% seem to recover; 6 to 10 years after treatment 40–50%, though improved, remain symptomatic; and the remaining 20–30% do not improve (American Psychiatric Association, 2000, p. 437).

Some individuals with agoraphobia become completely housebound; others show willingness to leave home if accompanied by a spouse, friend, child, or dog (Marks, 1970; Matthews, Gelder, & Johnston, 1981). One agoraphobic woman was willing to go to a restaurant as long as her husband agreed to stay by her side at all times; when he needed to use the restroom, she waited by the door of the restroom until he returned.

If a person confronts a realistic danger (e.g., a fire or an earthquake), that danger can upstage the person's anxiety about leaving home. In one dramatic example (Marks, 1970), a Jewish woman living in Vienna in the 1930s suffered such severe agoraphobia that she spent most of her time at home. When the Nazis came to power, she had to flee or else face a concentration camp. She did leave home, and even traveled to foreign countries for the next 2 years. She was tense, but not incapacitated. Eventually she settled in New York, where she established a new home. Then, when she was safe from persecution, her agoraphobia returned, leaving her housebound once again. Apparently, the woman was able to prioritize her anxieties, like the motorist described in chapter 3, who, in the face of a near-collision on the freeway, was cool and vigilant as he averted the danger. When the crisis had passed, however, anxiety emerged.

FACTORS THAT PRECIPITATE PANIC   Two kinds of events are known to precipitate a panic attack (which may later lead to agoraphobia). One is the loss, or threatened loss, of a significant person; the other is a physical disruption in the endocrine system (e.g., hyperthyroidism). A precipitating event, whether psychological or physiological, can lead to a massive discharge of the sympathetic division of the autonomic nervous system, causing panic.

- Interpersonal Loss. Agoraphobic anxiety is more likely to occur if the person is threatened with an interpersonal loss (A. J. Goldstein & Chambless, 1978; Marks, 1970; Matthews et al., 1981); for example, when a spouse threatens to leave a marriage or a parent has a terminal illness. For example, a fleeting but intensely disturbing thought may activate an existing template for anxiety. We therefore assume (a) that a person who is vulnerable to panic may have been sensitized by earlier experiences and (b) that severe anxiety can be activated by an anticipated loss (e.g., Harper & Roth, 1962; M. Sim & Houghton, 1966).
- Endocrine Disturbance. An endocrine malfunction can also trigger a panic attack (D. F. Klein, 1964; Liebowitz & Klein, 1979; Mendel & Klein, 1969; M. Sim & Houghton, 1966). An endocrine malfunction (e.g., following a hysterectomy, a thyroid malfunction, or childbirth) can also arouse panic. Early studies indicated that 30–50% of patients with agoraphobia had been having medical difficulties when panic first occurred (A. J. Goldstein & Chambless, 1978; D. F. Klein, 1964; Liebowitz & Klein, 1979).

No matter how the panic is activated, anxiety seems to spiral out of control. To use Goleman's (1995) term, an emotional hijacking occurs. Then the person hurries home for comfort. Not knowing how else to explain the panic, the person ascribes it to a variety of situations (e.g., crowded stores or supermarket lines). Individuals with agoraphobia usually fear another panic attack and develop a "fear of fear" (A. J. Goldstein & Chambless, 1978; Michelson, 1987). They also become hypervigilant to internal signs of anxiety. Staying home becomes a way to feel more comfortable (Barlow, 2002).

To summarize, it is important to distinguish between the following: (a) the stimulus situation that activated a template for anxiety—often interpersonal, like an impending death; (b) the person's explanation of the resulting panic attack—usually noninterpersonal, like a crowded store; and (c) the person's reason for staying at home—to avoid further panic. Thus, our interpretation of the disorder may differ from the person's own account.

A Characteristic Agoraphobic Personality?

We assume that people who are vulnerable to agoraphobia possess a template that predisposes them to uncontrollable anxiety when they experience a loss. The term *diathesis* is used to denote this kind of vulnerability or sensitivity, and the *diathesis-stress model* hypothesizes that people who possess the diathesis, when stressed, develop the disorder (Rosenhan & Seligman, 1995). If a very vulnerable person were moderately stressed by an impending loss, the person might develop the disorder; if the person were not stressed, the person would not develop the disorder. The syndrome would not be activated if the template or the precipitating event were weak.

Could we say that people with a template for anxiety share one or more personality traits? Not necessarily. A template for anxiety differs somewhat from person to person, so events that activate the syndrome would also differ somewhat from person to person. Some individuals with agoraphobia might describe themselves as anxious worriers, fearful of dangers in nature (e.g., Bowen & Kohout, 1979; Buglass, Clarke, Henderson, Kreitman, & Presley, 1977); others might describe themselves as socially anxious, afraid of being embarrassed or rejected (Arrindell, 1980; Foa et al., 1984; A. J. Goldstein & Chambless, 1978; Liebowitz & Klein, 1979; Marks & Herst, 1970). Three women, all vulnerable to anxiety, might report quite different concerns—for one, a potential loss of competence; for a second, a loss of face; for a third, the loss of a relationship.

At one time, many psychologists considered people with agoraphobia to be dependent people who had been overprotected as children (e.g., Barlow, 1988, p. 364; Matthews et al., 1981). Wolpe (1958), a behavior therapist, for example, described a woman with agoraphobia this way:

> (As) an only child, . . . she had been incredibly over-protected by her mother, who insisted on standing perpetually in attendance on her. She was permitted to do almost nothing for herself, forbidden to play games lest she get hurt, and even in her final year at high school was daily escorted . . . to and from school by her mother, who carried her school books for her. (p. 4)

Many subsequent studies have examined whether people with agoraphobia have been overprotected as children. These studies have yielded mixed results (Emmelkamp, 1988; Matthews et al., 1981). Whereas some have reported a high incidence of maternal overprotection and dependence (e.g., Solyom, Silberfeld, & Solyom, 1976), others have not (e.g., Parker, 1979). In one study the agoraphobic women described themselves as having been dependent as children; however, when they were evaluated objectively on a list of specific indicators of dependency (e.g., unusual conformity in school), they did not differ from the comparison group (Buglass et al., 1977). Thus, a template for anxiety does not seem to imply a single, uniform personality trait. Some people with the template seem timid, dependent, and afraid of natural disasters; others seem shy and socially anxious; still others seem controlling (as a way of managing their anxiety).

RELATION TO PERSONALITY DISORDERS   How does the avoidant, or dependent, personality disorder relate to these Axis I disorders? People with an avoidant or dependent personality disorder feel inadequate, have low self-esteem, and doubt their competence. Therefore, they have many opportunities to acquire a template for anxiety or depression, predisposing them to various Axis I disorders like major depressive disorder and panic disorder with agoraphobia. Indeed, *DSM–IV–TR* (American Psychiatric Association, 2000) notes that a person with an avoidant personality disorder is more likely than others to experience a depressive or anxiety disorder (p. 719), particularly a panic disorder with agoraphobia (720). On the other hand, many other people with a personality disorder are anxious or depressed, but they do not meet the full criteria for any particular Axis I disorder. Therefore, either may occur without the other.

PRECIPITATING FACTORS   What types of losses would activate a template and induce a panic attack? One type would be the impending death of a parent or spouse. Some people expect to feel so devastated by the loss that the expectation itself arouses panic. Another would be an anticipated loss of face—a rejection, criticism, or anticipated failure. In other cases, panic may occur as the person is about to initiate a separation. For example, imagine a person who desperately wants to become autonomous but whose initial steps in that direction activate a template for anxiety. The following case study illustrates this process. It describes an agoraphobic woman who had been overprotected but still could not be called dependent. It was reported in a book of case studies by M. J. Goldstein and Palmer (1975), and it illustrates how interpersonal factors can contribute to a person's template for anxiety and subsequent agoraphobia.

CASE EXAMPLE[1]   V. was a 27-year-old high-school teacher of mathematics who lived with her widowed mother. She regarded herself as a shy person who preferred to keep to herself. For several months she had been unable to leave home without feeling panicky, and her agoraphobia left her unable to continue teaching. The problem began about a year before when she and her mother had been Christmas shopping. Her mother was a loud-voiced person who would badger clerks and create a scene if she did not get the service she demanded. They were in the middle of a crowded department store when V. suddenly felt an impulse to flee. She panicked and drove home alone as fast as she could. Her mother was extremely angry, and V. was unable to explain what had happened. Over the next several weeks, she had several similar attacks—at a church party, at the grocery store, at a friend's house. Later the panic attacks occurred about

---

[1]From *The Experience of Anxiety: A Casebook, Expanded Edition* by Michael J. Goldstein and James O. Palmer, copyright © 1975 by Michael J. Goldstein and James O. Palmer. Used by permission of Oxford University Press, Inc.

once a week. Panic attacks seemed to occur only when she was in public, never when she was at home.

V.'s father was killed while serving in the military when she was 4 years old. Her mother was unable to cope, so V.'s maternal grandmother came to live with them. Her grandmother did the housework, her mother was preoccupied with her own thoughts, and V. played with her dolls. Her mother and grandmother overprotected her in several ways. For one thing, they always walked her to school and met her after school. She was warned again and again not to cross the street without an adult. She was the only child in school who had a raincoat every time a cloud appeared in the sky. She loved animals but was not allowed to have a pet, lest it bring germs into the house. Playmates were discouraged from visiting, and she had few or no playmates.

Although she was Protestant, she attended a Catholic girls' school until the 8th grade. Then she attended a public high school and was warned about the dangers. Her mother bought her new clothes, but she soon discovered that her mother's taste was different from that of the girls at school. She did not date and had very few girlfriends. In her senior year, however, she did form one close friendship with another girl who was aggressive and used vulgar language; her mother and grandmother disapproved of this friend, but V. secretly defied them by spending time with the girl.

Later, while she was attending the local 2-year college, her grandmother died, and her mother went into a second intense mourning. She discovered that her grandmother had been fairly well-to-do and that she and her mother inherited income property. Her mother claimed to be helpless about business matters, so V. had to straighten out the financial affairs; she prided herself on being a good businesswoman. She then went to the university, where she completed a degree in mathematics and obtained teaching credentials.

She met a man whom her mother encouraged her to marry. Her husband's parents planned the wedding. After the wedding she discovered that her husband had adopted a homosexual lifestyle before their marriage and wished to maintain it. This news left her feeling depressed and ashamed, as though she had been responsible for getting herself into such a situation. They divorced, and she then returned to live with her mother and obtained another teaching position. Before long she found herself feeling dissatisfied at home. For the first time in her life she began to resist some of her mother's demands. She even made plans to take a trip abroad with a friend, but canceled her plans at the last minute, feeling that she could not leave her mother alone. When her agoraphobia developed, her mother regarded it as something she fabricated and told her to "snap out of it."

ANALYSIS   V. may have been vulnerable to anxiety by temperament. Infants who are easily frightened may invite more protective behavior from adults than those who are bold. Furthermore, easily frightened children may more readily believe and heed an adult's warnings about danger. Numerous episodes involving fear would then contribute to a template for anxiety.

Two periods in V.'s life were especially distressing. One occurred in her preschool years during her mother's prolonged depression following the death of her husband. Another probably occurred after her shocking discovery of her

Table 8.1. Traits Used to Describe Veronica F's Mother

Category I	Category II
Domineering	Needy
Controlling	Vulnerable
Intrusive	Depressed
Demanding	Insecure
Overprotective	Helpless
Judgmental	Fearful
Opinionated	Incompetent

failed marriage, which her mother had encouraged. That experience may have reinforced doubts about her own judgment and ability to function as a fully competent adult.

In addition, her relationship with her mother would have provided fuel for a template for anxiety. Her mother was the person with whom she had interacted most often over the years. I once asked graduate students to read the original case history and describe the mother using common personality traits. The traits that were mentioned most often are shown in Table 8.1; they seemed to fall into two contrasting lists. Some described the mother as domineering, demanding, and overprotective (Category I); others described her as helpless, inept, fearful, and depressed (Category II). Thus, in some situations, the mother was strong-willed and apparently self-confident; in other situations, she seemed to be insecure and helpless.

Consider the messages conveyed by the mother's behavior. In some situations, the mother's controlling behavior invited the daughter to yield; and V. was very dutiful, heeding her mother's warnings and following her mother's advice. In other situations, however, the mother's helplessness apparently invited the daughter to take charge (as in financial matters), thereby protecting her mother from anxiety and helplessness. Moving out of her mother's house would thus have posed two kinds of threat: dangers to herself (the mother had been protecting her from a dangerous world) and dangers to her mother (she had been protecting her mother from anxiety and helplessness).

Should we describe V. as "dependent?" Probably not. After all, she was a very competent adult in important ways (e.g., able to oversee her family's property, able to manage the household finances, able to teach high school mathematics). We assume that she wanted greater autonomy after her own failed marriage; we also assume that her impulse to flee from her mother during the shopping center incident reflects that motive. In other words, we assume that she was trapped by a pair of conflicting motives depicted in Table 8.2: (a) to accept the status quo and continue living with her mother; or (b) to leave home and establish her own autonomous existence. Each option suggested a positive and a negative consequence:

1. If she remained at home with her mother, she would be secure in her mother's care (+), but that living arrangement would curtail her autonomy (−).

Table 8.2.   The Nature of Veronica F's Conflicting Motives

Options	Positive Consequence	Negative Consequence
Remain at home with mother	Mother is content; Veronica is protected	Veronica feels childlike
Leave home and be autonomous	Veronica feels adultlike	Mother is anxious; Veronica feels guilty; Veronica is anxious

2. If she left home to be more autonomous: She might achieve greater autonomy (+); but that step would open the floodgates to possible disaster, such as abandoning or betraying her mother; shirking her responsibility; exposing herself to danger; causing her mother to be displeased and anxious; causing herself to feel anxious and guilty. The more she might want to leave home, the more intense her anxiety and guilt.

The two options in Table 8.2 thus depict her conflict of motives. Her impulse to flee while shopping with her mother apparently touched quite a nerve, activated her template, and induced a panic. By returning home immediately (Option 1), she felt safer. Thus began her struggle with agoraphobia.

In this particular case, a communal motive apparently conflicted with an agentic motive: to accept the security of home, or to seek the autonomy of breaking away. Her "nearly enacted" autonomy (fleeing) dramatically exposed the dangers of being alone and the guilt of abandoning her mother, thereby inducing panic. In this particular case, then, the person's own motive to leave home seems to have induced the "anticipated loss" that triggered the panic.

Formulation

Several factors may be identified as contributors to a person's vulnerability to panic (Liotti, 1991). First, some children are temperamentally prone to anxiety. They are especially ready to perceive danger, internalize warnings, and adopt the worries of other people. Second, some children have a history of anxiety-arousing experiences (e.g., early losses, parental indifference, severe rejection) that contribute to their own unique template for anxiety. Third, some children have anxious, overprotective caretakers who keep rescuing them from imagined dangers, thereby undermining the child's competence and self-confidence.

The stimulus situation that first precipitates a panic attack may be physiological (e.g., a thyroid malfunction) or psychological (e.g., anticipating a threatened loss). Typical psychological stressors seem to include (a) a parent's impending death; (b) some other anticipated loss, including a loss of face; and (c) the person's own intense (but conflicted) desire to become autonomous. Whatever the trigger, panic ensues, and the person hurries home for comfort. Then the person ascribes the panic to incidental situations and avoids those situations by staying home.

According to the thesis of this book, a syndrome may arise from a frustrated motive. The frustrated motive leads to negative affect, which can activate an existing template. That motive, however, is not unique to the syndrome. Some people become depressed when a communal motive is frustrated, others when an agentic motive is frustrated. In the following chapter, we extend our discussion to two more syndromes and Axis I disorders.

9

Difficulty Regulating Impulses, Thoughts, and Behavior: Obsessive–Compulsive and Eating Disorders

In chapter 8 we examined two common syndromes, major depression and panic attack. Both of these syndromes reflect a loss of control over one's emotion. Now we examine two syndromes that reflect a loss of control over impulses, thoughts, or behaviors. In both cases, self-control has acquired a special significance for the person's self-image, so the loss of control is disturbing. Paradoxically, the harder the person tries to regulate the impulse, thought, or behavior, the more difficult it becomes to do so. We shall describe a theoretical mechanism that has been proposed to explain the process.

The first disorder is the obsessive–compulsive disorder (different from the obsessive–compulsive personality disorder). In one form of this disorder, the person is unable to regulate unwanted aggressive thoughts and urges. The second disorder is the binge-eating/purging type of anorexia nervosa, in which the over-controlled anorexic person periodically has uncontrollable eating binges. We begin the chapter with the obsessive–compulsive disorder and later examine the eating disorders. The explanation in each case draws on theories that are relevant to our interpersonal approach to psychopathology.

Obsessive–Compulsive Disorder and a Loss of Control

In the following sections we provide some definitions and examples. Then we examine several forms of the obsessive-compulsive disorder, including an obsessive urge to harm other people. This interpersonal form of the disorder is then examined more closely.

Definitions and Examples

The *DSM–IV–TR* (p. 457) defines an obsession as a persistent idea, thought, impulse, or image that the person finds intrusive and inappropriate, causing marked anxiety or distress. It may seem senseless to the person, but it is nonetheless distressing. One common example is the thought that "my hands are covered with dangerous germs." An obsession is said to be *ego-dystonic*, because the person regards it as "not the real me" (irrational, but still impossible to control). The person recognizes that the thought is self-generated (it is not attributed to someone else) and finds its occurrence puzzling. If the person did accept the idea as valid ("my hands really are covered with germs"), we would say that it was *ego-syntonic* and call it a *delusion* rather than an *obsession*.

A person who suffers from an obsession may try simply to ignore or suppress it. The person may also try to "undo" it through some act. A compulsion is a repeated act (e.g., handwashing) that temporarily relieves the distress caused by the obsession. By performing this act, the person feels better. The relief is short-lived, however; the obsession soon returns, and the cycle repeats itself. Obsessions and compulsions sometimes go together. A man might have a disturbing obsession that his hands are contaminated, and he compulsively washes his hands to remove the germs. According to *DSM–IV–TR* (p. 458), a person qualifies for the disorder only if the obsession or compulsion causes marked distress, is time-consuming, or significantly interrupts the person's normal routine or functioning.

Here are some typical obsessions drawn from clinical sources:

> Case 1. Shortly after his son was born, a man found that he had recurrent urges to throw his baby down a flight of stairs. He was troubled to discover such murderous impulses in himself, and after each episode, he felt that he had sinned.
>
> Case 2. A nurse kept thinking that her hands were covered with deadly germs and feared that she might contaminate patients she touched. Although she knew that her obsession was irrational, she washed her hands several times every hour throughout the day, scrubbing them with alcohol until they ached.
>
> Case 3. While delivering his weekly Sunday morning sermon, a minister frequently had an urge to tell a dirty joke. He recognized the inappropriateness of his impulse, but the urge was so intense that he worried that he might let the joke slip out one Sunday morning.
>
> Case 4. While driving along the freeway, a man found himself having a strong urge to crash his car into other cars. He felt very ashamed for having this urge.
>
> Case 5. A middle-aged woman regarded herself as gentle and kind, but whenever she drove her car, she had a strong impulse to run into bicyclists on the road. She felt especially ashamed of these impulses because they flew in the face of strong personal values.
>
> Case 6. A woman drove her children to school every weekday morning, picked them up at the end of the day, drove them to after-school activities, and then drove them home. After each trip, she felt that she might have run over a pedestrian. In order to reduce her tension, she had to make a second trip, retracing her earlier route. At first, her compulsive checking helped reduce her tension, but after a while she discovered another problem: The second trip eased her mind about the first trip, but she now needed a third trip to check for possible victims of her second trip.

The content of common obsessions seems to vary to some extent from era to era. Religious obsessions were once very common, but today the common themes often involve aggression and violence. The six examples given above reveal aggressive impulses, thoughts, or fantasies—harming, contaminating, shocking, crashing, murdering, or colliding with someone. The target may be a member of one's family, a friend, a stranger, or oneself. Typical compulsions include checking (e.g., checking the closet for hidden bombs), praying (to atone for offensive impulses), and washing (to eliminate dirt and germs).

Three Common Types of Obsessions

We select three common types of obsessions to illustrate their range. The first is clearly interpersonal; we call it *an urge to harm someone else* (a child, a spouse, a stranger, a pedestrian, a bicyclist). People with this kind of obsessive urge are usually highly socialized and conscientious, so they are not at all likely to commit the act and feel distressed to detect the aggressive impulse in themselves. Thus, the urge to harm someone else seems to violate the person's own standards, yet the person cannot shake it off. The person's "actual self" is at odds with the person's "ideal self" and "ought self," so the person is apt to feel distressed (cf. Higgins, 1987, 1996).

A second category is *a fear of harming others*. This type of obsession reflects a concern that "I might accidentally or unwittingly harm someone else" or that "I might already have done so". Some examples include worries about inadvertently running over someone, locking one's child in a closet, burning down the family home, or spreading disease. The aggression is not as explicit in this category as it is in the urge to harm someone, but still, it gives rise to shame or guilt. A person with this type of obsession worries about his or her potential to harm someone else. They often feel guilt and shame (e.g., about being criticized or making mistakes); in contrast, people with a simple phobia (e.g., a fear of elevators) worry more often about being harmed in noninterpersonal situations (R. M. Turner, Steketee, & Foa, 1979).

A third category may be called *a fear of harm to oneself*. These obsessions concern distressing thoughts such as "I might be physically harmed by an invisible danger." Examples include thoughts that "I may get tetanus by accidentally stepping on a rusty nail" and "I may get AIDS by eating food in a restaurant." These obsessions resemble simple phobias in that the person fears a threatening object, but that object (bacteria, a virus, dirt, poison, explosives) happens to be invisible. The unseen danger is especially difficult to avoid, so obsessive–compulsive people protect themselves by cleaning, washing, and checking—scrubbing their hands, cleaning their floors, scouring their eating utensils, checking for explosives, rusty nails, and signs of dirt. Even if the danger cannot be eliminated, the cleaning, washing, or checking at least provides a temporary sense of control.

An obsessive urge to harm someone else is one form of the obsessive–compulsive disorder that is unambiguous. It is an intense but troubling desire that involves other people. For a fleeting moment, the person has an impulse to commit a horrendous act—throw the baby down the stairs, shock the congregation with a dirty joke, harm bicyclists by driving into them. As a participant–observer, the person notes the aggressive impulse and feels horrified. The urge to harm someone else thus poses an important theoretical question: What is the origin of this (apparently antisocial) urge in a person who is otherwise so well socialized? To use the language of learning theorists, what reinforces an obsessive urge to harm someone else? Why does the urge take this particular form (e.g., to harm bicyclists)? Does the urge have meaning for the person, or is it meaningless? The psychoanalytic theory was developed, in part, to answer questions like these, so we briefly consider the psychoanalytic explanation.

Psychoanalytic Explanation of the Obsessive Urge to Harm Someone Else

The following sections briefly review the psychoanalytic explanation of an obsessive urge to harm someone else. We examine early and later versions of the psychoanalytic theory and then show how the theory has been applied to an obsessive urge to harm someone else.

Early Theory

The concept of energy played a major role in the early version of Freud's theory. Energy, a popular concept among 19th-century writers, was initially used to explain the flow of behavior throughout life: People take in energy when they eat, drink, and breathe, and expend energy in the course of living. According to the theory, some of this energy is used for processes under the control of the nervous system. The release or discharge of psychic energy was thought to produce pleasure. If psychic energy could not be released (because of inhibitions acquired in childhood), the feeling was one of tension or pressure, as reflected in everyday metaphors ("bottled up emotion," "choked with rage"). After the energy was released in a burst of anger, a surge of love, or a sexual orgasm, however, the person was thought to experience relief and pleasure. If the accumulated energy was not released directly, the person had to find indirect ways to do so. Dreams and psychiatric symptoms constitute two of these ways. According to the theory, an obsessive urge to harm someone might be an indirect way of discharging accumulated energy. For this reason, the obsessive urge might seem to provide momentary relief, pleasure, or satisfaction.

Later Theory

The energy concept, however, was controversial among later psychoanalytic theorists: Should we regard it literally as a transformation of physical energy, or was it meant to be a metaphor? As the theory matured, Freud drew less upon the energy concept and more upon the biological concept of instinct. According to that view, a person possesses numerous instincts (Freud never specified how many), like the hunger instinct. The body produces somatic "stimulations" (e.g., activations in the hypothalamus), which produce psychological experiences—including a desire for food, thoughts about food, and impulses to search for food. These psychological effects then drive behavior. According to the later theory, then, instincts bridge the world of body to the world of mind (Cameron & Rychlak, 1985). For every instinct, the person is apparently motivated to find a suitable object: for hunger, the object is a particular kind of food; for sex, a particular type of person. When the "aim" of the instinct is finally satisfied, bodily stimulations subside, producing a feeling of relief or pleasure.

According to this version of the theory, an obsessive urge to harm someone might be explained in terms of an aggressive instinct. When the person is provoked, bodily stimulations (caused, perhaps, by elevated levels of particular hormones) have psychological consequences—aggressive impulses, thoughts, feelings—which then prompt aggressive behavior. In the course of becoming socialized, however, people also learn to suppress aggression. Therefore, when we are sufficiently provoked, we experience a motivational conflict. Should we express aggressive behavior (satisfying biological pressures), or should we suppress aggressive impulses (satisfying social pressures)? The person needs to find a compromise between conflicting demands. Motivational conflict thus plays a fundamental role in the psychoanalytic explanation of this type of psychopathology. Because an obsessive urge to harm someone (a momentary mental state) stops short of overt behavior, it may be viewed as a compromise between conflicting motives: It acknowledges the aggressive tendency, without actually expressing the forbidden behavior.

Developmental Aspects of the Psychoanalytic Theory

The psychoanalytic theory also contained propositions about successive phases of a child's development. Writers like E. Erikson (1963) highlighted interpersonal themes that are associated with each phase of development. The first two phases, in particular, reflect two themes that were thought to be important developmentally.

The first phase (the oral dependent phase) extends from birth to 12–18 months. At that time infants are helplessly dependent on adults for food and care. A hungry newborn reflexively turns its mouth toward whatever stimulates its face. Once its lips grasp an object, it begins to suck; if the object yields milk, the newborn continues to suck until it is satisfied. From this beginning, the infant becomes increasingly skillful at interacting with the mother. According to Erikson (1963), this phase lays a foundation for trust or mistrust, depending on contingencies that the infant perceives. To say that a child trusts the parent is to say that the child expects to be fed and cared for. A child who begins life mistrusting the caregiver enters the next phase with a handicap.

By age 1 or 1 1/2, children are able to stand and walk, an achievement that helps them explore the world. As children become competently mobile, they can be more exploratory and self-assertive. Around this time, toilet training begins and the child enters the second phase, the anal phase. For the first time in life, the child is expected to regulate his or her body, to take note of internal sensations and exercise corresponding sphincter (and later bladder) control. Adults value this achievement and make their wishes and expectations clear to the child. It represents the beginning of self-control and self-regulation.

Learning sphincter and bladder control is not easy. If the parents become impatient, angry, or anxious, toilet training can become emotionally charged. It is not unusual for adults to express disapproval, and some adults unwittingly frighten the child with fictions (e.g., that scary monsters are lurking in the toilet, waiting to harm a dawdling child). Anxiety disrupts the delicate motor control that is required in toilet training, and opportunities abound for a template to form that involves anxiety and a lack of control over the body.

Another type of self-control is highlighted as well during this phase of life, namely, the control of emotions. A socialized child must learn to control negative emotions. The terrible twos are famous for temper tantrums (anger, rage, aggression, physical destructiveness), which the child must learn to suppress. In this domain as well, parents praise a child who shows self-control, and they scold, shame, or criticize a child who does not. When the discipline is particularly harsh and the struggle and tension are severe, fertile ground exists for an anxiety-based template.

Erikson (1963) called the interpersonal theme of the anal phase "autonomy versus shame and doubt" (p. 251). Does the child emerge from this phase with confidence about self-regulation, or does the child emerge harboring self-doubt? According to Erikson, shame leaves a person feeling self-conscious and "completely exposed and conscious of being looked at . . . with one's pants down, [having] an impulse to bury one's face" (p. 252). Doubt is the sibling of shame. It reflects an awareness that some quality of the self may be substandard. Criticism, shame, and defeat undermine a child's efforts to achieve a sense of autonomy, so the child has to be on guard, curbing impulses and avoiding transgressions. According to the psychoanalytic view, the attitudes, expectancies, feelings, and restraint acquired during childhood may help lay the foundation for an obsessive–compulsive disorder.

Conflicting Motives and Defensive Processes

No matter how self-restrained a person becomes, situations arise that push the limits. An unusually conscientious nurse cares for a nasty, unappreciative patient who mindlessly berates her. A real estate agent toils for years on behalf of a client who then buys the house from someone else. An architect devotes painstaking months designing an elegant building for a client who then demands ludicrous alterations. Even the most restrained person would understandably feel angry or wish to retaliate. The person's occasional lapses from restraint expose the conflict: to express aggression or suppress it? Conflict can arise over any form of self-control—sexual impulses, feelings of intimacy, feelings of anger, self-disclosures, and so on. Table 9.1 schematically depicts a hypothetical conflict over aggression. It shows the competing behaviors and hypothetical consequences of each.

To reduce the feeling of conflict, we often find a compromise solution. For example, we find ways to explain another person's offensive behavior and thereby reduce our anger: "No wonder she seems so crabby and unreasonable—she is terrified of dying." Psychoanalytic writers identified defense mechanisms that people commonly use to help reduce the feeling of conflict. Two mechanisms in particular are often associated with the obsessive–compulsive disorder: *reaction formation* and *undoing*. *Reaction formation* is a strategy for handling ambivalent feelings: The person accentuates positive reactions in order to camou-

Table 9.1. Nature of the Conflict Over Aggression

Options	Positive Consequence	Negative Consequence
Behave aggressively (e.g., criticize, blame, fight, object, rebel, oppose)	Relieves tension	Feels immoral, causes shame, guilt, anxiety
Suppress aggression	Feels civilized, noble, respectable	Feels weak, like a wimp, exploited

flage negative reactions. When the positive feelings are fortified, they obscure the negative feelings, and the person seems entirely loving, solicitous, and kind.

Undoing is a strategy by which a person first expresses a forbidden feeling, thought, or impulse and then symbolically negates it with a neutralizing act. The person might have a thought ("I could kill her") and then negate it with another thought ("I don't mean that, of course; what I really mean is, I will try to help her"). When this strategy works, the person first expresses aggression (satisfying the aggressive desire) and then neutralizes the aggression (satisfying the desire for self-control). When a person is under great stress, however, these strategies may stop working. The unacceptable thought or fantasy ("I could kill her") returns again and again, too often or too intensely to be denied, neutralized, or undone. Then the person would lose self-control, and we speak of an obsessive urge to harm someone. It seems paradoxical that a highly socialized, self-restrained person would ever lose control over aggressive impulses, thoughts, or fantasies. Why does this happen, and how does stress undermine self-restraint? These questions are examined in Wegner's (1994) theory of ironic processes.

Ironic Processes, Overload, and the Obsessive–Compulsive Urge

Wegner's (1994) theory concerns paradoxes in everyday life:

1. A tired insomniac, trying hard to fall asleep, finds himself all the more awake.
2. A person on a diet, trying hard not to think of food, becomes obsessed with a desire for apple pie.
3. A depressed person, trying hard to ignore a broken romance, cannot stop thinking about details of the breakup.

To explain these phenomena, Wegner postulated two separate components of self-regulation; he called one an *operating process*, the other a *monitoring process*. The operating process includes every action the person takes to produce the desired effect. A man trying to suppress sad feelings might (a) whistle a happy tune, (b) think positive, happy thoughts, (c) engage in pleasant, distracting activities, and (d) generate positive (cheering) explanations for his frustration. According to Wegner, these procedures are intentional and require de-

Table 9.2. Experimental Design of the Study

Condition	Period 1	Period 2	Period 3
Suppress first	Practice	Suppress	Express
Express first	Practice	Express	Suppress

Note. From "Paradoxical Effects of Thought Suppression," by D. M. Wegner, D. J. Schneider, S. C. Carter, and L. White, 1987, *Journal of Personality and Social Psychology, 53*, p. 7. Copyright © 1987 by the American Psychological Association. Adapted with permission of the author.

liberate, concentrated effort; they may be very complex. The other process, the monitoring process, involves nothing but a search for failures to produce the desired effect; it is relatively simple and can be carried out automatically and with little effort. When a failure is detected (e.g., a dieter mindlessly eats caloric food), the person has to begin the operating process again, perhaps trying harder or using a different strategy.

If an operating process works, the goal is attained. However, the operating process may be laborious. For example, a conscientious nurse might wish to control her anger, but the day's events are extremely taxing: a difficult patient piles one complaint upon another, a supervisor criticizes her work unfairly, a co-worker's absence increases her workload, a medical procedure is very demanding. Situations like these all compete for her attention—problems that draw resources from her operating process. As she approaches the limit of her processing capacity, she inadvertently utters a curse. Then her monitoring process immediately detects the slip and she feels guilty and remorseful. These internal states then interfere further with the operating process.

Attentional distractors thus interfere with the limited resources available to the operating process. In other words, distractors reduce the person's capacity to suppress unwanted thoughts, affect, or behavior. That is why dieting is so much more difficult for a person under stress. With every failure, emotional reactions add even more distractors, further impeding the operating process.

Because the monitoring process involves a search for failures, the person has to keep the undesired outcome in mind. According to Wegner's theory, when we keep that unwanted thought in mind, we make it all the more available and increase its probability of occurring. Thus, monitoring ironically increases the probability of occurrence of the very impulse, thought, or behavior that we are trying to suppress.

Wegner, Schneider, Carter, and White (1987) examined thought suppression experimentally. Participants were asked to describe their "stream of consciousness" for three successive 5-minute periods. They were instructed to describe whatever thoughts, sensations, images, memories, etc., came to mind. To begin the first 5-minute period (Period 1), the experimenter left the room, and the participants reported their stream of consciousness onto a tape recorder.

Each person was then assigned to one of two conditions: suppress-first and express-first. To begin the second 5-minute period (Period 2), the participants in the suppress-first condition were told: "In the next five minutes, please verbalize your thoughts as you did before, with one exception. This time, try NOT to think of a white bear. Every time you say 'white bear' or have 'white bear' come to mind, though, please ring the bell on the table before you." In order not

Table 9.3. Mean Number of Times Participants Reported Thinking of a White Bear During the 5-Minute Period

Condition	Suppress	Express
Suppress first	6.3	22.1
Express first	7.3	16.4

Note. From "Paradoxical Effects of Thought Suppression," by D. M. Wegner, D. J. Schneider, S. C. Carter, and L. White, 1987, *Journal of Personality and Social Psychology, 53*, p. 7. Copyright © 1987 by the American Psychological Association. Adapted with permission of the author.

to think of a white bear, the participants had to monitor that thought, thereby increasing its availability. Participants in the express-first condition received the same instructions, but the word *not* was omitted; that is, they were told to keep thinking of a white bear. Then in Period 3 (the last 5-minute period), the participants in each group received the instructions that the other group had just received. The full experimental design is shown in Table 9.2.

Table 9.3 shows the mean number of times that the participants in each condition rang the bell during Period 2 and Period 3. Table 9.3 contains two interesting results. First, the participants were relatively unsuccessful at suppressing the thought of a white bear during the suppress phase. Participants in each group thought of a white bear more than once a minute on average while they were trying to suppress it. Second, the two groups differed during the express phase (when they were free to think about a white bear). As shown in the second column of Table 9.3, the suppress-first group seemed to show a rebound effect; after suppressing the thought in Period 2, they reported more white bear thoughts in Period 3 than the other group had done during their express period. Apparently, by monitoring their thoughts while suppressing, they increased the occurrence of those thoughts.

Formulation of the Obsessive–Compulsive Disorder

This section summarizes our formulation of the obsessive-compulsive disorder. We begin with the obsessive urge to harm someone else. Then we consider why the formulation may not apply to other forms of the obsessive-compulsive disorder. Finally, we examine differences between the obsessive-compulsive disorder and the obsessive-compulsive personality disorder.

Obsessive Urge to Perform a Forbidden Act

An obsessive urge to perform a forbidden act may be organized around a motivational conflict about expressing (vs. suppressing) the forbidden behavior. Some candidates for this type of conflict would include aggressive behavior, sexual behavior, emotional expression, and eating. We assume that, during the person's formative years, the behavior was tagged as forbidden and became emotionally charged. As part of the socialization process, the person learned to suppress the behavior, exercising rigid self-control. In later years, however, the behavior may have been provoked, and stressors, negative affect, and other distractors have siphoned off resources needed for self-control. As a result, the operating process has faltered and slips have occurred.

Why would an obsessive urge take the specific form that it takes (e.g., an impulse to harm one's child, an impulse to harm bicyclists on the road)? Sometimes the content is easy to understand. If a man's 3-year-old child disturbed his marriage or caused intense frustration, an (unwanted) impulse to harm the child might be understandable. What about an urge to run over innocent bicyclists? To explain that, we would have to understand the broad meaning of *bicyclist* to the afflicted person. Consider a woman treated by the author. She had envied her two younger brothers throughout their childhood years. Whereas she herself was asthmatic and sickly, her brothers were very robust—praised for their good health, high energy, strong physiques, and athletic prowess. They were bicycle enthusiasts, and she vividly recalled her envy the day they set off together for a 100-mile bicycle marathon, surrounded by admiring well-wishers. Many years later, a stressful family dispute erupted, re-awakening her feelings of envy and precipitating her obsessive urge to run over bicyclists.

Other Types of Obsessive–Compulsive Disorders

An obsessive urge to perform a forbidden act is relatively easy to interpret because it directly exposes conflicting motives. However, obsessive fears are more ambiguous. How should we conceptualize an obsessive fear "that I may harm someone else"? Should we view it simply as a fear, like a fear of earthquakes or accidents ("I fear that my child might fall from the tree")? Or should we view it as a fear of one's own impulses, intentions, or wishes ("I fear that I could and might harm my own child")? In other words, a fear of harming someone could reflect a fear that arises (a) from a helpless lack of control or (b) from a forbidden desire. To choose between these interpretations, we would need more case-specific details: Is the person suffering primarily from a helpless sense of incompetence, or from a motivational conflict over a forbidden impulse?

An obsessive fear of being harmed may also be ambiguous. For example, Foa (1979) described an obsessive–compulsive man who feared contamination from "male germs" (germs acquired through contact with other men). Should we interpret this fear literally as a phobia, an irrational fear of catching germs from men, or should we interpret it as the man's fear of physical contact with men? If the latter, why would the man fear physical contact with men? Is he afraid, literally, of being harmed, or is he afraid of his own impulse to get close to another man? The two alternative interpretations highlight the inherent ambiguity in the original complaint: Is it a simple fear or a motivational conflict?

Relationship to the Obsessive–Compulsive Personality Disorder

An obsessive–compulsive urge to perform a forbidden act seems to have three prerequisites: (a) a history in which the person learned to suppress a specific class of behavior; (b) a habitual suppression of that behavior over the years; and (c) a current situation that provokes the forbidden behavior, exacerbates the conflict, and precipitates the syndrome. In other words, an obsessive urge to perform a forbidden act seems to result from conflicting motives that the now-overloaded system cannot control.

This formulation differs from our formulation (in chapter 7) of the obsessive–compulsive personality disorder. That formulation emphasized broad agentic themes: striving broadly for mental and interpersonal control, defining oneself as competent, careful, and beyond reproach. Thus, in formulating the personality disorder, we assumed that the person felt scrutinized or evaluated. Over time, the person has learned to concentrate, attend to detail, and aim for perfection; those capacities now help enhance the self-image.

In contrast, an obsessive urge to express a forbidden behavior seems more circumscribed and focused. The two disorders are compatible, but neither is a prerequisite for the other. A person does not have to be a perfectionist, detail-oriented, and hard-working to lose control of a formerly suppressed impulse. However, people who strongly value self-control may be a little more vulnerable to both disorders, so the two disorders may be weakly correlated. As described in *DSM–IV–TR*, the obsessive–compulsive disorder "*may* be associated with . . . the obsessive–compulsive personality disorder" (American Psychiatric Association, 2000, p. 458). In other words, each frequently occurs without the other. For this reason, we consider the two disorders to be distinct. Furthermore, some forms of the obsessive–compulsive disorder (e.g., obsessive fears of hidden dangers) seem to reflect a straightforward fear, not a normally suppressed behavior that reflects unfavorably on the person's self-image. There is no obvious reason for those forms of the obsessive–compulsive disorder to be associated with the obsessive–compulsive personality disorder.

Overload and Eating Binges

The section on eating disorders in *DSM–IV–TR* contains two primary diagnostic categories, anorexia nervosa and bulimia nervosa (see also Brownell & Fairburn, 1995; Fairburn, 1997; Garfinkel, Kenney, & Kaplan, 1995). Anorexic individuals are characterized by their refusal to eat enough food to maintain a minimally normal body weight. Despite strict control over themselves, however, many anorexic individuals have periodic lapses, or episodes of binge-eating in which they report losing control of their own eating behavior; they form the binge-eating/purging type of anorexia nervosa. After binge-eating, they typically "undo" their loss of control by self-induced vomiting or by using laxatives, diuretics, or enemas (Fairburn & Wilson, 1993; Garner, Garner, & Rosen, 1993).

Bulimic individuals are characterized by eating binges, but their weight is usually within the normal range. They are concerned about their weight and are typically on a diet; but periodically they have secret eating binges in which they ingest a huge quantity of (usually high-calorie) food. A binge is often triggered by a depressed mood or by an interpersonal stressor. The person feels ashamed of these binges and finds a way to undo the binge. The "purging type" of person with bulimia induces vomiting or uses laxatives, diuretics, or enemas; the "nonpurging type" uses exercise, fasting or some other compensatory measure.

Thus, individuals with bulimia, like those with the binge-eating/purging type of anorexia, strive to control their eating behavior. Under stress, however, they lose control (e.g., Grissett & Norvell, 1992). In that way, they resemble those obsessive–compulsive people who, under stress, lose control of aggressive thoughts or impulses. Both disorders highlight a dramatic loss of self-control. Furthermore, the explanatory mechanism seems similar: When the person is stressed, the operating process becomes overloaded. When it collapses, the person surrenders to a frenzy of eating. Finally, as in the obsessive–compulsive disorder, interpersonal factors seem to play an important role in the etiology and maintenance of the disorder.

People with anorexia who binge-eat are particularly striking because they display such iron-clad will power, yet they lose control from time to time. Anorexia is especially important because it can be life-threatening. We therefore examine the binge-eating/purging type of anorexia nervosa more closely. The principles apply to bulimia as well.

Anorexia Nervosa

Anorexia nervosa is particularly common among young women in late adolescence and early adulthood. According to *DSM–IV–TR*, anorexia is often triggered by a stressful life event. The disorder is defined by four criteria. First, the person refuses to maintain a body weight that is minimally normal for that person's age and height. The word *refuses* indicates that the disorder is not due to a loss of appetite. Second, the person is intensely afraid of gaining weight or becoming fat (even though the person, objectively speaking, is underweight). Third, the person has a distorted perception of the shape or weight of his or her body and keeps using a scale or mirror to check for fat. One gaunt anorexic woman, for example, said that, whenever she stood before a mirror, she immediately noticed a bulge in her abdomen that was slight, but in her opinion, disfiguring. Fourth, for females with anorexia, as the proportion of body fat decreases, a pituitary malfunction causes abnormally low levels of estrogen secretion, and the woman stops menstruating (amenorrhea). Self-starvation produces significant biochemical changes, such as mild anemia and hypercholesterolemia. The person may then report medical difficulties, such as constipation, abdominal pain, and lethargy. In time, she may need to be hospitalized in order to treat fluid and electrolyte imbalances and restore a normal weight. Among hospitalized individuals, more than 10% die as a result of starvation, suicide, or electrolyte imbalance (Hsu, 1995).

The *DSM–IV–TR* (p. 585) differentiates between a restricting type and a binge-eating/purging type of anorexia nervosa. During binge-eating, the person usually ingests an enormous amount of high-calorie food in a short period of time and then tries to "undo" the indulgence by purging (self-induced vomiting, laxatives, diuretics, or enemas).

Background Characteristics

Typically, a person with anorexia nervosa is a woman who grew up in a comfortable home, where she was a model child—a very good girl, obedient, cooperative, industrious, and bright, not at all rebellious, difficult, or oppositional.

Her parents remember her as "their perfect child," the one they never had to worry about. Bruch (1973, pp. 262–263; 1982) described a poignant case of a woman with anorexia who, at age 6, found the Christmas present that her parents had bought for her. Though very disappointed by the gift, she began dropping hints that that was the very gift she was hoping for. Her parents did not regard her goodness to be a problem, but, as an adult, she remembered feeling that she had no right to assert her own wishes.

In typical cases, a girl who becomes anorexic will decide that she is simply too fat and goes on a mild diet between the ages of 12 and 18. The diet is usually triggered by some stressor: Perhaps someone teases her or disparages her figure; perhaps she feels humiliated to see an unflattering photograph of herself; perhaps she feels embarrassed about her weight as she is about to leave for summer camp or college. Her dieting pays off, and people tell her how nice and thin she looks. She interprets the praise as a sign of respect and continues to diet. Gradually her dieting escalates, but instead of becoming more popular, she becomes socially withdrawn. No matter how gaunt she becomes, she feels that she must not eat. Eventually, she discovers additional ways to lose weight (self-induced vomiting, laxatives, diuretics, and enemas). According to *DSM–IV–TR*, the anorexic person's self-esteem becomes tied to her body shape and weight. Weight loss seems like an impressive achievement, a sign of extraordinary self-discipline; but weight gain seems like an unacceptable failure of self-control (APA, 2000). Because anorexic individuals are vulnerable to failure of this type, they are frequently depressed—socially withdrawn, irritable, low in self-esteem (e.g., see Ruderman & Besbeas, 1992).

Crisp, Hsu, Harding, and Hartshorn (1980) studied the course of the disorder in 105 hospitalized women with anorexia. On average, the women reached their maximum weight at age 15.6. At that time, their mean weight was 120.7 pounds (10 pounds heavier than a comparable normative sample). Mild dieting began at age 16.6, and the dieting got severe at age 17.3. They stopped menstruating at age 17.7 on average and reached their lowest weight at age 19.0, when their mean weight was 82.3 pounds (a 32% loss of their initial weight). They were hospitalized at age 20.8, on average. About half of them had eating binges and purged. They were all treated for anorexia nervosa, and by age 25–29, they had generally returned to a normal weight. Other investigators have reported similar outcomes (e.g., Eisler et al., 1997). However, the probability of relapse is high (Kordy et al., 2002), and problems with obsessions, compulsions, and social interaction often persist (Gillberg, Rastam, & Gillberg, 1995; Kasvikis, Tsakiris, Marks, Basoglu, & Noshirvani, 1986; Nilsson, Gillberg, Gillberg, & Rastam, 1999; also see Graber, Brooks-Gunn, Paikoff, & Warren, 1994; Heatherton, Mahamedi, Striepe, Field, & Keel, 1997; Herzog, Schellberg, & Deter, 1997).

Typical Formulation: Agentic Goals and Anorexia Nervosa

What would motivate a person to stop eating? As we noted in chapter 2, anorexia often highlights agentic motives that overpower the hunger drive (e.g., motives to earn the respect and admiration of others by attaining society's highest standard of beauty, motives to define the self as an effective person with self-control and self-determination). Before developing anorexia the individual always tried hard to please, and now, as her diet succeeds, she is exhilarated by feelings of power (including sexual power) and beauty.

Imagine a child who, for biological reasons, is slightly overweight and routinely receives demeaning bits of advice: "Will power, Mary Ann, will power!" "You would be so pretty, Mary Ann, if you just lost 10 pounds!" "No more you-know-what, Mary Ann (and you know why!)." Messages like these happen to match daily messages from television programs, magazine articles, and advertisements condemning overweight women. These messages proclaim that, for women especially, thin bodies are valued, admired, and rewarded.

Indeed, in American culture, the ideal female figure has become progressively thinner over the years (P. N. J. Myers & Biocca, 1992). Downs and Harrison (1985) studied over 4,000 television commercials and found a message about attractiveness in over 1,000 of them. According to the authors' estimate, the average person is exposed to 14 such messages every day (i.e., over 5,000 messages a year) denigrating excess weight in women (Lautman, 1991; P. N. J. Myers & Biocca, 1992; Silverstein, Perdue, Peterson, & Kelly, 1986).

No wonder a compliant girl, eager to please, internalizes those messages (Stice, 1994; Stice, Shupak-Neuberg, Shaw, & Stein, 1994; Striegel-Moore, 1995). Through introjection, a child who has been criticized comes to adopt both roles toward herself (criticizer and the target of criticism). The girl thus scolds herself for being fat and reacts with shame, guilt, and depression. As a result, her family, her culture, and now her very self all urge her to lose weight. She yields to these pressures and begins to diet; and as she achieves success, she is pleased with her own self-initiated control. Motivated by her own efficacy and feeling of power, she steps up the process, simplifying the rules of her diet: Perhaps initially she eliminated only sweets from her diet; in time, perhaps she restricted herself to grains, fruits, and vegetables; later, perhaps to vegetables only; still later, perhaps to lettuce. The simpler the rule, the easier the decision not to eat, the faster the weight loss, and the greater her pride. I once treated an anorexic woman who enjoyed working as a checker in a supermarket because it felt so good to contrast her own strict self-control with most customers' lax self-indulgence. Self-discipline and the achievement of thinness leave the person feeling important, like "a somebody" (Becker, 1973). Many individuals with anorexia take on other forms of self-control as well, such as jogging, swimming, karate, weight-lifting, and gymnastics.

However, the individual's victory over the self is a shaky one. After all, self-starvation takes resolve and vigilance. Therefore, stress (and related distractors) can overload the system, and a major stressor can bring on a mindless self-indulgence. One woman I treated had predictable eating binges whenever she quarreled with her boyfriend. Her self-indulgence then brought on self-blame, discouraging thoughts ("I blew it!"), a drop in resolve, and a surrender to binge-eating.

According to Wegner's theory, stress and negative affect overload a person's operating process, causing a collapse of self-control. Such failures are a constant reminder that thinness is a fragile and hard-won achievement. Apparently, individuals with anorexia generally lack confidence in their capacity to control their eating, but those who binge have concrete evidence that they easily lose control. Perhaps that is why people with anorexia who binge are harder to treat (Steinhausen, 1995).

Other Motives: Communal Goals and Anorexia Nervosa

The behaviors associated with anorexia can also help satisfy communal motives. As one example, Minuchin (1974; Minuchin, Rosman, & Baker, 1978), a family therapist, noted that a child's symptoms can preserve family harmony. In some families, for instance, aggression is tacitly forbidden; confrontation, fighting, and open disagreement are not permitted; and family members silently agree to conceal and deny evidence of conflict. Nonetheless, the parents may harbor quiet dissatisfactions with each other. Perhaps the father isolates himself in work, whereas the mother stoically manages the home alone. When their marital dissatisfactions do surface periodically, the child's anorexia can draw attention away from the conflict and direct it instead to a common cause, namely, the child's extreme thinness. Thus, the child's anorexia may help preserve harmony in the family.

The dependency motive is sometimes implicated in anorexia nervosa. In some families, the individual before she develops anorexia had been the special little girl. After she matures sexually, however, her status changes. She is expected to leave home, go to college, choose a career, and plan for adulthood. Some girls find this change in expectations disturbing and threatening. However, self-starvation reverses all that. As she loses weight, her adult feminine curves disappear, she stops menstruating, and people want to take care of her. After all, who could abandon a gaunt, apparently sick child in need of nourishment and sustenance? Thus, her anorexic condition may help restore her earlier status and satisfy her goal to be cared for.

Treatment

The most pressing goal of treatment is to help the anorexic individual gain weight (Rock & Curran-Celentano, 1996). The person may have to be hospitalized to be fed intravenously, treated for medical complications, or removed from a pathogenic social situation (Garner & Needleman, 1996). Medication per se does not seem to help, but strict behavior therapy is sometimes useful in getting the person to eat. For example, rewards, like the opportunity to have visitors, are sometimes made contingent on eating.

Treatment also must examine interpersonal issues, especially the agentic and communal meaning of self-starvation and thinness to the person. The person's motivational conflicts should be explored and clarified. The injurious consequences of self-starvation also must be made explicit. Russell, Szmukler, Dare, and Eisler (1987) have suggested that family therapy is more effective than individual therapy, at least for adolescents (see Humphrey, 1987); but, in general, no one type of treatment is highly effective. Only 50–60% of the patients treated for anorexia nervosa achieve a normal weight after treatment (Hsu, 1990; Steinhausen, 1995), and, even among those, eating continues to be a major preoccupation. For a further discussion of treatment, see Johnson, Tsoh, and Varnado (1996) and Wilson and Fairbern (1998).

Experimental Studies of the Conflict Over Eating

We have ascribed a lapse in self-control to an overtaxed operating process: A major rejection, for example, might trigger an eating binge. This mechanism can also be demonstrated experimentally in a nonclinical sample. Herman and Polivy (1975) developed an inventory that contains questions like "How often are you dieting?" "Do you give too much time and thought to food?" "Do you feel guilty after overeating?" On the basis of their responses, participants were classified as "restrained" or "unrestrained." Restrained people are apparently in conflict over eating; they report that they often think about food, frequently are on a diet, and typically feel guilty after overeating. In general, restrained people seem to eat less than unrestrained people, except when they are under stress. When they are depressed, for example, they eat more. In contrast, unrestrained people, when depressed, eat less (Polivy & Herman, 1976). Apparently, depression is one product of stress that overloads the operating process and undermines a restrained person's hard-won self-control.

Polivy and Herman (1976) tested this hypothesis experimentally by subjecting female college students to a high or low level of anxiety. Restrained and unrestrained participants were presented with three containers of ice cream, which they were to rate for the quality of flavor (chocolate, vanilla, and strawberry). They were told to take their time and sample each flavor five times. Then they were told that the purpose of the study was to learn how different sensory experiences influence one another, so they would now receive tactile stimulation to determine its effect on their taste preference. Women in the low-anxiety condition were told that they would periodically experience a mild tickle or tingle; those in the high-anxiety condition were told that they would receive a painful electric shock. As they waited for the next phase of the study, they were invited to have as much ice cream as they wanted. They waited 10 minutes; the anticipated tactile stimulation did not actually occur. During their wait, they were left alone so they might continue sampling the ice cream unobserved. Under low anxiety, the restrained and unrestrained participants did not differ in the amount of ice cream that they ate. Under high anxiety, however, the restrained group ate significantly more ice cream than the unrestrained group. High anxiety thus overloaded and interrupted their usual self-control.

The study was later extended by Heatherton, Herman, and Polivy (1991) to include an interpersonal stressor. Participants were randomly assigned to one of three experimental conditions or to a control condition. In one experimental condition (shock), the participants expected to receive a painful electric shock; in another (failure), they tried to solve an unsolvable problem; in a third condition (speech), they were told that they would have to give a 2-minute extemporaneous speech to a critical panel of judges. The mean amount of ice cream that the participants consumed is shown in Figure 9.1. First notice the results for participants in the control group. As expected, restrained people (who normally diet) ate less ice cream than the unrestrained people. In the three experimental conditions, however, the restrained participants (now under stress) ate more ice cream than the unrestrained participants. Interestingly, the condition that produced the greatest difference between the two groups was the one in which they anticipated having to speak before a panel of critical judges. This condition

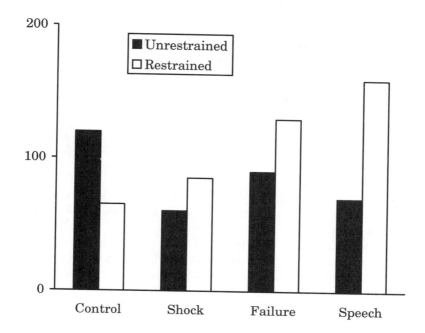

Figure 9.1. Amount of ice cream eaten by participants in each condition. From "Effects of Physical Threat and Ego Threat on Eating Behavior," by T. F. Heatherton, C. P. Herman, and J. Polivy, 1991, *Journal of Personality and Social Psychology, 60*, p. 140. Copyright © 1991 by the American Psychological Association. Adapted with permission of the author.

was the most directly interpersonal (criticism from a panel of peers), and it was the condition that interfered most with the participants' usual self-control.

Demanding cognitive tasks can also interfere with a restrained person's self-regulation. A. Ward and Mann (2000) demonstrated that, for restrained eaters, a heavy cognitive load interrupts the person's restraint against eating. In one study, participants were told that the investigator was examining the effect of mood on performance. To induce a pleasant mood, the investigator would ask them to consume some pleasant-tasting food (chocolate chip cookies, nacho chips, and M&M's). In the high-load condition, participants had to memorize a series of art slides and also perform a reaction time task (responding with a foot pedal to a beep emitted randomly by a computer). In the low-load condition, participants simply had to perform the reaction time task. Food was available throughout the task. Restrained eaters consumed more food when they were under a high cognitive load, whereas unrestrained eaters showed the opposite pattern.

Summary

This chapter has examined two syndromes that are associated with the obsessive–compulsive and eating disorders. Each of the particular syndromes that we examined reflects a motivational conflict. In each case, a motive has been suppressed in favor of an opposing motive to exercise and display self-control. However, under stress, the operating process seems to get overloaded, and the person loses control. As a result, the person displays unwanted behavior and experiences considerable distress.

Our theoretical analysis helps clarify why punishment generally backfires when used to treat disorders like these. For example, consider an early behavioral technique for treating the obsessive–compulsive disorder, a method called *thought-stopping* that made use of punishment. When thought-stopping was used, the person was to indicate whenever an unwanted thought had occurred. The therapist would then administer an electric shock, snap a rubber band, bang a fist on the table, or shout, "Stop!" Though crude, the procedure was said to be breath-taking in its directness and simplicity (Reed, 1985). However, the procedure proved to be ineffective, and we can now say why: Punishment attaches anxiety, disapproval, criticism, and other distracting emotional baggage to an already overloaded attempt to suppress forbidden behavior. It therefore undermines the very task that the treatment should be accomplishing. In contrast, effective treatments usually try to alleviate negative emotion like guilt and anxiety. They therefore come across as theoretically sounder (and more humane).

We have examined the interpersonal approach to a representative sample of personality disorders (part II) and, separately, to a representative sample of syndromes (part III). In part IV we consider personality disorders and syndromes that reflect an identity disturbance. An identity disturbance has interpersonal consequences, and it can play a critical role in the development of certain syndromes or personality disorders. If a particular syndrome and a particular personality disorder each requires the same type of identity disturbance, those two disorders would have an element in common, so they might have a greater-than-chance probability of co-occurring. The two disorders do not have to co-occur; in fact, they usually do not co-occur because each disorder has its own unique requirements as well. Without the critical identity disturbance, however, neither disorder could occur.

Part IV

Identity Disturbance: A Synthesis

10

Diffuse Identity and Lack of Long-Term Direction: The Histrionic Personality Disorder and Other Related Disorders

This chapter examines the histrionic personality disorder. People with this disorder seem to over-value communion at the expense of self-definition and autonomy. The person readily connects with others, but at a price: The person is left with a somewhat diffuse or vague identity. As described later in the chapter, a diffuse identity helps explain certain salient features of the person's behavior. Furthermore, some of these features help explain related Axis I disorders, which have elements in common with the histrionic personality disorder. We examine these Axis I disorders as well.

A clear self-definition helps a person plan long-term strategies for satisfying important motives; that is, a clear self-definition gives a person direction and purpose. It also helps a person adhere to a coherent set of values, ideals, and standards. In contrast, a person with a vague self-image seems to be more impulsive, pursuing short-term goals and immediate gratification. As a result, the person has difficulty describing long-term ambitions, values, and personal characteristics. Instead, yesterday's commitments seem to fall by the wayside, and the person is without direction or a clear sense of self. Interestingly, however, people with a diffuse self-image find it hard to tolerate being alone; when alone, they complain of feeling empty or bored.

A diffuse self-image is also associated with the antisocial personality disorder, and this chapter examines that condition as well. Whether for biological or environmental reasons, antisocial people seem to acquire a tenuous attachment to caretakers. This lack of attachment leaves them unconcerned with other people's rights, feelings, or wishes; they seem to experience little shame, guilt, or remorse. Thus, the histrionic and antisocial personality disorders resemble each other with respect to a diffuse self-image and long-range ambitions, but they differ in terms of their capacity to connect with other people.

We begin the chapter with the histrionic personality disorder (and related Axis I disorders). Our description will clarify the meaning of a diffuse identity. Then we examine the antisocial personality disorder, showing how it resembles and contrasts with the histrionic personality disorder.

Histrionic Personality Disorder

In this section we examine the diagnostic criteria of the histrionic personality disorder and a case example. Then we consider the etiology of the disorder to explain why the communal motive is so prominent. The histrionic personality disorder is associated with a particular attentional style, so we also examine that style and some of its interpersonal consequences. Finally, we summarize the section by formulating the disorder.

Description

DIAGNOSTIC CRITERIA   Exhibit 10.1 shows the eight diagnostic criteria of the histrionic personality disorder, as described in *DSM–IV–TR* (American Psychiatric Association, 2000). To qualify for the disorder, the person must meet five or more of these criteria (and also experience subjective distress or impaired functioning). People who meet the criteria are usually lively, dramatic people who wish to be the center of attention. They usually try to impress other people by their appearance; they spend a lot of time, energy, and money on clothes and accessories and then seek approval or admiration. They may also try to attract attention by being sexually provocative or inappropriately seductive. If they are not the center of attention, they sometimes make up stories, create a scene, or do something dramatic to attract attention. Initially, they charm other people with their apparent warmth and openness, but over time that charm wears thin.

Histrionic people are also described as emotional; they tend to display more sadness, anger, or delight than a given situation calls for. To observers, the person's emotional expression seems exaggerated (e.g., uncontrollable sobbing over a minor loss, temper tantrums over a minor frustration). For that reason the person is described as self-dramatizing and theatrical and may seem shallow or phony.

Two other characteristics are also included in the list of criteria. First, histrionic people tend to have a style of speech that is impressionistic and lacking in detail. For example, the person may express a very strong opinion and then provide only vague, diffuse, and unsupported reasons to substantiate the opinion. Second, histrionic people also tend to be highly suggestible; their opinions and feelings are easily influenced by other people and by current fads.

CASE EXAMPLE   Millon and Davis (2000, p. 237) described a single, 23-year-old woman whose gynecologist referred her for psychological assessment. She was described as outgoing, effusive, and "dressed to kill." She had been experiencing debilitating pain for over half a year, but the pain seemed to be medically unexplainable. Throughout the interview, she used facial and other nonverbal expressiveness to dramatize the meaning of her words. In describing her pain, for example, she said she felt as though "I will absolutely expire" as she closed her eyes and dropped her head forward to feign death. However, when asked about her pain, she became coquettish and was either unable or unwilling to provide details. She talked freely about topics tangential to the inter-

Exhibit 10.1.   Diagnostic Criteria for Histrionic Personality Disorder

A pervasive pattern of excessive emotionality and attention seeking, beginning by early adulthood and present in a variety of contexts, as indicated by five (or more) of the following:

(1) is uncomfortable in situations in which he or she is not the center of attention
(2) interaction with others is often characterized by inappropriate sexually seductive or provocative behavior
(3) displays rapidly shifting and shallow expression of emotions
(4) consistently uses physical appearance to draw attention to self
(5) has a style of speech that is excessively impressionistic and lacking in detail
(6) shows self-dramatization, theatricality, and exaggerated expression of emotion
(7) is suggestible, i.e., easily influenced by others or circumstances
(8) considers relationships to be more intimate than they actually are

Note. From *Diagnostic and Statistical Manual of Mental Disorders* (4th ed., Text Revision, p. 714) by the American Psychiatric Association, 2000, Washington, DC: Author. Reprinted with permission.

view, skipping quickly from topic to topic and periodically inserting sexual double entendres. She described her family as happy and well-adjusted but acknowledged conflict with her mother and complained that her older brothers treated her like a baby. She described herself as close to her parents and said that she calls home every day. She was not currently in a serious relationship, but stated with a giggle that most boys "find me very attractive," adding that they "just want me for my body." She also reported that she found it easy to get to know others. At the time of the interview, she was working as a dancer at an adult club; she particularly liked the attention and the money that the job provided. She felt that, in contrast to the other girls, she was an artist. Her family believed that she was teaching ballet.

This combination of traits—extraverted, attention-getting, emotional, vague, and suggestible—may seem puzzling. Why should an emotional and attention-getting person lack precision in explaining opinions? Why should such people be suggestible? A systematic account is needed to help clarify why these traits go together and how they can cause the kind of subjective distress we observe in a histrionic person. That is the purpose of the following sections.

Etiology

We assume that the histrionic person is biologically predisposed to histrionic traits. For example, children who are temperamentally extraverted can use that extraversion to help satisfy motives to engage and connect with others. If an extraverted child has a very strong need to connect with others (e.g., because of life experiences with an unavailable caretaker), the child's lively and outgoing friendliness may help the child connect. Similarly, an innately emotional person might use emotionality as a way of connecting. Emotional expressiveness enables a person to disclose private internal experiences, thereby engaging other people. Thus, extraversion and emotionality can both be used to satisfy communal goals. If these strategies are successful, the person does not develop a personality disorder.

A personality disorder implies (a) that the person has come to display the traits excessively, pervasively, and rigidly and (b) that the strategy has backfired so that it now thwarts, rather than satisfies, important motives. Indeed, other people might find excessive displays of emotion and self-disclosure aversive and avoid the person. In that case, the person might come to feel ignored or neglected and react to the frustrated motive with strong negative affect (sadness, anger).

How does a histrionic person acquire such a strong need to connect? Very few studies provide data on the etiology of the histrionic personality disorder. From the data that do exist, we assume that the person's caretakers were relatively unavailable during the child's formative years. In some cases, the mother was depressed and withdrawn during the person's childhood years; in other cases, the mother expressed a dislike for caretaking responsibilities (Fitzgerald, 1948; Krohn, 1978). In still other cases, the mother, though affable and sociable, did not meet the child's basic needs in significant ways (L. S. Benjamin, 1996). As a result, the child may have found and cultivated ways to attract an adult's attention. The child could be cute, entertaining, dramatic, or flirtatious, and that ability enabled the child to attract attention and connect. When the strategy worked, it helped the child engage otherwise unavailable people. L. S. Benjamin (1996) suggested that, in some cases, adult caretakers even discouraged the child from developing and displaying competence, so agentic goals were eclipsed by more pressing communal goals. In any case, connections and relationships came to acquire a high priority.

Attentional Style and Its Consequences

Histrionic people also show a characteristic attentional style, which may help the person connect with others (Shapiro, 1965). The style may be contrasted with that of the person with obsessive–compulsive personality disorder. Whereas the person with obsessive–compulsive personality disorder finds it easy to concentrate and focus attention on the figure of the attentional field, the histrionic person is very responsive to peripheral stimuli. As the person focuses on some object of attention, a peripheral stimulus (arising from internal experience or from the external environment) upstages the earlier object of attention. Thus, the new object displaces the earlier one to become the new figure of the attentional field (Shapiro, 1965). We say that histrionic people are more responsive to novel stimuli than other people and seem more lively and spontaneous.

As a result of this attentional style, the person is less apt to concentrate on a single target of attention for long and would find it hard to explain, justify, or describe a complex observation carefully, systematically, and coherently. This difficulty is particularly evident when a histrionic person is interviewed. For example, I once posed the following question to an intelligent young woman who had always lived with her parents: "You mentioned that your parents recently decided to get a divorce after 25 years of marriage. Tell me more about that. Why do you think they decided to divorce after all those years?" The woman considered the question briefly and then said, "I really don't know; they always seemed so happy together." Perhaps the woman had never observed, pondered, or digested information about her parents' marital unhappiness, or perhaps she was too distracted during the interview to formulate an answer.

As another example, an examiner administered a Rorschach test to an examinee, and during the inquiry phase, he asked a question: "You mentioned that this card looks like a bat. Tell me about that. What about the card made it look like a bat?" Most people would explain their perception in terms of the shape, color, or shading of the inkblot. The person replied, "It's hard to say; somehow the idea of a bat just popped into my head." As a third example, an interviewer asked a very intelligent woman to describe her boyfriend: "What is he like?" The woman replied with a smile, "My boyfriend? Well, he's like, Wow! I mean, like, Wow!" In all three cases, the answer contained surprisingly little detail for the person's apparent intelligence.

Because of this impressionistic style, histrionic people sometimes seem naïve. In some of his plays, the American playwright, Tennessee Williams, portrayed "southern belles" who display this quality. One character in Williams's play *A Streetcar Named Desire* (1947) was Blanche DuBois. When Blanche's parents died, the family's estate was willed to her and her younger sister. Blanche, the older sister, then found herself in charge of the property. Over the years, however, the property slipped through her hands and was somehow lost. When her brother-in-law confronted her about the loss, demanding an explanation, she simply reached into her trunk of papers and possessions and pulled out a disorganized jumble of legal documents, unwilling or unable to retrieve memories or focus on details that explained the loss. To summarize, we assume that criterion 5 of the histrionic personality disorder ("impressionistic style") results from the person's attentional style.

A second consequence is that another person's words (thoughts, beliefs, opinions) constitute novel stimuli that readily engage the histrionic person's attention. The person accepts the other person's novel suggestions, letting them upstage his or her prior beliefs and feelings. As a result, the histrionic person is said to be more suggestible than most people (criterion 7). Furthermore, in accepting the other person's suggestions, the histrionic person may feel better connected to that person. A histrionic woman once told me the following experience: "Yesterday I told my friend that I don't like my job as a typist; it's boring. My friend said, 'Melanie, you shouldn't be a typist; you're so outgoing and friendly—you could be an airline stewardess.'" The woman recalled that she then found herself thinking, "She's right... I *am* friendly and outgoing. I *should* be a stewardess. Why didn't I think of that?" Apparently, another person's words can have a strong momentary impact. Perhaps that is why people with a histrionic personality disorder are said to be more hypnotizable than other people (e.g., Spiegel & Fink, 1979).

Because the histrionic person accepts other people's words and suggestions so responsively, we say that the person readily relaxes interpersonal boundaries. The term *interpersonal boundaries* refers to the distinction we normally make between our own mental experiences (e.g., feelings, beliefs, attitudes, aspirations) and those of another person. Most people have no difficulty maintaining interpersonal boundaries. We hear someone rave about a movie that we disliked, and we easily retain our own reasons for disliking the movie.

Sometimes we choose to relax interpersonal boundaries. As we watch a play, we let ourselves identify with one of the characters and temporarily lose a sense of ourselves as observers. Or we listen to an orator espousing some view and feel at one with that view, as though we and the orator were jointly promoting the very same view. In cases like these, we take pleasure in temporarily surrendering our own separateness.

However, histrionic people seem to exercise less control over the process than most people do. By relaxing interpersonal boundaries, histrionic people surrender their sense of separateness. Later we shall consider costs to the person; here we examine its benefits. To begin with, the histrionic person feels temporarily at one with the other person. Second, the person comes across to others as warm, friendly, and engaged, thereby sustaining the relationship. Third, by relaxing interpersonal boundaries, the person is apparently able to act out particular interpersonal roles (American Psychiatric Association, 2000, p. 712) that deepen the connection to others. That is, the person seems to know what others expect of a "hapless victim," a "desperate suicidal person," a "sexy, foxy lady," a "deserving artist," a "high-born princess," or a "sick unfortunate." By being a hapless victim to a willing rescuer, for example, the person deepens the relationship. If the person were the hostess at a party or a church gathering, "hostessing" would be acted out convincingly and without self-consciousness, and guests would feel charmed and warmly welcomed.

Weak Interpersonal Boundaries and Identity Diffusion

Consider the price a person pays in relaxing interpersonal boundaries so readily. A sense of self is derived from consistent internal experiences: reasonably consistent beliefs, values, goals, interests, tastes, traits, and so on. If a person relaxes interpersonal boundaries too readily, the person's internal states frequently change to match those of someone else. Thus, the person does not experience enough consistency to have a clear sense of self. The term *identity diffusion* refers to a vague or blurry sense of self. Before we examine this concept, however, let us review the meaning of a clear sense of self.

A clear adult identity reflects a stable image of "me," an image that distinguishes oneself from other people. Naturally, some degree of inconsistency arises in everyone from time to time; we all vary to some extent across situations. Therefore, each person has to find ways to integrate conspicuous inconsistencies in order to feel reasonably coherent (Gergen, 1968). People might notice, for example, that their behavior changes systematically in different situations or roles (e.g., "I am serious at work, but I clown around with my friends at dinner"). In that way, the person transforms an observed inconsistency into a lawful regularity (e.g., Vallacher, 1980). That is, the person has differentiated the self (sometimes I am serious, sometimes I am a clown), but the two facets are now integrated into a more complex (yet coherent) regularity—serious-at-work-and-a-clown-with-friends. Self-differentiation and integration may go hand in hand to produce a more complex, yet coherent, conception of the self.

Asch and Zukier (1984) described methods that people normally use to integrate contrasting characteristics in themselves and other people. In one method, the person may "segregate" traits by situation or role ("I am bright in intellectual matters, but inept in practical matters"). In another method, the person may regard one trait as the "means" for achieving the other as the "end" ("I have to be mean [or strict or stern] to my son in order to be kind and ensure his future happiness). Through these and many other methods, the person creates a reasonably coherent image of the self.

How about a person who relaxes interpersonal boundaries too readily? Day after day, the person takes on other people's beliefs, opinions, hobbies, interests, and so on, continually changing the self-image. Newer values and goals keep replacing earlier ones. As a result, the person has to sacrifice the kind of consistency that provides a clear self-image. The person would have trouble describing long-term goals and ambitions. The person would lack the kind of direction a person achieves through long-term plans, purposes, and projects. The *DSM–IV–TR* alludes to a diffuse identity in the following features: suggestibility (criterion 7), rapidly shifting and shallow emotions (criterion 3), impressionistic speech lacking in detail (criterion 5), and relationships considered to be more intimate than they actually are (criterion 8).

A person whose self-image keeps changing would find it hard to describe the self. Some people who experience that say that they feel "confused about who I am." A diffuse identity can be very distressing. An intelligent and articulate woman in treatment complained that she seemed to lack "a core me." She said, "I seem to believe whatever other people tell me. I feel that I have no real opinions or convictions of my own. My sister's husband got me my job (which I do not like), and last week I became a vegetarian because my girlfriend is a vegetarian. But I ask myself, who am I?" L. S. Benjamin (1996) described a histrionic person who remarked, "I look in the mirror all the time just to be sure that somebody is there" (p. 171). People with a diffuse identity complain of feeling empty, hollow, or weak inside; they sometimes say that they feel unreal or like having a "false self." Feelings of emptiness seem to be more pronounced when the person is alone. Apparently, an interpersonal connection helps the person avoid a feeling of emptiness. Objective measures of identity diffusion have been proposed by Wilkinson-Ryan and Westen (2000) and S. Taylor and Goritsas (1994).

Formulation

We assume that people with a histrionic personality disorder have acquired an exaggerated desire to connect with others. This desire apparently stems from an insecurity acquired over many childhood years. If the primary attachment figure was relatively unavailable (e.g., depressed, withdrawn, or otherwise preoccupied), the child may have formed an anxious attachment and came to fear separation, loss, and isolation. Over the years, however, the person may have learned to use his or her innate talents to engage other people (e.g., by being cute, sociable, lively, vivacious, the life of the party). In brief, we organize the histrionic personality disorder around a need to feel close and connected. One strategy for connecting is to attract attention by being lively, dramatic, or emotional. Another is to relax interpersonal boundaries, thereby connecting with others through (momentarily) shared feelings and cognitions.

If the person relaxes interpersonal boundaries too readily, the person sacrifices a firm sense of self and seems to feel at sea when alone. Characteristic problems follow from the person's identity diffusion:

1. A histrionic person may be troubled by a lack of long-term goals and direction.
2. Short-term goals, commitments, and promises get forgotten, so the person may seem shallow or unreliable to others.
3. Because of an intense desire for connection, the person may seem needy or manipulative, leading others to reject the person.
4. Isolation may leave the person feeling lonely, empty, depressed, or anxious.

Comparison With the Dependent Personality Disorder

People with a histrionic personality disorder strongly desire contact with others and thus resemble people with a dependent personality disorder. Both categories include people who are uncomfortable alone. For this reason, the two disorders tend to co-occur (American Psychiatric Association, 2000, p. 712). However, the two disorders are thought to reflect different interpersonal histories. People with a dependent personality disorder were apparently overprotected during their childhood years and encouraged to surrender control to the care of others. In time, they learned to avoid risks and avoid the displeasure of others. Baker, Capron, and Azorlosa (1996) have shown differences in the family environments of the two groups. Compared to families of histrionic people, families of dependent people discouraged independence and de-emphasized achievement.

The interpersonal problems associated with the dependent personality disorder are located in the lower right-hand quadrant of the interpersonal space (too passive and too friendly); these problems are captured by such statements as "I try to please other people too much;" "I let other people take advantage of me too much;" and "it is hard for me to be firm when I need to be." In contrast, the interpersonal problems associated with the histrionic personality disorder are generally located in the upper right-hand quadrant of the interpersonal space (too controlling and too friendly); those problems are captured by such statements as "I open up to people too much;" "I want to be noticed too much;" and "I find it hard to stay out of other people's business." The histrionic person's strategies apparently involve more initiative and greater control over others.

Two Associated Axis I Disorders

Certain strategies for reducing stress can be either adaptive or maladaptive. For example, a person who is very able to sustain focused attention may use that strategy to gather information as a way of reducing stress. However, that very ability can backfire, producing an Axis I disorder like "hypochondriasis." In the same way, histrionic people possess abilities that can be used to reduce stress. Their ability to distract themselves and overlook anxiety-arousing details, for example, can help them avoid anxiety. However, that very same ability can backfire, producing an Axis I disorder. We now turn to two examples, "conversion disorder" and "somatization disorder.".

Conversion Disorder

A conversion disorder typically reflects a motor deficit (e.g., a paralysis) or a sensory deficit (e.g., a deafness) that cannot be explained by any known medical abnormality. Because it suggests a neurological condition, it is sometimes called *pseudoneurological*. Typical motor impairments include a weakness or paralysis of the arms or legs, difficulty swallowing, and difficulty talking. Typical sensory impairments include blindness, double vision, deafness, and a loss of touch or pain sensation. The symptom is not deliberately "faked," but it does not make sense medically. For example, a student, complaining of a writer's cramp, was unable to write, but she was able to use the very same muscles to shuffle a deck of cards. Another person could not use his vocal cords to speak, but he was able to cough with normal voicing.

It is important to rule out a medical explanation before making this diagnosis. Sometimes ingenuity is required. For example, Malmo and his colleagues (Malmo, Davis, & Barza, 1952; Malmo, Malmo, & Ditto, 2003) described a patient who reported deafness. When the examiner clapped his hands behind the patient's head, no startle reaction occurred. Then electrodes were attached to the patient's head, neck, and arms, and a loud sound was presented surreptitiously through earphones. Initially, the examiner observed muscle contractions, but those contractions disappeared on subsequent presentations. The woman had apparently "corrected" her earlier slip, inhibiting her own reflexive muscle contractions. Finally, the examiner devised a conditioning procedure to test the limits of the deafness: The patient was instructed to place her finger on a button. A mild electric shock was administered periodically, and the woman was asked to lift her finger whenever she felt a shock. Initially each trial consisted of the sound, then the shock, and then her finger lifting. After many conditioning trials, the shock was occasionally omitted from the sequence. If the woman truly heard nothing, she would not have acquired a conditioned response. Although she did not lift her finger on those trials, an electromyogram showed a burst of muscle activity in her finger, indicating that she had, in some sense, "heard" the sound.

The term *conversion disorder* implies that the symptom helps the person reduce stress, and so relevant psychological factors should be evident. For example, an unmarried young woman had recently had an abortion and had to return home to live with her disapproving mother, who was constantly berating her. In time she developed a "deafness" that conveniently helped her endure her mother's insults. Her deafness also discouraged her mother from talking and excused the daughter from listening. This stress-reduction is said to be the "primary gain" of a conversion disorder. In addition, the person is thought to receive "secondary gain" (e.g., unaccustomed support and nurturance). If the person also lacks a well-defined identity, the disability helps sharpen the person's identity as "a handicapped person," thereby providing another form of secondary gain.

Historically, the conversion disorder has been associated with the histrionic personality disorder, and one can see why. Several aspects of the formulation would facilitate a conversion disorder. Suggestibility is one. A fleeting, peripheral thought that might seem naïve, transparent, or whimsical to someone else is taken seriously: "If I were unable to hold a pencil, I would not have to take the examination: Hey, I think I am having trouble holding a pencil!" "If I were sick, I would not have to go to work: Hmm, I do feel kind of sick!" A suggestible person, through a kind of self-hypnosis, might assume the role of a sick or handicapped person. If the person were not suggestible and focused on bodily details, the person would probably not be able to pull it off. The *DSM–IV–TR* notes that conversion disorders occur more often among people with a histrionic personality disorder.

One should not diagnose a conversion disorder casually. Too often, the label has been applied to patients with a genuine as-yet-undetected medical condition (e.g., patients with a brain tumor too small to be detected). Slater, Beard, and Gitero (1965) studied patients over a 9-year period who had originally been diagnosed with a conversion disorder. Sixty percent of them later developed signs of a medical disease related to the nervous system (e.g., a brain tumor). Whitlock (1967) compared the incidence of organic brain disorder (a) in 56 patients originally diagnosed with a conversion disorder and (b) in 56 patients originally diagnosed with depression or anxiety disorder. He found that 62% of the first group showed later evidence of an organic brain disorder, whereas only 5% of the latter group did. Jones (1980) has reviewed other related studies. Thus, one must use the label with extreme caution.

Somatization Disorder

The somatization disorder is another disorder in which bodily symptoms are reported that cannot be ascribed to a known medical condition. In this disorder, the person expresses many (relatively minor) medical complaints rather than a single dramatic symptom. To meet the criteria listed in *DSM–IV–TR*, the person must have a history of pain associated with different bodily locations (e.g., head, abdomen, back, chest) or functions (e.g., menstruation, urination). In addition, the person must have a history of two or more gastrointestinal symptoms (e.g., nausea), one or more sexual or reproductive symptoms (e.g., in women, vomiting throughout pregnancy; in men, ejaculatory dysfunction), and a history of at least one symptom that suggests a neurological condition (e.g., difficulty swallowing). The *DSM–IV–TR* describes the disorder as "chronic but fluctuating" (p. 488). It rarely remits completely, and a year seldom passes without a medical consultation for some unexplained somatic complaint. It is diagnosed more often in women than in men in the United States, but it is commonly diagnosed in men in other cultures.

One patient diagnosed with somatization disorder was a singer who reported that her gums frequently bled during her performances. She experienced other somatic difficulties, including dizziness and blurry vision, but her bleeding gums were the most troublesome symptom since they interfered with her work as a singer. It was later discovered that the bleeding was unwittingly self-induced. She also reported, during the interview, that she found it stressful to compete professionally with other singers. Apparently, her symptom provided an escape from those pressures, as though she were saying, "No wonder I cannot make it as a singer—my gums bleed! Besides, I am too ill to perform!" Thus, her symptoms served a purpose.

People with a somatization disorder do not seem to be faking the disorder. In fact, most people could not induce a symptom like bleeding gums voluntarily. Certain characteristics of the histrionic personality disorder seem to be a prerequisite for the somatization disorder, and *DSM–IV–TR* notes that the two disorders tend to co-occur. For one thing, the person has to be suggestible, able to play the role of a sick person well and able to overlook disconfirming evidence. The histrionic attentional style probably helps the person maintain the illusion; the person does not sustain intense, concentrated attention to relevant bodily details. According to *DSM–IV–TR*, people with a somatization disorder describe their complaints in a dramatic way but are usually unable to provide specific factual details. This Axis I diagnosis would seem very doubtful in a person who did not show at least some of the relevant characteristics of the histrionic personality disorder.

Antisocial Personality Disorder

People with an antisocial personality disorder, like those with a histrionic personality disorder, seem to have a relatively diffuse sense of self. They have difficulty describing long-range goals, plans, and ambitions and complain that they feel empty and bored when alone. In addition, they are sometimes skillful at playing roles, particularly roles that enable them to deceive other people into gratifying their short-term goals. Even a love relationship seems to be a kind of "game-playing" to antisocial people (Arnold & Thompson, 1996), a manipulative love style that ultimately can be very hurtful to the partner.

Description

People with an antisocial personality disorder seem to lack empathy for others and have little remorse after hurting or mistreating other people. In other words, their conscience seems to be poorly developed. Exhibit 10.2 shows the diagnostic features (American Psychiatric Association, 2000). People with this diagnosis disregard and violate the rights of others. They steal, default on debts, harass others, pursue illegal occupations, and violate laws; they lie and deceive in order to get what they want. They also behave irresponsibly (e.g., miss work, impulsively quit their jobs, fail to provide child support). By late adolescence they have frequently had scrapes with the law and a poor work record (Rey, Singh, Morris-Yates, & Andrews, 1997).

Some antisocial people possess a superficial charm and glibness that they use to manipulate other people in order to satisfy their short-term goals. To people who know them well, however, they are cold, callous, even contemptuous of other people's feelings, wishes, rights, and suffering. They are generally

Exhibit 10.2.   Diagnostic Criteria for Antisocial Personality Disorder

---

A. There is a pervasive pattern of disregard for and violation of the rights of others occurring since age 15 years, as indicated by three (or more) of the following:
  (1) failure to conform to social norms with respect to lawful behaviors as indicated by repeatedly performing acts that are grounds for arrest
  (2) deceitfulness, as indicated by repeated lying, use of aliases, or conning others for personal profit or pleasure
  (3) impulsivity or failure to plan ahead
  (4) irritability and aggressiveness, as indicated by repeated physical fights or assaults
  (5) reckless disregard for safety of self or others
  (6) consistent irresponsibility, as indicated by repeated failure to sustain consistent work behavior or honor financial obligations
  (7) lack of remorse, as indicated by being indifferent to or rationalizing having hurt, mistreated, or stolen from another
B. The individual is at least age 18 years.
C. There is evidence of Conduct Disorder with onset before age 15 years.
D. The occurrence of antisocial behavior is not exclusively during the course of schizophrenia or a manic episode.

Note. From *Diagnostic and Statistical Manual of Mental Disorders* (4th ed., Text Revision, p. 706) by the American Psychiatric Association, 2000, Washington, DC: Author. Reprinted with permission

impulsive in satisfying short-term goals. They may be aggressive and get into physical fights or commit violent acts. Some show a reckless disregard for their own safety and that of others and impulsively drive at great speeds while intoxicated. Compared to other people, antisocial individuals are more apt to die prematurely from an accident or homicide and more apt to spend time in jail.

Most of the features in Exhibit 10.2 are behavioral—visible acts of deceit and criminality. One exception, though, is criterion 7: a lack of remorse. The person seems indifferent to having injured, mistreated, deceived, or stolen from someone else. If a person with the disorder clearly lacks remorse, the behavioral features are apt to be more severe (Goldstein et al., 1996): more impulsive behavior, a worse employment history, more irresponsibility over financial and parental obligations. Those who lack remorse also have a greater history of violence (e.g., using weapons in fights, being cruel to animals and people, forcing sexual activity). The overall prevalence of the disorder in the American population is about 3% among men and 1% among women.

One ability that is sometimes associated with the antisocial personality disorder is the ability to play roles in order to manipulate others. The person assumes the role with minimal anxiety or guilt and without self-consciousness. To illustrate this role-playing ability, we might consider a woman who was interviewed on a radio program *"Suckers"* (National Public Radio). The woman seemed to have a knack for "taking advantage of opportunities." As one example, she had purchased an inexpensive copy of a very expensive garment and later "returned" it (as though it were the original) to a fashionable retail store for a profit of nearly $2,000. In another incident she allowed herself to be tape-recorded as she tried to return a 4-year-old sweater without a receipt. When the store manager refused to provide a cash refund, she became quite upset, almost indignant, because she had apparently convinced herself that she deserved a refund. She then wrote letters to the CEO and CFO of the company (as well as to the mayor of New York), until she finally obtained a cash refund. Her role-playing capacity seemed to include an ability to "almost believe" that her false assertions were true.

Two Interpretations of the Antisocial Personality Disorder

Theoretically, antisocial features can arise from either biological or psychosocial causes—most likely, from a combination of the two. Consider a child who, for biological reasons, experiences minimal anxiety and little desire for human contact. That child would exhibit relatively little distress in separating from caretakers. If the child's caretakers were to react to the child's apparent indifference by ignoring the child, the child might not find much satisfaction in human interaction. Conversely, consider a child who was biologically normal but who had been so neglected or abused over a period of time that the child came to "de-activate" the attachment system. That child might also seem socially indifferent. Whether the original cause was biological or psychosocial (or both), the child would initiate relatively little contact, and other people might respond with the complement (indifference). In the following section we examine each of the two explanations.

THE ROLE OF ATTACHMENT   Much has been written to suggest that the attachment system can become de-activated as a result of prolonged and severe neglect, deprivation, rejection, or abuse (e.g., Dozier, Stovall, & Albus, 2000). Considerable evidence indicates that the family backgrounds of antisocial individuals are replete with parental neglect, indifference, and abuse (e.g., Farrington & Loeber, 1998; Loeber, 1990; Loeber et al., 1993; Luntz & Widom, 1994; Nichols, 1996; Norden, Klein, Donaldson, Pepper, & Klein, 1995). From interviews with criminals about their family backgrounds (and from other corroborating evidence), Marshall and Cooke (1999) demonstrated the salience of parental indifference, neglect, antipathy, inconsistent discipline, and psychological abuse. In general, the greater the number of risk factors, the greater the probability that the child becomes antisocial (Farrington, 1988; West & Farrington, 1977).

According to the attachment theory, a child who deactivates the attachment system is less apt to form strong attachments in adulthood (L. S. Benjamin, 1996; Bowlby, 1973; Millon & Davis, 2000). For example, imagine a child who is repeatedly moved from one foster home to another, so that incipient attachments are continually uprooted. After the child has deactivated the attachment system, the child would seem to be self-sufficient and indifferent to separation. The child would have learned not to rely on caretakers (Bowlby, 1973). Then, not needing caretakers for comfort and security, the child would have little reason to try to please them. Not needing to please them, the child would have little reason to anticipate their reactions, internalize their standards, or empathize with them.

A socially disconnected child would invite indifference from others. As a result, the child would not receive the normal benefits of social interaction. For example, less joint attention with the caretaker ("Look, Jimmy, the puppy really likes you!"), less empathic mirroring ("I bet you'd like to hold the puppy, right, Jimmy?"). Processes like joint attention and empathic mirroring probably help promote self-reflection. Compared to other people, the child might therefore be less apt to self-reflect. With a relatively diffuse self-definition, little desire to please others, and a lack of internalized standards, the child is apt to become more impulsive. During early childhood, a very skillful caretaker might be able to reverse the process, making social interaction so rewarding that the child finds pleasure in it and is eager to please the caretakers. Later in life, however, these kinds of deficits may be difficult to change.

Without a clear self-definition, a person is apparently guided more by here-and-now desires than by long-term goals. Without the restraint of a conscience, a person acts impulsively without remorse. Without self-reflection, a person lacks observing ego. Interestingly, though, antisocial individuals do seem to need the company of other people. When they are alone, they complain of feeling bored, as though their lack of self-definition is highlighted. To overcome this feeling of boredom, they crave excitement and stimulation. Fast, reckless driving, and the use of drugs and alcohol seem to help alleviate the sense of boredom.

THE ROLE OF BIOLOGICAL FACTORS   In his classic book *Mask of Sanity* (1941), Cleckley postulated a biological basis for some forms of the antisocial personality disorder. He used the term *primary psychopath* to describe a subset of antisocial individuals whose disorder seems to have biological roots. Today, the term *psychopath* connotes a biological origin, whereas the term *sociopath* connotes a psychosocial origin. The *DSM–IV–TR*, however, avoids the distinction altogether and does not use either term.

Hare (1991, 1999) constructed an instrument for measuring psychopathic behavior. He suggested that some children do not form attachments to their caretakers because of a malfunction of some brain structure or a surplus or deficit in some hormone or neurotransmitter (e.g., Raine et al., 1994). Biological hypotheses seem especially plausible when we observe a child who has been raised in a conventional and otherwise normal family and who, in contrast to the other siblings, later becomes a mass murderer or a cold, conniving con artist. In such cases, the disorder seems too profound to be ascribed entirely to hypothetical stressors within the family, especially if the stressors seem to have affected one child but not the others. Parents of such children frequently report that they had already detected a serious problem before the child started school (Hare, 1999, p. 157).

Therefore, researchers have tried to identify biological correlates of psychopathic behavior. It is now well-known that psychopathic people are slower than other people to acquire a conditioned fear reaction (Lykken, 1957; Newman & Kosson, 1986; Newman, Widom, & Nathan, 1985). They are also less sensitive to the emotional meaning of words. For example, Williamson, Harpur, and Hare (1991) presented a sequence of words or nonwords to participants, asking them to judge, as quickly as possible, whether each stimulus was a word or a nonword. Their reaction times and EEGs were measured. All participants, psychopathic and nonpsychopathic, reacted more quickly to words than to nonwords and showed a stronger EEG response. Some of the words, however, had negative emotional connotations (e.g., *death*), whereas other words did not (e.g., *paper*). Nonpsychopathic participants responded faster (and with a stronger EEG response) to the emotional words than the neutral words, but psychopathic individuals showed no difference. Apparently, psychopathic individuals are less sensitive than nonpsychopathic individuals to the emotional meaning of words.

Some researchers have also suggested that the frontal lobes of psychopathic people may differ from those of nonpsychopathic people. The frontal lobes are normally involved in goal-setting and planning. When a person's frontal lobes are damaged, the person becomes more impulsive (e.g., shoplifting). Therefore, some have suggested that psychopathic behavior may be due to congenital brain damage or dysfunction. However, recent research has not found evidence of frontal-lobe damage in psychopathic individuals (Hare, 1999). In general, studies of biological factors, like EEG abnormalities and brain dysfunctions, have produced equivocal results (Marshall & Cooke, 1999).

FORMULATION   We assume that biological factors interact with psychosocial factors to produce an antisocial personality disorder (Raine, Brennan, & Mednick, 1994; Raine, Brennan, Mednick, & Mednick, 1996). Because children differ innately in their susceptibility to anxiety (perhaps also in their desire for contact with others), some children, by nature, would experience much less distress over separation. That biological trait could have important consequences for a child's interactions with caretakers. If a caretaker reacted to a child's apparent indifference with neglect or deprivation, we might expect the child to adopt an avoidant style. With little encouragement from adults, the child's capacity for self-reflection would also be impaired, as would the child's internalization of parental and cultural standards. On the other hand, a very skillful caretaker might be able to make social interactions so rewarding that even a moderately limited child would find pleasure in social interaction. In any case, nature (in the form of temperament) and nurture (in the form of deprivation and other interpersonal stressors) probably work together to produce an antisocial personality disorder. Specific mechanisms, however, are still poorly understood.

This chapter has examined one type of identity disturbance, namely, a diffuse identity, that occurs in both the histrionic and antisocial personality disorders. A diffuse identity implies (a) a vague self-image without consistent values, (b) a lack of long-term goals or direction, (c) a feeling of emptiness or boredom when alone, and (d) a readiness to assume, without self-consciousness, roles that engage other people.

The term *identity disturbance* is used in another sense as well, namely, a "split identity." A split identity is particularly evident in the borderline personality disorder, where it seems to cause severe instabilities in the person's interpersonal behavior and affect. The following chapter examines that phenomenon, its interpersonal origins, and its psychological consequences. A split identity is also prominent in the Axis I disorder known as the *dissociative identity disorder*. We shall examine that disorder in the following chapter as well.

11

Split Identity and Instability: Borderline Personality Disorder and Related Conditions

In chapter 10 we discussed identity diffusion and some of the consequences of a diffuse self-image. Another type of identity disturbance is the "split" identity. A *split identity* refers to an unstable self-image. People with a borderline personality disorder, for example, seem to vacillate between contrasting images of the self that prevail at different times. At times the person may view the self positively, but then, following a real or imagined abandonment, the person shifts rather abruptly to an intensely negative view of the self. This shift from a positive to a negative self-image (with a corresponding shift in affect and behavior) seems to occur when the person feels abandoned, rejected, or unwanted (a communal loss).

In this chapter we first describe the borderline personality disorder. Then we ask how the person comes to acquire a split identity, and we formulate the disorder around it. We also consider the type of frustration that may cause a shift from one self-image to the other and the person's ways of coping with the resulting affect (particularly depression and rage). We also examine an Axis I syndrome that builds on a split identity. Finally, we examine the narcissistic personality disorder, which may also be viewed in terms of a split identity. We begin with the description of the borderline personality disorder in *DSM–IV–TR* (American Psychiatric Association, 2000).

Borderline Personality Disorder

The term *borderline personality* was once used to describe a condition thought to straddle the border between neurotic behavior and psychotic behavior. Today we do not use the term that way. It is generally believed that when people with a borderline personality disorder are under severe stress, they may exhibit temporary distortions of reality (e.g., paranoid ideas), but, in general, they are no more susceptible to schizophrenia or other psychotic disorders than other people.

Diagnostic Criteria

Exhibit 11.1 shows the diagnostic criteria. The first criterion (1) describes an organizing motive: "frantic efforts to avoid real or imagined abandonment." For

Exhibit 11.1. Diagnostic Criteria for Borderline Personality Disorder

A pervasive pattern of instability of interpersonal relationships, self-image, and affects, and marked impulsivity beginning by early adulthood and present in a variety of contexts, as indicated by five (or more) of the following:

(1) frantic efforts to avoid real or imagined abandonment. *Note:* Do not include suicidal or self-mutilating behavior covered in Criterion 5.
(2) a pattern of unstable and intense interpersonal relationships characterized by alternating between extremes of idealization and devaluation
(3) identity disturbance: markedly and persistently unstable self-image or sense of self
(4) impulsivity in at least two areas that are potentially self-damaging (e.g., spending, sex, substance abuse, reckless driving, binge eating.) *Note.* Do not include suicidal or self-mutilating behavior covered in Criterion 5.
(5) recurrent suicidal behavior, gestures, or threats, or self-mutilating behavior
(6) affective instability due to a marked reactivity of mood (e.g., intense episodic dysphoria, irritability, or anxiety usually lasting a few hours and only rarely more than a few days)
(7) chronic feelings of emptiness
(8) inappropriate, intense anger or difficulty controlling anger (e.g., frequent displays of temper, constant anger, recurrent physical fights)
(9) transient, stress-related paranoid ideation or severe dissociative symptoms

Note. From *Diagnostic and Statistical Manual of Mental Disorders* (4th ed., Text Revision, p. 710) by the American Psychiatric Association, 2000, Washington, DC: Author. Reprinted with permission.

example, the person may be strongly affected by a perceived rejection. Some criteria in Exhibit 11.1 describe the person's reaction to abandonment: abrupt and conspicuous shifts in identity (3), affect (6), and interpersonal relationships (2). When borderline people feel abandoned, they seem to change rather markedly; for example, fighting with people they once loved, viewing the self very negatively, becoming enraged, depressed, or anxious. A once-idealized friend might now become an object of hate. The borderline person might lash out unexpectedly with uncontrollable anger (8). During a temper tantrum, the person might even become physically violent, hitting the other person, throwing things, biting, yelling obscenities, and so on. For this reason the person may be described as unstable—unstable in identity, unstable in affect, and unstable in interpersonal relationships. Interpersonal relationships are full of commotion, leading to broken friendships, interpersonal rejections, the loss of jobs, and broken marriages. Negative life events are common in the person's life.

Other criteria in Exhibit 11.1 describe the person's attempts to feel better (i.e., to reduce negative affect). For example, the person might engage in impulsive eating binges, spending sprees, promiscuous sex, reckless driving, or substance abuse (4). Borderline people might also mutilate themselves (e.g., by cutting their wrists) in an effort to feel better (Kemperman, Russ, & Shearin, 1997), and they may exhibit suicidal behavior, gestures, or threats (5). Self-mutilation and suicidal gestures can have different meanings to different people; the person may be expressing self-loathing, punishing the self, or manipulating others into being more nurturant by inducing guilt or sympathy in others. The

DSM–IV–TR notes that people with a borderline personality disorder exhibit a higher than average probability of premature death from suicide. They are also prone to have physical handicaps from their own self-mutilation or failed suicide attempts.

To qualify for the disorder, an individual must exhibit at least five of the nine features. According to *DSM–IV–TR*, the disorder occurs in about 2% of the general population, more often among women than men. It is diagnosed in about 10% of the outpatients at mental health clinics and in about 20% of psychiatric inpatients.

Case Example

Millon and Davis (2000, p. 434) described an attractive woman of 47 who sought treatment because she felt depressed about the impending end of her third marriage. Although she had not yet obtained a divorce, she and her husband were living apart. She had been phoning him four or five times a day until he eventually changed his telephone number and moved away. She felt angry at him for leaving and worthless for being left alone. She also reported that she was spending her time shopping, buying what she could not afford, drinking too much, and looking for someone to replace her husband. Her personality seemed to pose contrasting sides: At times she appeared hard, calculating, and bitter, but at other times she seemed like a teenager immersed in an existential crisis, trying to discover who she really was. Sometimes she described her husband as "an asshole," other times as "the most loving person." Her history was full of instability. Her mother had been married numerous times, and she acquired many half-siblings and step-siblings. Her family life was full of conflict and dissension. Whenever her mother remarried, she and her mother had to move and she felt uprooted. Friendships ended, and her schoolwork suffered. She had attempted suicide twice and had been hospitalized three times. At the time of the interview she was in therapy, but she felt angry because her therapist would not see her more than twice a week.

Empirical Study of the Features

Like all personality disorders, the borderline personality disorder is a fuzzy category. No single feature is essential for membership in the category. The five features that one person exhibits may have little overlap with the five features that another person exhibits. As shown in the following study, however, some features do occur more often than others.

Clarkin, Widiger, Frances, Hurt, and Gilmore (1983) interviewed 76 outpatients at a psychiatric clinic in New York who met the criteria for a personality disorder. Patients in the sample were then interviewed in greater depth, and raters judged whether each patient exhibited each of the borderline features. Some features occurred more often than others. The relative frequency of each feature is shown in Table 11.1. At the time of the study, the third edition of the *Diagnostic and Statistical Manual of Mental Disorders* (*DSM–III*; American

Table 11.1. Relative Frequency of Each Borderline Feature in a Sample of 76 Patients With Personality Disorders

Feature	Relative frequency
Unstable relationships	.34
Identity disturbance	.29
Affective instability	.50
Uncontrollable anger	.47
Impulsivity	.49
Physically self-damaging acts	.36
Feeling of emptiness	.33
Intolerance of being alone	.17

Note. From "Prototypic Typology and the Borderline Personality Disorder," by J. F. Clarkin, T. A. Widiger, A. Frances, S. Hurt, and M. Gilmore, 1983, *Journal of Abnormal Psychology, 92,* pp. 267–269. Copyright © 1983 by the American Psychological Association. Reprinted with permission of the author.

Psychiatric Association, 1980) was in use, rather than *DSM–IV–TR*; it contained only eight rather than nine criteria. In addition, the earlier criterion, *intolerance of being alone,* was replaced by *fear of abandonment.* The features that the 76 patients reported most often were "impulsivity," "affective instability," and "uncontrollable anger."

Then the investigators counted the number of features that every patient met. Some patients did not show any borderline features; some showed every feature on the list. Table 11.2 shows how many patients showed no features, how many one feature, how many two features, and so on. Notice that the frequency distribution is continuous; there are no gaps. Two patients showed all of the features; these patients closely approximated the prototype (or theoretical ideal) of the borderline personality disorder. At the other extreme, 17 patients did not show any borderline features.

How many patients in the sample actually met the criteria for the borderline personality disorder? That is, how many possessed five or more features? From the data in Table 11.2, 20 patients (= 2 + 5 + 8 + 5) met the five-feature criterion; they comprise 20/76 = .26 of the sample. Thus, approximately one-fourth of the patients in the sample received the borderline diagnosis. They were comparable to the other 56 (nonborderline) patients with respect to gender (mostly female), age, marital status, education, and type of job.

For convenience, we speak of borderline and nonborderline patients, but the two groups are not truly dichotomous. The patients varied continuously in the degree to which they approximated the theoretical ideal. The cutoff point that separates borderline from nonborderline patients was arbitrarily chosen to be five features. The difference between a person with four features (not-borderline) and a person with five features (borderline) is very slight; it certainly does not reflect a qualitative discontinuity.

Suppose a person meets the criteria and fits the diagnostic category. What is the probability that that person has each feature on the list? To answer this question, the investigators examined the frequency of each feature (a) among the 20 borderline patients and (b) among the 56 nonborderline patients. As one

Table 11.2.   Relative Frequency of Each Degree of Approximating the Theoretical Ideal of the Borderline Personality Disorder

Number of features	Frequency	Proportion of sample
8	2	.03
7	5	.07
6	8	.11
5	5	.07
4	8	.11
3	12	.16
2	7	.09
1	11	.14
0	17	.22
	76 cases	1.00

Note. From "Prototypic Typology and the Borderline Personality Disorder," by J. F. Clarkin, T. A. Widiger, A. Frances, S. Hurt, and M. Gilmore, 1983, *Journal of Abnormal Psychology, 92,* pp. 267–269. Copyright © 1983 by the American Psychological Association. Reprinted with permission of the author.

example, consider the feature "unstable interpersonal relationships" shown in Table 11.3. This feature occurred in 18 of the 20 borderline patients (the proportion, 18/20 = .90, is called the *sensitivity* of the feature), but it occurred in only 8 of the 56 nonborderline patients (that proportion is 8/56 = .14). Clearly, patients with a borderline diagnosis had a greater likelihood of having the feature than nonborderline patients: .90 versus .14. Thus, *unstable interpersonal relationships* turned out to be the single most discriminating feature in this study.

For patients who had a feature, what proportion qualified for the full borderline diagnosis? For example, how many patients with the feature "unstable interpersonal relationships" actually met the diagnosis? Table 11.3 answers that question, too. Of the 26 patients who showed unstable relationships, 18 had the borderline diagnosis; this proportion (18/26 = .69) is called the *positive predictive power* of the feature. It may be compared to the proportion of people without the feature who had the borderline diagnosis (2/50 = .04). Clearly, a patient with unstable relationships had a greater chance of receiving the borderline diagnosis: .69 versus .04. Similar results have been obtained by other investigators (e.g., Modestin, 1987). Table 11.4 shows the positive predictive power of each of the eight features.

The investigators also asked whether any pair of features could discriminate borderline from nonborderline patients. Did any pair of features exist such that every person who possessed those two features received the borderline diagnosis? The answer to this question was yes. Everyone in the sample with "unstable interpersonal relationships" *and* "identity disturbance" had enough other features to qualify for the diagnosis. (These two features, then, were sufficient conditions for the diagnosis. However, they were not necessary for the diagnosis: Some people satisfied the criteria in other ways.) Still, "unstable interpersonal relationships" and "identity disturbance" do seem to be very characteristic of borderline patients.

Table 11.3. Frequency of "Unstable Relationships" Among Patients With Borderline and Non-Borderline Diagnosis

Relationship	Borderline	Not borderline	Total
Unstable	18	8	26
Stable	2	48	50
Total	20	56	76

Note. From "Prototypic Typology and the Borderline Personality Disorder," by J. F. Clarkin, T. A. Widiger, A. Frances, S. Hurt, and M. Gilmore, 1983, *Journal of Abnormal Psychology, 92*, pp. 267–269. Copyright © 1983 by the American Psychological Association. Reprinted with permission of the author.

Origin of the Borderline Personality Disorder

One explanation of the borderline personality disorder comes from the object relations school of psychoanalysis (see J. R. Greenberg & Mitchell, 1983), which emphasizes the interpersonal origins of the disorder. According to these writers, a child must have reasonably consistent parenting in order to acquire a stable, unitary self-image. If the child is treated inconsistently (e.g., sometimes abusively, sometimes nurturantly), the child's image of the self and others is affected in profound ways.

The borderline personality disorder has been the most thoroughly studied of all the personality disorders (Clarkin, Marziali, & Munroe-Blum, 1992), and early abuse seems to be very pronounced (e.g., Berelowitz & Tarnopolsky, 1993; Zanarini & Frankenburg, 1997). For example, Laporte and Guttman (1996) studied the hospital records of 751 female patients between the ages of 16 and 45; 366 of them had a borderline personality disorder. From information in the records, the investigators reported an extremely high incidence of verbal, physical, and sexual abuse in their histories. Fossati, Madeddu, and Maffei (1999) summarized 21 studies (totalling nearly 2,500 individuals) showing the high frequency of childhood sexual abuse.

Insecure attachment styles are also very common among borderline people (e.g., Melges & Swartz, 1989; Sack, Sperling, Fagen, & Foelsch, 1996; West, Keller, Links, & Patrick, 1993). Borderline people frequently report a chronic fear of interpersonal loss, a protest over separation, compulsive care seeking, and an angry separation from a disappointing other (Sack et al., 1996). They also describe both parents very negatively (Baker, Silk, Westen, Nigg, & Lohr, 1992). In chapter 3, we examined a form of insecure attachment in childhood that is thought to arise from very inconsistent parenting, namely, the disorganized (Type D) attachment pattern. As described earlier, children who have been both nurtured and frightened by the same caretaker seem to display dazed or disorganized behavior in the strange situation. We now examine the mechanism by which inconsistent treatment might lead to instability in adulthood.

Consider a caretaker whose behavior is sometimes very loving (nurturant, caring, admiring) and sometimes very hostile (cold, rejecting, sadistic). Harris (1967, p. 163), in his book *I'm OK—You're OK*, provided examples of a parent who would sometimes beat the child and sometimes applaud the child, producing overwhelming inconsistency in the child's view of the parent and the self.

Table 11.4. Probability of Borderline Diagnosis in Patients Given Individual Features (Positive Predictive Power)

Feature	Feature present	
	Yes	No
Impulsivity	.59	.00
Unstable relationships	.69	.04
Uncontrollable anger	.50	.05
Identity disturbance	.59	.13
Affective instability	.50	.03
Intolerance of being alone[a]	.38	.24
Physically self-damaging acts	.56	.10
Feeling of emptiness	.64	.08

Note. From "Prototypic Typology and the Borderline Personality Disorder," by J. F. Clarkin, T. A. Widiger, A. Frances, S. Hurt, and M. Gilmore, 1983, *Journal of Abnormal Psychology, 92,* pp. 267–269. Copyright © 1983 by the American Psychological Association. Reprinted with permission of the author. [a] In *DSM–IV* this feature was changed to "Frantic efforts to avoid abandonment."

For example, Harris described a preschooler whose mother was alcoholic. While drunk, the mother would cuddle, stroke, tickle, and lovingly play with the child, clapping her hands and laughing hysterically. Later she would pass out, abandoning the child who was now alone and hungry. Still later, when she awakened, she would feel dyspeptic, dysphoric, logy, sluggish, and nauseated. Now irritable, easily provoked, and bugged by the child, she would scold, hit, and reject the child. The next day the cycle would repeat itself.

POLARIZED IMAGES We might list the caretaker's attributes during each extreme state. When the caretaker is nice, loving, and friendly, the child perceives that the caretaker "likes me, takes care of me, wants to be with me." Exhibit 11.2 lists a set of perceptions that apply when the caretaker behaves lovingly. This global perception has been called metaphorically *the good mother.* When the caretaker is rejecting, cold, or hostile, the child perceives that the caretaker "hates me, hurts me, does not want me around." That global perception has been called *the bad mother.* The attributes within a column cohere with each other and form a single, unitary image that has meaning for the child. However, the two images are distinct and disparate; one is friendly, loving, and kind, the other is unfriendly, unloving, and unkind. Because they contrast so sharply, the features in one list seem to negate features in the other.

When a preschool child frequently experiences both images in succession— first one, then the contrasting one—the child would be unable to integrate them into a single composite of one person (Adler & Buie, 1979; Kernberg, 1985). In a sense, the child's experience resembles that of a red toy car that is moved behind a dark filter (abruptly turning black) and then moved outside the filter (abruptly turning red). Apparently, the child's understanding permits a magical change (that is, the child is not troubled by a logical contradiction), so the abrupt change from red to black to red again does not pose a conceptual problem. Similarly, the caretaker is one person physically, but the person's attributes abruptly change. When the good image is activated, the child feels secure and loved; when the bad image is activated, the child feels insecure and unloved.

Exhibit 11.2. Attributes of "The Good Mother" and "The Bad Mother"

The good mother	The bad mother
gives to me	punishes me
likes me	hates me
takes care of me	hurts me
welcomes me	throws me out
is kind toward me	is cruel to me
makes me feel good	makes me feel bad
supports me	scolds me
defends me	criticizes me
attends to my needs	ignores my needs
cares about me	doesn't care about me
comforts me	disappoints me

Contrasting perceptions seem to have an "either–or" quality, like the reversible figure in Figure 11.1. The figure can be perceived either as a youngish, pleasant-looking woman with a normal-sized nose or as an oldish, haggish woman with an over-sized nose. We can oscillate from one clear perception to the other, but we cannot experience both simultaneously. The preschool child who holds very contradictory images of the same person is not likely to integrate them into a single image (Kegan, 1982).

For comparison, consider a child who is treated with reasonable consistency. Every so often the caretaker might get angry and punish the child, but those negative experiences are relatively infrequent; the positive image is much sharper and more salient. Over time, the child can expand the positive image and incorporate occasional negative characteristics: "My mother is usually caring, kind, and loving; but when she is tired and provoked, she has a very short fuse." In other words, the normal child can build on a reasonably strong, favorable image to include the less frequent negative instances. As a result, the normal child acquires a subtler, better integrated, and more complex image of the caretaker.

Before ages 10–11, children seem to find it hard to imagine contradictory emotions toward the same target person. Harter (1986) had children view two photographs portraying a person who was expressing two different emotions about something. In one condition the emotions were similar (e.g., happy and proud); in the other condition, they were contrasting (e.g., mad and glad). The children, who ranged in age from 4 to 12, were asked to give an example showing how the two emotions could be occurring at the same time. At age 5, the children denied that a person could have two feelings at the same time (according to one child, "it's hard to think of two feelings at the same time because you only have one mind!"). By age 7, they could imagine two positive or two negative feelings toward the same target (e.g., "If your brother hit you, you would be both mad and sad"). By age 10 they could imagine contradictory feelings toward different targets (e.g., "I was mad at my brother for hitting me, but glad that my father let me hit him back"). Finally, by age 11 they could conceive contradictory feelings toward the very same target ("I was happy that I got a present but mad that it was not what I wanted").

Figure 11.1. Example of a reversible figure.

To summarize, the capacity to experience ambivalent feelings toward the same person seems to develop slowly over the childhood years. A child who has experienced intensely negative and intensely positive feelings toward the same person seems to acquire separate images that are difficult to integrate. When the child later describes or recalls early experiences, the child seems to recall them one way or the other, as though through a positive or a negative filter. For example, it is often said that prisoners who have been abused by their mothers sometimes describe their mothers in idealized terms—a "wonderful, loving woman"—but after they return home and their mother's behavior activates a negative image, the image becomes entirely negative. Contrasting images that have this "either–or" quality are said to be "polarized" or "split."

GENERALIZING TO OTHER PEOPLE   Polarized images can apparently generalize to other important people later in life. Through identification and recapitulation, the person replays old interactional patterns with significant others, sometimes idealizing, sometimes vilifying friends, lovers, coworkers, children. Apparently, the person continues to "split," unable to perceive the target person as a blend of negative and positive qualities. For the person who splits, negative characteristics are not just a part of the whole person; they are the whole person (at that instant). In this way, a once-idealized object of love can become an object of hate.

CONSEQUENCES FOR THE SELF-IMAGE   A person who has been treated inconsistently is likely to acquire split images of the self. A self-image, after all, is derived in part from the person's experience with others, and a person who has been treated inconsistently has received contradictory messages about the self. A "good mother" communicates a message that "you are loved and valued," whereas a "bad mother" communicates a message that "you are disliked and disposable." For this reason, the person may acquire split images of the self.

When a negative self-image is activated, the person might blame the self (and feel depressed) or blame others (and feel enraged). Therefore, borderline people are often severely depressed or enraged. To dispel these negative emotions, they may turn to drugs and alcohol, promiscuous sex, eating binges, shopping sprees. They may also harm themselves (e.g., by cutting, burning, hitting, or poisoning themselves) in an effort to feel better. Suicidal gestures, threats, and behaviors are sometimes viewed as dysfunctional ways of regulating negative affect (Kehrer & Linehan, 1996; Linehan, 1993; A. W. Wagner & Linehan, 1999; Westen, 1991).

SPLITTING VERSUS AMBIVALENCE   The term *ambivalence* refers to the simultaneous presence of positive and negative characteristics (Sincoff, 1990), whereas *splitting* refers to an oscillation between extremes. A psychoanalytic concept like reaction formation presupposes the capacity to experience ambivalence—the person accentuates positive feelings as a way of concealing coexisting negative feelings. Therefore, we would not usually speak of reaction formation in a person who seemed to split.

As noted before, the "either–or" quality of split images resembles the "either–or" perception of a reversible figure. A reversible figure may be perceived one way or the other, but not both ways simultaneously (Kegan, 1982). Likewise, a person who splits seems to perceive the self (or a significant other) one way or the other, but not both ways simultaneously. When I was a trainee learning about psychotherapy, I treated a young man who had recently quarreled with his roommate-friend. The man had become so enraged that he broke his friend's ribs. The next day, however, he could scarcely remember what the fight was about. The incident left him feeling very bad and prompted him to seek psychotherapy. As a beginning interviewer, I (naïvely) tried to comment on the man's "ambivalence," using a metaphor of the day: "Part of you seems to be very fond of your roommate, but another part of you seems to be very angry at him." The young man, however, interpreted the remark as a comment about splitting and wondered how I knew that he had "two different sides, a 'good me' and a 'bad me'". He then described his split images, including separate names for each. Later in the chapter, we consider dissociative identity disorder (multiple personality disorder), which also requires a split self-image.

The composer Robert Schumannn appears to have had split self-images. He, too, had separate names for each, Florestan and Eusebius (Ostwald, 1985). In dedicating one of his compositions for piano (the *Davidsbündlertänze*), he wrote: "To Walther von Goethe, from Robert Schumann (Florestan and Eusebius)." Florestan was a powerful, fiery, aggressive hero of an opera by Beethoven; Eusebius was a gentle, sensitive, depressed early Christian martyr. The composition contains individual pieces, and Schumann placed an "F" or an "E" at the end of each piece to credit the appropriate "composer." The work may be viewed as an oscillation (perhaps a musical struggle) between an aggressive self-image and a depressed one. Schumann himself apparently had had very harsh early experiences, suffered emotionally, and ended his life in suicide (Ostwald, 1985).

Formulation

In formulating the borderline personality disorder, we assume that the person suffered intermittent, but intense physical, verbal, or sexual abuse in childhood. Such abuse can have two consequences. First, the person may acquire split images of the self and important others, causing abrupt shifts in behavior and affect. Second, the person may become extremely sensitive to rejection and abandonment, causing strong emotional reactions to apparent abandonment—depression, rage, and anxiety (Masterson, 1972). Then, in an effort to reduce negative affect, retaliate, or prevent further abandonment, the person may make use of self-defeating behaviors, such as suicidal and self-injurious behavior.

Comparison of Borderline and Histrionic Personality Disorders

Two criteria of the histrionic personality disorder are very similar to criteria of the borderline personality disorder. Both describe an emotional person. The histrionic person displays "rapidly shifting emotions" (3) and "exaggerated expression of emotion" (6), which include temper tantrums and uncontrollable sobbing (*DSM–IV–TR*, p. 711). The borderline person displays "affective instability" (6) and "inappropriate, intense anger" (8). Not surprisingly, these two disorders also tend to co-occur (*DSM–IV–TR*, p. 712).

One difference between the two disorders, however, is that the histrionic person strives to become connected by being the center of attention (1, 4), whereas the borderline person strives to avoid becoming disconnected (1). The two motives, getting attention and avoiding abandonment, are both communal, and so they are very compatible. Still, our formulation of the borderline individual emphasizes early abuse, splitting, and a split identity, whereas our formulation of the histrionic individual (chapter 10) emphasizes early neglect and unavailable others. In reality, however, the same caretakers may abuse and neglect a child, so the young person might well adopt the strategies associated with each disorder.

Split Identity Versus Diffuse Identity

The term *identity disturbance* is used to describe either a split identity or a diffuse identity (or both). We examined the meaning of a diffuse identity in chapter 10 and the meaning of a split identity in this chapter. We now reconsider why they might co-occur in the same person.

Clarkin, Caligor, Stern, and Kernberg (2002) created a structured interview that included questions about each type of identity disturbance. Questions about splitting might include: "Do you find that your relationships can be unstable—that you sometimes feel positive towards a person, but at other times you feel angry and mistrustful of that person?" "Does your self-esteem alternate between feeling special at times and feeling small and defective at other times?" Questions about identity diffusion might include: "Do you find yourself feeling confused about who you are or the kind of person you are?" "Do your ambitions and goals often change?" "Do you ever feel that your opinions are borrowed from other people and are not your own?"

Wilkinson-Ryan and Westen (2000) created a questionnaire to help therapists describe the identity disturbance of patients whom they knew well. From a factor analysis of the therapists' responses, different sets of items emerged. The items of one set reflected splitting, inconsistency, and instability; for example, "the patient frequently behaves in ways that seem inconsistent or contradictory;" "the patient feels like a different person depending on whom he or she is with." Items of the other set described a diffuse identity; for example, the patient "tends to feel that he or she does not know who his or her own self is;" "tends to feel empty inside;" "fears losing own identity in close relationships;" "fears he or she would no longer exist or would lose own identity if close relationship were to end."

Could a single person exhibit both identity diffusion (vagueness) and splitting (inconsistency)? As noted above, the salient motives of the borderline and histrionic individuals are compatible. Both arise from a desperate desire for connection (communion). However, the borderline person is thought to have experienced early abuse, whereas the histrionic person is thought to have experienced early neglect and unavailable caretakers. Because abuse and neglect are not incompatible, the two kinds of identity disturbance may occur in the same person. Further empirical research is needed to understand the relationship between them.

Dissociative Identity Disorder (Axis I Disorder)

Most people seem to have a reasonably unitary identity composed of reasonably coherent perceptions, values, goals, and personal memories. Most people do not have split images or feel like different people on different occasions. When they detect a significant contradiction in the self (e.g., behaving in ways that clash with everyday values), they find a way to reconcile the discrepancy. For example, a person whose atypical behavior happens to violate everyday standards might explain the contradiction by saying, "I was not my usual self today—that was not the real me." In this way, the person explains the aberrant behavior and maintains a unitary self-image.

In contrast, splitting exposes a conspicuous inconsistency. In extreme cases, the person shifts so abruptly from one split state to another that the person feels like two (or more) different people and cannot explain the contradiction. Such extreme shifts are observed in the Axis I disorder labeled *dissociative identity disorder* (multiple-personality disorder). In this disorder, a person who normally seems refined and gentle, when sufficiently stressed, might become so crude, tough, and aggressive that the person seems (and feels) like a different person.

People with a dissociative identity disorder typically report that they were horribly abused (physically or sexually) during their childhood years (e.g., Durand & Barlow, 2003; Gleaves, 1996; Putnam, Guroff, Silberman, Barban, & Post, 1986; C. A. Ross, 1997). The disorder itself may be viewed as an extreme elaboration of split identities. The person's usual identity (e.g., mild, restrained, soft-spoken) serves the person well in appeasing potential abusers, but a secondary identity (e.g., loud, coarse, aggressive) enables the person to act boldly from time to time without having to own up to the behavior. Sometimes the secondary identity begins as an imaginary playmate during childhood, such as a tough friend, who (at least in fantasy) protects the child from bullies and aggressors. Over time, this alter ego becomes elaborated and internalized, allowing the person, from time to time, to shift to the bolder self-system (with bold feelings, thoughts, mannerisms, speech styles, and behaviors) and to revert later to the safer, more usual identity. Some people extend the process to more than two identitites. The disorder is diagnosed more often in women than in men.

According to *DSM–IV–TR* (American Psychiatric Association, 2000), four criteria define the dissociative identity disorder (formerly called the *multiple-personality disorder*):

1. Two or more distinct identities or personality states exist within the person.
2. Each recurrently takes control of the person's behavior.
3. The person cannot recall important personal information, and this memory deficit is too extensive to be explained by ordinary forgetfulness.
4. The condition cannot be ascribed to the physiological effects of alcohol, drugs, or a general medical condition.

Apparently, the person experiences each identity as though it had its own unique history. The primary identity (typically passive, dependent, or depressed) contrasts with the secondary identity (typically assertive, aggressive, or hostile). The two differ not only with respect to behavior, cognitive styles, mannerisms, and attitudes, but also in physiological functioning (e.g., in pain tolerance, symptoms of asthma, handedness, optical functioning, or sensitivity to allergens; Kluft, 1987, 1991, 1999; S. D. Miller, 1989). Modern functional magnetic resonance imaging (fMRI) procedures show changes in brain function when different identifies are dominant (Tsai, Condie, Wu, & Chang, 1999). The various identities may also differ with respect to reported age, gender, and predominant affect (American Psychiatric Association, 2000). Each identity may regard the other as a friend, as an adversary, or as an unknown stranger. Ludwig, Brandsma, Wilbur, Bendfeldt, and Jameson (1972) tested the same person on an intelligence test under each identity. The person obtained similar overall IQ scores, but the pattern of subtest scores differed markedly. Many differences observed in the two states cannot be intentionally simulated (Armstrong, 1995; Eich, Macaulay, Loewenstein, & Dihle, 1997; S. D. Miller et al., 1991; Putnam, Zahn, & Post, 1995).

When the primary identity prevails, memories of the secondary self are usually hard to retrieve. The person may have to fabricate facts to fill in the memory gaps. Memory gaps are particularly evident when the person reports an event differently from other eye witnesses. Also, one identity may "know" more details about the other than vice versa (American Psychiatric Association, 2000). In general, a passive identity tends to be less aware of an aggressive or dominating identity than the other way around.

In the first half of the 20th century, *dissociative identity disorder* and *conversion disorder* were classified together as *hysterical neurosis*. It is easy to see why they were classified together. For one thing, people with both disorders are generally often hypnotizable; the symptoms can be induced or removed under hypnosis. Second, both seem to involve skillful role-playing. Third, both may be used to help resolve a conflict. A person with a conversion disorder can turn a deaf ear to a parent's criticism without offending the parent. A timid or meek person with a dissociative identity disorder can be aggressive without having to feel responsible for the unaccustomed boldness.

Later the two disorders were differentiated. The revised third edition of the *Diagnostic and Statistical Manual of Mental Disorders* (*DSM–III–R*; American Psychiatric Association, 1987) included a comment that histrionic traits are common in the conversion disorder (p. 257) and that borderline traits tend to accompany the multiple-personality disorder (p. 272). Nowadays, *DSM–IV–TR* notes that the histrionic and borderline personality disorders frequently co-occur (p. 712). In addition, *DSM–IV–TR* reports that the histrionic personality disorder is a correlate of the conversion disorder (p. 495) and that the borderline personality disorder is a correlate of the dissociative identity disorder (p. 527).

Narcissistic Personality Disorder

People with a narcissistic personality disorder sometimes exhibit a split identity, too, although they are often able to conceal their negative self-image. According to *DSM–IV–TR*, the narcissistic personality disorder reflects "a pervasive pattern of grandiosity, need for admiration, and lack of empathy" (p. 714). Narcissistic people shift between extremes of agency—feeling "superior and special" and feeling "inferior and ordinary." This shift, like that of the borderline person, may be ascribed to split images of the self (Kernberg, 1985; Millon & Davis, 2000; Summers, 1994). To an outsider, the person appears to have an inflated sense of self-importance, entitlement, or "specialness." However, the person's self-esteem is very fragile. When frustrated, the person may privately experience a deep sense of shame, inferiority, or worthlessness and become enraged or depressed. The extremes are thought to arise from a history of incon-

Exhibit 11.3.   Diagnostic Features of the Narcissistic Personality Disorder

A pervasive pattern of grandiosity (in fantasy or behavior), need for admiration, and lack of empathy, beginning by early adulthood and present in a variety of contexts, as indicated by five (or more) of the following:

(1) has a grandiose sense of self-importance (e.g., exaggerates achievements and talents, expects to be recognized as superior without commensurate achievements)

(2) is preoccupied with fantasies of unlimited success, power, brilliance, beauty, or ideal love

(3) believes that he or she is "special" and unique and can only be understood by, or should associate with, other special or high-status people (or institutions)

(4) requires excessive admiration

(5) has a sense of entitlement, i.e., unreasonable expectation of especially favorable treatment or automatic compliance with his or her expectations

(6) is interpersonally exploitative, i.e., takes advantage of others to achieve his or her own ends

(7) lacks empathy: is unwilling to recognize or identify with the feelings and needs of others

(8) is often envious of others or believes that others are envious of him or her

(9) shows arrogant, haughty behaviors or attitudes

Note. From *Diagnostic and Statistical Manual of Mental Disorders* (4th ed., Text Revision, p. 717) by the American Psychiatric Association, 2000, Washington, DC: Author. Reprinted with permission.

sistent treatment: The person has been, at times, lavishly admired and praised but, at other times, degraded and shamed.

Features of the narcissistic personality disorder are shown in Exhibit 11.3. To qualify for the diagnosis, a person should exhibit five or more features. The first emphasizes a grandiose sense of self-importance—overestimating one's own abilities and accomplishments, assuming that others are favorably disposed, being surprised when praise is not forthcoming. Although narcissistic people are often envious of others, they also devalue other people's accomplishments to protect their own self-esteem. They seem to invite admiration (e.g., fishing for compliments) and frequently display a sense of entitlement (e.g., expecting special privileges).

The *DSM–IV–TR* also notes that narcissistic people generally lack empathy for others; they seem to have difficulty recognizing the needs, desires, and feelings of other people. They sometimes seem contemptuous of people with problems and may find it hard to provide social support (e.g., boasting about their own good health to someone who is sick). They are often arrogant or haughty, displaying disdain, snobbishness, or a patronizing attitude (e.g., commenting within earshot of a clumsy waiter that he is stupid).

Many traits of the narcissistic person seem to show a struggle with self-esteem. Although the person's grandiosity suggests high self-esteem, the person is vulnerable to criticism, defeat, shame, and humiliation. A casual remark or observation can frustrate a desire for admiration, deflating the person's self-image and causing severe negative affect (rage, disdain, defiant counterattack). Interpersonal difficulties arise because the person lacks empathy, needs excessive admiration, and displays a sense of entitlement.

The narcissistic personality disorder, like the borderline personality disorder, seems to arise from inconsistent treatment during childhood. In this case, however, the formulation emphasizes agency and self-definition. Apparently, the child was praised as brilliant, gifted, and superior (at times) and degraded as shameful, inferior, and disappointing (at other times). Brilliance and inferiority are difficult to integrate, causing split images of the self. The adult narcissist thus strives desperately to sustain an exceptional self-image, bolstered by fantasies of success, grandiosity, a sense of self-importance, and a sense of entitlement.

The other side of the split (intense inferiority) is often kept concealed because, in the narcissistic person's view, exposing shame, humiliation, or depression would itself be humiliating. Therefore, to an outside observer, the person may seem to have uniformly high self-esteem. For similar reasons, the narcissistic person would not reveal any weaknesses, including suicidal or self-injurious behavior or temper tantrums. Certainly the person is capable of intense anger, envy, and rage, but displaying those states might violate the very image that the person is trying to project.

Summary

In this chapter, we have examined the role of splitting in two personality disorders. The split in the borderline personality disorder seems to highlight the importance of communion (relationships). In the narcissistic personality disorder, it seems to highlight the importance of agency (self-definition). Splitting also plays a major role in the Axis I dissociative identity disorder, where the person, under stress, shifts to a fully developed secondary identity. Thus, the inconsistency that arises from a split identity joins the vagueness of a diffuse identity as a second form of identity disturbance. The two kinds of identity disturbance are not mutually exclusive and may even co-occur.

We assume that both forms of identity disturbance have evolved out of interpersonal experiences. Borderline people desperately need to avoid abandonment because splitting produces such rage and depression. Histrionic people desperately need to engage other people's attention because the self, without the company of others, feels empty, aimless, and bare. Narcissistic people desperately need the admiration of others because the alternative to feeling special is to feel shamefully inferior. In all three cases, the person needs other people to help satisfy these motives. Unfortunately, however, the strategies used to satisfy such motives can also drive others away.

Identity disturbance also clarifies another class of disorders, namely, the (Axis I) schizophrenic disorders. In those disorders, the person has a fragile sense of self and, under stress, becomes anxiously preoccupied with the self: "Will my already vague self vanish completely?" "Will my self be transformed into a very different self?" This anxiety produces a real dilemma for the person (whether to relate to other people or not), further complicating the person's everyday life. In the next chapter we turn to schizophrenia and related disorders.

12

Schizophrenia and Related Disorders

Schizophrenia is an Axis I disorder that frequently reflects an identity disturbance. A prerequisite to schizophrenia seems to be a biological predisposition,
but, as described below, interpersonal processes are relevant as well. The chapter also describes two personality disorders that seem to be related to schizophrenia.

Schizophrenia illustrates the diathesis-stress model with exceptional clarity. According to the diathesis-stress model, certain people are especially vulnerable to schizophrenia. Their vulnerability seems to stem from a biological
predisposition combined with certain kinds of environmental experiences involving the self and other people. Then, when the highly vulnerable person
encounters severely stressful situations, he or she succumbs to schizophrenia.
The most severe stressors seem to be interpersonal. If a person is not vulnerable or if a vulnerable person is not sufficiently stressed, the person does not
seem to develop schizophrenia. Thus, schizophrenia helps to expose the role of
interpersonal interactions in the development of psychopathology (Erickson,
Beiser, Iacono, Felming, & Lin, 1989).

In this chapter we first define schizophrenia. Then we show that people
who are prone to schizophrenic episodes have an attentional difficulty: they are
very distractible on laboratory tasks requiring concentration. In many cases,
the parents (non-schizophrenic) of people with schizophrenia also exhibit the
same attentional difficulty. Furthermore, when both generations are affected,
deviant communication patterns exist within the family that may contribute to
the development of schizophrenia in the younger generation.

Definition of Schizophrenia

At one time, schizophrenia was said to be a thought disorder (e.g., Bleuler, 1950;
Cameron, 1938). However, the term *thought disorder* has two different meanings. Sometimes it refers to a problem in the form of thinking: The person lacks
the ability to control or direct the flow of thoughts. For example, a person trying
to formulate a thought might become distracted by some irrelevant stimulus.
Terms like *loose associations* and *incoherent speech* imply that the person's ideas
shift fluidly and abruptly from one topic to another.

The other meaning of *thought disorder* refers to peculiar content in the
person's thoughts, such as bizarre delusions and auditory hallucinations. The
content may be peculiar in that the person may lose the usual boundary that
separates self from nonself. For example, a person might believe that someone
is inserting thoughts into his or her head (a bizarre delusion). Or the person

might "hear" his or her own thoughts as though they were spoken aloud by someone else (an auditory hallucination).

Both types of thought disorder have profound interpersonal consequences. People who cannot control the sequence of their thoughts cannot make themselves understood. Their verbalizations may be odd and confusing, and other people, feeling perplexed, may avoid contact with them (Nisenson & Berenbaum, 1998). The person then comes to feel anxious about social interactions and withdraws. Similarly, people who have bizarre delusions or hear auditory hallucinations also suffer interpersonal consequences. If a man believed that other people could transform his "self", he would understandably feel threatened and anxious, leading to a mistrust and avoidance of other people. Not surprising, the person might try to keep a low profile—speak little, initiate little activity, and express little affect. The resulting constellation of symptoms and signs might affect many psychological functions, producing severe anxiety, social withdrawal, flattened affect, a paucity of communication, and a drop in interpersonal motivation.

The diagnostic features of schizophrenia are listed in Exhibit 12.1. The major features include disorganized or incomprehensible speech, delusions, and hallucinations. These are said to be positive signs of schizophrenia. Negative signs reflect a diminution or absence of normal processes: The person may speak very little (*alogia*), initiate little goal-directed behavior (lack volition), or display little emotion (*flat affect*). To meet the criteria, the person should exhibit two or more of the five features continuously over a one-month period; at least some signs of disturbance should be evident for at least six months. In addition, the person's social or occupational functioning should be significantly impaired. Finally, the symptoms should not be explainable in other ways (e.g., being the result of a general medical condition). Nearly 1% of the American population experiences an episode of schizophrenia at some time in their lives.

To summarize, both types of thought disorder may induce other signs of schizophrenia. We begin with the attentional difficulty and then show that the same vulnerability may appear in the non-schizophrenic parents of people with schizophrenia. We then examine stressful consequences that contribute to schizophrenia.

Severe Attentional Distractibility

Many people who have experienced schizophrenia have written a personal account of their experience. Freedman (1974) compiled 50 firsthand, autobiographical accounts and systematically tabulated the most common symptoms that were mentioned. The single most common symptom was a severe attentional problem: difficulty concentrating and focusing attention. Some people said that their minds wandered excessively; others said they could not keep their minds on a single line of thought; others said they could not differentiate important from unimportant objects of attention. One woman said that she felt as though her attention were "being pulled in different directions by some external force;" her problem, she noted, was not merely "keeping to the point," but rather, that there were so many points, all having equal urgency and significance (p. 336). Another woman said, "If I am talking to somebody, they need only to cross their

Exhibit 12.1.   Diagnostic Criteria for Schizophrenia

A. *Characteristic symptoms:* Two (or more) of the following, each present for a significant portion of time during a 1-month period (or less if successfully treated):
   (1) delusions
   (2) hallucinations
   (3) disorganized speech (e.g., frequent derailment or incoherence)
   (4) grossly disorganized or catatonic behavior
   (5) negative symptoms, i.e., affective flattening, alogia, or avolition
   Note. Only one Criterion A symptom is required if delusions are bizarre or hallucinations consist of a voice keeping up a running commentary on the person's behavior or thoughts, or two or more voices conversing with each other.
B. *Social/occupational dysfunction:* For a significant portion of the time since the onset of the disturbance, one or more major areas of functioning such as work, interpersonal relations, or self-care are markedly below the level achieved prior to the onset (or when the onset is in childhood or adolescence, failure to achieve expected level of interpersonal, academic, or occupational achievement).
C. *Duration:* Continuous signs of the disturbance persist for at least 6 months. This 6-month period must include at least 1 month of symptoms (or less if successfully treated) that meet Criterion A (i.e., active-phase symptoms) and may include periods of prodromal or residual symptoms. During these prodromal or residual periods, the signs of the disturbance may be manifested by only negative symptoms or two or more symptoms listed in Criterion A present in an attenuated form (e.g., odd beliefs, unusual perceptual experiences).
D. *Schizoaffective and Mood Disorder exclusion:* Schizoaffective Disorder and Mood Disorder With Psychotic Features have been ruled out because either (1) no Major Depressive, Manic, or Mixed Episodes have occurred concurrently with the active-phase symptoms; or (2) if mood episodes have occurred during active-phase symptoms, their total duration has been brief relative to the duration of the active and residual periods.
E. *Substance/general medical condition exclusion:* The disturbance is not due to the direct physiological effects of a substance (e.g., a drug of abuse, a medication) or a general medical condition.
F. *Relationship to a Pervasive Developmental Disorder:* If there is a history of Autistic Disorder or another Pervasive Developmental Disorder, the additional diagnosis of Schizophrenia is made only if prominent delusions or hallucinations are also present for at least a month (or less if successfully treated).

Note. From *Diagnostic and Statistical Manual of Mental Disorders* (4th ed., Text Revision, p. 312), by the American Psychiatric Association, 2000, Washington, DC: Author. Reprinted with permission.

legs or scratch their heads, and I am distracted and forget what I was saying" (p. 336).

A related problem is called *racing thoughts*. People with this problem have so many thoughts simultaneously that they cannot select a single thought as the object of focus. Their thoughts move so quickly that the person is constantly drawn from one thought to an unrelated thought. One woman commented that her thoughts "were whirling around, wild and free, distinctly out of control" (p. 335). Another spoke of thoughts wandering around in circles without going anywhere; she noted that it took ages to read a paragraph in a book because each bit "starts me thinking in ten different directions at once" (p. 335). In describing the experience, people frequently used words that express confusion: confused, foggy, bewildered, dazed, disoriented, feeling hazy.

Perhaps the worst case of attentional distractibility occurs in the famous *word salad*. Each phrase that the person utters seems to arouse a tangential thought that upstages the earlier thought, so the person's speech is altogether incoherent and unintelligible. Bleuler (1950) illustrated the word salad with a fragment from a letter written by a schizophrenic man:

> One must have arisen sufficiently early and then there is usually the necessary appetite present. "L'appetit vient en mangeant," says the Frenchman. With time and years the individual becomes so lazy in public life that he is not even capable of writing any more. On such a sheet of paper, one can squeeze many letters if one is careful not to transgress by one "square shoe." In such fine weather one should be able to take a walk in the woods. (p. 20)

The text begins "One must have arisen sufficiently early," suggesting the idea of breakfast, which seems to elicit the thought "and then there is usually the necessary appetite present." The idea of appetite, in turn, suggests the proverb "L'appetit vient en mangeant," written in French, so it arouses thoughts of state and government. And so on. The person is apparently unable to inhibit irrelevant associations.

Sometimes attentional difficulties are evident in a person's responses on an intelligence test. For example, a person may answer rather difficult questions correctly but occasionally miss very easy questions. As one example, a person was asked, "Who was the first president of the United States?" and responded, "the White House" (Arieti, 1974, p. 263). Lapses of this kind would lead an examiner to consider the possibility of a significant attentional problem.

A Laboratory Measure of Attentional Distractibility

Simple laboratory tasks have been developed to study attentional distractibility. Oltmanns and Neale (1975; 1978), for example, had participants listen to strings of digits recorded in a woman's voice that were presented at a two-second rate into the participant's left ear (e.g., 7-4-9-1-8-3). After hearing a given string, the participant was to repeat the digits verbatim. The participant was told to ignore any message that was presented to the right ear. On some trials, nothing was presented to the participant's right ear ("no distractor" trials). On other trials, competing strings of digits in a man's voice were presented to the right ear ("distractor" trials). Distractors generally impair everyone's recall, so anyone (whether or not they had schizophrenia) would find it harder to recall a string of digits if a distractor was competing for the person's attention; but the impairment should be greater for those with schizophrenia than for those without the disorder. Therefore, two groups of participants (matched for gender, age, and education) were studied: patients with schizophrenia and inmates without schizophrenia from a New York City correctional institution.

Table 12.1. Mean Proportion of Strings Correctly Recalled

String	Participant	
	Nonschizophrenic	Schizophrenic
6 digits, no distractors	.82	.74
6 digits, with distractors	.69	.48

Note. From "Schizophrenic Performance When Distractors Are Present," by T. F. Oltmanns and J. M. Neale, 1975, *Journal of Abnormal Psychology, 84,* p. 207. Copyright © 1975 by the American Psychological Association. Reprinted with permission of the authors.

Table 12.1 shows the mean proportion of six-digit strings that the participants in each group recalled correctly. Not surprising, the participants without schizophrenia recalled more strings correctly, with or without distractors. Furthermore, both groups showed a significant decrement due to the distractors, but the decrement was significantly greater for participants with schizophrenia than for those without the disorder: For individuals without schizophrenia, the difference was .82 − .69 = .13; for individuals with schizophrenia, that difference was twice as large: .74 − .48 = .26. Thus, distractors affected both groups, but the impairment was substantially greater for individuals with schizophrenia. In another study, the investigators showed that the degree of impairment caused by distractors was correlated with the presence of symptoms like incoherence and loose associations.

A Measure of Associative Distractibility

Chapman and his associates (e.g., Rattan & Chapman, 1973) devised another measure of attentional distractibility. They prepared a multiple-choice test in which every item contained a stimulus of the form "Word W means the same as" plus four choices. The participant had to select the best answer. One of the more difficult items, for example, was the following:

> *SHOOT* means the same as: (A) book; (B) rug; (C) sprout;
> (D) none of the above.

Shoot (as in *bamboo shoot*) means the same as *sprout* (as in *alfalfa sprout*), so the correct answer is (C). Another version of the item contained a distractor:

> *SHOOT* means the same as: (A) rifle; (B) rug; (C) sprout;
> (D) none of the above.

In this form of the item, *rifle*, a strong associate of *SHOOT*, is one of the incorrect choices. *Rifle* attracts the attention of a schizophrenic patient: It seems so strongly related to SHOOT that it upstages an important detail in the instructions—namely, "means the same as"—and is selected more often by individuals with schizophrenia than by individuals without schizophrenia.

Two forms of the test were prepared. Each form listed 30 items with a distractor and 30 items without a distractor; an item that appeared one way in one form appeared the other way in the other form.

With a distracting associate:
SHOOT means the same as:
(A) rifle (associate)
(B) rug (irrelevant)
(C) sprout (correct)
(D) none of the above

Without a distracting associate:
SHOOT means the same as:
(A) book (irrelevant)
(B) rug (irrelevant)
(C) sprout (correct)
(D) none of the above

The test was administered to three groups of participants: a group of men hospitalized with schizophrenia and two comparison groups. Because schizophrenia impairs the person's performance, the patients were compared with two comparison groups, one comparable in intelligence to the participants with schizophrenia and one lower in intelligence. Men in the group with schizophrenia, on the average, had completed 11.3 years of school. Those in the first comparison group had completed 11.9 years of school, those in the second comparison group, 9.4 years.

Table 12.2 shows the mean number of items (out of 60) of each type that participants in each group answered correctly. Neither comparison group was affected by the presence of a distracting associate; their performance was similar with or without a distractor. Only the participants with schizophrenia made more errors when a distractor was present. Their performance on the "no distractor" items was comparable to that of the dull control participants, but their performance on the "distractor" items was significantly worse. Boland and Chapman (1971) showed that additional errors occurred because the individuals with schizophrenia more often selected the distracting associate.

"Attentional slippage" caused by an attention-getting associate can be observed in people without schizophrenia as well when the pull of the distracting associate is strong enough. The following example illustrates the process:

The string of letters P-O-L-K is pronounced "poke" with a silent "l." F-O-L-K is pronounced "foke," also with a silent "l." And the white of an egg is pronounced how? _____.

It is a rare person who remembers, under these conditions, that the white of an egg is pronounced *albumen*. The associative pull from *POLK* and *FOLK* to *YOLK* is so strong that we lose track of the task itself, namely, to find a word that *means the same as* the white of an egg. Powerful associates compel our attention and upstage details of the original task.

Attentional Distractibility in Relatives of People With Schizophrenia

CHILDREN OF PARENTS WITH SCHIZOPHRENIA   Similar tasks have been used to study attentional distractibility in the "not-yet-old-enough-to-have-schizophrenia" children of people with schizophrenia. The probability is approximately

Table 12.2.   Mean Number of Correct Responses in Each Condition

Condition	With distractor	Without distractor
Comparison group 1 (nonclinical)	36.4	35.3
Comparison group 2 (dull, nonclinical)	27.9	28.0
Schizophrenic individuals	22.4	28.0

Note. From "Associative Intrusions in Schizophrenic Verbal Behavior," by R. B. Rattan and L. J. Chapman, 1973, *Journal of Abnormal Psychology, 82,* p. 171. Copyright © 1973 by the American Psychological Association. Adapted with permission of the author.

.01 that a child selected at random from the general population will one day be diagnosed with schizophrenia. That probability increases to .15 for people whose mothers have (or have had) schizophrenia. In general, schizophrenia does not manifest itself until late in adolescence or early adulthood, typically between the late teens and the mid-30s, so children whose mothers have had schizophrenia are said to be at risk for schizophrenia. The following study tested the attentional distractibility of children of mothers with schizophrenia before any of them exhibited symptoms of schizophrenia.

Asarnow, Steffy, MacCrimmon, and Cleghorn (1977) compared three groups of children who were 15 to 16 years old. The children of one group were born to mothers with schizophrenia but raised in a foster home from the age of 8 or 9; they formed a *high-risk foster group.* The children of a second group had been separated from their parents (without schizophrenia) at approximately the same age; they formed a *foster control group.* The children of a third group had always lived with their biological parents; they formed a *never-separated control group.* The task required each child to watch the center of a screen on which a T or F periodically flashed, and the child had to name the target letter. On some trials distracting letters appeared briefly in peripheral locations on the screen. The number of distractors varied from trial to trial—0, 2, 4, or 9 distractor letters. The child was instructed to ignore the distractors and report the target letter. As the number of distracting letters increased, the child's performance in every group declined. However, the impairment was greatest for the high-risk children. Other studies using other methods (e.g., Griffith, Mednick, Schulsinger, & Diderichsen, 1980) have shown a similar vulnerability among children who are biologically at risk.

PARENTS OF PEOPLE WITH SCHIZOPHRENIA   Parents of people with schizophrenia also seem to have attentional difficulties even if they do not have schizophrenia. In a series of studies, Singer and Wynne (1965a, 1965b; Wynne, 1977) examined families in which the son or daughter had developed schizophrenia. As the researchers met with the families, they observed many cryptic and ambiguous communications between family members. The following excerpt from a family therapy session illustrates the problem.

> Teenage daughter: Nobody will listen to me. Everybody is trying to still me.
> Mother: Nobody wants to kill you.
> Father: If you're going to associate with intellectual people, you'll have to remember that still is a noun and not a verb.

Sadly, the daughter wanted to say something important to them, but the parents' replies deflected attention away from her statement. Singer and Wynne hypothesized that the parents of children with schizophrenia (including those who had never had schizophrenia) may have attentional difficulties of their own, thereby aggravating the son or daughter's attentional problem. According to their hypothesis, parents usually help children establish a shared focus of attention, but parents with attentional difficulties are less able to perform this parental function. If a child is burdened with (and frustrated by) attentional difficulties, cryptic communications from a distractible parent might compound the problem.

To study attentional difficulties, Singer and Wynne administered the Rorschach Inkblot Test to the parents of recovering children with schizophrenia. When a person takes the test, the person has to attend to each inkblot, achieve and sustain a reasonably clear perception, and then describe that perception to the examiner. Sustained attention is essential. The investigators first identified 20 families in which the son or daughter had developed schizophrenia as a young adult and 15 other families in which the son or daughter had been hospitalized for some other psychiatric disorder (e.g., a severe obsessive-compulsive disorder). No parent in either group had ever been diagnosed with schizophrenia. The Rorschach responses of each parent were transcribed verbatim, and a clinical psychologist judged whether the responses of each set of parents seemed to reflect an attentional difficulty. From this information the psychologist tried to guess whether the son or daughter of that family was apt to have schizophrenia. Of the 20 families with a son or daughter with schizophrenia, 17 were identified correctly as schizophrenic from the parents' responses; of the 15 other families, 13 were identified correctly as not schizophrenic.

Here are some examples of Rorschach responses that suggested attentional difficulties (Singer & Wynne, 1965a). The first illustrates a problem in sustaining and describing a perception.

> [Rorschach Card I] This thing here makes you want to—these sort of handles here, make you want to—that wouldn't—might not be—doors closing, closed doors or something. Although that line—isn't as definite and straight as would be if it were doors, I don't know, I don't think—but I don't know. This could be—no, I guess not. Mmm, it could be. . . (p. 193)

Here is another example in which the parent could not sustain the original perception.

> [Rorschach Card I] That looks like a bat. The more I look at it, the less it seems like that, I guess. I'm not sure about that bat anymore. (p. 194)
> [Rorschach Card VIII] As I look at that card, it's changing. (p. 195)

In other cases the parent described a perception and immediately rejected it (i.e., a perception and then a denial of that perception).

> [Rorschach Card II] That's not a dog, and it's not a sheep, and it's not a crocodile. (p. 194)

[Rorschach Card III] Couldn't be a tree, no ground there; couldn't be hawks' claws, not enough claws. (p. 194)

Other early studies showed similar attentional and communication difficulties among the parents of people with schizophrenia. Feinsilver (1970) devised a procedure in which a parent without schizophrenia was seated back-to-back with his or her (recovered) son or daughter. A series of objects were shown to one member of the dyad, and that person was instructed to name characteristics of each object to help the other person guess what it was. The 30 objects included a battery, a bell, a magnifying glass, a whistle, and so on. The speaker's communications were studied. One parent of a person with schizophrenia, for example, described the bell by saying, "It's circular to make a noise." This wording confusingly suggests that the object's circularity causes the sound. Another parent said of a spool of white thread, "It's white and tight." Juxtaposing the two ideas ("the thread is white" and "the thread is wound tight") into a highly condensed rhyme seems to confuse, rather than enlighten. Unclear communications were common among the parents (without schizophrenia) of people with schizophrenia, leading the son or daughter to misidentify the object. Similar results were reported by Wild, Shapiro, and Goldenberg (1975).

The term *communication deviance* (CD) refers to these various anomalies: unclear, amorphous, fragmented, or ambiguous language that obscures meaning and blurs the focus of attention (Segrin, 2001). It is frequently observed among biological relatives of people who develop schizophrenia. Miklowitz et al. (1991) administered the Thematic Apperception Test to patients and their parents shortly after the patients were discharged from the hospital and scored the responses for CD. The family also spent 10 minutes discussing family problems, and the family discussions were transcribed and scored for CD. In general, parents who showed high levels of CD on one task showed high levels on the other task. Table 12.3 shows different types of CD observed in the first 10 minutes of family discussions. The most frequent forms were idea fragments and odd word usage. We return to this measure in the next section when we examine family interactions more closely.

Schizotypal Personality Disorder

Observations like these have led to an Axis II diagnosis called the *schizotypal personality disorder*. People classified this way show the odd thinking and vague, digressive speech that seems so familiar among the relatives of individuals with schizophrenia. To use an example from the *DSM–IV–TR*, the person might say "I wasn't very talkable at work today," combining *talkative* and *sociable* into the nonword *talkable*. Similar peculiarities may be observed in the person's physical appearance or behavior. To others the person seems odd or eccentric. In addition, people with schizotypal personality disorder often seem to be socially anxious—stiff, inappropriate, or constricted socially. Intense social anxiety seems to prevent intimate contact with others, so a person with schizotypal personality disorder typically lacks a close friend.

It is possible that these characteristics—odd thinking, odd behavior, social anxiety, and a lack of friends—reinforce one another. People who seem a little

Table 12.3. Examples of Communication Deviance

ICD code	Definition	Example	Occurrences Parents M	Parents SD	Patients M	Patients SD	Reliability[a]
Idea fragments	Speaker abandons ideas or abruptly ends comments without returning to them	"But the thing is as I said, there's got . . . you can't drive in the alley."	3.15	2.78	2.02	2.75	.90
Unintelligible remarks	Comments are incomprehensible in the context of conversation	"Well, that's just *probably a real closing spot.*"	<1	0.51	<1	0.71	.78
Contradictions or retractions	Speaker contradicts earlier statements or presents mutually inconsistent alternatives	"No, that's right, she does."	<1	0.48	<1	0.73	.67
Ambiguous references	Speaker uses sentences with no clear object of discussion	"Kid stuff that's one thing but *something else is different too.*"	1.91	1.83	1.65	2.15	.72
Extraneous remarks	Speaker makes off-task comments	"I wonder how many rooms they have like this?"	<1	0.46	<1	1.48	.85
Tangential inappropriate response	Nonsequitur replies or speaker does not acknowledge others' statements	Patient: "Sometimes I work on the back yard." Mother: "Let's talk about your schoolwork."	<1	0.50	<1	0.45	.80
Odd word usage or odd sentence construction	Speaker uses words in odd ways, leaves out words, puts words out of order, uses many unnecessary words	"It's gonna be *up and downwards along the process all the while to* go through something like this."	4.10	3.50	3.85	4.84	.96

Note. ICD = International Classification of Diseases. From "Communication Deviance in Families of Schizophrenic and Manic Patients," by D. J. Miklowitz, D. I. Velligan, M. J. Goldstein, K. H. Neuchterlein, et al., 1991, *Journal of Abnormal Psychology, 100,* p. 167. Copyright © 1991 by the American Psychological Association. Reprinted with permission of the authors. [a]Based on percentage of agreements.

odd tend to be shunned by others, even as children. They receive fewer social invitations from others, and other people avoid and reject them. They therefore find social interactions aversive, come to doubt themselves socially, and become socially anxious. Their social anxiety then exacerbates their apparent oddness, and they are shunned even more.

Later in this chapter we consider other consequences of odd thinking, odd behavior, social anxiety, and social isolation. For now, we simply list the features described in *DSM–IV–TR* (see Exhibit 12.2). The person may acquire odd beliefs or exhibit magical thinking. For example, the person may believe that he or she has special powers to read other people's thoughts or to sense events before they happen. One person described in *DSM–IV–TR* believed that his spouse was taking the dog out for a walk because an hour earlier he himself had thought that it needed to be done.

The person with schizotypal personality disorder may be superstitious or strongly believe in clairvoyance, telepathy, or a "sixth sense." Furthermore, individuals with the disorder express ideas of reference; that is, they incorrectly interpret events as having a particular relevance, meaning, or significance to themselves. For example, an individual with schizotypal personality disorder may conclude that two strangers talking on the street are talking about him. According to *DSM–IV–TR* (American Psychiatric Association, 2000, p. 699), the schizotypal personality disorder occurs in approximately 3% of the general population and is more prevalent among the first-degree biological relatives of individuals with schizophrenia than among the general population (p. 699); moreover, it sometimes precedes the onset of schizophrenia (p. 304).

Marker Versus Symptom of Schizophrenia

A symptom (or sign) of schizophrenia is evident during a schizophrenic episode, but a "marker" of the disorder refers to an indicator that the person is vulnerable to schizophrenia (not necessarily warranting a diagnosis of schizophrenia). Rosenbaum, Shore, and Chapin (1988) devised a simple laboratory procedure that differentiates one from the other. The task they used was a simple reaction time task. At the beginning of a trial, a buzzer tells the participant to get ready. The participant places his or her forefinger on a telegraph key and waits for a stimulus light to appear. The moment the light appears, the participant releases the telegraph key as quickly as possible. The participant's reaction time is the amount of time between the onset of the light and the participant's response. The sequence is then repeated on many successive trials.

Ready signal (buzzer)	→	Participant presses telegraph key	→	Stimulus light appears	→	Participant releases telegraph key

Consider the interval of time between the ready signal (the buzzer) and the appearance of the stimulus light (the *preparatory interval*). If the length of the interval changes from trial to trial, the participant cannot tell exactly when the light will appear: The interval might be 4 seconds long, 10 seconds long, even 20

Exhibit 12.2.   Diagnostic Criteria for Schizotypal Personality Disorder

A. A pervasive pattern of social and interpersonal deficits marked by acute discomfort with, and reduced capacity for, close relationships as well as by cognitive or perceptual distortions and eccentricities of behavior, beginning by early adulthood and present in a variety of contexts, as indicated by five (or more) of the following:
  (1) ideas of reference (excluding delusions of reference)
  (2) odd beliefs or magical thinking that influences behavior and is inconsistent with subcultural norms (e.g., superstitiousness, belief in clairvoyance, telepathy, or "sixth sense"; in children and adolescents, bizarre fantasies or preoccupations)
  (3) unusual perceptual experiences, including bodily illusions
  (4) odd thinking and speech (e.g., vague, circumstantial, metaphorical, overelaborate, or stereotyped)
  (5) suspiciousness or paranoid ideation
  (6) inappropriate or constricted affect
  (7) behavior or appearance that is odd, eccentric, or peculiar
  (8) lack of close friends or confidants other than first-degree relatives
  (9) excessive social anxiety that does not diminish with familiarity and tends to be associated with paranoid fears rather than negative judgments about self
B. Does not occur exclusively during the course of schizophrenia, a mood disorder with psychotic features, another psychotic disorder, or a pervasive developmental disorder.

Note. If criteria are met prior to the onset of schizophrenia, add "premorbid" (e.g., "Schizotypal Personality Disorder [Premorbid]"). From *Diagnostic and Statistical Manual of Mental Disorders* (4th ed., Text Revision, p. 701), by the American Psychiatric Association, 2000, Washington, DC: Author. Reprinted with permission.

seconds long. In that case, the person's reaction time from trial to trial would be very similar, no matter how long the preparatory interval. For control participants, this reaction time is approximately 260 milliseconds.

Suppose, however, the preparatory interval were the same on every trial in a block of trials. For example, suppose the time between the buzzer (the signal to get ready) and the light were always four seconds long. Then participants would be able to keep their attention sustained for four seconds, knowing that the light will appear in four seconds, and they would be able to react more quickly to the light. For control participants, this reaction time is approximately 220 milliseconds. Thus, a fixed (constant) preparatory interval that is four seconds long shortens the reaction time from 260 milliseconds to 220 milliseconds.

If the preparatory interval were 7.5 seconds on every trial in a block, the participants could use that interval to advantage, but the advantage would not be as great because it is harder to keep one's attention sustained for 7.5 seconds. The reaction time in that case would be reduced from 260 milliseconds to 230 milliseconds. If the preparatory interval were very long (say, 20 or 30 seconds), the person's attention would start to wander, and the person would be unprepared when the stimulus light appeared. In that case, the reaction time would be approximately 260 milliseconds (no advantage). These values are shown in Figure 12.1.

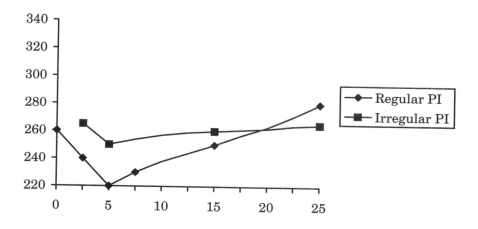

Figure 12.1. Reaction time for control participants (students) as a function of preparatory interval (PI).

The two curves in Figure 12.1 cross at 17.7 seconds. That means that control participants can take advantage of a preparatory interval up to 17 or 18 seconds, but a preparatory interval longer than that would be of no use. This upper limit, 17.7 seconds, is called the *crossover point*. The investigators compared three groups: control participants, participants with schizotypal personality disorder, and participants with schizophrenia. As shown in Table 12.4, participants with either schizotypal personality disorder or schizophrenia both had a substantially lower crossover point than control participants. Because of their difficulty sustaining attention, a preparatory interval longer than eight or nine seconds provides no advantage. The crossover point thus differentiates control participants from the two vulnerable groups, so it is considered to be a marker of schizophrenia.

In addition, the investigators assessed each participant's overall reaction time. As shown in Table 12.4, the mean reaction time was similar for control participants and participants with schizotypal personality disorder (neither group had the handicap observed for participants with schizophrenia). Participants with schizophrenia took much longer to respond. Thus, the mean reaction time differentiated participants with schizophrenia from those in the two groups without schizophrenia. To summarize, the crossover point differentiated the two vulnerable groups from the control group; it constituted a marker of schizophrenia. However, the reaction time was greater only for those with schizophrenia so it constituted a symptom of schizophrenia.

Interpersonal Interactions Across Two Generations

Consider families in which a primary caretaker and a child are both vulnerable to schizophrenia. In a classic study, Waring and Ricks (1965) identified people who, as children, had received treatment at a particular child guidance clinic. At that time, they were, on average, 14 years old. No one in the sample developed schizophrenia at age 14, but some of them were later hospitalized for schizo-

Table 12.4.   Mean Crossover Point and Reaction Time (RT) for Each Group of Participants

RT	Schizophrenic	Schizotypal	Control
Crossover point (seconds)	8.9	8.6	17.7
Overall RT (milliseconds)	467	265	260

Note. From "Attention Deficit in Schizophrenia and Schizotypy," by G. Rosenbaum, D. L. Shore, and K. Chapin, 1988, *Journal of Abnormal Psychology, 97,* p. 45. Copyright © 1988 by the American Psychological Association. Reprinted with permission of the authors.

phrenia. (The median age of hospitalization was 21.) The investigators identified two samples of people who had been treated at the clinic: 50 who later developed schizophrenia (Group S) and 50 who did not (Group N). The two groups were matched for gender, IQ, ethnic background, social class, age at the time of treatment, and symptoms for which they had been treated. Then the investigators examined the childhood records compiled at the clinic. These records contained detailed information about the parents' personalities, the nature of the parents' marriage, and the parent–child relationships.

The records contained sparse information about the fathers because many of the fathers had refused to be interviewed or were absent from the family because of divorce, desertion, or death. More information existed about the mothers' personalities. Although the term *schizotypal personality disorder* had not yet been coined, the traits that we now associate with that disorder stood out. The mothers of Group S were more often described by terms like *odd, vague, incoherent, evasive,* and *peculiar*. They were also frequently described as fearful, nervous, worried, and withdrawn.

The investigators also examined descriptions of the mother–child relationship. The term *symbiotic union* was used to describe one prominent feature of Group S families. This term implied that the mother seemed to overstep boundaries that normally separate two people; that is, she seemed to regard the child's thoughts, feelings, and wishes as an extension of her own and, as a result, unintentionally undermined the child's sense of self as separate, autonomous, and independent. In cases that I have known, one mother dressed herself and her daughter alike, read every book that the daughter was reading, and stated that she had exactly the same interests and feelings that her daughter expressed. In another case the mother was unwittingly intrusive into her son's affairs, regarding it as perfectly natural to ask him about personal matters and also share with him details of her own gynecological problems. In a third case the mother would benignly rephrase feelings, thoughts, and wishes that her son had expressed, so that they matched her own,

Measures of Family Atmosphere

In more recent years, three measures of the family atmosphere have been developed that may help clarify the origin of schizophrenia: CD, expressed emotion (EE), and affective style. We next consider each of these measures of the family atmosphere and the hints they offer about the origin of a schizophrenic disorder.

COMMUNICATION DEVIANCE As described earlier, CD refers to odd or amorphous wording of communications that blurs meaning, obscures the focus of attention, and befuddles the listener. In general, CD occurs more often among the parents of people with schizophrenia than among the parents of people without schizophrenia (Miklowitz, 1994). M. J. Goldstein (1981, 1987) studied a sample of adolescent children (on average, approximately 16 years old) who were in treatment for behavioral difficulties; none of them showed signs of schizophrenia at that time. The investigators also assessed the amount of CD in the speech of their parents. Five years later, when the participants were young adults, they were retested to determine which participants were now showing definite signs of schizophrenia. The parents' level of CD was the best predictor of these signs of schizophrenia. Eight of the 40 participants (now 21 years old, on average) were showing signs of the disorder, and all of them were from families that had exhibited a high level of CD. J. M. Lewis, Rodnick, and Goldstein (1981) showed that high-CD families exhibit other (nonverbal) anomalies as well. For example, high-CD parents more often avoid eye contact with their son or daughter than do low CD parents.

Suppose a biologically vulnerable child were raised in a low-CD family. The child would have a predisposing diathesis, but suppose the atmosphere at home were not stressful. Would that child be likely to develop schizophrenia? Or suppose a nonvulnerable child were raised in a high-CD family: That child would lack a predisposing diathesis, but suppose the atmosphere at home were quite stressful. Would that child be prone to schizophrenia? To answer these questions, investigators in Finland identified children who had been given up for adoption between 1960 and 1979 (Wahlberg et al., 1997). There were two groups of adoptees: (a) a "high-risk" sample of 58 whose biological mothers had been hospitalized for schizophrenia and (b) a "low-risk" (comparison) sample of 96 others. Children in the two samples were matched in various ways (e.g., age of adoptive parents, gender of child, age at placement, socioeconomic status). On average, the adoptees were 15 months old when they were placed in the adoptive family. Later, when they were young adults (approximately 21 years old), the members of each family were interviewed and tested. A measure of CD was computed for the adoptive parents in each family, and the two groups of adoptive parents did not differ significantly on average.

Finally, the investigators evaluated each adoptee for signs of odd or incipiently disordered thinking and correlated this outcome with the family's degree of CD. For the "high-risk" (vulnerable) sample, the two variables showed a striking relationship. That is, high-risk offspring adopted into a family with parents with high CD showed substantial disordered thinking, whereas high-risk offspring adopted into a family with parents with low CD showed little disordered thinking. For the "low-risk" (comparison) sample, the two variables were uncorrelated.

Communication deviance seems to reflect a biological vulnerability that is transmitted genetically. However, the child's vulnerability seems to be exacerbated if the parents' style of communicating is cryptic, amorphous, or unfocused. In other words, the combination of a vulnerable child in a high-CD family environment may be especially noxious. Perhaps that is why a measure of the family's CD also helps us predict relapse. If an individual who has recovered from schizophrenia returns home to a family that is high in CD, the person is more likely than other individuals who have recovered from schizophrenia to have a relapse within one year (Rund, Oie, Borchgrevink, & Fjell, 1995; Velligan et al., 1996).

EXPRESSED EMOTION   A second measure of family atmosphere has been called *expressed emotion*. This measure, which seems to be relatively independent of CD (N. M. Docherty, 1995; Miklowitz et al., 1986), reflects emotional attitudes toward a patient within a family (Cutting & Docherty, 2000). Each relative's EE is assessed in a one- to two-hour semistructured interview. The interviewer asks the relative about the patient's psychiatric history, symptoms, and daily activities. The interview is audiotaped, and several characteristics of the responses are evaluated. The primary ingredient in the measure is the number of critical comments made about the patient—6 or more critical comments constitute a high score. A second ingredient is the hostility expressed. Whereas a criticism concerns the patient's actions, hostility reflects a global feeling about the whole person (e.g., "I can't stand to be around her"). A third ingredient is called *emotional over-involvement*. An over-involved relative may be overprotective toward the patient or very dramatic about the patient's illness. Of the three ingredients, the number of critical comments seems to carry the greatest weight.

C. E. Vaughn and Leff (1981) studied the attitudes more closely that distinguish high- from low-EE relatives. They noted, first, that schizophrenic patients are often uncomfortable with interpersonal closeness, and low-EE relatives seem to respect the patient's desire for social distance. High-EE relatives are more intrusive; they make repeated attempts to establish contact, and they keep offering unsolicited (often critical) advice. Second, low-EE relatives seem more confident, less anxious about the patient's illness. They seem to cope with crises effectively and exert a calming influence on the patient and other family members. High-EE relatives, on the other hand, respond to the patient's illness with more distress or anger. Third, low-EE relatives consider the patient to be suffering from a legitimate illness, whereas high-EE relatives seem to doubt that the patient is genuinely ill; they frequently blame the patient for the condition. Finally, low-EE relatives are generally tolerant of the patient's symptoms and impairments, whereas high-EE relatives are less tolerant and more impatient.

A striking finding keeps appearing in the literature relating EE to a patient's relapse. When schizophrenic patients recover and are discharged from the hospital, those who return to a household with at least one high-EE relative are more apt to relapse within a year than those who return to a low-EE home (G. W. Brown, Birley, & Wing, 1972; G. W. Brown, Carstairs, & Topping, 1958). This result has been confirmed many times. Butzlaff and Hooley (1998) reported a meta-analysis that combined the results of 23 studies and showed a robust effect. Similarly, Bebbington and Kuipers (1994) aggregated data from 25 studies and reached the same conclusion. They showed a 50% relapse rate for patients who returned to high-EE households, but only a 21% relapse rate for those who returned to low-EE households. Two other protective factors help prevent a relapse—patients do better if they (a) take their medication regularly and (b) have less face-to-face contact with a high-EE parent. The strongest protective factor, however, seems to be a low-EE household (M. J. Goldstein &

Strachan, 1987). The importance of EE is not unique to schizophrenia; a low-EE environment also prevents relapse in depression, anorexia, and bipolar disorder (Hooley & Hiller, 1997).

AFFECTIVE STYLE   A third measure of family atmosphere has been described by Doane, West, Goldstein, Rodnick, and Jones (1981). This measure, like EE, concerns emotional attitudes. Whereas EE is assessed by interviewing a relative, affective style is based on the verbatim transcript of a family discussion involving the patient and other family members. Various positive and negative categories are scored that include personal criticisms (e.g., "You have an ugly, arrogant attitude"), guilt induction (e.g., "You cause our family an awful lot of trouble"), critical intrusiveness (e.g., "You enjoy being mean to others"), and a lack of support. This measure also predicts relapse (Doane, Falloon, Goldstein, & Mintz, 1985; Doane, Goldstein, Miklowitz, & Falloon, 1986). It seems to overlap with EE but requires judgments that are harder to rate reliably (Hooley & Hiller, 1997).

Why do these factors affect relapse? To begin with, CD probably reflects a biological vulnerability that causes problems with selective attention and related processes. This difficulty seems to manifest itself in impulsive or unfocused thinking. The vulnerability alone need not be pathogenic, but in a high-CD household, the child may struggle to be understood (and thus feel inept about making perceptions and wishes known). The child may also struggle to decipher the meanings, intentions, and wishes of others. Therefore, a child in this situation may be burdened with interpersonal frustrations. If the child also happens to provoke criticism, anger, and guilt-induction from family members (high EE, negative affective style), interpersonal interactions would adversely affect the person's self-image and generate stress. At the very time when the person needs repose and support, the household may intensify the level of stress.

Possible Consequences for a Vulnerable Child

What would a vulnerable child experience if, day after day, an adult were vague, unclear, or tangential and then chided the child for not paying attention? What would the experience be like if, day after day, a well-meaning adult, affected by his or her own fluid associations, challenged, distorted, and "corrected" the child's feelings, thoughts, and wishes, as though the child kept misreading internal states of self and others? Different children learn to cope in different ways. Some children would probably withdraw in self-defense. Ellison, van Os, and Murray (1998) reviewed a substantial literature that examined the childhood behavior of individuals who later were diagnosed with schizophrenia. The literature not only highlights the preschizophrenic child's poor concentration and passivity; it also reveals substantial social withdrawal. For example, children who later become schizophrenic show a preference for solitary play by ages 4 to 6; by ages 13–15, teachers describe them as retiring, aloof, timid, and socially anxious.

A child who withdraws must also pay a price for social isolation. Consider a typical example of the experience of a child without schizophrenia: A four-year-old child that I once knew was away from his mother for several hours, playing at the home of a friend, when he began to feel uneasy. He was sure that his mother was worrying about him and insisted that he be taken home. When the suggestion was made that he telephone his mother to ask how she was and to let her know that he was safe, he rejected the proposal on the grounds that he could "feel" his mother worrying. Upon his arrival home, his mother greeted him—cheerful, intact, and completely unworried. They talked about his concern, his mother reassured him that she was safe and happy, and, following this bit of reality testing, he revised his earlier hypothesis. Had he been a more isolated child, he would not have had the opportunity to verbalize, test, and alter the belief that he could "feel" his mother worrying.

As noted before, adults regularly help children label and describe internal states, thereby sharpening their sense of self as distinct and valid. A mother might say, "I know you don't like mashed potatoes, but try these; they are different." The statement acknowledges, labels, and validates the child's dislike, thereby affirming the child's sense of self. Similarly, the question "Do you want to keep this old blanket, or may I throw it out" acknowledges a private internal state that only the child is privy to. Such comments acknowledge the uniqueness and consistency of the child's inner experience. In contrast, an isolated child would have fewer such exchanges, and the self would be less sharply defined.

Some dysfunctional beliefs concern the person's vulnerability to outside influence. As described in chapter 1, some people acquire an intense fear that their existence is threatened by other people's influence, that their self might vanish or be overtaken. This fear, which we have called *ontological insecurity*, is the intense worry that another person might overpower and encompass one's self. Such fears amount to a fear of dying and generate intense anxiety.

To summarize, cognitions acquired in childhood—such as a belief that "I can feel another person's feelings," that "other people can read my thoughts," or that "I can be transformed into someone else"—can be quite disturbing. When a vulnerable person is isolated, the person lacks opportunities for reality testing, and dysfunctional beliefs go unchallenged, persist over time, and thrive under stress.

Ontological Insecurity and Schizophrenia

Most people take the self for granted. We feel real and alive and expect to continue existing day after day. We differentiate between our "body" and our "self" as co-existing entities that came into existence when we were born, and we generally regard the self as consistent, unique, and permanent. R. D. Laing (1965) first used the term *ontological security* to denote a sense of security that the self will continue existing as long as the body is alive. Not everyone feels ontologically secure, however. Some people regard the self as insubstantial and fragile; they worry that the self might change beyond recognition or stop existing altogether. They feel so vulnerable to outside influence and so responsive to other people's suggestions that, in self-defense, they cannot permit other people to get close.

Variations of this theme get expressed in treatment. One man felt that the treatment process could rob him of his individuality. Early in the treatment he believed that he was unable to resist anything the therapist said and feared that he would gradually be transformed into a replica of the therapist. Another patient became anxious and angry if others did not recognize her uniqueness. If a friend proposed an activity together that the patient happened not to enjoy, the patient complained that her friend "has no idea who I am" and that her friend was dismissively trying to take her over.

Laing (1965) described several variations of the problem. In one, which he called *engulfment*, the person worries that the self might be engulfed by another more powerful person, as though the person's original self might become just an extension of the engulfer's self. Patients in therapy sometimes say that they feel "enclosed," "swallowed up," "drowned," "eaten up," "smothered," or "stifled" by people who get too close. In another variation, which Laing called *implosion*, the person believes that forces in the external world are about to crash in, obliterate the self, and leave a vacuum that other people's ideas, feelings, and wishes can rush in and fill, like a gas filling a vacuum. The panic aroused by these beliefs might resemble a nonschizophrenic person's panic in confronting his or her unanticipated impending death.

People with ontological insecurity find ways to preserve the self. One patient was reassured by his own strong body odor, which kept other people away and provided evidence that his self was still there. Another patient early in treatment remarked that her anger and depression helped her feel intact. Her therapist, trying to be encouraging, had commented that people do change and she did not have to remain depressed and angry indefinitely. However, she found the comment disturbing and replied that she could not let go of her anger and depression, for if she did, she would lose her identity.

People who suffer from ontological insecurity have a major conflict. On the one hand, they have good reason to keep themselves isolated and separate from other people—to protect and preserve the self. On the other hand, when they are isolated, they also feel lonely, stressed, and unsupported. Having to choose between the two poses a terrible dilemma.

Schizoid Personality Disorder

If a person desperately needed to avoid social contact (e.g., to preserve the self), the person might misinterpret other people's intentions and facial expressions (Mandal, Pandey, Prasad, 1998), become withdrawn and detached, and display little emotion. The schizoid personality disorder describes this pattern of detachment. In some cases it is an antecedent to schizophrenia. Exhibit 12.3 lists its features. Overtly, people with schizoid personality disorder seem to have no desire for intimacy; they have few friends and often do not marry. They appear cold and aloof and seem not to care what others think of them. Occasionally, when a person with schizoid personality disorder becomes comfortable enough to reveal private feelings, the person may acknowledge painful feelings related to social interactions (American Psychiatric Association, 2000, p. 695).

Exhibit 12.3.   Diagnostic Criteria for Schizoid Personality Disorder

A.   A pervasive pattern of detachment from social relationships and a restricted range of expression of emotions in interpersonal settings, beginning by early adulthood and present in a variety of contexts, as indicated by four (or more) of the following:
(1)   neither desires nor enjoys close relationships, including being part of a family
(2)   almost always chooses solitary activities
(3)   has little, if any, interest in having sexual experiences with another person
(4)   takes pleasure in few, if any, activities
(5)   lacks close friends or confidants other than first-degree relatives
(6)   appears indifferent to the praise or criticism of others
(7)   shows emotional coldness, detachment, or flattened affectivity
B.   Does not occur exclusively during the course of schizophrenia, a mood disorder with psychotic features, another psychotic disorder, or a pervasive developmental disorder and is not due to the direct physiological effects of a general medical condition.

Note. If criteria are met prior to the onset of schizophrenia, add "premorbid" (e.g., "Schizoid Personality Disorder [Premorbid]"). From *Diagnostic and Statistical Manual of Mental Disorders* (4th ed., Text Revision, p. 697), by the American Psychiatric Association, 2000, Washington, DC: Author. Reprinted with permission.

Case Example of Edvard Munch

In chapter 2, we referred to the art of the Norwegian expressionist painter, Edvard Munch (1863–1944). Munch deliberately tried to represent some of his internal experiences on canvas in an effort to free himself of disturbing feelings and images (Steinberg & Weiss, 1954). From letters and other available information, he has been described as extremely lonely. According to Steinberg and Weiss:

> closeness whether it involved friendship with a man, sexual intimacy with a woman, or even looking at a person, was frightening to him . . . A sustained sexual relationship was impossible for him since he felt it would "sap his strength." His concept of closeness between two individuals . . . was of a destructive incorporation of one by the other. [He also believed that] human beings are like empty vessels capable of being filled by waves which emanate from everything. By flowing into people, these waves affect their minds and change their bodies. (p. 410)

Munch's mother died of tuberculosis when he was five years old. He witnessed her having a pulmonary hemorrhage before she died, a grotesque image that probably lasted a lifetime. His mother wrote him a letter before she died, warning her children to avoid evil and follow their father's religious teachings; the letter offered the hope of reuniting with her after death (Munch, 1949). He apparently had fantasies of reuniting with his mother, but in time came to believe that this reunion would cause his own death. Perhaps that idea fueled his view that closeness is dangerous. Seven years after his mother died, his sister also died, again from tuberculosis. Because Munch was himself a sickly child, his sister's death was probably all the more frightening.

Munch's father was a physician who worked in the slums of Oslo and would not accept money from the poor. He was apparently a difficult and unpredictable person. As quoted by Deknatel (1950), Munch wrote that his father:

> had a difficult temper . . . with periods of religious anxiety which could reach the borders of insanity . . . When anger did not possess him, he could be like a child and joke and play with us . . . When he punished us, he could be almost insane in his violence. (p. 10)

Munch became psychotic in 1908–1909 when he was 46 years old. His work during the 15-year period before his breakdown is considered unusual, creative, and disturbingly macabre. A theme that keeps re-appearing is the incorporation or engulfment of one person by another. In chapter 2 (Figure 2.1), we presented an example; "Lovers in the Waves" displays a woman's face, torso, and long hair, with a man's face buried in her hair. Similar themes appear in other paintings of Munch's. In many paintings, the woman's hair binds the man to her, apparently symbolizing engulfing tendencies that Munch ascribed to women. His intense anxiety is itself depicted in one of his most famous paintings, *The Scream*, showing a man in terror (presumably because of interpersonal dangers like engulfment).

Munch recovered from his psychosis in later years, when he became even more isolated. His paintings at that time were colorful and decorative but less creative. He also developed a change in his personal relationship to his pictures; they became his companions, and

> [h]e referred to them as his children and would rarely be persuaded to part with them . . . Occasionally if he was dissatisfied with a painting, he beat it with a whip, claiming that this "horse treatment" improved its character . . . [Once, when he did agree to sell a painting, he said to the buyer], "Go in and fetch your love. She has been strutting with pride all day because you like her." [He] could scarcely do anything when he was separated from his paintings. He was restless and bored until he was with them again. (Steinberg & Weiss, 1954, p. 421)

Earlier in life he had been terrified by interpersonal relationships, but later he apparently did form a tolerable relationship (to his pictures). They were less threatening than people since they were, after all, a product of his own self.

Thought Disorder and Subtypes of Schizophrenia

Two main themes have helped us organize our thinking about schizophrenia: attentional distractibility, which emphasizes a deficit in the process of thinking, and delusional content, which emphasizes devastating beliefs about the vulnerability of the self. These two themes appear to different degrees in the subtypes of schizophrenia described in *DSM–IV–TR*. There are four subtypes:

the disorganized type, the paranoid type, the catatonic type, and the undifferentiated type. Let us consider each type.

The disorganized type of schizophrenia highlights attentional distractibility—loose associations, incoherent and disorganized speech, neologisms, and word salad. Although minidelusions do occur in this form of schizophrenia, they are not elaborated; they lack unity or an integrating theme and usually seem transitory and silly. The *DSM–IV–TR* lists three essential features: disorganized speech, disorganized behavior, and flat or inappropriate affect. Because the person's thoughts and intentions are so easily derailed by interfering thoughts and lost intentions, we know very little about the person's actual thoughts. We only know the surface manifestation—unintelligible speech, unintelligible behavior, and unintelligible affect. The disorganized type of schizophrenia has a relatively early and insidious onset without significant remissions and a relatively poor prognosis.

The paranoid type of schizophrenia highlights ontological insecurity. It is the most common form of schizophrenia today. It has a later onset than the disorganized type, and its prognosis may be more favorable. In contrast to the disorganized type, it is often expressed as a bizarre delusion about being overtaken. The person construes casual observations as referring to oneself (ideas of reference). For example, seeing two people laughing, the person might infer that "they are laughing at me." Elaborate persecutory delusions also focus on the self (e.g., "my physician is conspiring with God to transform my soul"). Persecutory delusions clarify the reason for the person's anxiety and rouse the person to action as a way of saving the self. Persecutory delusions also generate anger, and the combination of the two may produce homicidal impulses and impel the person to violence.

Grandiose delusions (e.g., being selected by God for a special purpose) can also help define the self in a protective way. The Schreber case, described by S. Freud (1911/1963), shows how persecutory and grandiose delusions work together. Schreber was a prominent judge in Germany who became psychotic. He believed that God had attached Himself to Schreber's nerves and was transforming Schreber from a man into a woman. In his delusion, God planned eventually to impregnate him so that he would deliver God's children and begin a super-race of human beings. Although Schreber dreaded the impending transformation, he felt proud to be selected for God's mission.

The catatonic type of schizophrenia is extremely rare today, but it, too, seems to arise from ontological insecurity. The essential feature is a marked psychomotor disturbance, such as immobility, muteness or an apparent stuperous condition. (Catatonic frenzies may also occur; they are marked by excessive motor activity.) When extremely inactive, the person may refuse to talk, move, eat, or dress; the person may also assume and maintain odd poses for a long duration and seem to be stubborn, oppositional, and resistant to instructions.

In some cases, at least, it is clear that a bizarre delusion has inspired the catatonic behavior. I once worked with a catatonic patient who, after recovering, explained that he had understood the universe to be organized into five basic dimensions: the three spatial dimensions, time, and a fifth dimension that threatened his existence. He believed that any words he spoke would draw him into this fifth dimension and place him in a state of purgatory. When he came to feel safer in the hospital, he was willing to write and later was willing to talk again. Given his delusion, his catatonic behavior made sense.

Finally, the undifferentiated type of schizophrenia refers to a miscellaneous category. It includes other individuals who manifest symptoms of schizophrenia but do not meet the criteria for one of the first three categories. The undifferentiated category, for example, would include people who are sometimes delusional and sometimes incoherent.

Anxiety Aroused by Demand for Closeness

According to many researchers, a schizophrenic person experiences intense anxiety over interpersonal closeness (e.g., Cameron, 1947; Haley, 1963; Sullivan, 1953). When the relevant template is activated, the person's anxiety level rises, and schizophrenic symptoms (e.g., neologisms, tangential associations, illogical thought sequences, and delusions) increase. This hypothesis was tested experimentally by Shimkunas (1972) and replicated by Levy (1976). In Shimkunas's study, 60 men and women, all patients in a hospital, were interviewed; 20 were diagnosed with paranoid schizophrenia, 20 had nonparanoid schizophrenia, and 20 were nonpsychotic psychiatric patients. The experimenter explained to each patient that he was trying to develop a new method of interviewing: He would show the patient a series of cards, and a different topic would appear on each card. First, he would talk about the topic himself, reporting his own feelings and attitudes, and then the patient was to talk about the topic. There were eight different topics altogether, all interpersonal topics: getting angry at people; helping other people; depending on people; being rejected by people; and so on. The experimenter's statement about each topic constituted the experimental manipulation. In one condition (the personal disclosure condition), the experimenter's statement was personal: He spoke of himself, using words like *I*, *me*, and *my*, and vividly described his own feelings. From the principle of complementarity, this high level of self-disclosure (high communion) invited the patient to do the same. In the other condition (the impersonal disclosure condition), the experimenter was impersonal: He spoke only about other people (*someone*, *they*, *people*) and described their feelings more vaguely.

The following examples illustrate the difference between the two conditions on the topic "getting angry at people."

> Personal Disclosure Condition: "When I'm angry at somebody, it's hard for me to know what to do about it. There was one time when I was in a group discussion, and every time I told my real feelings about something, this one guy would make hateful, cruel remarks about what I would say, and he'd keep giving me this ugly, dirty look for no reason at all. He really made me feel uncomfortable in front of all the other people; he made me feel like a real fool. I really despised him for doing that to me; I was scared to death that I could feel that way, but I could have killed that dirty bastard for what he did to me."
>
> Impersonal Disclosure Condition: "When people are angry at somebody, it seems hard for them to know what to do about it. Once somebody was in a

Table 12.5.   Mean Amount of Personal Disclosure for Patients in Each Condition

Condition	Schizophrenic		Nonpsychotic patients
	Paranoid	Other	
Personal	14.0	12.3	24.9
Impersonal	12.4	8.4	13.1

Note. From "Demand for Intimate Self-Disclosure and Pathological Verbalizations in Schizophrenia," by A. M. Himkunas, 1972, *Journal of Abnormal Psychology, 80,* p. 203. Copyright © 1972 by the American Psychological Association. Reprinted with permission of the author.

group discussion, and every time he gave his opinion, this one guy would make remarks that weren't very nice about what was said, and he appeared to give him a cross look for no reason. He appeared to make this person seem uncomfortable in front of the group; he seemed to make him feel bad. This person seemed rather displeased with this other guy. He didn't think much of him, and it appeared that he might want to do something to him. But he seemed to be uneasy about his opinions of the other guy. Anyway, he might have wanted to tell the other guy that he didn't like what he did." (Shimkunas, 1972; p. 200)

Statements in the personal disclosure condition contained self-references and emotional words, revealing the speaker's feelings, reactions, attitudes, and thoughts. In contrast, statements in the impersonal disclosure condition excluded personal reactions and feelings; those statements were bland and revealed little about the speaker's inner state. The interviewer and patient took turns on each topic; the interviewer always spoke first. Raters then rated each patient's response along several dimensions of interest and summed the ratings. With a 7-point rating scale (0 to 6) to assess a dimension, the total rating across 8 topics could range from 0 to 48.

One measure of interest was the actual level of self-disclosure in the patient's response. A low score reflected little disclosure. The mean rating of disclosure is reported in Table 12.5 for each condition. Nonpsychotic patients followed the experimenter's example and were more revealing in the personal disclosure condition. However, the schizophrenic patients disclosed little in both experimental conditions. Their mean level of self-disclosure in both conditions resembled that of the nonpsychotic patients in the impersonal condition. Thus, the schizophrenic patients were uniformly impersonal in their responses.

However, the invitation to disclose (and the stress it induced) did affect their responses. Another measure assessed the presence of peculiar or illogical thinking in the patients' responses. High ratings indicated a lot of peculiar or illogical thinking—bizarre content, illogical and tangential associations, unintelligible thought sequences. As shown in Table 12.6, the mean rating for the nonpsychotic group was low regardless of experimental condition. However, the schizophrenic participants showed more peculiar thinking in the personal disclosure condition. Apparently, the stress induced by the pressure to disclose exacerbated the signs of their thought disorder.

Another measure assessed the presence of delusional thinking in the patients' responses. Table 12.7 shows the mean ratings for that measure. Delusional thinking was particularly evident in the responses of paranoid schizophrenic patients in the personal disclosure condition. Thus, the results may be

Table 12.6. Mean Amount of Peculiar or Illogical Thinking for Patients in Each Condition

Condition	Schizophrenic		Nonpsychotic patients
	Paranoid	Other	
Personal	12.6	21.3	0.6
Impersonal	3.4	6.9	1.0

Note. From "Demand for Intimate Self-Disclosure and Pathological Verbalizations in Schizophrenia," by A. M. Himkunas, 1972, *Journal of Abnormal Psychology, 80*, p. 203. Copyright © 1972 by the American Psychological Association. Reprinted with permission of the author.

summarized this way: Schizophrenic patients were never as self-disclosing as the nonpsychotic patients were in response to the experimenter's personal disclosure. However, the schizophrenic patients did apparently feel pressured to self-disclose, and, under that pressure, their psychotic symptoms became more evident. These results have been replicated by Levy (1976), who demonstrated the same effect for patients receiving medication.

Case Illustration

A graduate student working as a psychiatric technician in a hospital had a puzzling encounter with a patient, a 25-year-old unemployed man who had been hospitalized for anxiety and depression. The patient was described as intelligent but socially clumsy. He had been unable to find a job since graduating from college, and after a year, he gave up, withdrew socially, and spent most of his time alone in his apartment. One day, after seeing his therapist, he was feeling angry and panicky, and his therapist suggested that he be hospitalized. In the hospital he was assigned to a psychiatric technician who later wrote a report of his observations. The following is an edited excerpt from his unpublished report.

> On the third day of his hospitalization, Richard told me that he felt scared. He said that he had been sitting outside on the grass talking to a female patient when he had a strong urge to rape her. We sat in silence for a while, and I asked him what he was feeling. He said he felt really sad. "You look as if you could cry," I said. To my surprise, he began to cry. I tried to give him physical and emotional comfort by sitting next to him and from time to time, I put my arm around him. I reinforced his crying, say it was OK, and to "let it out, let it go." When his sobbing subsided, I asked him again what he was feeling, what he was experiencing. He said it felt painful and he recalled himself as a little boy sitting in a highchair. He broke into periodic sobbing, as he recalled "and I dropped a bottle, and my mother started to slap me and slap me and slap me." When his story was finished, he was overcome with a sobbing. I asked him again what he was feeling, what he was experiencing, and he let out an enormous scream. He looked fierce during and after this scream. This was soon followed by a panicky state. For the next 15 or 20 minutes, he bounced from "I feel pain" to "I feel anger," from deep despair with tears and sobbing to the height of a fierce anger, accompanied by swearing and screaming. At times he would make sounds and postures like a 5-year-old child; at other times, he seemed confused and at other times he was hunched over, sad and in despair.

Table 12.7.   Mean Amount of Delusional Thinking for Patients in Each Condition

Condition	Schizophrenic		Nonpsychotic patients
	Paranoid	Other	
Personal	7.7	2.0	1.7
Impersonal	1.0	1.8	1.3

Note. From "Demand for Intimate Self-Disclosure and Pathological Verbalizations in Schizophrenia," by A. M. Himkunas, 1972, *Journal of Abnormal Psychology, 80,* p. 203. Copyright © 1972 by the American Psychological Association. Reprinted with permission of the author.

The psychiatric technician was working from a hypothesis that catharsis would be helpful. However, by repeatedly inviting the patient to tell what he was feeling, he was asking the patient to share private feelings and become intimate. In my view, the demand for self-disclosure in a case like this arouses severe anxiety and is counterproductive.

Beginning Treatment With a Schizophrenic Patient: A Case Study

Arieti's (1974) classic book on schizophrenia describes a young man, Mark, who became schizophrenic (pp. 637–645). In describing the case, Arieti showed how a therapist, early in the treatment, can be warm, supportive, and respectful without demanding self-disclosure.

Mark, a shy, married man and the father of a three-year-old son, had previously been in treatment because he felt lonely and had difficulty making friends. When he had his schizophrenic episode, he was 25 years old and thought he was having a heart attack. He felt that he had to pray to God for his survival by spinning around; if he stopped moving, he thought, he would die. In his view, his eyes were pointing in different directions because the muscles that controlled them were mixed up in his skull. He also felt that his brain tissue was being torn apart and that his heart was not supported in his body and was going to fall down. Therefore, he would lie on the floor, pull up his legs, and lean them against the wall to keep his heart from falling down. He also expected his heart and blood vessels to explode into a thousand pieces.

While in the hospital, he was withdrawn and apprehensive. He heard other patients talking disparagingly about him and overheard some female patients stating that he was "not masculine" and refer to him as *she*. At times people seemed to be saying what he was thinking. He could not look people in the eyes because they would find out things of which he was ashamed. Arieti learned that he had recently been fired from his job because he was spending too much time discussing the stock market with his stock broker. After he was fired, he went to work for his father, a successful businessman, who seemed to berate and criticize him constantly.

Early in the treatment, the only topic that Mark seemed comfortable talking about was the stock market, a topic about which he was knowledgeable and felt competent. Arieti let him talk about the stock market. Arieti reported that he himself learned a lot about Wall Street from these conversations and let Mark know that. In addition, Mark would sometimes express worries (e.g., that he was a poor husband and father and therefore ought to end his marriage). In response, Arieti would reassure him that this was not the time to make major decisions: He had been through a harrowing experience and first needed to recover. Big decisions could wait until he was feeling better. Later, when Mark recalled the early stage of treatment, he commented, "You made me feel at ease, you were receptive, uncritical; you accepted me with all my faults." He improved considerably and most of his somatic delusions disappeared.

The important point here is that early in the treatment, Arieti did not ask Mark about his thoughts and feelings, nor did he pressure Mark to provide details about his early life. Instead, he found a neutral, impersonal topic (the stock market) that they could discuss together, allowing Mark to display his competence to an interested audience. An important goal early in treatment was to reduce Mark's anxiety. In addition to prescribing anxiety-reducing medication, Arieti tried to remove the pressure associated with long-term decisions. He reassured Mark that all pressing decisions could (and would) be resolved in time. No doubt Arieti's manner also conveyed confidence that Mark would recover, and Arieti's reassuring confidence may have helped reduce Mark's anxiety as well.

Eventually, Mark described his family background. His parents were unhappily married; his father was a good provider, but distant, remote, and critical of those around him. When his parents fought, Mark sided with his mother because he felt that she would protect him from his father. He felt that she was the only person with whom he could communicate. She alone knew his feelings, needs, and thoughts. She could interpret the world to him and protect him from the many dangers and threats that she had warned him about. He also felt that he owed it to her to listen to and accept her views, even when they did not quite jibe with his own impressions.

Toward the end of his childhood, the situation improved, and he had a few friends. He completed college successfully, secured a job as an engineer, and at the age of 22 married Rosette; he became as dependent on Rosette as he had been on his mother. The couple had a child during their first year of marriage. Later, however, Mark was fired from his job because he was too slow in getting work done, and he did not get along with people. Then, he accepted his father's suggestion and began to work for him. However, the two of them did not get along; he came to see his father as the monster that his mother had depicted. His father seemed to criticize everything he did, reducing Mark's confidence and causing him to make mistakes. His wife also seemed to be growing more demanding, and he felt that something was fundamentally wrong with him. That was when he had a psychotic episode.

Mark made progress early in treatment, but, unfortunately, the stock market at that time fell. He lost his own profits as well as those of relatives whose money he had invested. He felt very diminished in other people's eyes, and his self-esteem was shattered. He became discouraged and depressed, but this time, delusions and hallucinations did not reappear. Still, he believed that people were laughing at him, and he became increasingly afraid to be around people. In crowds he saw eyes looking at him and people talking about him. When someone looked at him, he had to drop his eyes or look elsewhere.

In time the treatment began to address these symptoms. He came to recognize that he saw people laughing at him when he expected to see them laughing, and he expected to see them laughing because he believed that they should laugh at him. He came to understand that his fear of people and his feeling of inadequacy were correlated; each reinforced the other. The more fearful he was, the more inadequate he felt; and the more inadequate he felt, the more fearful he became.

Impulsive Thinking in Schizophrenic Individuals

Psychotic beliefs arouse intense anxiety, and when a person feels intensely anxious, inferences tend to become rash and impulsive. Writers have sometimes tried to portray the impulsive reasoning of schizophrenic individuals as an invalid form of syllogism. Von Domarus (1944), for example, argued that a schizophrenic person might reason as follows:

1. All As are C.
2. B is a C.
3. Therefore, B is an A.

(A concrete example would be: Idiots make mistakes; I make mistakes; therefore, I am an idiot.) Although this form of syllogism is invalid, we do use reasoning of this type to generate hypotheses. In doing so, though, we qualify the inference with words like *maybe, perhaps,* and *I wonder whether* to emphasize its tentativeness. Thus, we say to ourselves: "Schizophrenic individuals show incoherent or illogical thinking; Jones shows incoherent or illogical thinking; therefore, I wonder whether Jones perhaps has schizophrenia." Under intense anxiety, however, the qualifiers get lost or overlooked. Hence, a severely anxious person like Mark would draw the kind of hasty inference that supports a base of delusional beliefs. As therapy progresses, however, and the person comes to feel less anxious, it is often possible to identify and re-examine some everyday inferences, labeling them as *hypotheses*. After they are designated hypotheses, they can be tested empirically and, in time, confirmed or disconfirmed.

Summary

We have interpreted schizophrenia in terms of the diathesis–stress model. According to this hypothesis, a biological predisposition combines with life experiences to leave the person vulnerable to schizophrenia. This vulnerability is reflected, in part, by an attentional difficulty that is observed in schizophrenic individuals and in their parents. Then, when a highly vulnerable person encounters severely stressful situations, the person has a relatively higher probability of exhibiting the syndrome.

When two generations within a family both exhibit the attentional difficulty, amorphous communication patterns seem more likely. Family patterns may also include intrusiveness, a confusion of boundaries, and severely critical or hostile control. In that case, family interactions may also lead to dysfunctional beliefs (including ontological insecurity) and cause intense stress for the young person. As a result, the child may become isolated, socially awkward, and very anxious. Demands for closeness may further intensify the person's anxiety. Then, when sufficiently stressed, the vulnerable person succumbs to schizophrenia.

The diathesis–stress model probably applies as well to other disorders described in this book. In the following chapter, we conclude the book by summarizing several themes. Among those themes, we show that the diathesis–stress model may be applied broadly to less severe forms of psychopathology as well.

Part V

Conclusions

13

The Interpersonal View of Psycopathology

This book has stressed the role of interpersonal motives in explaining phenomena of psychopathology. It has emphasized communion and agency as two broad categories of interpersonal motives. If psychologists want to explain why a message is ambiguous, why an event is stressful, or why a person reacts emotionally, it is important to understand what the person is trying to achieve. The very same syndrome or behavior may have different interpretations, depending on the motive behind it. Agoraphobia, self-starvation, and self-injurious behavior cannot be understood unless we understand the motive behind the behavior.

Many personality disorders illustrate the importance of interpersonal motives. Frequently, a particular interpersonal motive helps organize criteria of a personality disorder, enabling us to formulate the disorder in interpersonal terms. In this chapter, I first review some of these organizing motives (themes). I show that the criteria of a personality disorder often describe a threatened motive, strategies for satisfying the motive, and reactions when the motive is frustrated. I also show that personality disorders and Axis I disorders alike typically reflect a Person × Situation interaction, which helps explain why diagnostic categories so often require a fuzzy definition. We begin the chapter with the personality disorders.

Personality Disorders and Characteristic Vulnerabilities

The criteria of most personality disorders explicitly mention a specific vulnerability. The clearest examples are the dependent, avoidant, borderline, narcissistic, histrionic, and paranoid personality disorders. For each of these disorders, the different criteria fall into one of the following categories: (a) the fundamental vulnerability—a salient or easily threatened motive; (b) strategies that the person uses to satisfy that motive; (c) negative affect that occurs when the motive is frustrated; and (d) ways in which the person tries to regulate the negative affect.

Personality Disorders for Which a Motive Is Specified

THE FUNDAMENTAL VULNERABILITY   The organizing motive reflects a wish to attain a desired state or avoid an aversive one. For example, one criterion of the borderline personality disorder (criterion 1) describes a severe fear of being abandoned. A prominent criterion of the histrionic personality disorder (criterion 1) describes an acute discomfort when the person is not the center of attention. A criterion of the narcissistic personality disorder (criterion 4) describes an excessive need for admiration. A criterion of the paranoid personality disorder (criterion 3) mentions a motive to protect the self from malice, humiliation, and exploitation by others.

Criteria of the avoidant personality disorder emphasize feelings of inadequacy and the person's desire to avoid rejection, disapproval, criticism, and ridicule (criteria 1, 2, 3, 4). Criteria of the dependent personality disorder emphasize an intense sense of helplessness and inadequacy and a desire to have others take charge (criteria 2, 4, 5, 8). These motives all stem from a sense of vulnerability in relating to other people. Although *DSM–IV–TR* generally tries to minimize clinical inference, the criteria described above all describe an intense motive to attain a desired state (another person's attention, admiration) or an intense motive to avoid an aversive state (abandonment, rejection, helplessness, or the malice of others).

STRATEGIES FOR SATISFYING THE MOTIVE   Other diagnostic criteria describe behaviors designed to satisfy the motive. For example, a person with a histrionic personality disorder typically uses physical appearance (criterion 4) and exaggerated emotion (criterion 6) to draw attention to the self. A narcissistic person exploits other people (criterion 6), adopts a sense of self-importance (criterion 1), fantasizes unlimited success, power, brilliance, or beauty (criterion 2), and holds beliefs about being special and entitled (criteria 3, 5). In these two disorders the person is apparently trying to attain a desired state (other people's attention in one, admiration in the other). In treatment, histrionic and narcissistic people seem to want something from the clinician, and clinicians, at least initially, report feeling more connected to those patients than to patients with any other personality disorder (Wagner, Riley, Schmidt, McCormick, & Butler, 1999).

People with other personality disorders exhibit defensive strategies for avoiding an aversive state. An avoidant person strives to avoid rejection by minimizing social contact (criterion 1); the person limits intimacy, new relationships, and risks (criteria 3, 5, 7). A dependent person strives to avoid helplessness by getting others to take charge (criterion 2) and finding ways to keep others happy (criteria 3, 5). A paranoid person strives to avoid humiliation by guarding against possible malice (criterion 1), disloyalty (criteria 2, 7), and abusive acts (criteria 3, 4, 5, 6).

REACTIONS WHEN THE MOTIVE IS FRUSTRATED   A third set of criteria describes the person's reaction when the motive is frustrated. A dependent person becomes uncomfortable, anxious, or helpless when alone (criterion 6). A borderline person shifts abruptly into a contrasting state of affect, identity, and interpersonal relationships (criteria 2, 3, 6, 8). A narcissistic person becomes envious (criterion 8). A paranoid person gets angry at signs of malice (criterion 6).

WAYS OF COPING WITH NEGATIVE AFFECT   The remaining criteria describe how the person copes with the negative affect produced by a frustrated motive.

The dependent person urgently seeks another relationship when a close relationship has ended (criterion 7). The borderline person acts out on the self or others through impulsive or suicidal behavior (criteria 4, 5). The narcissistic person becomes arrogant and haughty (criterion 9), perhaps also exploitative (criterion 6). The paranoid person counterattacks (criterion 6). Kemperman, Russ, and Shearin (1997), for example, showed that people often mutilate themselves (e.g., by cutting their wrists) explicitly in an effort to reduce negative affect.

Personality Disorders for Which a Motive Is Only Implied

Criteria of the obsessive–compulsive and schizoid personality disorders also suggest motives, but *DSM–IV–TR* does not explicitly name them. A person with an obsessive–compulsive personality disorder may be striving to protect the self from criticism and obtain approval. Most of the criteria of this disorder describe strategies for demonstrating that the person is beyond reproach: perfectionism (criterion 2), devotion to work (criterion 3), conscientiousness (criterion 4), and a rigid (criterion 8) and detailed focus on rules and order (criterion 1).

A person with a schizoid personality disorder may be very uncomfortable with closeness and may strive to keep separate from other people. Using Edvard Munch as an example, we suggested that a schizoid person minimizes contact with others in order to preserve the intactness of the self. If a motive "to preserve the self" is considered fundamental to the schizoid personality disorder, it clarifies why the person chooses solitary activities (criterion 2), shows little interest in sexual experiences (criterion 3), appears indifferent to praise or criticism (criterion 6), and is emotionally cold or detached (criterion 7).

Personality Disorders Without an Integrating Motive

People with an antisocial personality disorder seem to feel little guilt or remorse (criterion 7). Other criteria of this diagnostic category primarily describe antisocial acts that reflect this lack of conscience, such as committing unlawful acts (criterion 1); deceiving other people (criterion 2); and behaving impulsively, aggressively, and irresponsibly (criteria 3, 4, 6). The criteria do not seem to imply an easily threatened motive.

Criteria of the schizotypal personality disorder also seem to lack any integrating motive. Instead, those criteria resemble mild symptoms of the schizophrenic disorders: ideas of reference (criterion 1), odd beliefs and magical thinking (criterion 2), unusual perceptual experiences (criterion 3), odd thinking and speech (criterion 4), inappropriate affect (criterion 6), and eccentric behavior (criterion 7). For the antisocial and schizotypal personality disorders, then, one cannot argue that the criteria describe a self-protective interpersonal motive, strategies for satisfying the motive, or reactions when the motive is frustrated. Therefore, those two categories seem qualitatively different from the other eight personality disorders.

To summarize, most personality disorders highlight an important interpersonal motive: to connect with other people by getting attention (histrionic), to connect as a way of avoiding helplessness (dependent), to get admiration from other people (narcissistic), to keep other people at a distance (schizoid), to avoid feeling abandoned (borderline), to avoid contact with people who might reject or disapprove (avoidant), to defend oneself against the malice of others (paranoid), and to obtain approval and avoid criticism (obsessive–compulsive).

Clinicians sometimes speak of a *maladaptive interpersonal pattern* in describing the personality disorders (L. S. Benjamin, 1996; Carson, 1969; Kiesler, 1983, 1996; Leary, 1957; McLemore & Brokaw, 1987; Pincus & Wiggins, 1990: Strupp & Binder, 1984; Sullivan, 1953). That term is generally used to highlight the person's self-defeating interpersonal behavior. In this book I have tried to highlight specific ways in which the person's behavior is maladaptive. When a person meets the criteria for a personality disorder, the behavioral strategies for satisfying an interpersonal motive are not working. Because behavior is ambiguous, a behavioral strategy may backfire: the histrionic person, rather than attracting others, seems manipulative; the obsessive–compulsive person, rather than appearing perfect, seems pedantic; the dependent person, rather than inviting nurturance, seems needy; the avoidant person, rather than protecting the self from rejection, seems disinterested in other people. Then, as the person's efforts backfire, they frustrate the very motive that they were meant to satisfy. As a result, the person experiences subjective distress, which the person tries to alleviate in non-constructive ways (e.g., self-injurious behavior, counterattacking other people). A treatment needs to focus on each aspect of the formulation—the self-protective interpersonal motive, the ineffective strategies for satisfying the motive, the resulting (uncontrollable) negative affect, and the self-defeating ways of coping with negative affect.

The Central Role of Motives in the Personality Disorders

In this book I have assumed that most personality disorders result from a frustrated interpersonal motive. A motive, however, is not directly observable. It is always inferred from the person's self-report and overt behavior. To provide a valid self-report, a person must be somewhat psychologically minded, possess a capacity for self-reflection, and be willing to self-disclose. Some people are probably unable or unwilling to provide the kind of information that identifies the relevant motive.

Suppose a person is prone to frequent displays of temper and depression and seems to meet every criterion of the borderline personality disorder, with one exception: The person denies any concern over (or desire to avoid) real or imagined abandonment. That is, suppose the person claims to be unconcerned about abandonment, rejection, or the loss of close relationships. This hypothetical person, then, would possess 8 of the 9 criteria of a borderline personality disorder but would be claiming that other people's intentions or actions have nothing to do with his or her mood shifts, identity shifts, displays of temper, impulsive behavior, feelings of emptiness, and unstable relationships. If we accepted the self-report as valid, would we still judge the person to have a borderline personality disorder? Perhaps not. Interpersonal theorists, at least, would probably search for some other explanation and diagnosis—perhaps a purely biological explanation that did not require concepts like a fear of abandonment or frustrated interpersonal motives. In particular, an interpersonal theorist would probably not use the label "borderline personality disorder" to describe someone whose traits were best explained biologically. For an interpersonal theorist, the interpersonal motive would make a significant difference both in diagnosis and in treatment.

On the other hand, an interpersonal theorist might question the validity of the person's claim to be unconcerned about abandonment. It is possible that the person who displayed 8 of the 9 borderline criteria was, for some reason, unable to recognize, acknowledge, or describe the fundamental motive. An inference about an organizing motive is always a tentative hypothesis, not a logical deduction or observable fact. It is simply a guide to further inquiry. Like any hypothesis, it needs to be tested and either confirmed over time or rejected. If it is confirmed, it clarifies the person's problem, focuses the goal of treatment, and helps us empathize with the person's experience. If it is disconfirmed, however, it needs to be abandoned in favor of an alternate formulation of the case.

Sometimes a person qualifies (or nearly qualifies) for more than one personality disorder and may therefore be affected by more than one sensitized motive. For example, the very same person might crave attention (a histrionic motive) and also strive to avoid abandonment (a borderline motive). Indeed, the histrionic and borderline personality disorders frequently co-occur (Davila, 2001; D. C. Watson & Sinha, 1998). A person might also crave attention (a histrionic motive) as well as admiration (a narcissistic motive). It is very common for a person who qualifies for one personality disorder to qualify for another as well (Marinangeli et al., 2000). It is even possible for two salient motives to be in conflict (e.g., motives associated with the dependent and narcissistic personality disorders), further complicating the person's life.

Threatened Motives and the Person × Situation Interaction

How does an interpersonal motive become salient? What makes an interpersonal motive so pressing that its frequent frustration leads to a personality disorder? For one thing, the person may acquire significant self-doubts as a result of accumulated frustrations over many years—e.g., doubts about one's appeal to others, doubts about one's efficacy, doubts about one's respect from others. To disconfirm these unwanted hypotheses and dispel self-doubts, the person may become very sensitive to potentially relevant evidence: Am I unappealing to others? Will I be abandoned by others? Am I not respected by others? Can I protect myself from humiliation? In brief, the person may acquire a need to keep testing and disconfirming negative hypotheses, thereby reassuring the self. The greater the person's self-doubt, the greater the need (or motive) for reassurance.

Furthermore, the pressing motive may induce cognitive biases, which sustain the maladaptive cycle. Motives to avoid abandonment, rejection, humiliation, criticism, and disapproval, for example, serve a self-protective function. To protect the self from malice, a person with a paranoid personality disorder is highly suspicious of others. Suspiciousness seems to lower a person's objectivity. The paranoid person has a single-minded purpose—namely, to avoid humiliation by detecting evidence of cheating, deceiving, exploiting, betraying, and so on. Therefore, the person conducts a biased search; evidence to the contrary is simply ignored. When individuals with a paranoid personality disorder detect hints of malice, they quickly become convinced that their suspicion has been confirmed. This "discovery" then reinforces the original need for vigilance.

To some extent, a cognitive bias may be associated with every personality disorder that is organized around a desperate motive to protect the self. A person with a borderline personality disorder may be biased toward perceiving signs of abandonment; an avoidant person, signs of rejection; an obsessive–compulsive person, signs of criticism; a schizoid person, signs that other people wish to connect; and so on. The resulting false alarms increase the sense of frustrated motive and negative affect, thereby increasing the probability of some maladaptive way of reducing distress.

The pressing motive constitutes a vulnerability or diathesis; it may be a trait-like "person variable" that is acquired gradually through an interplay of temperament (biological endowment) and experience. Some vulnerable people are fortunate in that they do not often encounter situations that frustrate the now salient motive. Though vulnerable, they are spared the emotional distress of a frequently frustrated motive. Thus, psychopathology may arise from two types of interactions.

In the following section we consider two types of interaction: first, the vulnerability itself (attributable to a Heredity × Environment interaction) and then, the personality disorder (related to a Vulnerability × Situation interaction). We begin with personality disorders and later examine Axis I syndromes.

How the Vulnerability Develops: Temperament × Experience Interaction

The term *temperament* refers to personality traits that are biologically determined but modifiable through experience. Children who are distress-prone at 10 days of age are greatly affected by early experiences with the caretaker. As described in chapter 3, van den Boom (1994) studied infants who were distress-prone shortly after birth. Without any intervention, the mothers, in self-defense, frequently ignored the child except when the child was in distress. Then, when the infants were tested in the strange situation at 1 year of age, many were insecurely attached. If the mothers received special training, however, and learned to handle a distress-prone child, they were more responsive to the child and the child was usually securely attached. Thus, the child's "heredity" in combination with a particularly unresponsive environment produced a vulnerable (insecurely attached) child.

Biologically determined characteristics often shape a child's environment. Consider children who (for biological reasons) are easily distracted. Highly distractible children may have a very negative impact on their caretakers (Hallowell & Ratey, 1994, chapter 5). A squirmy, distractible child may irritate the adult, leading to criticism, blame, and rebuke for behaving that way. This combination of biology and its interpersonal consequences can adversely affect a child's self-image, self-confidence, and resulting competence.

As a third example, consider a child who is biologically prone to anxiety. This child would perceive danger and threat in situations that bolder children take in stride. If the anxious child were then often left alone, the child might easily acquire cognitions about hidden dangers, beliefs about his or her own inability to cope, and views about the undependability of others. These cognitions and accompanying feelings and bodily sensations might well sensitize a child to abandonment. In this way, heredity and environment could work together to produce a salient and easily threatened motive.

Personality Disorders and the Vulnerability×Situation Interaction

A person's vulnerability, in turn, interacts with situations to produce a personality disorder. Some vulnerable people are fortunate in that they do not often encounter frustrating situations. Although vulnerable, these fortunate people are spared emotional distress or impaired functioning. An ideally suited spouse or best friend, for example, might reliably satisfy the motive, thereby shielding the vulnerable person from a borderline, dependent, or histrionic personality disorder. Other vulnerable people, however, are less fortunate and repeatedly encounter situations that frustrate the motive.

In chapter 6 we considered a study by Shoda et al. (1994) to illustrate a Person × Situation interaction among children at a summer camp. Highly aggressive children displayed aggressive behavior, but each child did so in an idiosyncratic profile of situations. In the same way, we might expect some paranoid individuals to be particularly sensitive to put-downs from co-workers (e.g., hidden messages that demean the person's competence), whereas other paranoid individuals might be especially sensitive to a breach of communion by friends and family (e.g., hints of disloyalty).

Application to Axis I Disorders

The Person × Situation interaction also helps us understand Axis I disorders. For example, we have suggested that a template for depression arises from a combination of biological determinants and interpersonal experiences. This template constitutes the person's vulnerability. When a highly vulnerable person then encounters a very stressful situation (e.g., a communal loss, an agentic defeat), the template gets activated, producing a major depressive episode. People who are not vulnerable and people who rarely encounter stressful situations would seem less apt to exhibit the syndrome.

Schizophrenia illustrates another form of the Person × Situation interaction. A person is vulnerable to schizophrenia if the person possesses a biological predisposition together with a particular class of relevant experiences. When a highly vulnerable person then encounters major stressors (e.g., a major setback at work, turmoil in a relationship), a schizophrenic episode occurs. If the person were not vulnerable or if a vulnerable person did not encounter stress, a schizophrenic episode would probably not occur.

We have explained many Axis I disorders this way—panic disorder with agoraphobia, obsessive–compulsive disorder, major depressive disorder, anorexia nervosa, conversion disorder, and schizophrenic disorders. In each case, a

Heredity × Environment interaction seems to produce the vulnerability, and the syndrome occurs when a vulnerable person encounters significant stress.

According to this book, then, frustrated interpersonal motives play a role in Axis I as well as Axis II disorders. Perhaps that is why people who have an Axis I disorder so often have an Axis II disorder as well (e.g., Davila, 2001; Docherty, Fiester, & Shea, 1986; Segrin, 2001; Widiger, 1989). Corruble, Ginestet, and Guelfi (1996) have reported that 20–50% of inpatients and 50–85% of outpatients who had a major depressive disorder also had a personality disorder. Shea, Glass, Pilkonis, Watkins, & Docherty (1987) found that 35% of patients with a major depressive disorder had one or more personality disorders. No doubt there are many additional people who could be diagnosed with one disorder and exhibit many of the traits associated with the other (without actually meeting all of its criteria).

Personality Disorders in an Interpersonal Space

If the criteria of a personality disorder can be organized around a particular interpersonal motive, that disorder should occupy a particular location in the two-dimensional interpersonal space. For example, the histrionic motive ("to connect with other people by getting their attention") implies a desire to connect with and influence other people. This disorder should therefore occupy the upper right quadrant (connect and influence). Similarly, the dependent motive ("to connect with others and get them to take charge") implies that the dependent personality disorder should occupy the lower right quadrant (connect and yield to influence).

Several studies have scaled and graphed the personality disorders. Pincus and Wiggins (1990) administered questionnaires to a large sample of undergraduate students in order to assess the interpersonal problems (frustrated motives) associated with different personality disorders. Figure 13.1 shows, for each of six personality disorders, the graphical location of typical interpersonal problems. People with histrionic, antisocial, and narcissistic personality disorders, by their own report, tend to take charge of other people too readily (high agency). Those with a histrionic personality disorder also tend to connect with others too readily (high communion), whereas those with an antisocial personality disorder do not connect (low communion). People with a dependent, schizoid, and avoidant personality disorder tend to yield too readily as a result of feeling inferior and inadequate (low agency). Those with a dependent personality disorder also connect too readily (high communion), whereas those with a schizoid personality disorder avoid connecting (low communion).

Other authors have obtained similar results for both patients and students (Blackburn, 1998; DeJong, Van den Brink, Jansen, & Schippers, 1989; Matano & Locke, 1995; Morey, 1985; Overholser, 1996; J. P. Sim & Romney, 1990; Soldz, Budman, Demby, & Merry, 1993; Trull, Useda, Conforti, & Doan, 1997). As summarized by C. C. Wagner, Riley, Schmidt, McCormick, and Butler (1999), the following graphical locations are typical. People with a narcissistic personality disorder are high in agency and neutral in communion (they want respect and admiration). Those with a paranoid or antisocial personality disorder are high in agency and low in communion (they want to influence others without connecting). Those with an avoidant, schizoid, or schizotypal personality disorder are low in both (they want to protect the self by remaining passive and

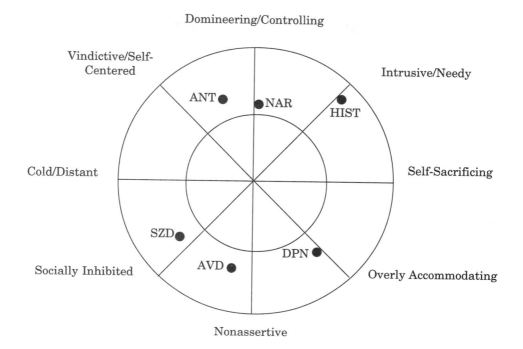

Figure 13.1. Location of personality disorders in the two-dimensional interpersonal space. ANT = antisocial; AVD = avoidant; DPN = dependent; HIST = historic; NAR = narcissistic; SZD = schizophrenic. From "Interpersonal Problems and Conceptions of Personality Disorders," by A. L. Pincus and J. S. Wiggins, 1990, *Journal of Personality Disorders, 4*, p. 348. Copyright © 1990 by Guilford. Adapted with permission.

disconnected). Those with a dependent personality disorder are low in agency and high in communion (they want others with whom they are connected to take charge). Those with a histrionic personality disorder are high in both (they want to influence others to become connected). The borderline personality disorder, with its many instabilities, does not seem to occupy a consistent graphical location.

Matano and Locke (1995) studied alcohol-dependent patients who had a personality disorder. According to their results, subjective distress is greater for people with a sense of inadequacy. Therefore, people with a dependent, avoidant, or schizoid personality disorder generally report more overall distress than people with a narcissistic, antisocial, or histrionic personality disorder. The authors also noted that those patients who are motivated to influence others (narcissistic, antisocial, and paranoid people) seem to "have a hard time relinquishing autonomy and control—whether to a treatment program or to a higher power in Alcoholics Anonymous" (p. 66). On the other hand, patients with a dependent personality disorder—who are too ready to relinquish control—seem to "have a hard time resisting social pressures to drink" (p. 66). The authors also suggested that patients who are highly communal (histrionic and dependent people) seem to "have a hard time respecting or maintaining boundaries in therapy," (p. 66) whereas, those who are more disconnected (schizoid, avoidant, paranoid, and antisocial patients) seem to have problems allowing themselves to engage with others. Those people may therefore find it hard to self-disclose as a way of promoting interpersonal relatedness in individual and group therapy.

The graphical arrangement of disorders also helps us predict which disorders are apt to co-occur. Disorders that are near one another are more likely to co-occur than disorders that are farther apart. Disorders that are diametrically apart, like the antisocial and dependent personality disorders, are negatively related. The motive associated with one contrasts with that of the other. The same is true for the histrionic and schizoid personality disorders. Thus, an interpersonal formulation helps organize the criteria of most personality disorders, thereby highlighting similarities, differences, and patterns of co-occurrence among them.

The Fuzzy Concept in Psychopathology

To end this chapter, we return to the concept of a "fuzzy category," which characterizes so many diagnostic categories. If a category were precisely defined, all criteria would be individually necessary and jointly sufficient; that is, every person who qualified for membership in the category would exhibit the same defining criteria. However, the members of a fuzzy category are heterogeneous. Their criteria overlap but are not identical. Why can we not define these diagnostic categories more precisely? We can now answer this question.

Personality Disorders

When a person is trying to satisfy an important motive, the person can do so in alternate ways. Two people with an obsessive–compulsive personality disorder may both wish desperately to avoid criticism, but one may do so by being neat, careful, and orderly, whereas others may do so by working night and day. Their goal is the same, but their strategies differ.

Similarly, people in the same diagnostic category may react differently when the motive is frustrated. Two people with a borderline personality disorder may both feel abandoned, but one may get depressed, whereas the other may become enraged. They both display negative affect, but they differ in the specific type of affect. Third, different people may cope with negative affect in different ways: one with eating binges, a second with vengeful rages, a third with suicidal gestures. Thus, a disorder may be attributed to a particular frustrated motive, but it may express itself in different ways—through different strategies, emotional reactions to frustration, and ways of coping with negative affect. Because of these different manifestations, the diagnostic category requires a fuzzy definition.

Axis I Syndromes

Axis I syndromes like panic attack and major depressive episodes also require a fuzzy definition. According to our interpretation, a network of associated elements forms a template—a central element plus associated feelings, cognitions, and bodily sensations. Because every person's history is unique, the exact elements differ somewhat from person to person, and the syndrome requires a fuzzy definition.

This book began with the following assertion: "Interpersonal communications can be very powerful. The message one person conveys to another, whether verbal or nonverbal, may gratify a salient motive, causing joy; it may frustrate that motive, causing distress." We have classified interpersonal motives as communal or agentic (or both), and throughout the book we have examined interpersonal behaviors in terms of these motives. A behavior is ambiguous if the motive behind it is uncertain.

Interpersonal motives are related to a person's image of the self and image of others, and these cognitions further explain why certain motives have become so salient. Most personality disorders may be organized around that motive, and many Axis I syndromes may be understood in terms of a template that results from a history of frustrated motives. Thus, frustrated interpersonal motives (together with biological factors) shape a person's vulnerability, and psychopathology arises in vulnerable people when sensitized motives are frustrated further.

This view has an obvious implication for clinical practice, and I offer that as my concluding remark. Whenever clinicians formulate a case, they must always address two basic questions: What, interpersonally, is the person trying to achieve? and How have those motives come to be frustrated? If we cannot answer these two questions, we cannot claim to understand the person's psychopathology.

Appendix _____

Some Statistical Properties
of a Circumplex

This appendix describes some statistical properties of any set of circumplex scales. We illustrate those properties using the Inventory of Interpersonal Problems (IIP-64; Horowitz, Alden, Wiggins, & Pincus, 2000; Horowitz, Strauss, & Kordy, 1994) and Locke's (2000) measure of interpersonal goals, as described in chapter 6. We also explain the theory in more detail.

Cosine Curve

We begin with Locke's measure of interpersonal goals. In collecting normative data, Locke administered the measure to nearly 600 people and then correlated the scores on each of the eight scales with scores on each of the other scales (Locke, 2000). As one example, consider Scale 7 (see Figure 6.1; p. 119). What degree of correlation would one expect between the scores on this scale and scores on each of the other scales?

First consider the correlation between Scale 7 and the adjacent variable, Scale 8. That correlation should be positive because both variables reflect strong communal motives: A person with a high score on Scale 7 should obtain a high score on Scale 8. In Locke's data, $r = .46$. For similar reasons, a positive correlation coefficient would be expected for every pair of adjacent variables.

Now consider the degree of correlation between Scale 7 and Scale 3. These two variables are diametrically opposite each other. In Figure 6.1, one reflects positive communion, the other reflects negative communion. Scale 7 reflects a motive for the presence of communion, Scale 3, a motive for the absence of communion. Therefore, those two scales should be negatively correlated. In Locke's data, this correlation coefficient was $-.67$. Similarly, a negative correlation coefficient would be expected for every pair of opposite variables.

What is the correlation between Scale 7 and Scale 1? Those two variables should be uncorrelated because one reflects a motive for communion, whereas the other reflects a motive for agency; they are said to be orthogonal. In Locke's data, that correlation coefficient was .00. Similarly, a nonsignificant correlation coefficient would be expected for every pair of orthogonal variables.

The following list shows the degree of correlation between Scale 7 and each of the other scales.

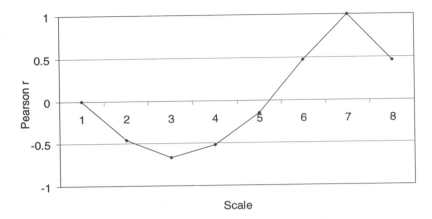

Figure A.1.   Pearson r between Scale 7 and each of the eight scales.

Correlation of Scale 7 with:

Scale	Pearson r
Scale 1	.00
Scale 2	−.46
Scale 3	−.67
Scale 4	−.52
Scale 5	−.15
Scale 6	.47
Scale 7 (itself)	1.00
Scale 8	.46

These correlation coefficients are shown graphically in Figure A.1. Notice the wavelike pattern. The general pattern (Figure A.1) is said to approximate a cosine curve. The correlation coefficients are highest for adjacent variables, lowest for diametrically opposite variables, and intermediate for variables in between. (We explain the reason later.) For each of the eight variables in a circumplex, the pattern of correlations with the other variables approximates a cosine curve.

Here is one implication of this principle. Suppose we wanted to understand the interpersonal motives of people who are shy. Shyness reflects an interpersonal motive (e.g., to avoid humiliation and embarrassment), so a measure of shyness ought to correlate with Locke's scales, forming a pattern that approximates a cosine curve—highest with the scale that measures a shy person's primary motive and lowest with the scale opposite it. Therefore, we might administer a measure of shyness to a group of people and correlate their scores on the shyness measure with their scores on each of Locke's eight scales. Which of Locke's scales would show the highest correlation with the measure of shyness? Shy people are likely to obtain high scores on the interpersonal goals of Scale 4 (e.g., "It is important to me not to say something stupid," "not to expose myself to ridicule," "to keep my thoughts or feelings to myself"). In other words, scores on the shyness measure should correlate most highly with scores on Scale 4. However, scores on the shyness measure should correlate negatively with scores on Scale 8 (the diametrically opposite scale that emphasizes goals like "It is

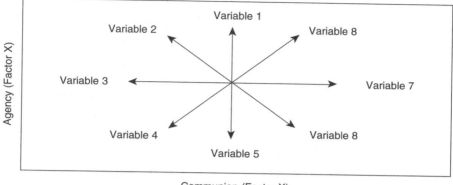

Figure A.2.   Theoretical composition of the 8 variables.

important to me to express myself openly," "that others listen to what I have to say," "that others show me respect"). Intermediate scales, like Scale 6 and Scale 2, would be unrelated to shyness and therefore should be uncorrelated with the measure of shyness. The pattern would thus resemble a cosine curve.

In the same way we could examine other constructs that seem to be interpersonal (e.g., assertiveness, dependency, intrusiveness, competitiveness). For example, consider the Masculinity scale of the Bem Sex Role Inventory (BSRI; Bem, 1974). Is "masculinity" an interpersonal construct? If so, its correlations with Locke's scales should approximate a cosine curve. They do. Locke correlated scores on that measure with scores on each of his eight scales of interpersonal motives. The highest correlation was with Scale 1 (purely agentic goals). Beginning with Scale 1, the correlation coefficients were .38, .17, .05, −.19, −.32, −.15, −.08, .18. This pattern suggests that the Masculinity scale of the BSRI, at least to some extent, measures an interpersonal motive: People with high scores on the Masculinity scale have strong agentic goals (Scale 1, $r = .38$) and weaker goals on the opposite scale (Scale 5, $r = −.32$). Locke also examined scores on the Femininity scale of the BSRI. Scores on that scale also approximated a cosine curve, but the highest correlation was with Scale 7 (communal goals). Apparently, the Femininity scale, at least to some extent, measures interpersonal goals for communion (Scale 7).

Suppose we were creating a new measure of some interpersonal construct (e.g., empathy, loneliness, shyness, assertiveness, narcissism, trust, and so on). After creating the measure, we might administer it to a group of people along with eight interpersonal reference scales. If it is measuring an interpersonal construct, its pattern of correlation coefficients with the eight reference scales should approximate a cosine curve.

Theory

Consider the two-dimensional interpersonal space in Figure A.2. It is organized around the two basic interpersonal factors, communion (X) and agency (Y). For simplicity, we refer to them as *Factor X* and *Factor Y*. Now imagine a set of eight reference variables (traits, motives, interpersonal problems), and let us assume that each variable reflects some combination of Factor X and/or Factor Y (nothing else). We shall call the 8 variables *Variable 1*, *Variable 2*, and so on, up to *Variable 8*.

According to the theory, every interpersonal variable (1 through 8) can be represented graphically as composed entirely of Factor X, entirely of Factor Y, or a combination of both. Variable 7, for example, reflects nothing but the presence of Factor X: The more of Factor X, the higher the level of Variable 7. Variable 3 reflects nothing but the absence of Factor X: The less of Factor X, the higher the level of Variable 3. Variable 1 and Variable 5 reflect nothing but Factor Y: The more of Factor Y, the higher the level of Variable 1; the less of Factor Y, the higher the level of Variable 5. All other variables are a combination of the two factors. Variable 8, for example, requires Factor X and Factor Y in equal amounts (Eq. A1):

$$\text{Variable 8} = .5 \text{ Factor X} + .5 \text{ Factor Y} \qquad (A1)$$

Similarly, and as depicted in Equation A2, Variable 2 requires an absence of Factor X (coldness) and the presence of Factor Y (dominance).

$$\text{Variable 2} = -.5 \text{ Factor X} + .5 \text{ Factor Y} \qquad (A2)$$

In this way, each variable can be expressed as a combination of the two underlying interpersonal factors. Each variable is represented by a vector shown in the graph of Figure A.2.

We assume for the moment that each of the eight interpersonal variables can be measured perfectly without measurement error. Suppose we wanted to examine some new interpersonal measure, like a new measure of empathy, dependency, or competitiveness. We call this new measure *Measure M*, which we assume, for the moment, to be error-free. Now suppose we correlate scores on the hypothetical Measure M with scores on each of the eight (error-free) reference scales. What degree of correlation would one expect, theoretically, between scores on Measure M and scores on each of the eight reference scales?

If M is truly an interpersonal construct (composed of nothing but Factor X, Factor Y, or both), it should be most highly correlated with one of the reference scales. For example, suppose M is like Variable 7 and consists entirely of communion. Then it should correlate perfectly with Variable 7. Like Variable 7, M would be represented by a vector along the X-axis. That is, M and Variable 7 would coincide. The angular separation between them would be 0°, and the correlation between them would be 1.00.

How about the theoretical correlation between M and Variable 3 (diametrically opposite Variable 7)? M increases as Factor X increases, Variable 3 increases as Factor X diminishes; therefore, the correlation between them should be −1. The angular separation between the vector for M and the vector for Variable 3 is 180° and the correlation between the two is −1.00.

How about the theoretical correlation between M and Variable 1? Those two vectors are orthogonal. That is, they are 90° apart; one consists exclusively

Table A.1. Theoretical Correlation Between M and the Scale

Variable	Angular of separation (degree)	Expected correlation
7	0	1
1	90	0
3	180	−1

of Factor X, the other exclusively of Factor Y. Therefore, the correlation between them should be .00. Table A.1 summarizes the theoretical correlation coefficients between Variable M and three of the eight reference variables.

Notice that the expected correlation coefficient happens to be equal to the cosine of the angle that separates M from the variable in question (see Eq. A3).

$$\cos 0° = 1;$$
$$\cos 90° = 0; \qquad (A3)$$
$$\cos 180° = -1.$$

Thus, the correlation between a variable and M (which, in this example, consists exclusively of Factor X) seems to depend upon the angular separation between M and the corresponding scale (Eq. A4):

$$r = \cos \theta, \qquad (A4)$$

where θ is the angular separation between the two measures of interest.

For example, consider the correlation between M and the scale that is 45° away, namely, Variable 8. Because "cos 45°" is .707, the correlation between M and Variable 8 would seem to be .707. Why would that correlation equal .707? M, in this example, consists entirely of Factor X. However, Variable 8 consists equally of Factor X and Factor Y. Therefore, the two variables overlap with respect to Factor X, but not with respect to Factor Y; that is, they have half of their variance in common. A squared correlation coefficient tells the proportion of variance that the two variables share (in this case, .50). Therefore, r, theoretically, should equal the square root of .50, or .707. The statement "$r = \cos 45° = .707$" tells the degree of correlation theoretically expected between two variables that are separated by 45°.

Table A2 tells the expected correlation coefficient between M and each of the eight variables.

The graph in Figure A.3a shows the theoretical correlation coefficients between an external variable M (which consists only of Factor X) and each of the 8 interpersonal reference variables. This graph is called a *cosine curve*. We say that a variable is interpersonal if the form of its correlation coefficients with the reference variables approximates this theoretical pattern. The scale that has the highest degree of correlation with M identifies the interpersonal construct that M most closely resembles. In Figure A.3a, the highest point corresponds to Variable 7 because M, like Variable 7, consists entirely of Factor X (communion). The lowest point corresponds to Variable 3, which is diametrically opposite Variable 7.

Table A.2. Relationship Between the Angular Separation of Two Variables and Their Theoretical Correlation

Variable	Angular of separation (degree)	$\cos \theta$ = theoretical r
1	90	.000
2	135	−.707
3	180	−1.000
4	225	−.707
5	270	.000
6	315	.707
7	0	1.000
8	45	.707

We express the general form of the cosine curve in Figure A.3a this way (Eq. A5):

$$r_i = \cos \theta_i \qquad (A5)$$

In this equation the subscript "i" refers to the different reference scales—1, 2, ..., 8—and θ_i refers to the angle that separates the vector of Measure M from the corresponding reference scale.

In practice, other (noninterpersonal) factors as well as random error of measurement reduce the magnitude of the correlation coefficients. Therefore, in practice, the cosine curve is not likely to range fully from −1 to +1. Instead, all correlation coefficients are attenuated to some degree. Perhaps they would range from −0.6 through 0 to +0.6. Errors of measurement and irrelevant (noninterpersonal) factors reduce the amplitude of the cosine curve. The letter "a" is used to represent the actual amplitude of the cosine curve, and the equation may be revised this way: (Eq. A6)

$$r_i = a \cos \theta_i \qquad (A6)$$

If the amplitude equals .6, the correlations would range from −.6 (the lowest) through 0 to + .6 (the highest). The graph of this cosine curve is shown in Figure A.3b. It is flatter than the one in Figure A.3a, but it still shows the characteristic interpersonal pattern of correlation coefficients. The greater the amplitude, the greater the range of correlation coefficients.

The cosine curve is affected by another factor as well. On questionnaires, people are often asked to rate each item on a rating scale (say, a 5-point rating scale from 0 to 5). However, different people use the scale differently. Some people use relatively low ratings in responding to all items, whereas other people use relatively high ratings in responding to all items. As a result, some people have relatively low scores on all eight scales, and other people have relatively high scores on all eight scales. This style of responding causes some degree of positive correlation across all scales, elevating the magnitude of all correlation coefficients. The cosine pattern of correlation coefficients still holds, but all val-

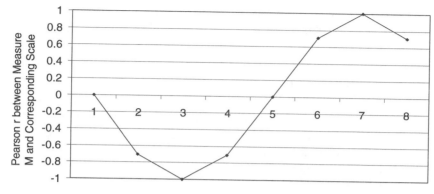

Figure A.3a. Theoretical cosine curve.

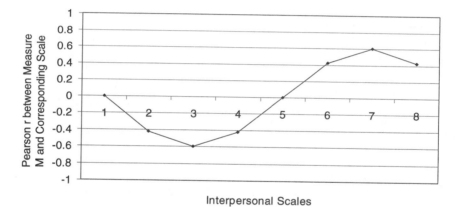

Figure A.3b. Same curve when a = .6.

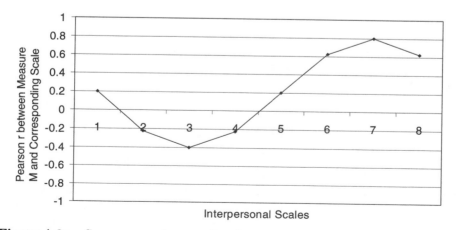

Figure A.3c. Same curve when a = .6 and e = .2.

ues are elevated to some degree. The formula therefore becomes as follows (Eq. A7):

$$r_i = a \cos \theta_i + e, \tag{A7}$$

where e (for "elevation") tells the degree to which all correlation coefficients are elevated. If e equals .20, for example, every value of r would increase by .20. In the previous example, "a," the amplitude, equaled .60, and the values of r ranged from −.60 through 0 to +.60. If all values were elevated by .20 because people use the scale differently, the resulting correlations would now range from −.40 to +.80. That graph is shown in Figure A.3c. Gurtman (1993, 1994, 1995, 1996; Gurtman & Bakarishnan, 1998; Pincus & Gurtman, 1995) has discussed the cosine curve in greater detail with many applications.

Comparing Different Instruments

Imagine two different tests of the same construct—two different tests of dependency, or two tests of trust, or two tests of assertiveness. Even though two measures have the same name (e.g., "dependency"), they are not necessarily measuring exactly the same construct. In one case, dependency might emphasize a strong need for a leader; in a second case, it might emphasize a strong need to accommodate or please other people; in a third case, it might emphasize a strong need to be close to or involved with other people. Therefore, we might want to compare different tests that purportedly measure the same construct by correlating them with the same reference scales. The IIP-64 has been used in this way.

Gurtman (1991, 1992a, 1992b) administered two measures of "dependency" to a group of people along with the eight scales of the IIP-64. He showed that each measure produced a cosine curve pattern of correlation coefficients with the eight scales of the IIP-64, but one had its highest correlation with Scale 6 (overly accommodating), whereas the other had its highest correlation with Scale 5 (nonassertive). He also compared two different measures of "trust." Again, each measure produced a cosine curve pattern of correlations with the reference scales, but one had its highest correlation with Scale 6 of the IIP-64 (overly accommodating), whereas the other had its highest correlation with Scale 7 of the IIP (self-sacrificing). Thus, scales with the same name sometimes measure slightly different constructs.

Some Useful Summary Statistics

In chapter 6, we examined the IIP-64 scores of Ms. D, a woman with a dependent personality disorder (see Figures 6.4). We reported the eight scores as standardized T-scores. Standardized T-scores can always be reduced to z-scores by subtracting 50 and dividing by 10. For simplicity, we now express Ms. D's scores as z-scores. Beginning with Scale 1 (Domineering/Controlling), Ms. D's eight z-scores are as follows: .6, .4, .7, 1.0, 2.1, 2.7, .8, and .4. All eight scores reflect above-average distress (that is, every z-score > 0); the highest score occurred on Scale 6 (overly accommodating), where "z = 2.7" tells us that Ms. D's distress on that scale was 2.7 standard deviations above the mean of the standardization group. In Figure A.4, the length of each vector corresponds to the z-score for that scale.

Ms. D's eight z-scores may be combined in a way that shows her "net distress" along each underlying dimension—along communion (X) and along agency (Y). Figure A4 shows the vector corresponding to each scale. The length of each vector represents the amount of distress on that scale. Every vector may be analyzed into an X-component and a Y-component, so we can separately average the X-components and the Y-components. First consider the X-component of each vector. The X-component of a vector is computed by multiplying that vector by the cosine of its angle with the X-axis. The vector of Scale 8, for example, makes a 45° angle with the X-axis. To determine its X-component, we multiply the vector by cos 45° (which equals .7). Because the length of the vector for Scale 8 is .4, the length of its X-component is (cos 45°) (.4) = (.7) (.4) = .28. The cosine is positive in some cases (too much communion, as in the problems of Scales 6, 7, and 8) and negative in other cases (too little communion, as in the problems of Scales 2, 3, and 4). After we have determined the X-component of each vector, we sum the eight values algebraically to determine the net amount of communal distress: $\sum z_i (\cos \theta_i)$.

In Equation A8 we spell out the individual terms. The vectors for Scale 1 and Scale 5 both have cosines equal to 0 so they do not appear (for Scale 1, cos 90° = 0; for Scale 5, cos 270° = 0). In other words, Scales 1 and 5 measure only agentic (Y) distress.

$$\text{Net Communal Distress} = .7 \text{ Scale } 6 + \text{Scale } 7 + .7 \text{ Scale } 8$$
$$- .7 \text{ Scale } 2 - \text{Scale } 3 - .7 \text{ Scale } 4 \tag{A8}$$

The vector of Scale 7 makes an angle of 0° with the X-axis, and cos 0° = 1. Therefore, the distress on that scale is weighted by 1; it measures nothing but communal distress. The vector of Scale 3 makes an angle of 180°, and cos 180° = −1, so Scale 3 is weighted by −1.

We apply this formula to Ms. D's z-scores (Eq. A9):

$$\text{Net Communal (X) Distress} = .7 (2.7) + 1 (.8) + .7 (.4) - .7 (.4) - 1 (.7) - .7 (1.0)$$
$$= 1.89 + .80 + .28 - .28 - .70 - .70$$
$$= 1.29 \tag{A9}$$

The net amount of communal distress is positive, indicating that Ms. D experienced more distress from excessive connectedness than from a lack of connectedness.

Now consider the Y-component of each vector. To compute the Y-component of a vector, we multiply that vector by the sine of its angle with the X-axis. For example, Scale 8 is at a 45° angle, so we multiply the vector by sin 45° (which equals .7). Because Ms. D's z-score on Scale 8 is .4, the Y-component of the vector is as follows: (sin 45°) (.4) = (.7) (.4) = .28. The sine of the angle is

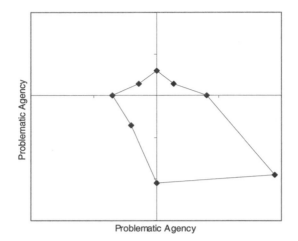

Figure A.4. Ms. D's z-score on each scale.

positive in some cases (Scales 8, 1, and 2) and negative in other cases (Scales 4, 5, and 6). Then we algebraically sum the Y-components: $\Sigma z_i (\sin \theta_i)$.

We spell out the individual terms (see Equation A10). The vectors for Scale 3 and Scale 7 both have a sine equal to 0 so they do not appear in the formula (for Scale 7, $\sin 0° = 0$; for Scale 3, $\sin 180° = 0$). These two scales measure only communal (X) distress.

$$\text{Net Agentic (Y) Distress} = .7 \text{ Scale } 8 + \text{Scale } 1 + .7 \text{ Scale } 2$$
$$- .7 \text{ Scale } 4 - \text{Scale } 5 - .7 \text{ Scale } 6 \qquad \text{(A10)}$$

Scale 1 and Scale 5 are purely agentic (one is positive, the other is negative). They are therefore counted fully; $\sin 90° = 1$, and $\sin 270° = -1$.

We apply this formula to Ms. D's data (Eq. A11):

$$\text{Net Agentic Distress} = .7 (.4) + 1 (.6) + .7 (.4)$$
$$- .7 (1.0) - 1 (2.1) - .7 (2.7)$$
$$= .28 + .6 + .28 - .70 - 2.10 - 1.89$$
$$= -3.53 \qquad \text{(A11)}$$

Thus, the net amount of agentic distress is negative (distress related to a lack of agency). To summarize, Ms. D's net distress on communion was positive, and her net distress on agency was negative. Her overall net distress therefore lies in the lower right quadrant of the interpersonal space (as expected for someone with a dependent personality disorder).

Finally, we can imagine a point that represents the location of Ms. D's net distress. Dividing each quantity by 4 allows us to interpret the length of the summary vector as a z-score. Following Leary (1957), the resulting values are sometimes called *LOV* and *DOM* (Eq. 12).

$$\text{LOV} = 1.29/4 = .32$$
$$\text{DOM} = -3.53/4 = -.88. \qquad \text{(A12)}$$

The location of this point, [.32, −.88], is shown on the graph in Figure A4. We can draw a vector from the origin to this point to depict the locus of Ms. D's average distress. This "summary" vector may be regarded as an average of the 8 vectors describing Ms. D's distress.

The length of the summary vector is computed as follows (Eq. A13):

$$\text{Vector Length} = \sqrt{(\text{LOV})^2 + (\text{DOM})^2}$$
$$= \sqrt{(.32)^2 + (-.88)^2} \quad \text{(A13)}$$
$$= .94.$$

The vector length can be interpreted as a z-score. The amount of distress it describes is nearly 1 standard deviation above average. We can also determine the angle that the summary vector makes with the Y-axis. The Y-coordinate divided by the X-coordinate gives the tangent of its angle with the X-axis (Eq. A14):

$$\tan \theta = -.88/.32 = -2.75 \quad \text{(A14)}$$

The angle with the tangent "−2.75" lies 290° from the X-axis (lower right quadrant).

We can use the same procedure to describe the scores of Ms. A, the woman with an avoidant personality disorder. Figures 6.5 and 6.6 reported her standardized T-scores. The same data may be expressed as z-scores: Beginning with Scale 1, these z-scores are .7, .9, 1.2, 3.2, 2.1, 1.0, .5, .3. (Notice that every z-score is above 0.) First we multiply each z-score by its corresponding cosine (0, −.7, −1, −.7, 0, .7, 1, .7). The X-component of each vector is: 0, −.63, −1.20, −2.24, 0, .70, .50, and .21; and their algebraic sum is: −2.66. Then we multiply each z-score by its corresponding sine (1, .7, 0, −.7, −1, −.7, 0, .7). The Y-component of each vector is: .70, .63, 0, −2.24, −2.10, −.70, 0, and .21; and their algebraic sum is: −3.50. Dividing each sum by 4, we compute the coordinates of the summarizing point [−0.66, −0.88]. The vector from the origin to this point represents an average of the eight vectors. This vector is in the lower left quadrant. The vector length is: $\sqrt{(-0.66)^2 + (-0.88)^2} = \sqrt{1.21} = 1.1$, which can be interpreted as a z-score. Finally, we compute the tangent of the summary vector's angle with the X-axis: (−0.88)/(−0.66) = 1.33. The angle with that tangent is 233°, which places Mrs. A's overall distress in the lower left quadrant, as expected for someone with an avoidant personality disorder.

References

Abramson, L. Y., Seligman, M. E. P., & Teasdale, J. (1978). Learned helplessness in humans: Critique and reformulation. *Journal of Abnormal Psychology, 87,* 49–74.

Addis, L. (1981). Dispositions, explanation and behavior. *Inquiry, 24,* 205–227.

Adler, G., & Buie, D. H. (1979). Aloneness and borderline psychopathology: The possible relevance of child development issues. *International Journal of Psychoanalysis, 60,* 83–96.

Ainsworth, M. D. S. (1982). Attachment: Retrospect and prospect. In C. M. Parkes & J. Stevenson-Hinde (Eds.), *The place of attachment in human behavior* (pp. 3–30). New York: Basic Books.

Ainsworth, M. D. S. (1991). Attachments and other affectional bonds across the life cycle. In C. M. Parkes, J. Stevenson-Hinde, & P. Marris (Eds.), *Attachment across the life cycle* (pp. 33–51). London: Routledge.

Ainsworth, M. D. S., & Bell, S. M. (1970). Attachment, exploration, and separation: Illustrated by the behavior of one-year-olds in a strange situation. *Child Development, 41,* 49–67.

Alden, L. E., & Capreol, M. J. (1992). *Interpersonal problem patterns in avoidant personality disordered outpatients: Prediction of treatment response.* Unpublished manuscript.

Alden, L. E., & Capreol, M. J. (1993). Avoidant personality disorder: Interpersonal problems as predictors of treatment response. *Behavior Therapy, 24,* 357–376.

Alden, L. E., Wiggins, J. S., & Pincus, A. L. (1990). Construction of circumplex scales for the Inventory of Interpersonal Problems. *Journal of Personality Assessment, 55,* 521–536.

Allport, F. (1937). Teleonomic description in the study of personality. *Character and Personality, 5,* 202–214.

Allport, G. W. (1937). *Personality: A psychological interpretation.* New York: Holt, Rinehart & Winston.

Alston, W. P. (1975). Traits, consistency, and conceptual alternatives for personality theory. *Journal for the Theory of Social Behaviour, 5,* 17–48.

Altman, J. H., & Wittenborn, J. R. (1980). Depression-prone personality in women. *Journal of Abnormal Psychology, 89,* 303–308.

American Psychiatric Association. (1968). *Diagnostic and statistical manual of mental disorders* (2nd ed.). Washington, DC: Author.

American Psychiatric Association. (1980). *Diagnostic and statistical manual of mental disorders* (3rd ed.). Washington, DC: Author.

American Psychiatric Association. (1987). *Diagnostic and statistical manual of mental disorders* (3rd ed., rev.). Washington, DC: Author.

American Psychiatric Association. (2000). *Diagnostic and statistical manual of mental disorders* (4th ed., text revision). Washington, DC: Author.

Amitay, O. A., Mongrain, M., & Fazaa, N. (2001). *Love and control: Self-criticism from parents to daughters and consequences for relationship partners.* Unpublished manuscript.

Anders, T. F. (1978). Home-recorded sleep in two and nine-months old infants. *Journal of the Academy of Child Psychiatry, 17,* 421–432.

Anderson, C. A., Jennings, D. L., & Arnoult, L. H. (1988). The validity and utility of attributional style construct at a moderate level of specificity. *Journal of Personality and Social Psychology, 55,* 979–990.

Andrews, B. (1995). Bodily shame as a mediator between abusive experiences and depression. *Journal of Abnormal Psychology, 104,* 277–285.

Andrews, G. C., Tennant, D., Hewson, D., & Vaillant, G. (1978). Life event stress, social support, coping style, and risk of psychological impairment. *Journal of Nervous and Mental Disease, 166,* 307–316.

Angyal, A. (1941). *Foundations for a science of personality.* New York: Commonwealth Fund and Harvard University Press.

Arieti, S. (1974). *Interpretation of schizophrenia* (2nd ed.). New York: Basic Books.

Arieti, S., & Bemporad, J. (1980). The psychological organization of depression. *American Journal of Psychiatry, 136,* 1365–1369.

Aristotle. (1952). Physics, Book II. In R. M. Hutchins (Ed.), *Great books of the Western world* (Vol. 8; pp. 268–278). Chicago: Encyclopaedia Britannica.

Arkin, R. M., & Oleson, K. C. (1998). Self-handicapping. In J. Darley & J. Cooper (Eds.), *Attribution and social interaction: The legacy of Edward M. Jones* (pp. 313–347). Washington, DC: American Psychological Association.

Arkowitz, H., Lichtenstein, E., McGovern, K., & Hines, P. (1975). The behavioral assessment of social competence in males. *Behavior Therapy, 6,* 3–13.

Armstrong, J. (1995). Psychological assessment. In J. L. Spira (Ed.), *Treating dissociative identity disorder* (pp. 3–37). San Francisco: Jossey-Bass.

Arnold, M. E., & Thompson, B. (1996). Love style perceptions in relation to personality function. *Journal of Social Behavior and Personality, 11,* 425–438.

Arrindell, W. A. (1980). Dimensional structure and psychopathology correlates of the fear survey schedule (FSS-III) in a phobic population: A factorial definition of agoraphobia. *Behaviour Research and Therapy, 18,* 229–242.

Arroyo, C. G., & Zigler, E. (1995). Racial identify, academic achievement, and the psyschological well-being of economically disadvantaged adolescents. *Journal of Personality and Social Psychology, 69,* 903–914.

Asarnow, R. F., Steffy, R. A., MacCrimmon, D. J., & Cleghorn, J. M. (1977). An attentional assessment of foster children at risk for schizophrenia. *Journal of Abnormal Psychology, 86,* 267–275.

Asch, S. E., & Zukier, H. (1984). Thinking about persons. *Journal of Personality and Social Psychology, 46,* 1230–1240.

Aspinwall, L. G., & Taylor, S. E. (1997). A stitch in time: Self-regulation and proactive coping. *Psychological Bulletin, 121,* 417–436.

Austin, J. T., & Vancouver, J. B. (1996). Goal constructs in psychology: Structure, process, and content. *Psychological Bulletin, 120,* 338–375.

Bakan, D. (1966). *The duality of human existence: Isolation and communion in western man.* Boston: Beacon.

Baker, J. D., Capron, E. W., & Azorlosa, J. (1996). Family environment characteristics of persons with histrionic and dependent personality disorders. *Journal of Personality Disorders, 10*, 82–87.

Baker, L., Silk, K. R., Westen, D., Nigg, J. T., & Lohr, N. E. (1992). Malevolence, splitting and parental ratings by borderlines. *The Journal of Nervous and Mental Disease, 180*, 258–264.

Baldwin, D. A. (1995). Understanding the link between joint attention and language. In C. Moore & P. J. Dunham (Eds.), *Joint attention: Its origins and role in development* (pp. 131–158). Hillsdale, NJ: Erlbaum.

Baldwin, J. (1897). *Social and ethical interpretations in mental development.* New York: Macmillan.

Bandura, A. (1977). Self-efficacy: Toward a unifying theory of behavioral change. *Psychological Review, 84*, 191–215.

Bandura, A. (1982). Self-efficacy mechanism in human agency. *American Psychologist, 37*, 122–147.

Bandura, A. (1986). *Social foundations of thought and action: A social cognitive theory.* Englewood Cliffs, NJ: Prentice-Hall.

Bandura, A. (1997). *Self-efficacy: The exercise of control.* New York: Freeman.

Barlow, D. H. (1988). *Anxiety and its disorders: The nature and treatment of anxiety and panic.* New York: Guilford.

Barlow, D. H. (2002). *Anxiety and its disorders: The nature and treatment of anxiety and panic* (2nd ed.). New York: Guilford.

Bartholomew, K. (1990). Avoidance of intimacy: An attachment perspective. *Journal of Social and Personal Relationships, 7*, 147–178.

Bartholomew, K., & Horowitz, L. M. (1991). Attachment styles among young adults: A test of a model. *Journal of Personality and Social Psychology, 61*, 226–244.

Bartrop, R. W., Luckhurst, E., Lazarus, L., Kiloh, L. G., & Penny, R. (1977). Depressed lymphocyte function after bereavement. *The Lancet, 1*, 834–836.

Bates, J. E., Bayles, K., Bennett, D. S., Ridge, B., & Brown, M. M. (1991). Origins of externalizing behavior problems at eight years of age. In D. J. Pepler & K. H. Rubin (Eds.), *The development and treatment of childhood aggression* (pp. 93–120). Hillsdale, NJ: Erlbaum.

Bates, J. E., Maslin, C. A., & Frankel, K. A. (1985). Attachment security, mother–child interaction, and temperament as predictors of behavior problem ratings at age three years. In I. Bretherton & E. Waters (Eds.), Growing points of attachment theory and research. *Monographs of the Society for Research in Child Development, 50*(1-2, Serial No. 209), 167–193.

Bebbington, P., & Kuipers, L. (1994). The predictive utility of expressed emotion in schizophrenia: An aggregate analysis. *Psychological Medicine, 24*, 707–718.

Beck, A. T. (1967). *Depression: Clinical, experimental and theoretical aspects.* New York: Hoeber.

Beck, A. T. (1983). *Cognitive therapy and the emotional disorders.* New York: International Universities Press.

Beck, A. T., & Freeman, A. F. (1990). *Cognitive therapy of personality disorders.* New York: Guilford.

Becker, E. (1973). *The denial of death.* New York: Free Press.

Beeghly, M., & Cicchetti, D. (1994). Child maltreatment, attachment, and the self-system: Emergence of an internal state lexicon in toddlers at high social risk. *Development and Psychopathology, 6*, 5–30.

Bellack, A. S., & Morrison, R. L. (1982). Interpersonal dysfunction. In A. S. Bellack, M. Hersen, & A. E. Kazdin (Eds.), *International handbook of behavior modification and therapy* (pp. 717–747). New York: Plenum.

Bem, S. L. (1974). The measurement of psychological androgeny. *Journal of Consulting and Clinical Psychology, 42*, 165–176.

Benjamin, L. S. (1974). Structural analysis of social behavior. *Psychological Review, 81*, 392–425.

Benjamin, L. S. (1977). Structural analysis of a family in therapy. *Journal of Consulting and Clinical Psychology, 45*, 391–406.

Benjamin, L. S. (1986). Adding social and intrapsychic descriptors to Axis I of *DSM–III*. In T. Millon & G. Klerman (Eds.), *Contemporary issues in psychopathology* (pp. 599–638). New York: Guilford.

Benjamin, L. S. (1996). *Interpersonal diagnosis and treatment of personality disorders* (2nd ed.). New York: Guilford.

Berelowitz, M., & Tarnopolsky, A. (1993). The validity of borderline personality disorder: An updated review of recent research. In P. Tryer & G. Stein (Eds.), *Personality disorder reviewed* (pp. 90–112). London: Royal College of Psychiatrists Publications Office.

Berkman, L. F., & Syme, S. L. (1979). Social networks, host resistance, and mortality: A nine-year follow-up study of Alameda County residents. *American Journal of Epidemiology, 109*, 186–204.

Berne, E. (1964). *Games people play*. New York: Ballantine Books.

Berzins, J. I. (1977). Therapist–patient matching. In A. S. Gurman & A. M. Razin (Eds.), *Effective psychotherapy* (pp. 221–251). New York: Pergamon.

Beutler, L. E. (1979). Toward specific psychological therapies for specific conditions. *Journal of Consulting and Clinnical Psychology, 47*, 882–897.

Bierman, R. (1969). Dimensions of interpersonal facilitation in psychotherapy and child development. *Psychological Bulletin, 72*, 338–352.

Birtchnell, J. (1993). *How humans relate*. London: Praeger Publishers.

Blackburn, R. (1998). Relationship of personality disorders to observer ratings of interpersonal style in forensic psychiatric patients. *Journal of Personality Disorders, 12*, 77–85.

Blascovich, J., & Tomaka, J. (1991). Measures of self-esteem. In J. P. Robinson, P. R. Shaver, & L. S. Wrightsman (Eds.), *Measures of personality and social psychological attitudes* (pp. 115–160). New York: Academic Press.

Blatt, S. J. (1974). Levels of object representation in anaclitic and introjective depression. *The Psychoanalytic Study of the Child, 24*, 107–157.

Blatt, S. J. (1990). Interpersonal relatedness and self-definition: Two personality configurations and their implications for psychopathology and psychotherapy. In J. L. Singer (Ed.), *Repression and dissociation* (pp. 299–335). Chicago: University of Chicago Press.

Blatt, S. J., D'Afflitti, J. P., & Quinlan, D. M. (1976). Experiences of depression in normal young adults. *Journal of Abnormal Psychology, 85*, 383–389.

Blatt, S. J., & Schichman, S. (1983). Two primary configurations of psychopathology. *Psychoanalysis and Contemporary Thought, 6*, 187–254.

Blatt, S. J., & Zuroff, D. C. (1992). Interpersonal relatedness and self-definition: Two prototypes for depression. *Clinical Psychology Review, 12*, 527–562.

Blehar, M. C., Lieberman, A. F., & Ainsworth, M. D. S. (1977). Early face-to-face interaction and its relation to later infant–mother attachment. *Child Development, 48*, 182–194.

Bleuler, E. (1950). *Dementia praecox on the group of schizophrenias* (J. Zinkin, Trans.). New York: International Universities Press.

Bluhm, C., Widiger, T., & Miele, G. (1990). Interpersonal complementarity and individual differences. *Journal of Personality and Social Psychology, 58*, 464–471.

Blumberg, S. R., & Hokanson, J. E. (1983). The effects of another person's response style on interpersonal behavior in depression. *Journal of Abnormal Psychology, 92*, 196–209.

Boland, T. B., & Chapman, L. J. (1971). Conflicting predictions from Broen's and Chapman's theories of schizophrenic thought disorder. *Journal of Abnormal Psychology, 78*, 52–58.

Boswell, P. C., & Murray, E. J. (1981). Depression, schizophrenia, and social interaction. *Journal of Consulting and Clinical Psychology, 49*, 641–647.

Bowen, R. C., & Kohout, I. (1979). The relationship between agoraphobia and primary affective disorders. *Canadian Journal of Psychiatry, 24*, 317–322.

Bower, G. H. (1981). Mood and memory. *American Psychologist, 36*, 129–148.

Bowlby, J. (1944). Forty-four juvenile thieves: Their characters and home life. *International Journal of Psycho-Analysis, 25*, 19–52, 107–127.

Bowlby, J. (1951). *Maternal care and mental health* (WHO Monograph No. 2). Geneva: World Health Organization.

Bowlby, J. (1969). Affectional bonds: Their nature and origin. In H. Freeman (Ed.), *Progress in mental health* (pp. 319–327). London: J. & B. Churchill.

Bowlby, J. (1973). *Attachment and loss: Vol. 2. Separation: Anxiety and anger.* New York: Basic Books.

Bowlby, J. (1977). The making and breaking of affectional bonds: I. Aetiology and psychopathology in the light of attachment theory. *British Journal of Psychiatry, 130*, 201–210.

Bowlby, J. (1980). By ethology out of psychoanalysis: An experiment in interbreeding. *Animal Behavior, 28*, 649–656.

Bowlby, J. (1982). *Attachment and loss: Vol. 1. Attachment.* New York: Basic Books. (Original work published 1969)

Bradley, G. W. (1978). Self-serving biases in the attribution process: A reexamination of the fact and fiction question. *Journal of Personality and Social Psychology, 36*, 56–71.

Brennan, K. A., Clark, C. L., & Shaver, P. R. (1998). Self-report measurement of adult attachment: An integrative overview. In J. A. Simpson & W. S. Rholes (Eds.), *Attachment theory and close relationships* (pp. 46–76). New York: Guilford.

Brennan, T. (1982). Loneliness at adolescence. In L. A. Peplau & D. Perlman (Eds.), *Loneliness: A sourcebook of current theory, research and therapy* (pp. 269–290). New York: Wiley.

Bretherton, I. (1984). *Symbolic play: The development of social understanding.* New York: Academic Press.

Bretherton, I. (1985). Attachment theory: Retrospect and prospect. *Monographs of the Society for Research in Child Development, 50,* 3–35.

Bretherton, I., & Munholland, K. A. (1999). Internal working models in attachment relationships: A construct revisited. In J. Cassidy & P. R. Shaver (Eds.), *Handbook of attachment: Theory, research, and clinical applications* (pp. 89–111). New York: Guilford.

Breznitz, Z. (1992). Verbal indicators of depression. *Journal of General Psychology, 199,* 351–363.

Briere, J. (1992). *Child abuse trauma: Theory and treatment of the lasting effects.* Newbury Park, CA: Sage.

Brigham, N. L., Kelso, K. A., Jackson, M. A., & Smith, R. H. (1997). The roles of invidious comparisons and deservingness in sympathy and schadenfreude. *Basic and Applied Social Psychology, 19,* 363–380.

Brim, O. G., Jr. (1976). Life-span development of the theory of oneself: Implications for child development. In H. W. Reese (Ed.), *Advances in child development* (Vol. 11, pp. 241–251). New York: Academic Press.

Brouwers, M. C., & Sorrentino, R. M. (1993). Uncertainty orientation and protection motivation theory: The role of individual differences in health compliance. *Journal of Personality and Social Psychology, 65,* 102–112.

Brown, D. R. (1996). Marital status and mental health. In H. W. Neighbors & J. S. Jackson (Eds.), *Mental health in Black America* (pp. 77–94). Thousand Oaks, CA: Sage.

Brown, G. W., Bifulco, A., & Harris, T. O. (1987). Life events, vulnerability and onset of depression: Some refinements. *British Journal of Psychiatry, 150,* 30–42.

Brown, G. W., Birley, J. L. T., & Wing, J. K. (1972). Influence of family life on the course of schizophrenic disorders: A replication. *British Journal of Psychiatry, 121,* 241–258.

Brown, G. W., Carstairs, G. M., & Topping, G. (1958). Post-hospital adjustment of chronic mental patients. *Lancet, 2,* 685–689.

Brown, J., Cohen, P., Johnson, J. G., & Smailes, E. M. (1999). Childhood abuse and neglect: Specificity of effects on adolescent and young adult depression and suicidality. *Journal of the American Academy of Child and Adolescent Psychiatry, 38,* 1490–1496.

Brown, J. D. (1998). *The self.* New York: McGraw-Hill.

Brown, P., & Levinson, S. (1987). *Politeness: Some universals in language usage.* New York: Cambridge University Press.

Brownell, K. D., & Fairburn, C. G. (Eds.). (1995). *Eating disorders and obesity: A comprehensive handbook.* New York: Guilford.

Bruch, H. (1973). *Eating disorders: Obesity, anorexia nervosa, and the person within.* New York: Basic Books.

Bruch, H. (1982). Anorexia nervosa: Therapy and theory. *American Journal of Psychiatry, 132,* 1531–1538.

Buglass, D., Clarke, J. F., Henderson, A. S., Kreitman, N., & Presley, A. S. (1977). A student of agoraphobic housewives. *Psychological Medicine, 7,* 73–86.

Burgess, E. P. (1969). The modification of depressive behaviors. In R. D. Rubin & D. Franks (Eds.), *Advances in behavior therapy* (pp. 193–199). New York: Academic Press.

Burleson, B. R. (1994). Comforting messages: Significance, approaches, and effects. In B. R. Burleson, T. L. Albrecht, & I. G. Sarason (Eds.), *Communication of social support* (pp. 3–28). Thousand Oaks, CA: Sage.

Burleson, B. R., Albrecht, T. L., & Sarason, I. G. (1994). *Communication of social support*. Thousand Oaks, CA: Sage.

Burns, L. E., & Thorpe, G. A. (1977). The epidemiology of fears and phobias (with particular reference to the National Survey of Agoraphobics). *Journal of International Medical Research, 5,* 1–7.

Buss, A. H., & Plomin, R. (1984). *Temperament: Early developing personality traits*. Hillsdale, NJ: Erlbaum.

Buss, D. M., & Craik, K. H. (1983). The act frequency approach to personality. *Psychological Review, 90,* 105–126.

Butler, J., & Haigh, G. (1954). Changes in the relation between self-concepts consequent upon client centered counseling. In C. R. Rogers & R. Dymond (Eds.), *Psychotherapy and personality change* (pp. 55–75). Chicago: University of Chicago Press.

Butzlaff, R. L., & Hooley, J. M. (1998). Expressed emotion and psychiatric relapse. *Archives of General Psychiatry, 55,* 547–552.

Caldji, C., Tannenbaum, B., Sharma, S., Francis, D., Plotsky, P. M., & Meaney, M. J. (1998). Maternal care during infancy regulates the development of neural systems mediating the expression of fearfulness in the rat. Proceedings of the National Academy of Science.

Cameron, N. (1938). Reasoning, regression and communication in schizophrenics. *Psychological Monographs, 50,* issue 221.

Cameron, N. (1947). *The psychology of behavior disorders: A biosocial interpretation*. Cambridge, MA: Mifflin.

Cameron, N. (1963). *Personality development and psychopathology*. Boston: Houghton Mifflin.

Cameron, N., & Rychlak, J. F. (1985). *Personality development and psychopathology: A dynamic approach* (2nd ed.). Boston: Houghton Mifflin.

Campbell, J. D., Assanand, S., & Di Paula, A. (2000). Structural features of the self-concept and adjustment. In A. Tesser, R. B. Felson, & J. M. Suls (Eds.), *Psychological perspectives on self and identify* (pp. 67–87). Washington, DC: American Psychological Association.

Campbell, J. D., Assanand, S., & Di Paula, A. (2003). The structure of the self-concept and its relation to psychological adjustment. *Journal of Personality, 71,* 116–140.

Campos, J. J., Barrett, K., Lamb, M. E., Goldsmith, H. H., & Stenberg, C. (1983). Socioemotional development. In P. H. S. E. Mussen, M. M. Haith, & J. J. V. E. Campos (Eds.), *Handbook of child psychology: Vol. 2. Infancy and developmental psychobiology* (4th ed., pp. 783–815). New York: Wiley.

Cantor, N., & Kihlstrom, J. F. (1987). *Personality and social intelligence*. Englewood Cliffs, NJ: Prentice Hall.

Cantor, N., Smith, E., French, R. D. S., & Mezzich, J. (1980). Psychiatric diagnosis as prototype categorization. *Journal of Abnormal Psychology, 89,* 181–193.

Carlson, V., Chicchetti, D., Barnett, D., & Braunwald, K. (1989). Disorganized/disoriented attachment relationships in maltreated infants. *Developmental Psychology, 25*, 525–531.

Carpenter, M., Akhtar, N., & Tomasello, M. (1998). Sixteen-month-old infants differentially imitate intentional and accidental actions. *Infant Behavioral Development, 21*, 315–330.

Carson, R. C. (1969). *Interaction concepts of personality*. Chicago: Aldine.

Carter, H., & Glick, P. C. (1976). *Marriage and divorce: A social and economic study* (2nd ed.). Cambridge, MA: Harvard University Press.

Carver, C. S. (1989). How should multifaceted personality constructs be tested? *Journal of Personality and Social Psychology, 56*, 577–585.

Carver, C. S., Pozo, C., Harris, S. D., Noriega, V., Scheier, M. F., Robinson, D. S., et al. (1993). How coping mediates the effects of optimism on distress: A study of women with early stage breast cancer. *Journal of Personality and Social Psychology, 65*, 375–390.

Carver, C. S., & Scheier, M. F. (1994). Situational coping and coping dispositions in a stressful transaction. *Journal of Personality and Social Psychology, 66*, 184–195.

Caspar, F. (1995). *Plan analysis: Toward optimizing psychotherapy*. Seattle: Hogrefe & Huber.

Caspar, F. (1997). Plan analysis. In T. Eells (Ed.) *Handbook of psychotherapy case formulation*. New York: Guilford.

Cassidy, J. (1999). The nature of the child's ties. In J. Cassidy & P. R. Shaver (Eds.), *Handbook of attachment: Theory, research, and clinical applications* (pp. 3–20). New York: Guilford.

Chambless, D. L. (1982). Characteristics of agoraphobia. In D. L. Chambless & A. J. Goldstein (Eds.), *Agoraphobia* (pp. 1–18). New York: Wiley.

Cherry, C. (1953). Some experiments on the recognition of speech with one and with two ears. *Journal of the Acoustical Society of America, 25*, 975–979.

Christensen, A. J., Dornink, R., Ehlers, S. L., & Schultz, S. K. (1999). Social environment and longevity in schizophrenia. *Psychosomatic Medicine, 61*, 141–145.

Cicchetti, D., & Barnett, D. (1991). Attachment organization in maltreated preschoolers. *Development and Psychopathology, 3*, 397–411.

Cicchetti, D., Lynch, M., Schonk, S., & Todd-Manly, J. (1992). An organizational perspective on peer relations in maltreated children. In R. D. Parke & G. M. Ladd (Eds.), *Family–peer relationships: Modes of linkage* (pp. 345–383). Hillsdale, NJ: Erlbaum.

Clarkin, J. F., Caligor, E., Stern, B., & Kernberg, O. F. (2002). *Structured interview of personality organization (STIPO)*. Unpublished manuscript.

Clarkin, J. F., Marziali, E., & Munroe-Blum, H. (1992). *Borderline personality disorder: Clinical and empirical perspectives*. New York: Guilford.

Clarkin, J. F., Widiger, T. A., Frances, T. A., Hurt, S. W., & Gilmore, M. (1983). Prototypic typology and the borderline personality disorder. *Journal of Abnormal Psychology, 92*, 263–275.

Cleckley, H. (1941). *The mask of sanity*. St. Louis, MO: Mosby.

Clyne, M. B. (1966). *Absent: School refusal as an expression of disturbed family relationships*. London: Tavistock Institute of Human Relations.

Coates, D., & Wortman, C. B. (1980). Depression maintenance and interpersonal control. In A. Baum & J. E. Singer (Eds.), *Advances in environmental psychology* (pp. 149–182). Hillsdale, NJ: Erlbaum.

Cobb, S. (1976). Social support as a moderator of life stress. *Psychosomatic Medicine, 38,* 300–314.

Cofer, D. H., & Wittenborn, J. R. (1980). Personality characteristics of formerly depressed women. *Journal of Abnormal Psychology, 89,* 309–314.

Cohen, F., & Lazarus, R. S. (1973). Active coping processes, coping dispositions, and recovery from surgery. *Psychosomatic Medicine, 35,* 375–389.

Collins, A. M., & Loftus, E. F. (1975). A spreading-activation theory of semantic processing. *Psychological Review, 82,* 407–428.

Collins, W. A., Maccoby, E. E., Steinberg, L., Hetherington, E. M., & Bornstein, M. H. (2000). Contemporary research on parenting: The case for nature and nurture. *American Psychologist, 55,* 218–232.

Compas, B. E., Malcarne, V. L., & Fondacaro, K. M. (1988). Coping with stressful events in older children and young adolescents. *Journal of Consulting and Clinical Psychology, 56,* 405–411.

Cooley, C. H. (1902). *Human nature and the social order.* New York: G. Scribner's Sons.

Coopersmith, S. (1967). *The antecedents of self-esteem.* San Francisco: Freeman.

Coopersmith, S. (1975). *Coopersmith Self-Esteem Inventory, technical manual.* Palo Alto, CA: Consulting Psychologists Press.

Corruble, E., Ginestet, D., & Guelfi, J. D. (1996). Comorbidity of personality disorders and unipolar major depression: A review. *Journal of Affective Disorders, 37,* 157–170.

Covington, M. V. (1992). *Making the grade: A self-worth perspective on motivation and school reform.* New York: Cambridge University Press.

Coyne, J. (1976a). Depression and the response of others. *Journal of Abnormal Psychology, 85,* 186–193.

Coyne, J. (1976b). Toward an interactional description of depression. *Psychiatry, 39,* 28–39.

Coyne, J., Aldwin, C., & Lazarus, R. S. (1981). Depression and coping in stressful episodes. *Journal of Abnormal Psychology, 90,* 439–447.

Cramer, P. (1991). Anger and the use of defense mechanisms in college students. *Journal of Personality, 59,* 39–55.

Cramer, P. (1999). Personality, personality disorders, and defense mechanisms. *Journal of Personality, 67,* 535–554.

Cramer, P. (2000). Defense mechanisms in psychology today: Further processes for adaptation. *American Psychologist, 55,* 637–646.

Cramer, P., & Block, J. (1998). Preschool antecedents of defense mechanism use in young adults. *Journal of Personality and Social Psychology, 74,* 159–169.

Craske, M. G., & Barlow, D. H. (1993). Panic disorder and agoraphobia. In D. H. Barlow (Ed.), *Clinical handbook of psychological disorders* (2nd ed.). New York: Guilford.

Crick, N. R., & Dodge, K. A. (1994). A review and reformation of social information-processing mechanisms in children's social adjustment. *Psychological Bulletin, 115,* 74–101.

Crisp, A. H., Hsu, L. K. G., Harding, B., & Hartshorn, J. (1980). Clinical features of anorexia nervosa: A study of consecutive series of 102 female patients. *Journal of Psychosomatic Research, 24*, 179–191.

Crits-Christoph, P., & Connolly, M. B. (2001). Relational interpretations. *Psychotherapy, 38*, 423–428.

Crittenden, P. M. (1988). Relationships at risk. In J. Belsky & T. Nezworski (Eds.), *Clinical implications of attachment* (pp. 136–176). Hillsdale, NJ: Erlbaum.

Crockenberg, S. B., & Acredolo, C. (1983). Infant temperament ratings: A functon of infants, or mothers, or both? *Infant Behavior and Development, 6*, 61–72.

Cronbach, L. J., Gleser, G. C., Nanda, H., & Rajaratnam, N. (1972). *The dependability of behavioral measurements: Theory of generalizability for scores and profiles.* New York: Wiley.

Cropanzano, R., James, K., & Citera, M. (1992). A goal hierarchy model of personality, motivation, and leadership. In L. L. Cummings & B. M. Staw (Eds.), *Research in organizational behavior* (Vol. 15, pp. 267–322). Greenwich, CT: JAI Press.

Cross, T. L., Coleman, L. J., & Terhaar-Yonkers, M. (1991). The social cognition of gifted adolescents in schools: Managing the stigma of giftedness. *Journal for the Education of the Gifted, 15*, 44–55.

Cutrona, C. E., Russell, D., & Jones, R. D. (1985). Cross-situational consistency in causal attributions: Does attributional style exist? *Journal of Personality and Social Psychology, 47*, 1043–1058.

Cutrona, C. E., & Suhr, J. A. (1992). Controllability of stressful events and satisfaction with spouse support behaviors. *Communication Research, 19*, 154–174.

Cutrona, C. E., & Suhr, J. A. (1994). Social support communication in the context of marriage: An analysis of couples' supportive interactions. In B. R. Burleson, T. L. Albrecht, & I. G. Sarason (Eds.), *Communication of social support* (pp. 113–135). Thousand Oaks, CA: Sage.

Cutting, L. P., & Docherty, N. M. (2000). Schizophrenia outpatients' perceptions of their parents: Is expressed emotion a factor? *Journal of Abnormal Psychology, 109*, 266–272.

Davila, J. (2001). Paths to unhappiness: The overlapping courses of depression and romantic dysfunction. In S. R. H. Beach (Ed.), *Marital and family processes in depression: A scientific foundation for clinical practice* (pp. 71–87). Washington, DC: American Psychological Association.

Dean, A., & Lin, N. (1977). The stress-buffering role of social support. *Journal of Nervous and Mental Disease, 165*, 403–417.

Deaton, J. D., Berg, S. W., Richlin, M., & Litrownik, A. J. (1977). Coping activities in solitary confinement of U.S. Navy POWs in Vietnam. *Journal of Applied Social Psychology, 7*, 239–257.

DeJong, C. A. T., Van den Brink, W., Jansen, J. A. M., & Schippers, G. M. (1989). Interpersonal aspects of *DSM–III* Axis II: Theoretical hypotheses and empirical findings. *Journal of Personality Disorders, 3*, 135–146.

Deknatel, F. B. (1950). *Edvard Munch.* New York: Chanticleer.

DeLongis, A., Coyne, J. C., Dakof, G., Folkman, S., & Lazarus, R. S. (1982). Relation of daily hassles, uplifts, and major life events to health status. *Health Psychology, 1*, 119–136.

DeVoge, J., & Beck, S. (1978). The therapist–client relationship in behavior therapy. In M. Hersen, R. M. Eisler, & P. M. Miller (Eds.), *Progress in behavior modification* (Vol. 6, pp. 203–248). New York: Academic Press.

Doane, J. A., Falloon, I. R. H., Goldstein, M. J., & Mintz, J. (1985). Parental affective style and the treatment of schizophrenia: Predicting course of illness and social functioning. *Archives of General Psychiatry, 42*, 34–42.

Doane, J. A., Goldstein, J. J., Miklowitz, D. J., & Falloon, I. R. H. (1986). The impact of individual and family treatment on the affective climate of families of schizophrenics. *British Journal of Psychiatry, 148*, 279–287.

Doane, J. A., West, K. L., Goldstein, M. J., Rodnick, E. H., & Jones, J. E. (1981). Parental communication deviance and affective style: Predictors of subsequent schizophrenia spectrum disorders in vulnerable adolescents. *Archives of General Psychiatry, 38*, 679–685.

Docherty, J., Fiester, S., & Shea, T. (1986). Syndromes: Diagnosis and personality disorder. In R. Hales & A. Frances (Eds.), *Psychiatric update: American Psychiatric Association annual review* (Vol. 5, pp. 315–355). Washington, DC: American Psychiatric Association.

Docherty, N. M. (1995). Expressed emotion and language disturbances in parents of stable schizophrenia outpatients. *Schizophrenia Bulletin, 21*, 411–418.

Dodge, K. A. (1993). Social–cognitive mechanisms in the development of conduct disorder and depression. *Annual Review of Psychology, 44*, 559–584.

Dodge, K. A., & Cole, J. D. (1987). Social-information-processing factors in reactive and proactive aggression in children's peer groups. *Journal of Personality and Social Psychology, 53*, 1146–1158.

Donahue, E. M., Robins, R. W., Roberts, B. W., & John, O. P. (1993). The divided self: Concurrent and longitudinal effects of psychological adjustment and social roles on self-concept differentiation. *Journal of Personality and Social Psychology, 64*, 834–846.

Donovan, J. E., Jessor, R., & Costa, F. M. (1988). Syndrome of problem behavior in adolescence: A replication. *Journal of Consulting and Clinical Psychology, 56*, 762–765.

Dooley, P. A. (1995). Perceptions of onset controllability of AIDS and helping judgments: An attributional analysis. *Journal of Applied Social Psychology, 25*, 858–869.

Dow, M. G., & Craighead, W. E. (1987). Social inadequacy and depression: Overt behavior and self-evaluation processes. *Journal of Social and Clinical Psychology, 5*, 99–113.

Downey, G., & Feldman, S. I. (1996). Implications of rejection sensitivity for intimate relationships. *Journal of Personality and Social Psychology, 70*, 1327–1343.

Downs, A. C., & Harrison, S. K. (1985). Embarrassing age spots or just plain ugly? Physical attractiveness stereotyping as an instrument of sexism on American television commercials. *Sex Roles, 13*, 9–19.

Dozier, M., Stovall, K. C., & Albus, K. E. (2000). Attachment and psychopathology in adulthood. In J. Cassidy & P. R. Shaver (Eds.), *Handbook of attachment: Theory, research, and clinical applications* (pp. 497–519). New York: Guilford.

Dryer, D. C., & Horowitz, L. M. (1997). When do opposites attract? Interpersonal complementarity versus similarity. *Journal of Personality and Social Psychology, 72,* 596–603.

Durand, V. M., & Barlow, D. H. (2003). *Essentials of abnormal psychology* (3rd ed.). Pacific Grove, CA: Wadsworth-Thomson Learning.

Dweck, C. S., Chiu, C., & Hong, Y. (1995). Implicit theories and their role in judgments and reactions: A world from two perspectives. *Psychological Inquiry, 6,* 267–285.

Dweck, C. S., & Leggett, E. (1988). A social–cognitive approach to motivation and personality. *Psychological Review, 95,* 256–273.

Edson, M. (1999). *Wit.* New York: Faber and Faber.

Edwards, J. A., Weary, G., & Reich, D. A. (1998). Causal uncertainty: Factor structure and relation to the Big Five personality factors. *Personality and Social Psychology Bulletin, 24,* 451–462.

Eells, T. (Ed.). (1997). *Handbook of psychotherapy case formulation.* New York: Guilford.

Egeland, B., & Farber, E. A. (1984). Infant–mother attachment: Factors related to its development and changes over time. *Child Development, 55,* 731–771.

Egeland, B., & Sroufe, L. A. (1981a). Attachment and early maltreatment. *Child Development, 52,* 44–52.

Egeland, B., & Sroufe, L. A. (1981b). Development sequelae of maltreatment in infancy. In R. Rizley & D. Cicchetti (Eds.), *Developmental perspectives on child maltreatment* (pp. 77–92). San Francisco: Jossey-Bass.

Eich, E., Macaulay, D., Loewenstein, R. J., & Dihle, P. H. (1997). Memory, amnesia, and dissociative identity disorder. *Psychological Science, 8,* 417–422.

Eisler, I., Dare, C., Russell, G. F. M., Szmukler, G., LeGrange, D., & Dodge, E. (1997). Family and individual therapy in anorexia nervosa: A 5-year follow-up. *Archives of General Psychiary, 54,* 1025–1030.

Ekman, P., & Friesen, W. V. (1972). Hand movements. *Journal of Communication, 22,* 353–374.

Ekman, P., & Friesen, W. V. (1974). Nonverbal behavior and psychopathology. In R. J. Friedman & M. M. Mintz (Eds.), *The psychology of depression* (pp. 203–224). Washington, DC: Winston.

Ellison, Z., van Os, J., & Murray, R. (1998). Special feature: Childhood personality characteristics of schizophrenia: Manifestations of, or risk factors for, the disorder? *Journal of Personality Disorders, 12,* 247–261.

Ellring, H. (1986). Nonverbal expression of psychological states in psychiatric patients. *European Archives of Psychiatry and Neurological Sciences, 236,* 31–34.

Ellring, H., & Scherer, K. R. (1996). Vocal indicators of mood change in depression. *Journal of Nonverbal Behavior, 20,* 83–110.

Emde, R., & Walker, S. (1976). Longitudinal study of infant sleep: Results of 14 subjects studied at monthly intervals. *Psychophysiology, 13,* 456–461.

Emmelkamp, P. M. G. (1988). Phobic disorders. In C. G. Last & M. Hersen (Eds.), *Handbook of anxiety disorders* (pp. 66–86). New York: Pergamon.

Emmons, R. A. (1989). The personal striving approach to personality. In L. A. Pervin (Ed.), *Goal concepts in personality and social psychology* (pp. 87–126). Hillsdale, NJ: Erlbaum.

Epstein, S. (1973). The self-concept revisited—or a theory of a theory. *American Psychologist, 28*, 404–416.

Erickson, D. H., Beiser, M., Iacono, W. G., Fleming, J. A. E., & Lin, T. (1989). The role of social relationships in the course of first-episode schizophrenia and affective psychosis. *American Journal of Psychiatry, 146*, 1456–1461.

Erikson, E. H. (1963). *Childhood and society* (2nd ed.). New York: Norton.

Erickson, M. F., Sroufe, L. A., & Egeland, B. (1985). The relationship between quality of attachment and behavior problems in preschool in a high-risk sample. *Monographs of the Society for Research in Child Development, 50*(1-2, Serial No. 209), 147–156.

Exline, J. J., & Lobel, M. (1999). The perils of outperformance: Sensitivity about being the target of a threatening upward comparison. *Psychological Bulletin, 125*, 307–337.

Fagot, B. I., & Kavanaugh, K. (1990). The prediction of antisocial behavior from avoidant attachment classifications. *Child Development, 61*, 864–873.

Fairburn, C. G. (1997). Eating disorders. In D. M. Clark & C. G. Fairburn (Eds.), *Science and practice of cognitive behaviour therapy* (pp. 209–241). New York: Oxford University Press.

Fairburn, C. G., Welch, S. L., Doll, H. A., Davies, B. A., & O'Connor, M. E. (1997). Risk factors for bulimia nervosa: A community-based-control study. *Archives of General Psychiatry, 54*, 509–517.

Fairburn, C. G., & Wilson, G. T. (Eds.). (1993). *Binge eating: Nature, assessment and treatment*. New York: Guilford.

Farrington, D. P. (1988). Social, psychological and biological influences on juvenile delinquency and adult crime. In W. Buikhuisen & S. Mednick (Eds.). *Explaining criminal behavior* (pp. 68–89). Leiden: E. J. Brill.

Farrington, D. P., & Loeber, R. (1998). Transatlantic replicability of risk factors in the development of delinquency. In P. Cohen, C. Slomkowski, & L. N. Robins (Eds.). *Where and when: Geographic and generational influence on psychopathology* (pp. 299–329). Mahwah, NJ: Erlbaum.

Feinsilver, D. (1970). Communication in families of schizophrenic patients. *Archives of General Psychiatry, 22*, 143–148.

Fitzgerald, O. (1948). Love deprivation and the hysterical personality. *Journal of Mental Science, 94*, 701–717.

Flavell, J. H. (1986). The development of children's knowledge about the appearance–reality distinction. *American Psychologist, 41*, 418–425.

Flavell, J. H., Flavell, E. R., & Green, F. L. (1983). Development of the appearance–reality distinction. *Cognitive Psychology, 15*, 95–120.

Flavell, J. H., Green, F. L., & Flavell, E. R. (1986). Development of knowledge about the appearance–reality distinction. *Monographs of the Society for Research in Child Development, 51*, 1–68.

Fleming, B. (1990). Dependent personality disorder. In A. T. Beck & A. Freeman (Eds.), *Cognitive therapy of personality disorders* (pp. 283–308). New York: Guilford.

Foa, E. B. (1979). Failure in treating obsessive–compulsives. *Behaviour Research and Therapy, 17*, 169–176.

Foa, E. B., Steketee, G. S., Grayson, J. B., Turner, R. M., & Latimer, P. R. (1984). Deliberate exposure and blocking of obsessive–comulsive rituals: Immediate and long-term effects. *Behavior Therapy, 15*, 450–472.

Foersterling, F. (1985). Attributional training: A review. *Psychological Bulletin, 98*, 495–512.

Fossati, A., Madeddu, F., & Maffei, C. (1999). Borderline personality disorder and childhood sexual abuse: A meta-analytic study. *Journal of Personality Disorders, 13*, 268–280.

Fossi, L., Faravelli, C., & Paoli, M. (1984). The ethological approach to the assessment of depressive disorders. *Journal of Nervous and Mental Disease, 172*, 332–341.

Fox, N. A., & Card, J. A. (1999). Psychophysiological measures in the study of attachment. In J. Cassidy & P. R. Shaver (Eds.), *Handbook of attachment: Theory, research, and clinical applications* (pp. 181–197). New York: Guilford.

Fraley, R. C., Waller, N. G., & Brennan, K. A. (2000). An item response theory analysis of self-report measures of adult attachment. *Journal of Personality and Social Psychology, 78*, 350–365.

Freedman, B. J. (1974). The subjective experience of perceptual and cognitive disturbances in schizophrenia. *Archives of General Psychiatry, 30*, 333–340.

French, R. D. (1981). *Interpersonal problem solving skill in lonely people.* Stanford University, Stanford, CA. [unpublished dissertation]

Freud, A. (1966). *Normality and pathology in childhood: Assessment of development.* New York: International Universities Press.

Freud, S. (1963). Mourning and melancholia. In P. Rieff (Ed.), *General psychological theory: Papers on metapsychology* (pp. 164–179). New York: Collier Books. (Original work published in 1917)

Freud, S. (1963). On the mechanisms of paranoia. In P. Rieff (Ed.), *General psychological theory: Papers on metapsychology* (pp. 29–48). New York: Collier Books. (Original work published 1911)

Funder, D. C., & Dobroth, K. M. (1987). Differences between traits: Properties associated with interjudge agreement. *Journal of Personality and Social Psychology, 52*, 409–418.

Gaebel, W., & Wolwer, W. (1992). Facial expression and emotional face recognition in schizophrenia and depression. *European Archives of Psychiatry and Clinical Neuroscience, 242*, 46–52.

Gallup, G. G. J. (1970). Chimpanzees: Self-recognition. *Science, 167*, 86–87.

Gallup, G. G. J. (1991). Toward a comparative psychology of self-awareness: Species limitations and cognitive consequences. In G. R. Goethals & J. Strauss (Eds.), *The self: An interdisciplinary approach* (pp. 121–135). New York: Springer-Verlag.

Garfinkel, P. E., Kenney, S. H., & Kaplan, A. S. (1995). Views on classification and diagnosis of eating disorders. *Canadian Journal of Psychiatry, 40*, 445–456.

Garner, D. M., Garner, M. V., & Rosen, L. W. (1993). Anorexia nervosa "restrictors" who purge: Implications for subtyping anorexia nervosa. *International Journal of Eating Disorders, 13*, 171–185.

Garner, D. M., & Needleman, L. D. (1996). Stepped-care and decision-tree models for treating eating disorders. In J. K. Thompson (Ed.), *Body image, eating disorders, and obesity* (pp. 225–252). Washington, DC: American Psychological Association.

Gergen, K. J. (1968). Personal consistency and the presentation of self. In C. Gordon & J. Gergen (Eds.), *The self in social interaction* (pp. 299–308). New York: Wiley.

Gifford, R. (1994). A lens-mapping framework for understanding the encoding and decoding of interpersonal disposition in nonverbal behavior. *Journal of Personality and Social Psychology, 66*, 398–412.

Gillberg, I. C., Rastam, M., & Gillberg, C. G. (1995). Anorexia nervosa 6 years after onset: I. Personality disorders. *Comprehensive Psychiatry, 36*, 61–69.

Glasgow, R. E., & Arkowitz, H. (1975). The behavioral assessment of male and female social competence in dyadic heterosexual interactions. *Behavior Therapy, 6*, 488–498.

Gleaves, D. H. (1996). The sociocognitive model of dissociative identity disorders: A reexamination of the evidence. *Psychological Bulletin, 120*, 42–59.

Goldberg, S., Lojkasek, M., Minde, K., & Corter, C. (1990). Predictions of behavior problems in children born prematurely. *Development and Psychopathology, 1*, 15–30.

Goldsmith, D. J. (1994). The role of facework in supportive communication. In B. R. Burleson, T. L. Albrecht, & I. G. Sarason (Eds.), *Communication of social support* (pp. 29–49). Thousand Oaks, CA: Sage.

Goldstein, A. J., & Chambless, D. L. (1978). A reanalysis of agoraphobia. *Behavior Therapy, 9*, 47–59.

Goldstein, M. J. (1981). Family factors associated with schizophrenia and anorexia nervosa. *Journal of Youth and Adolescence, 10*, 385–405.

Goldstein, M. J. (1987). Family interaction patterns that antedate the onset of schizophrenia and related disorders: A further analysis of data from a longitudinal prospective study. In K. Hahlweg & M. J. Goldstein (Eds.), *Understanding major mental disorder: The contribution of family interaction research* (pp. 11–32). New York: Family Process Press.

Goldstein, M. J., & Palmer, J. O. (1975). *The experience of anxiety: A casebook* (2nd ed.). New York: Oxford University Press.

Goldstein, M. J., & Strachan, A. M. (1987). The family and schizophrenia. In T. Jacob (Ed.), *Family interaction and psychopathology: Theories, methods and findings* (pp. 481–508). New York: Plenum.

Goldstein, R. B., Powers, S. I., McCusker, J., Lewis, B. F., Mundt, K. A., & Bigelow, C. (1996). Lack of remorse in antisocial personality disorder among drug abusers in residential treatment. *Journal of Personality Disorders, 10*, 321–334.

Goleman, D. (1995). *Emotional intelligence*. New York: Bantam Books.

Gore, S. (1978). The effect of social support in moderating the health consequences of unemployment. *Journal of Health and Social Behavior, 19*, 157–165.

Gotlib, I. H., & Beatty, M. (1985). Negative responses to depression: The role of attributional style. *Cognitive Therapy and Research, 9*, 91–103.

Gotlib, I. H., & Robinson, L. A. (1982). Responses to depressed individuals: Discrepancies between self-report and observer-rated behavior. *Journal of Abnormal Psychology, 91*, 231–240.

Graber, J. A., Brooks-Gunn, J., Paikoff, R. L., & Warren, M. P. (1994). Prediction of eating problems: An 8-year study of adolescent girls. *Developmental Psychology, 30*, 823–834.

Grawe, K. (2003). *Psychological therapy*. Seattle: Hogrefe & Huber.

Greenberg, J. R., & Mitchell, S. A. (1983). *Object relations in psychoanalytic theory*. Cambridge, MA: Harvard University Press.

Greenberg, M. T. (1999). Attachment and psychopathology in childhood. In J. Cassidy & P. R. Shaver (Eds.), *Handbook of attachment: Theory, research and clinical applications* (pp. 469–496). New York: Guilford.

Griffith, J. J., Mednick, S. A., Schulsinger, F., & Diderichsen, B. (1980). Verbal asssociative disturbances in children at high risk for schizophrenia. *Journal of Abnormal Psychology, 89*, 125–131.

Grinker, R. R. (1964). Communications by patients in depressive states. *Archives of General Psychiatry, 10*, 576–580.

Grissett, N. I., & Norvell, N. K. (1992). Perceived social support, social skills and quality of relationships in bulimic women. *Journal of Consulting and Clinical Psychology, 60*, 293–299.

Gross, J. J. (1999). Emotion and emotion regulation. In L. A. Pervin & O. P. John (Eds.), *Handbook of personality: Theory and research* (2nd ed., pp. 525–552). New York: Guilford.

Grosse Holtforth, M., & Grawe, K. (2002). *Fragebogen zur Analyse motivationaler Schemata (FAMOS)—Handanweisung*. Goettingen, Germany: Hogrefe.

Grosse Holtforth, M., Grawe, K., & Egger, O. (2003). *Reducing the dreaded: Change of avoidance motivation in psychotherapy*. Unpublished manuscript.

Gurtman, M. B. (1987). Depressive affect and disclosures as factors in interpersonal rejection. *Cognitive Therapy and Research, 11*, 87–100.

Gurtman, M. B. (1991). Evaluating the interpersonalness of personality scales. *Personality and Social Psychology Bulletin, 17*, 670–677.

Gurtman, M. B. (1992a). Construct validity of interpersonal personality measures: The interpersonal circumplex as a nomological net. *Journal of Personality and Social Psychology, 63*, 105–118.

Gurtman, M. B. (1992b). Trust, distrust, and interpersonal problems: A circumplex analysis. *Journal of Personality and Social Psychology, 62*, 989–1002.

Gurtman, M. B. (1993). Constructing personality tests to meet a structural criterion: Application of the interpersonal circumplex. *Journal of Personality, 61*, 237–263.

Gurtman, M. B. (1994). The circumplex as a tool for studying normal and abnormal personality: A methodological primer. In S. Strack & M. Lorr (Eds.), *Differentiating normal and abnormal personality* (pp. 243–263). New York: Springer.

Gurtman, M. B. (1995). Personality structure and interpersonal problems: A theoretically-guided item analysis of the Inventory of Interpersonal Problems. *Assessment, 1*, 343–361.

Gurtman, M. B., & Bakarishnan, J. D. (1998). Circular measurement redux: The analysis and interpretation of interpersonal circle profiles. *Clinical Psychology: Science and Practice, 5*, 344–360.

Hale, W. W., Jansen, J. H. C., Bouhuys, A. L., Jenner, J. A., & van der Hoofdakker, R. H. (1997). Non-verbal behavioral interactions of depressed patients with partners and strangers: The role of behavioral social support and involvement in depression persistence. *Journal of Affective Disorders, 44*, 111–122.

Haley, J. (1963). *Strategies of psychotherapy*. New York: Grune & Stratton.

Hallowell, E. M., & Ratey, J. J. (1994). *Driven to distraction*. New York: Simon & Schuster.

Hammen, C., & Peters, S. D. (1978). Interpersonal sequences of depression: Responses to men and women enacting a depressed role. *Journal of Abnormal Psychology, 87*, 322–332.

Hampshire, S. (1953). Dispositions. *Inquiry, 14*, 5–11.

Hansson, R. O., & Jones, W. H. (1981). Loneliness, cooperation, and conformity among American undergraduates. *Journal of Social Psychology, 115*, 103–108.

Hare, R. D. (1991). *The Hare psychopathy checklist—revised manual*. Toronto: Multi-Health Systems.

Hare, R. D. (1998). Psychopathy, affect and behavior. In D. J. Cooke, A. E. Forth, & R. D. Hare (Eds.), *Psychopathy: Theory, research, and implications for society* (pp. 105–137). Dordrecht, Netherlands: Kluwer.

Hare, R. D. (1999). *Without conscience: The disturbing world of the psychopaths among us*. New York: Guilford.

Harlow, H. F. (1958). The nature of love. *American Psychologist, 13*, 673–685.

Harper, M., & Roth, M. (1962). Temporal lobe epilepsy and the phobia-anxiety-depersonalization syndrome. *Comprehensive Psychiatry, 3*, 129–151.

Harris, T. A. (1967). *I'm OK—you're OK*. New York: Avon Books.

Harter, S. (1986). Cognitive–developmental processes in the integration of concepts about emotions and the self. *Social Cognition, 4*, 119–151.

Harter, S. (1999). *The construction of the self: A developmental perspective*. New York: Guilford.

Hartshorne, H., & May, A. (1928). *Studies in the nature of character, Vol. 1. Studies in deceit*. New York: Macmillan.

Hays, R. D., & Ellickson, P. L. (1996). Associations between drug use and deviant behavior in teenagers. *Addictive Behaviors, 21*, 291–302.

Hazan, C., & Shaver, P. R. (1987). Romantic love conceptualized as an attachment process. *Journal of Personality and Social Psychology, 52*, 511–524.

Hazan, C., & Shaver, P. R. (1990). Love and work: An attachment theoretical perspective. *Journal of Personality and Social Psychology, 59*, 270–280.

Heatherton, T. F., Herman, C. P., & Polivy, J. (1991). Effects of physical threat and ego threat on eating behavior. *Journal of Personality and Social Psychology, 60*, 138–143.

Heatherton, T. F., Mahamedi, F., Striepe, M., Field, A. E., & Keel, P. (1997). A 10-year longitudinal study of body weight, dieting, and eating disorder symptoms. *Journal of Abnormal Psychology, 106*, 117–125.

Heinicke, C. M., & Westheimer, I. J. (1965). *Brief separations*. New York: International Universities Press.

Helgeson, V. S. (2002). *The psychology of gender*. Upper Saddle River, NJ: Prentice Hall.

Helsing, K. J., Szklo, M., & Comstock, G. W. (1981). Factors associated with mortality and widowhood. *American Journal of Public Health, 71,* 802–809.

Herman, C. P., & Polivy, J. (1975). Anxiety, restraint, and eating behavior. *Journal of Abnormal Psychology, 84,* 666–672.

Hersov, L. A. (1960). Refusal to go to school. *Child Psychology and Psychiatry, 1,* 137–145.

Hertsgaard, L., Gunnar, M., Erickson, M. F., & Nachmias, M. (1995). Adrenocortical response to the strange situation in infants with disorganized/disoriented attachment relationships. *Child Development, 66,* 1100–1106.

Herzog, W., Schellberg, D., & Deter, H. C. (1997). First recovery in anorexia nervosa patients in the long-term course: A discrete-time survival analysis. *Journal of Consulting and Clinical Psychology, 65,* 169–177.

Higgins, E. T. (1987). Self-discrepancy: A theory relating self and affect. *Psychological Review, 94,* 319–340.

Higgins, E. T. (1996). Ideals, oughts, and regulatory focus: Affect and motivation from distinct pains and pleasures. In P. M. Gollwitzer & J. A. Bargh (Eds.), *The psychology of action: Linking cognition and motivation to behavior* (pp. 91–114). New York: Guilford.

Hinchcliffe, M. K., Hooper, D., & Roberts, J. F. (1978). *The melancholy marriage: Depression in marriage and psychosocial approaches to therapy.* New York: Wiley.

Hobson, C. J., Kamen, J., Szostek, J., Nethercut, C. M., Tiedmann, J. W., & Wojnarowicz, S. (1998). Stressful life events: A revision and update of the Social Readjustment Rating Scale. *International Journal of Stress Management, 5,* 1–23.

Hokanson, J. E., Sacco, W. P., Blumberg, S. R., & Landrum, G. C. (1980). Interpersonal behavior of depressive individuals in a mixed-motive game. *Journal of Abnormal Psychology, 89,* 320–332.

Holmes, D. S. (1968). Dimensions of projection. *Psychological Bulletin, 69,* 248–268.

Holmes, D. S. (1978). Projection as a defense mechanism. *Psychological Bulletin, 85,* 677–688.

Holmes, D. S., & McCaul, K. D. (1989). Laboratory research on defense mechanisms. In R. W. J. Neufeld (Ed.), *Advances in the investigation of psychological stress* (pp. 161–192). New York: Wiley.

Holmes, T. H., & Rahe, R. H. (1967). The Social Readjustment Rating Scale. *Journal of Psychosomatic Research, 11,* 213–218.

Holtzworth-Munroe, A., & Hutchinson, G. (1993). Attributing negative intent to wife behavior: The attributions of maritally violent versus nonviolent men. *Journal of Abnormal Psychology, 102,* 206–211.

Hooley, J. M., & Hiller, J. B. (1997). Family relationships and major mental disorder: Risk factors and preventive strategies. In S. Duck (Ed.), *Hand-*

book of personal relationships (2nd ed., pp. 621–648). Chichester, England: Wiley.

Hooley, J. M., & Hiller, J. B. (1998). Expressed emotion and the pathogenesis of relapse in schizophrenia. In M. F. D. Lenzenweger, & R. H. Dworkin (Eds.), *Origins and development of schizophrenia* (pp. 447–468). Washington, DC: American Psychological Association.

Hope, S., Power, C., & Rodgers, B. (1999). Does financial hardship account for elevated psychological distress in lone mothers? *Social Science and Medicine, 49,* 1637–1649.

Horney, K. (1945). *Our inner conflicts.* New York: Norton.

Horowitz, L. M. (1994). Schemas, psychopathology, and psychotherapy research. *Psychotherapy Research, 4,* 1–17.

Horowitz, L. M., Alden, L. E., Wiggins, J. S., & Pincus, A. L. (2000). *Inventory of interpersonal problems.* San Antonio, TX: The Psychological Corporaton.

Horowitz, L. M., French, R. D. S., & Anderson, C. A. (1982). The prototype of a lonely person. In L. Peplau & D. Perlman (Eds.), *Loneliness: A sourcebook of current theory, research, and therapy* (pp. 183–205). New York: Wiley Interscience.

Horowitz, L. M., Krasnoperova, E. N., Tatar, D. G., Hansen, M. B., Person, E. A., Galvin, K. L., & Nelson, K. L. (2001). The way to console may depend on the goal: Experimental studies of social support. *Journal of Experimental Social Psychology, 37,* 49–61.

Horowitz, L. M., Locke, K. D., Morse, M. B., Waiker, S. V., Dryer, D. C., Tarnow, E., & Ghannam, J. (1991). Self-derogations and the interpersonal theory. *Journal of Personality and Social Psychology, 61,* 68–79.

Horowitz, L. M., Post, D. L., French, R. D. S., Wallis, K. D., & Siegelman, E. Y. (1981). The prototype as a construct in abnormal psychology: II. Clarifying disagreement in psychiatric judgments. *Journal of Abnormal Psychology, 90,* 575–585.

Horowitz, L. M., Rosenberg, S. E., Baer, B. A., Ureño, G., & Villaseñor, V. S. (1988). Inventory of interpersonal problems: Psychometric properties and clinical applications. *Journal of Consulting and Clinical Psychology, 56,* 885–892.

Horowitz, L. M., Strauss, B., & Kordy, H. (1994). *Das Inventar zur Erfassung interpersonaler Probleme—Deutsche Version.* Weinheim, Germany: Beltz Test Gesellschaft.

Horowitz, L. M., & Vitkus, J. (1986). The interpersonal basis of psychiatric symptoms. *Clinical Psychology Review, 6,* 443–469.

Horowitz, L. M., Wright, J. C., Lowenstein, E., & Parad, H. W. (1981). The prototype as a construct in abnormal psychology: I. A method for deriving prototypes. *Journal of Abnormal Psychology, 90,* 568–574.

Horvath, A. O., & Luborsky, L. (1993). The role of the therapeutic alliance in psychotherapy. *Journal of Consulting and Clinical Psychology, 61,* 561–573.

House, J. S., Robbins, C., & Metzner, H. L. (1982). The association of social relationships and activities with mortality: Prospective evidence from the Tecumseh Community health study. *American Journal of Epidemiology, 116,* 123–140.

Howes, J. J., & Hokanson, J. E. (1979). Conversational and social responses to depressive interpersonal behavior. *Journal of Abnormal Psychology, 88,* 625–634.

Hsu, L. K. G. (1990). *Eating disorders.* New York: Guilford.

Hsu, L. K. G. (1995). Outcome of bulimia nervosa. In K. D. Brownell & C. G. Fairburn (Eds.), *Eating disorders and obesity: A comprehensive handbook* (pp. 238–244). New York: Guilford.

Hudley, C., & Graham, S. (1993). An attributional intervention to reduce peer-directed aggression in African American boys. *Child Development, 64,* 124–138.

Humphrey, L. L. (1987). Comparison of bulimic-anorexia and nondistressed families using structural analysis of social behavior. *Journal of the American Academy of Child and Adolescent Psychiatry, 26,* 248–255.

Ingram, R. E. (2003). Origins of cognitive vulnerability to depression. *Cognitive Therapy and Research, 27,* 77–88.

Ingram, R. E., Miranda, J., & Segal, Z. V. (1998). *Cognitive vulnerability to depression.* New York: Guilford.

Jacobson, N. S., & Margolin, G. (1979). *Marital therapy: Strategies based on social learning and behavior exchange principles.* New York: Brunner/Mazel.

James, W. (1892). *Psychology: The briefer course.* New York: Holt.

Jefferson, G., & Lee, J. R. E. (1992). The rejection of advice: Managing the problematic convergence of a "troubles-telling" and a "service encounter." In P. Drew & J. Heritge (Eds.), *Talk at work* (pp. 521–571). Cambridge, England: Cambridge University Press.

Johnson, A. M., Falstein, E. I., Szurek, S. A., & Svendsen, M. (1941). School phobia. *American Journal of Orthopsychiatry, 11,* 702–711.

Johnson, W. G., Tsoh, J. Y., & Varnado, P. J. (1996). Eating disorders: Efficacy of pharmacological and psychological interventions. *Clinical Psychology Review, 16,* 457–478.

Joiner, T. E., Jr., Katz, J., & Lew, A. (1999). Harbingers of depressotypic reassurance seeking: Negative life events, anxiety, and self-esteem. *Personality and Social Psychology Bulletin, 25,* 630–637.

Jones, E. E., & Berglas, S. (1978). Control of attributions about the self through self-handicapping strategies: The appeal of alcohol and the role of underachievement. *Personality and Social Psychology Bulletin, 4,* 200–206.

Jones, I. H., & Pansa, M. (1979). Some nonverbal aspects of depression and schizophrenia occurring during the interview. *Journal of Nervous and Mental Disease, 167,* 402–409.

Jones, M. M. (1980). Conversion reaction: Anachronism or evolutionary form? A review of the neurologic, behavioral, and psychoanalytic literature. *Psychological Bulletin, 87,* 427–441.

Jones, W. H., Hobbs, S. A., & Hockenbury, D. (1982). Loneliness and social skill deficits. *Journal of Personality and Social Psychology, 42,* 682–689.

Kachin, K. E., Newman, M. G., & Pincus, A. L. (2001). An interpersonal problem approach to the division of social phobia subtypes. *Behavior Therapy, 32,* 479–501.

Kagan, J. (1994). *Galen's prophecy: Temperament in human nature.* New York: Basic Books.

Kagan, J., Reznick, J. S., & Snidman, N. (1988). Biological bases of childhood shyness. *Science*, *240*(4849), 161–171.

Karen, R. (1994). *Becoming attached*. New York: Warner.

Kasvikis, Y. G., Tsakiris, F., Marks, I. M., Basoglu, M., & Noshirvani, H. V. (1986). Past history of anorexia nervosa in women with obsessive–compulsive disorders. *International Journal of Eating Disorders*, *5*, 1069–1075.

Kaufman, J., & Cicchetti, D. (1989). The effects of maltreatment on school-aged children's socioemotional development: Assessments in a day camp setting. *Developmental Psychology*, *15*, 516–524.

Kazdin, A. E., Moser, J., Colbus, D., & Bell, R. (1985). Depressive symptoms among physically abused and psychiatrically disturbed children. *Journal of Abnormal Psychology*, *94*, 298–307.

Kazdin, A. E., Sherick, R. B., Esveldt-Dawson, K., & Rancurello, M. D. (1985). Nonverbal behavior and childhood depression. *Journal of the American Academy of Child Psychiatry*, *24*, 303–309.

Kegan, R. (1982). *The evolving self: Problem and process in human development*. Cambridge, MA: Harvard University Press.

Kehrer, C. A., & Linehan, M. M. (1996). Interpersonal and emotional problem solving skills and parasuicide among women with borderline personality disorder. *Journal of Personality Disorders*, *10*, 153–163.

Kemperman, I., Russ, M. J., & Shearin, E. (1997). Self-injurious behavior and mood regulation in borderline patients. *Journal of Personality Disorders*, *11*, 146–157.

Kendall-Tackett, K. A., Williams, L. M., & Finkelhor, D. (1993). Impact of sexual abuse on children: A review and synthesis of recent empirical studies. *Psychological Bulletin*, *113*, 164–180.

Kennedy, W. A. (1965). School phobia: Rapid treatment of fifty cases. *Journal of Abnormal Psychology*, *70*, 285–289.

Kernberg, O. (1985). *Borderline conditions and pathological narcissism*. Northvale, NJ: Aronson.

Kiecolt-Glaser, J. K., Garner, W., Speicher, C., Penn, G. M., Holliday, B. S., & Glaser, R. (1984). Psychosocial modifiers of immunocompetence in medical students. *Psychosomatic Medicine*, *46*, 7–14.

Kiecolt-Glaser, J. K., & Glaser, R. (1987). Psychosocial moderators of immune function. *Annals of Behavioral Medicine*, *9*, 16–20.

Kiecolt-Glaser, J. K., Ricker, D., George, J., Messick, G., Speicher, C. E., Garner, W., & Glaser, R. (1984). Urinary cortisol levels, cellular immunocompetency, and loneliness in psychiatric patients. *Psychosomatic Medicine*, *46*, 15–23.

Kiesler, D. J. (1983). The 1982 interpersonal circle: A taxonomy for complementarity in human transactions. *Psychological Review*, *90*, 185–214.

Kiesler, D. J. (1996). *Contemporary interpersonal theory and research: Personality, psychopathology and psychotherapy*. New York: Wiley.

Kiesler, D. J., Schmidt, J. A., & Wagner, C. C. (1997). A circumplex inventory of impact messages: An operational bridge between emotion and interpersonal behavior. In R. Plutchik & H. R. Conte (Eds.), *Circumplex models of personality and emotions* (pp. 221–244). Washington, DC: American Psychological Association.

Killingmo, B. (1989). Conflict and deficit: Implications for technique. *International Journal of Psychoanalysis, 70*, 65–79.

King, D. A., & Heller, K. (1984). Depression and the response of others: A re-evaluation. *Journal of Abnormal Psychology, 93*, 477–480.

Klein, D. F. (1964). Delineation of two drug-responsive anxiety syndromes. *Psycopharmacologia, 5*, 397–408.

Klein, E. (1945). The reluctance to go to school. *The Psychoanalytic Study of the Child, 1*, 263–279.

Klinger, E. (1987). Current concerns and disengagement from incentives. In F. Halisch & J. Kuhl (Eds.), *Motivation, intention, and volition* (pp. 337–347). Heidelberg, Germany: Springer-Verlag.

Kluft, R. P. (1987). An update on multiple personality disorder. *Hospital and Community Psychiatry, 38*, 363–373.

Kluft, R. P. (1991). Multiple personality disorder. In A. Tasman & S. M. Goldinger (Eds.), *Review of psychiatry* (Vol. 10, pp. 161–188). Washington, DC: American Psychiatric Press.

Kluft, R. P. (1999). Current issues in dissociative identity disorder. *Journal of Practical Psychology and Behavioral Health, 5*, 3–19.

Kobak, R. (1999). The emotional dynamics of disruptions in attachment relationships: Implications for theory, research, and clinical intervention. In J. Cassidy & P. R. Shaver (Eds.), *Handbook of attachment: Theory, research, and clinical applications* (pp. 21–43). New York: Guilford.

Koestner, R., Zuroff, D. C., & Powers, T. A. (1991). The family origins of adolescent self-criticism and its continuity into adulthood. *Journal of Abnormal Psychology, 100*, 191–197.

Kohut, H. (1984). *How does analysis cure?* Chicago: University of Chicago Press.

Kordy, H., Kraemer, B., Palmer, R. L., Papezova, H., Pellet, J., Richard, M., Treasure, J., & COST Action B6. (2002). Remission, recovery, relapse, and recurrence in eating disorders: Conceptualization and illustration of a validation strategy. *Journal of Clinical Psychology, 58*, 833–846.

Kraus, A. S., & Lillienfeld, A. M. (1959). Some epidemiologic aspects of the high mortality rate in the young widowed group. *Journal of Chronic Diseases, 19*, 207–217.

Krohn, A. (1978). Hysteria. *Psychological Issues, 45*, 129–155.

LaForge, R., & Suczek, R. F. (1955). The interpersonal dimension of personality: III. An interpersonal check list. *Journal of Personality, 24*, 94–112.

Laing, R. D. (1965). *The divided self: An existential study in sanity and madness.* London: Penguin Books.

Lamb, M. E., Thompson, R. A., Gardner, W., & Charnov, E. L. (1985). *Infant–mother attachment: The origins and developmental significance of individual differences in strange situation behavior.* Hillsdale, NJ: Erlbaum.

Laporte, L., & Guttman, H. (1996). Traumatic childhood experiences as risk factors for borderline and other personality disorders. *Journal of Personality Disorders, 10*, 247–259.

LaRocco, J. M., House, J. S., & French, J. R. P., Jr. (1980). Social support, occupational stress, and health. *Journal of Health and Social Behavior, 21,* 202–218.

Lautman, M. (1991). End–benefit segmentation and prototypical bonding. *Journal of Advertising Research, 31,* 9–18.

Lazarus, A. A. (1960). The elimination of children's phobias by deconditioning. In H. J. Eysenck (Ed.), *Behavior therapy and the neuroses.* Oxford, England: Pergamon.

Lazarus, R. S. (1991). *Emotion and adaptation.* New York: Oxford University Press.

Leary, T. F. (1957). *Interpersonal diagnosis of personality.* New York: Ronald.

Lefcourt, H. (1992). Durability and impact of the locus of control construct. *Psychological Bulletin, 112,* 411–414.

Lehman, D. R., Ellard, J. H., & Wortman, C. B. (1986). Social support for the bereaved: Recipients' and providers' perspectives on what is helpful. *Journal of Consulting and Clinical Psychology, 54,* 438–446.

Lehman, D. R., & Hemphill, K. J. (1990). Recipients' perceptions of support attempts and attributions for support attempts that fail. *Journal of Social and Personal Relationships, 7,* 563–574.

Levine, S. (1983). A psychobiological approach to the ontogeny of coping. In N. Garmezy & M. Rutter (Eds.), *Stress, coping, and development in children* (pp. 107–131). New York: McGraw-Hill.

Levine, S., Coe, C. L., Smotherman, W. P., & Kaplan, J. N. (1978). Prolonged cortisol evaluation in the infant squirrel monkey after reunion with the mother. *Physiology and Behavior, 20,* 7–10.

Levy, S. M. (1976). Schizophrenic symptomatology: Reaction or strategy? A study of contextual antecedents. *Journal of Abnormal Psychology, 85,* 435–445.

Lewinsohn, P. M., & Rosenbaum, M. (1987). Recall of parental behavior by acute depressives, remitted depressives and nondepressives. *Journal of Personality and Social Psychology, 52,* 611–619.

Lewis, J. M., Rodnick, E. H., & Goldstein, J. J. (1981). Intrafamilial interactive behavior, parental communication deviance, and risk for schizophrenia. *Journal of Abnormal Psychology, 90,* 448–457.

Lewis, M., Feiring, C., McGuffog, C., & Jaskir, J. (1984). Predicting psychopathology in six-year-olds from early social relations. *Child Development, 55,* 123–136.

Liebowitz, M. R., & Klein, D. F. (1979). Assessment and treatment of phobic anxiety. *Journal of Clinical Psychiatry, 40,* 486–492.

Lin, N., Simeone, R. S., Ensel, W. M., & Kuo, W. (1979). Social support, stressful life events, and illness: A model and an empirical test. *Journal of Health and Social Behavior, 20,* 108–119.

Lindsay-Hartz, J., de Rivera, J., & Mascolo, M. F. (1995). Differentiating guilt and shame and their effects on motivation. In J. P. Tangney & K. W. Fischer (Eds.), *Self-conscious emotions* (pp. 274–300). New York: Guilford.

Linehan, M. M. (1993). Cognitive–behavioral treatment for bordeline personality disorder. New York: Guilford.

Linn, P., & Horowitz, F. (1983). The relationship between infant individual differences and mother–infant interaction during the neonatal period. *Infant Behavior and Development, 6,* 415–427.

Linville, P. W. (1985). Self-complexity and affective extremity: Don't put all of your eggs in one cognitive basket. *Social Cognition, 3,* 94–120.

Liotti, G. (1991). Insecure atachment and agoraphobia. In C. M. Parkes (Ed.), *Attachment across the life cycle* (pp. 216–233). New York: Tavistock/Routledge.

Little, B. R. (1983). Personal projects: A rationale and method for investigation. *Environment and Behavior, 15,* 273–309.

Liu, D., Diorio, J., Tannenbaum, B., Caldji, C., Francis, D., Freedman, J. A., Sharma, S., Pearson, P., Plotsky, P. M., & Meaney, M. J. (1997). Maternal care, hippocampal glucocorticoid receptors and hypothalmic–pituitary–adrenal responses to stress. *Science, 277,* 1659–1662.

Livesley, W. J., Schroeder, M. L., Jackson, D. N., & Jang, K. L. (1994). Categorical distinctions in the study of personality disorder: Implications for classification. *Journal of Abnormal Psychology, 103,* 6–17.

Lizardi, H., Klein, D. N., Ouimette, P. C., Riso, L. P., Anderson, R. L., & Donaldson, S. K. (1995). Reports of the childhood home environment in early-onset dysthymia and episodic major depression. *Journal of Abnormal Psychology, 104,* 132–139.

Locke, K. D. (2000). Circumplex scales of interpersonal values: Reliability, validity, and applicability to interpersonal problems and personality disorders. *Journal of Personality Assessment, 75,* 249–267.

Locke, K. D. (2003). H as a measure of complexity of social information processing. *Personality and Social Psychology Review, 7,* 268–280.

Locke, K. D., & Horowitz, L. M. (1990). Satisfaction in interpersonal interactions as a function of similarity in level of dysphoria. *Journal of Personality and Social Psychology, 58,* 823–831.

Loeber, R. (1990). Development and risk factors of juvenile antisocial behaviour and delinquency. *Clinical Psychology Review, 10,* 1–41.

Loeber, R., Wung, P., Keenan, K., Giroux, B., Stouthamer-Loeber, M., Van Kammen, W. B., & Maughan, B. (1993). Developmental pathways in disruptive child behavior. *Development and Psychopathology, 5,* 103–133.

Lopata, H. Z. (1969). Loneliness: Forms and components. *Social Problems, 17,* 248–262.

Lorenz, K. (1957). *Instinctive behavior.* New York: International Universities Press.

Lorr, M., & Strack, S. (1990). Wiggins' Interpersonal Adjective Scales: A dimentional view. *Personality and Individual Differences, 11,* 423–425.

Lowenstein, E. (1984). *Social perceptions of the depressed person: The effects of perceived responsibility and response to advice.* Unpublished doctoral dissertation. Stanford University: Stanford, CA.

Luborsky, L., & Crits-Christoph, P. (1998). *Understanding transference: The Core Conflictual Relationship Theme method (2nd Ed.).* Washington, DC: American Psychological Association.

Ludwig, A. M., Brandsma, J. M., Wilbur, C. B., Bendfeldt, F., & Jameson, D. H. (1972). The objective study of a multiple personality. *Archives of General Psychiatry, 26,* 298–310.

Luntz, B. K., & Widom, C. S. (1994). Antisocial personality disorder in abused and neglected children grown up. *American Journal of Psychiatry, 151*, 670–674.

Lykken, D. T. (1957). A study of anxiety in the sociopathic personality. *Journal of Abnormal and Social Psychology, 55*, 6–10.

Lyons-Ruth, K., Connell, D., Zoll, D., & Stahl, J. (1987). Infants at social risk: Relations among infant maltreatment, maternal behavior, and infant attachment behavior. *Developmental Psychology, 23*, 223–232.

Lyons-Ruth, K., & Jacobvitz, D. (1999). Attachment disorganization: Unresolved loss, relational violence, and lapses in behavioral and attentional strategies. In J. Cassidy & P. R. Shaver (Eds.), *Handbook of attachment: Theory, research and clinical applications* (pp. 520–554). New York: Guilford.

Lyons-Ruth, K., Zoll, D., Connell, D., & Grunebaum, H. (1989). Family deviance and family disruption in childhood: Associations with maternal behavior and infant maltreatment during the first two years of life. *Development and Psychopathology, 1*, 219–236.

Mahler, M. S., Pine, F., & Bergman, A. (1975). *The psychological birth of the human infant*. New York: Basic Books.

Main, M. (1995). Recent studies in attachment: Overview with selected implications for clinical work. In S. Goldberg, R. Muir, & J. Kerr (Eds.), *Attachment theory: Social, developmental, and clinical perspectives* (pp. 407–474). Hillsdale, NJ: Analytic Press.

Main, M., Kaplan, N., & Cassidy, J. (1985). Security in infancy, childhood, and adulthood: A move to the level of representation. *Monographs of the Society for Research in Child Development, 50*, 66–106.

Main, M., & Solomon, J. (1986). Discovery of a new, insecure–disorganized/disoriented attachment pattern. In T. B. Brazelton & M. W. Yogman (Eds.), *Affective development in infancy* (pp. 95–124). Norwood, NJ: Ablex.

Main, M., & Solomon, J. (1990). Procedures for identifying infants as disorganized/disoriented during the Ainsworth strange situation. In M. T. Greenberg, D. Cicchetti, & E. M. Cummings (Eds.), *Attachment in the preschool years: Theory, research, and intervention* (pp. 121–160). Chicago: University of Chicago Press.

Malle, B. F., & Knobe, J. (1997). Which behaviors do people explain? A basic actor–observer asymmetry. *Journal of Personality and Social Psychology, 72*, 288–304.

Malmo, R. B., Davis, J. F., & Barza, S. (1952). Total hysterical deafness: An experimental case study. *Journal of Personality, 21*, 188–204.

Malmo, R. B., Malmo, H. P., & Ditto, B. (2003). On reversible deafness, generalized anxiety disorder, and the motoric brain: A psychophysiological perspective. *International Journal of Psychophysiology, 48*, 97–113.

Mandal, M. K., Pandey, R., & Prasad, A. B. (1998). Facial expression of emotions and schizophrenia: A review. *Schizophrenia Bulletin, 24*, 399–412.

Marinangeli, M. G., Butti, G., Scinto, A., DiCicco, L., Petruzzi, C., Daneluzzo, E., & Rossi, A. (2000). Patterns of comorbidity among *DSM–III–R* personality disorders. *Psychopathology, 32*, 69–74.

Marks, I. M. (1970). Agoraphobic syndrome (phobic anxiety state). *Archives of General Psychiatry, 23*, 538–553.

Marks, I. M., & Herst, E. (1970). The open door: A survey of agoraphobics in Britain. *Social Psychiatry, 1*, 16–24.

Marshall, L. A., & Cooke, D. J. (1999). The childhood experiences of psychopaths: A retrospective study of familial and societal factors. *Journal of Personality Disorders, 13*, 211–225.

Masterson, J. (1972). *Treatment of the borderline adolescent: A developmental approach.* New York: Wiley.

Matano, R. A., & Locke, K. D. (1995). Personality disorder scales as predictors of interpersonal problems of alcoholics. *Journal of Personality Disorders, 9*, 62–67.

Matlin, M. (2002). *Cognition* (5th ed.). Orlando, FL: Harcourt College Publishers.

Matthews, A. M., Gelder, M. G., & Johnston, D. W. (1981). *Agoraphobia: Nature and treatment.* New York: Guilford.

McAdams, D. P. (1988). Personal needs and personal relationships. In S. Duck (Ed.), *Handbook of research on personal relationships* (pp. 7–22). New York: Wiley.

McAllister, H. (1996). Self-serving bias in the classroom: Who shows it? Who knows it? *Journal of Educational Psychology, 88*, 123–131.

McClelland, D. C. (1985). *Human motivation.* Glenview, IL: Scott, Foresman.

McCranie, E. W., & Bass, J. D. (1984). Childhood family antecedents of dependency and self-criticism: Implications for depression. *Journal of Abnormal Psychology, 93*, 3–8.

McGee, L., & Newcomb, M. D. (1992). General deviance syndrome: Expanded hierarchical evaluations at four ages from early adolescence to adulthood. *Journal of Consulting and Clinical Psychology, 60*, 766–776.

McKinney, W. T. (1974). Primate social isolation: Psychiatric implications. *Archives of General Psychiatry, 31*, 422–426.

McLemore, C. W., & Brokaw, D. W. (1987). Personality disorders as dysfunctional interpersonal behavior. *Journal of Personality Disorders, 1*, 270–285.

McWilliams, N. (1994). *Psychoanalytic diagnosis.* New York: Guilford.

Mead, G. H. (1934). *Mind, self, and society.* Chicago: University of Chicago Press.

Melges, F. T., & Swartz, M. S. (1989). Oscillations of attachment in borderline personality disorder. *American Journal of Psychiatry, 146*, 1115–1120.

Meltzoff, A. (1995). Understanding the intentions of others: Re-enactment of intended acts by 18-month-old children. *Developmental Psychology, 31*, 838–850.

Mendel, J. G. C., & Klein, D. F. (1969). Anxiety attacks with subsequent agoraphobia. *Comprehensive Psychiatry, 10*, 190–195.

Michelson, L. (1987). Cognitive–behavioral assessment and treatment of agoraphobia. In L. Michelson & L. M. Ascher (Eds.), *Anxiety and stress disorders* (pp. 213–279). New York: Guilford.

Midgley, C., Arunkumar, R., & Urdan, T. C. (1996). "If I don't do well tomorrow, there's a reason": Predictors of adolescents' use of academic self-handicapping strategies. *Journal of Educational Psychology, 88*, 423–434.

Miklowitz, D. J. (1994). Family risk indicators in schizophrenia. *Schizophrenia Bulletin, 20*, 137–149.

Miklowitz, D. J., Strachan, A. M., Goldstein, M. J., Doane, J. A., Snyder, K. S., Hogarty, G. E., & Falloon, I. R. H. (1986). Expressed emotion and communication deviance in the familities of schizophrenics. *Journal of Abnormal Psychology, 95,* 60–66.

Miklowitz, D. J., Velligan, D. I., Goldstein, M. J., Nuechterlein, K. H., Gitlin, M. J., Ranlett, G., & Doane, J. A. (1991). Communication deviance in families of schizophrenic and manic pataients. *Journal of Abnormal Psychology, 100,* 163–173.

Miller, M. A., & Rahe, R. H. (1997). Life changes scaling for the 1990s. *Journal of Psychosomatic Research, 43,* 279–292.

Miller, S. D. (1989). Optical differences in cases of multiple personality disorder. *Journal of Nervous and Mental Disease, 177,* 480–486.

Miller, S. D., Blackburn, T., Scholes, G., White, G. L., & Mamalis, N. (1991). Optical differences in multiple personality disorder: A second look. *Journal of Nervous and Mental Disease, 179,* 132–135.

Miller, S. M. (1979). Coping with impending stress: Physiological and cognitive correlates of choice. *Psychophysiology, 16,* 572–581.

Miller, S. M. (1987). Monitoring and blunting: Validation of a questionnaire to assess styles of information-seeking under threat. *Journal of Personality and Social Psychology, 52,* 345–353.

Miller, S. M., & Mangan, C. D. (1983). The interacting effects of information and coping style in adapting to gynecologic stress: Should the doctor tell all? *Journal of Personality and Social Psychology, 45,* 223–236.

Millon, T. (1981). *Disorders of personality:* DSM–III, *Axis II.* New York: Wiley.

Millon, T., & Davis, R. (2000). *Personality disorders in modern life.* New York: Wiley.

Milner, J. S. (1993). Social information processing and physical child abuse. *Clinical Psychology Review, 13,* 275–294.

Minuchin, S. (1974). *Families and family therapy.* Cambridge, MA: Harvard University Press.

Minuchin, S., Rosman, B. L., & Baker, L. (1978). *Psychosomatic families.* Cambridge, MA: Harvard University Press.

Miranda, J., & Persons, J. B. (1988). Dysfunctional attitudes are mood-state dependent. *Journal of Abnormal Psychology, 97,* 76–79.

Miranda, J., Persons, J. B., & Byers, C. N. (1990). Endorsement of dysfunctional beliefs depends on current mood state. *Journal of Abnormal Psychology, 99,* 237–241.

Mirsky, A. (1968). Communication of affects in monkeys. In D. C. Glass (Ed.), *Environmental influences* (pp. 129–137). New York: Rockefeller University Press and Russell Sage Foundation.

Mischel, W., Cantor, N., & Feldman, S. (1996). Principles of self-regulation: The nature of willpower and self-control. In E. T. Higgins & A. Kruglanski (Eds.), *Social psychology: Handbook of basic principles* (pp. 329–360). New York: Guilford.

Mischel, W., & Shoda, Y. (1998). Reconciling processing dynamics and personality dispositions. *Annual Review of Psychology, 49,* 229–258.

Modestin, J. (1987). Quality of interpersonal relationships: The most characteristic *DSM–III* BPD criterion. *Comprehensive Psychiatry, 28,* 397–402.

Mongrain, M. (1998). Parental representations and support-seeking behaviors related to dependency and self-criticism. *Journal of Personality*, *66*, 151–173.

Mongrain, M., Vettese, L. C., Shuster, B., & Kendal, N. (1998). Perceptual biases, affect, and behavior in the relationships of dependents and self-critics. *Journal of Personality and Social Psychology*, *75*, 230–241.

Moore, C., & Dunham, P. J. (Eds.). (1995). *Joint attention: Its orgins and role in development*. Hillsdale, NJ: Erlbaum.

Moore, T., & Ucko, L. (1957). Night waking in early infancy. *Archives of Disease in Childhood*, *32*, 333–342.

Moos, R. H. (1995). Development and applications of new measures of life stressors, social resources, and coping responses. *European Journal of Psychological Assessment*, *11*, 1–13.

Moos, R. H., & Moos, B. S. (1997). Life Stressors and Social Resources Inventory: A measure of adults' and youths' life contexts. In C. P. Zalaquett & R. J. Wood (Eds.), *Evaluating stress: A book of resources* (pp. 177–190). Lanham, MD: Scarecrow.

Morey, L. C. (1985). An empirical comparison of interpersonal and *DSM–III* approaches to classification of personality disorders. *Psychiatry*, *48*, 358–364.

Moriyama, I. M., Krueger, D. E., & Stamler, J. (1971). *Cardiovascular diseases in the United States*. Cambridge, MA: Harvard University Press.

Moskowitz, D. S. (1994). Cross-situational generality and the interpersonal circumplex. *Journal of Personality and Social Psychology*, *66*, 921–933.

Moskowitz, D. S. (1996). *Social behavior inventory*. Montreal, Quebec, Canada: McGill University.

Moskowitz, D. S., & Coté, S. (1995). Do interpersonal traits predict affect? A comparison of three models. *Journal of Personality and Social Psychology*, *69*, 914–924.

Mullen, B., & Riordan, C. A. (1988). Self-serving attributions for performance in naturalistic settings: A meta-analytic review. *Journal of Applied Social Psychology*, *18*, 3–22.

Munch, I. (Ed.). (1949). *Edvard Munch's letters to his family*. Oslo: Johan Grundt Tanum.

Murray, B. (1997). School phobias hold many children back. *APA Monitor*, *28*, 38–39.

Murray, H. A. (1938). *Explorations in personality*. New York: Oxford University Press.

Murray, H. A. (1943). *Manual of Thematic Apperception Test*. Cambridge, Mass: Harvard University Press.

Myers, P. N. J., & Biocca, F. A. (1992). The elastic body image: The effect of television advertising and programming on body image distortions in young women. *Journal of Communication*, *42*, 108–133.

Nasby, W., & Read, N. W. (1997). The inner and outer voyages of a solo circumnavigator: An integrative case study. *Journal of Personality*, *65*, 985–1068.

Naslund, B., Persson-Blennow, I., McNeil, T., Kaij, L., & Malmquist-Larsson, A. (1984). Offspring of women with nonorganic psychosis: Infant attachment to the mother at one year of age. *Acta Psychiatrica Scandinavia, 69,* 231–241.

Newman, J. P., & Kosson, D. S. (1986). Passive avoidance learning in psychopathic and nonpsychopathic offenders. *Journal of Abnormal Psychology, 95,* 252–256.

Newman, J. P., Widom, C. S., & Nathan, S. (1985). Passive avoidance in syndromes of disinhibition: Psychopathy and extraversion: *Journal of Personality and Social Psychology, 48,* 1316–1327.

Nichols, W. C. (1996). Persons with antisocial and histrionic personality disorders in relationships. In F. W. Kaslow (Ed)., *Handbook of relational diagnosis and dysfunctional family patterns* (pp. 287–299). New York: Wiley.

Nilsson, E. W., Gillberg, C., Gillberg, I. C., & Rastam, M. (1999). Ten year follow-up of adolescent-onset anorexia nervosa: Personality disorders. *Journal of American Academy of Child and Adolescent Psychiatry, 38,* 1389–1395.

Nisenson, L. G., & Berenbaum, H. (1998). Interpersonal interactions in individuals with schizophrenia: Individual differences among patients and their partners. *Psychiatry, 61,* 2–11.

Norden, K. A., Klein, D. N., Donaldson, S. K., Pepper, C. M., & Klein, L. M. (1995). Reports of the early home environment in *DSM–III–R* personality disorders. *Journal of Personality Disorders, 9,* 213–223.

Nowinski, V. W. (1999). *Empathic responding and self-affirmation: What do empathy seekers want?* Unpublished doctoral dissertation, Stanford University, Stanford, CA.

O'Brien, T. B., & DeLongis, A. (1996). The international context of problem-emotion-, and relationship-focused coping: The role of the Big Five personality factors. *Journal of Personality, 64,* 775–813.

O'Connor, M. J., Sigman, M., & Brill, N. (1987). Disorganizatoin of attachment in relation to maternal alcohol consumption. *Journal of Consulting and Clinical Psychology, 55,* 831–836.

O'Connor, T. G., Rutter, M., Beckett, C., Keaveney, L., Kreppner, J. M., & the English and Romanian Adoptees Study Team. (2000). The effects of global severe privation on cognitive competence: Extension and longitudinal follow-up. *Child Development, 71,* 376–390.

Oliver, J. M., Handal, P. J., Finn, T., & Herdy, S. (1987). Depressed and nondepressed students and their siblings in frequent contact with their families: Depression and perceptions of the family. *Cognitive Therapy and Research, 11,* 501–515.

Oltmanns, T. F., & Neale, J. M. (1975). Schizophrenic performance when distractors are present: Attentional deficit or differential task difficulty? *Journal of Abnormal Psychology, 84,* 205–209.

Oltmanns, T. F., & Neale, J. M. (1978). Distractibility in relation to other aspects of schizophrenic disorder. In S. Schwartz (Ed.), *Language and cognition in schizophrenia* (pp. 117–143). Hilldale, NJ: Erlbaum.

Ordway, N. K., Leonard, M. F., & Ingles, T. (1969). Interpersonal factors in failure to thrive. *Southern Medical Bulletin, 57,* 23–28.

Orford, J. (1986). The rules of interpersonal complementarity: Does hostility beget hostility and dominance, submission? *Psychological Review, 93,* 365–377.

O'Shaughnessy, B. (1970). The powerlessness of dispositions. *Analysis, 31,* 1–15.

Ostwald, P. F. (1985). *Schumann: The inner voices of a musical genius.* Boston: Northeastern University Press.

Overholser, J. C. (1996). The dependent personality and interpersonal problems. *Journal of Nervous and Mental Disease, 184,* 8–16.

Parker, G. (1979). Parental characteristics in relation to depressive disorders. *British Journal of Psychiatry, 134,* 138–147.

Patterson, R. J., & Moran, G. (1988). Attachment theory, personality development, and psychotherapy. *Clinical Psychology Review, 8,* 611–636.

Paykel, E. S., Myers, J. K., Denelt, M. N., Klerman, G. L., Lindenthal, J. J., & Pepper, M. P. (1969). Life events and depression. *Archives of General Psychiatry, 21,* 753–760.

Paykel, E. S., & Tanner, J. (1976). Life events, depressive relapse and maintenance treatment. *Psychological Medicine, 6,* 481–485.

Peplau, L. A., Miceli, M., & Morasch, B. (1982). Loneliness and self-evaluation. In L. A. Peplau & D. Perlman (Eds.), *Loneliness: A sourcebook of current theory, research, and therapy* (pp. 135–151). New York: Wiley.

Peplau, L. A. & Perlman, D. (Eds.) (1982). *Loneliness: A sourcebook of current theory, research and therapy.* New York: Wiley & Sons.

Perry, J. C. (2001). A pilot study of defenses in adults with personality disorders. *The Journal of Nervous & Mental Disease, 189,* 651–660.

Peterson, C. (1991). The meaning and measurement of explanatory style. *Psychological Inquiry, 2,* 1–10.

Peterson, C., Maier, S., & Seligman, M. E. P. (1993). *Learned helplessness: A theory for the age of personal control.* New York: Oxford University Press.

Pike, K. M. (1998). Long-term course of anorexia nervosa: Response, relapse, remission, and recovery. *Clinical Psychology Review, 18,* 447–475.

Pike, K. M., & Rodin, J. (1991). Mothers, daughters, and disordered eating. *Journal of Abnormal Psychology, 101,* 198–204.

Piliavin, I., Rodin, J., & Piliavin, J. (1969). Good samaritanism: An underground phenomenon? *Journal of Personality and Social Psychology, 13,* 289–299.

Pilkonis, P. A. (1988). Personality prototypes among depressives: Themes of dependency and autonomy. *Journal of Personality Disorders, 2,* 144–152.

Pilkonis, P. A., & Frank, E. (1988). Personality pathology in recurrent depression: Nature, prevalence, and relationship to treatment response. *American Journal of Psychiatry, 145,* 435–441.

Pincus, A. L., & Ansell, E. B. (2003). Interpersonal theory of personality. In T. Millon & M. Lerner (Eds.), *Comprehensive handbook of psychology: Personality and social psychology* (Vol. 5, pp. 209–229). New York: Wiley.

Pincus, A. L., & Gurtman, M. B. (1995). The three faces of interpersonal dependency: Structural analyses of self-report dependency measures. *Journal of Personality and Social Psychology, 69,* 744–758.

Pincus, A. L., & Wiggins, J. S. (1990). Interpersonal problems and conceptions of personality disorders. *Journal of Personality Disorders, 4,* 342–352.

Piper, W. E., Joyce, A. S., McCallum, M., & Azim, H. F. A. (1993). Concentration and correspondence of transference interpretations in short-term psychotherapy. *Journal of Consulting and Clinical Psychology, 61,* 586–595.

Piper, W. E., Joyce, A. S., McCallum, M., Azim, H. F., & Ogrodniczuk, J. S. (2001). *Interpretive and supportive psychotherapies : Matching therapy and patient personality.* Washington, DC: American Psychological Association.

Polivy, J., & Herman, C. P. (1976). Clinical depression and weight change. *Journal of Abnormal Psychology, 85,* 338–340.

Pollak, J. M. (1979). Obsessive–compulsive personality: A review. *Psychological Bulletin, 86,* 225–241.

Pollak, J. M. (1987). Obsessive–compulsive personality: Theoretical and clinical perspectives and recent research findings. *Journal of Personality Disorders, 1,* 248–262.

Putnam, F. W., Guroff, J. J., Silberman, E. K., Barban, L., & Post, R. M. (1986). The clinical phenomenology of multiple personality disorder: Review of 100 recent cases. *Journal of Clinical Psychiatry, 47,* 285–293.

Putnam, F. W., Zahn, T. P., & Post, R. M. (1995). Differential autonomic nervous system activity in multiple personality disorder. *Psychiatry Research, 31,* 251–260.

Rabkin, J. G., & Struening, E. L. (1976). Life events, stress, and illness. *Science, 194,* 1013–1020.

Radke-Yarrow, M., Cummings, E. M., Kuczynski, L., & Chapman, M. (1985). Patterns of attachment in two- and three-year olds in normal families with parental depression. *Child Development, 56,* 884–893.

Rafaeli-Mor, E., Gotlib, I. H., & Revelle, W. (1999). The meaning and measurement of self-complexity. *Personality and Individual Differences, 27,* 341–356.

Raine, A., Brennan, P., & Mednick, S. A. (1994). Birth complications combined with early maternal rejection at age 1 year predispose to violent crime at age 18 years. *Archives of General Psychiatry, 51,* 984–988.

Raine, A., Brennan, P., Mednick, B., & Mednick, S. A. (1996). High rates of violence, crime, academic problems, and behavioral problems in males with both early neuromotor deficits and unstable family environments. *Archives of General Psychiatry, 53,* 544–549.

Raine, A., Buchsbaum, M. S., Stanley, J., Lottenberg, S., Abel, L., & Stoddard, J. (1994). Selective reductions in prefrontal glucose metabolism in murderers. *Biological Psychiatry, 36,* 365–373.

Ranelli, C. J., & Miller, R. E. (1981). Behavioral predictors of amitriptyline response in depression. *American Journal of Psychiatry, 138,* 30–34.

Rattan, R. B., & Chapman, L. J. (1973). Associative intrusions in schizophrenic verbal behavior. *Journal of Abnormal Psychology, 82,* 169–173.

Ratti, L. A., Humphrey, L. L., & Lyons, J. S. (1996). Structural analysis of families with a polydrug-dependent, bulimic, or normal adolescent daughter. *Journal of Consulting and Clinical Psychology, 64,* 1255–1262.

Raver, C. C., & Leadbeater, B. J. (1995). Factors influencing joint attention between socioeconomically disadvantaged adolescent mothers and their infants. In C. Moore & P. J. Dunham (Eds.), *Joint attention: Its origins and role in development* (pp. 251–271). Hillsdale, NJ: Erlbaum.

Reed, G. F. (1985). *Obsessional experience and compulsive behavior.* Toronto: Academic Press.

Reich, W. (1949). *Character analysis* (3rd ed.). New York: Farrar, Straus, and Giroux.

Renken, B., Egeland, B., Marvinney, D., Mangelsdorf, S., & Sroufe, L. A. (1989). Early childhood antecedents of aggression and passive-withdrawal in early elementary school. *Journal of Personality, 5,* 257–281.

Rey, J. M., Singh, M., Morris-Yates, A., & Andrews, G. (1997). Referred adolescents as young adults: The relationship between psychosocial functioning and personality disorder. *Australian and New Zealand Journal of Psychiatry, 31,* 219–226.

Robbins, B., Strack, S., & Coyne, J. (1979). Willingness to provide feedback to depressed persons. *Social Behavior and Personality, 7,* 199–203.

Robins, C. J., Block, P., & Peselow, E. D. (1989). Relations of sociotropic and autonomous personality characteristics to specific symptoms in depressed patients. *Journal of Abnormal Psychology, 98,* 86–88.

Rock, C. L., & Curran-Celentano, J. (1996). Nutritional management of eating disorders. *The Psychiatric Clinics of North America, 19,* 701–713.

Rodriguez, V. B., Cafias, F., Bayon, C., Franco, B., Salvador, M., Graell, M., & Santo-Domingo, J. (1996). Interpersonal factors in female depression. *European Journal of Psychiatry, 10,* 16–24.

Roid, G. H., & Fitts, W. H. (1988). *Tennessee Self-Concept Scale* (revised manual). Los Angeles: Western Psychological Services.

Rosch, E., Mervis, C. B., Gray, W. D., Johnson, D. M., & Boyes-Braem, P. (1976). Basic objects in natural categories. *Cognitive Psychology, 8,* 382–439.

Rosenbaum, G., Shore, D. L., & Chapin, K. (1988). Attention deficit in schizophrenia and schizotypy: Marker versus symptom variables. *Journal of Abnormal Psychology, 97,* 41–47.

Rosenberg, M. (1965). *Society and the adolescent self-image.* Princeton, NJ: Princeton University Press.

Rosenhan, D. L., & Seligman, M. E. P. (1995). *Abnormal psychology* (3rd ed.). New York: Norton.

Ross, C. A. (1997). *Dissociative identity disorder.* New York: Wiley.

Rothbart, M. K., & Ahadi, S. A. (1994). Temperament and the development of personality. *Journal of Abnormal Psychology, 103,* 55–66.

Rothbart, M. K., & Park, B. (1986). On the confirmability and disconfirmability of trait concepts. *Journal of Personality and Social Psychology, 50,* 131–142.

Rotter, J. B. (1966). Generalized expectancies for internal versus external control of reinforcement. *Psychological Monographs, 80*(1, Whole No. 609).

Rubin, K. H., Fein, G. G., & Vandenberg, B. (1983). Play. In E. M. Hetherington (Ed.), *Handbook of child psychology: Vol. 4. Socialization, personality, and social development* (pp. 693–774). New York: Wiley.

Rubinow, D. R., & Post, R. M. (1992). Impaired recognition of affect in facial expression in depressed patients. *Biological Psychiatry, 31,* 947–953.

Ruderman, A. J., & Besbeas, M. (1992). Psychological characteristics of dieters and bulimics. *Journal of Abnormal Psychology, 101,* 383–390.

Rund, B. R., Oie, M., Borchgrevink, T. S., & Fjell, A. (1995). Expressed emotion, communication deviance and schizophrenia. *Psychopathology, 28,* 220–228.

Russell, G. F. M., Szmukler, G. I., Dare, C., & Eisler, I. (1987). An evaluation of family therapy in anorexia nervosa and bulimia nervosa. *Archives of General Psychiatry, 44,* 1047–1056.

Rutter, M. (1998). Developmental catch-up, and deficit, following adoption after severe global early privation. *Journal of Child Psychology and Psychiatry and Allied Disciplines, 39,* 465–476.

Rychlak, J. F. (1977). *The psychology of rigorous humanism.* New York: Wiley-Interscience.

Sack, A., Sperling, M. B., Fagen, G., & Foelsch, P. (1996). Attachment style, history, and behavioral contrasts for a borderline and normal sample. *Journal of Personality Disorders, 10,* 88–102.

Sadler, P., & Woody, E. (2003). Is who you are who you're talking to? Interpersonal style and complentarity in mixed-sex interaction. *Journal of Personality and Social Psychology, 84,* 80–96.

Safran, J. D., & Muran, J. C. (1996). The resolution of ruptures in the therapeutic alliance. *Journal of Consulting and Clinical Psychology, 64,* 447–458

Salzman, L. (1975). Interpersonal factors in depression. In F. F. Flach & S. C. Draghi (Eds.), *The nature and treatment of depression* (pp. 43–56). New York: Wiley.

Santor, D. A., & Zuroff, D. C. (1997). Interpersonal responses to threats to status and interpersonal relatedness: Effects of dependency and self-criticism. *British Journal of Clinical Psychology, 36,* 521–541.

Sarason, I. G., Sarason, B. B., & Pierce, G. R. (1990). *Social support: An interactional view.* New York: Wiley.

Scheier, M. F., Weintraub, J. K., & Carver, C. S. (1986). Coping with stress: Divergent strategies of optimists and pessimists. *Journal of Personality and Social Psychology, 51,* 1257–1264.

Schone, B. S., & Weinick, R. M. (1998). Health-related behaviors and the benefits of marriage for elderly persons. *Gerontologist, 38,* 618–627.

Schwartz, R. M., & Gottman, J. M. (1976). Toward a task analysis of assertive behavior. *Journal of Consulting and Clinical Psychology, 44,* 910–920.

Searles, H. (1956). The psychodynamics of vengefulness. *Psychiatry, 19,* 31–39.

Segrin, C. (2001). *Interpersonal processes in psychological problems.* New York: Guilford.

Segrin, C., & Flora, J. (1998). Depression and verbal behavior in conversations with friends and strangers. *Journal of Language and Social Psychology, 17,* 494–505.

Seligman, M. E. P. (1975). *Helplessness.* San Francisco: W. H. Freeman.

Shapiro, D. (1965). *Neurotic styles.* New York: Basic Books.

Shapiro, D. (1981). *Autonomy and rigid character.* New York: Basic Books.

Shaver, P. R., & Hazan, C. (1988). A biased overview of the study of love. *Journal of Social and Personal Relationships, 5,* 473–501.

Shaw, D. S., Owens, E. B., Vondra, J. I., Keenan, K., & Winslow, E. B. (1997). Early risk factors and pathways in the development of early disruptive behavior problems. *Development and Psychpathology, 8,* 679–700.

Shaw, D. S., & Vondra, J. I. (1995). Infant attachment security and maternal predictors of early behavior problems: A longitudinal study of low-income families. *Journal of Abnormal Child Psychology, 23,* 335–357.

Shaw, G. B. (1916). *Pygmalion*. London: Penguin Books.

Shea, M. T., Glass, D. R., Pilkonis, P. A., Watkins, J., Docherty, J. P. (1987). Frequency and implications of personality disorders in a sample of depressed outpatients. *Journal of Personality Disorders, 1*, 27–42.

Shechtman, N. (2002). *Talking to people versus talking to computers: Interpersonal goals as a distinguishing factor*. Unpublished doctoral dissertation, Stanford University, Stanford, CA.

Shechtman, N., & Horowitz, L. M. (2003, April). *Media inequality in conversation: How people behave differently when interacting with computers and people*. Paper presented at the Conference on Human Factors in Computing Systems, Ft. Lauderdale, FL.

Shimkunas, A. M. (1972). Demand for intimate self-disclosure and pathological verbalizations in schizophrenia. *Journal of Abnormal Psychology, 80*, 197–205.

Shoda, Y., Mischel, W., & Wright, J. C. (1994). Intraindividual stability in the organization and patterning of behavior: Incorporating psychological situations into the idiographic analysis of personality. *Journal of Personality and Social Psychology, 67*, 674–687.

Shye, D., Mullooly, J. P., Freeborn, D. K., & Pope, C. R. (1995). Gender differences in the relationship between social network support and mortality: A longitudinal study of an elderly cohort. *Social Science and Medicine, 41*, 935–947.

Siever, L. J., & Davis, K. L. (1991). A psychobiological perspective on the personality disorders. *American Journal of Psychiatry, 148*, 1647–1658.

Silverstein, B., Perdue, L., Peterson, B., & Kelly, E. (1986). The role of mass media in promoting a thin standard of bodily attractiveness for women. *Sex Roles, 14*, 519–532.

Sim, J. P., & Romney, D. M. (1990). The relationship between a circumplex model of interpersonal behaviors and personality disorders. *Journal of Personality Disorders, 4*, 329–341.

Sim, M., & Houghton, H. (1966). Phobic anxiety and its treatment. *Journal of Nervous and Mental Disease, 143*, 484–491.

Sincoff, J. B. (1990). The psychological characteristics of ambivalent people. *Clinical Psychology Review, 10*, 43–68.

Singer, M. T., & Wynne, L. C. (1965a). Thought disorder and family relations of schizophrenics: III. Methodology using projective techniques. *Archives of General Psychiatry, 12*, 187–200.

Singer, M. T., & Wynne, L. C. (1965b). Thought disorder and family relations of schizophrenics: IV. Results and implications. *Archives of General Psychiatry, 12*, 201–212.

Skinner, B. F. (1938). *The behavior of organisms: An experimental analysis*. New York: Appleton-Century-Crofts.

Slater, E., Beard, W. A., & Gitero, E. (1965). A follow-up of patients diagnosed as suffering from hysteria. *Journal of Psychosomatic Research, 9*, 9–13.

Slocum, J. (1972). *Sailing alone around the world*. New York: Sheridan House.

Smedslund, J. (1988). *Psycho-logic*. New York: Springer-Verlag.

Smedslund, J. (1997). *The structure of psychological common sense*. Mahwah, NJ: Erlbaum.

Solano, C. H., Batten, P. G., & Parish, E. A. (1982). Loneliness and patterns of self-disclosure. *Journal of Personality and Social Psychology, 43*, 524–531.

Soldz, S., Budman, S., Demby, A., & Merry, J. (1993). Representation of personality disorders in circumplex and five-factor space: Explorations with a clinical sample. *Psychological Assessment, 5*, 41–52.

Solyom, L., Silberfeld, M., & Solyom, C. (1976). Maternal overprotection in the etiology of agoraphobia. *Journal of the Canadian Psychiatric Association, 21*, 109–113.

Sorenson, R. L., Gorsuch, R. L., & Mintz, J. (1985). Moving targets: Patients' changing complaints during psychotherapy. *Journal of Consulting and Clinical Psychology, 53*, 49–54.

Spain, J. S., Eaton, L. G., & Funder, D. C. (2000). Perspectives on personality: The relative accuracy of self versus others for the prediction of emotion and behavior. *Journal of Personality, 68*, 837–867.

Spangler, G., & Grossmann, K. E. (1993). Behavioral organization in securely and insecurely attached infants. *Child Development, 64*, 1439–1450.

Sperling, M. (1967). School phobias: Classification, dynamics, and treatment. *The Psychoanalytic Study of the Child, 22*, 375–401.

Sperry, L., Gudeman, J. E., Blackwell, B., & Faulkner, L. R. (1992). *Psychiatric case formulations*. Washington, DC: American Psychiatric Press.

Spiegel, D., & Fink, R. (1979). Hysterical psychosis and hypnotizability. *American Journal of Psychiatry, 136*, 777–781.

Spieker, S. J., & Booth, C. (1988). Maternal antecedents of attachment quality. In J. Belsky & T. Nezworski (Eds.), *Clinical implications of attachment* (pp. 300–323). Hillsdale, NJ: Erlbaum.

Spitz, E. H. (1994). *Museums of the mind*. New Haven, CT: Yale University Press.

Spitz, R. A. (1945). Hospitalization—An inquiry into the genesis of psychiatric conditions in early childhood. *The Psychoanalytic Study of the Child, 1*, 53–74.

Squires, R. (1968). Are dispositions causes? *Analysis, 29*, 45–47.

Squires, R. (1970). Are dispositions lost causes? *Analysis, 31*, 15–18.

Sroufe, L. A. (1983). Infant–caregiver attachment and patterns of adaptation in preschool: The roots of maladaptation and competence. In M. Perlmutter (Ed.), *Minnesota Symposia on Child Psychology: Vol. 16. Development and policy concerning children with special needs* (pp. 41–83). Hillsdale, NJ: Erlbaum.

Sroufe, L. A. (Ed.). (1990). *Pathways to adaptation and maladaptation: Psychopathology as developmental deviation*. Hillsdale, NJ: Erlbaum.

Sroufe, L. A., Egeland, B., & Kreutzer, T. (1990). The fate of early experience following developmental change: Longitudinal approaches to individual adaptation in childhood. *Child Development, 61*, 1363–1373.

Sroufe, L. A., Waters, E., & Matas, L. (1974). Contextual determinants of infant affective response. In M. Lewis & L. A. Rosenblum (Eds.), *The origins of fear* (pp. 49–72). New York: Wiley.

Stayton, D. J., & Ainsworth, M. D. S. (1973). Individual differences in infant responses to brief, everyday separations as related to other infant and maternal behaviors. *Developmental Psychology, 9*, 226–235.

Steinbeck, J. (1939). *The grapes of wrath*. New York: Penguin Books.

Steinberg, S., & Weiss, J. (1954). The art of Edvard Munch and its function in his mental life. *The Psychoanalytic Quarterly, 23*, 409–423.

Steinhausen, H. (1995). The course and outcome of anorexia nervosa. In K. G. Brownell & C. G. Fairburn (Eds.), *Eating disorders and obesity: A comprehensive handbook* (pp. 234–237). New York: Guilford.

Stephens, R. S., Hokanson, J. E., & Welker, R. (1987). Responses to depressed interpersonal behavior: Mixed reactions in a helping role. *Journal of Personality and Social Psychology, 52*, 1274–1282.

Stern, D. (1977). *The first relationship: Infant and mother*. Cambridge, MA: Harvard University Press.

Stice, E. (1994). Review of the evidence for a sociocultural model of bulimia nervosa and an exploration of the mechanisms of action. *Clinical Psychology Review, 14*, 633–661.

Stice, E., Shupak-Neuberg, E., Shaw, H. E., & Stein, R. I. (1994). Relation of media exposure to eating disorder symptomatology: An examination of mediating mechanisms. *Journal of Abnormal Psychology, 103*, 836–840.

Stiles, W. B., Shapiro, D., & Elliott, R. (1986). Are all psychotherapies equivalent? *American Psychologist, 41*, 165–180.

Stone, M. H. (1993). *Abnormalities of personality: Within and beyond the realm of treatment*. New York: Norton.

Strack, S. (1987). Development and validation of an adjective checklist to assess the Millon personality types in a normal population. *Journal of Personality Assessment, 51*, 572–587.

Strack, S., & Coyne, J. C. (1983). Social confirmation of dysphoria: Shared and private reactions to depression. *Journal of Personality and Social Psychology, 44*, 798–806.

Strack, S., Lorr, M., & Campbell, L. (1990). An evaluation of Millon's circular model of personality disorders. *Journal of Personality Disorders, 4*, 353–361.

Strauss, B., Buchheim, A., & Kaechele, H. (Eds.) (2002). *Klinische Bindungsforschung*. Stuttgart, Germany: Schattauer.

Strauss, B., Eckert, J., & Ott, J. (1993). Interpersonale Probleme in der stationaeren Gruppenpsychotherapie. *Gruppenspsychotherapie und Gruppendynamik, 29* (3) (Themenheft).

Striegel-Moore, R. H. (1995). A feminist perspective on the etiology of eating disorders. In K. D. Brownell & C. G. Fairburn (Eds.), *Eating disorders and obesity: A comprehensive handbook* (pp. 224–229). New York: Guilford.

Strong, S. R., & Hills, H. I. (1986). *Interpersonal communication rating scale*. Richmond: Virginia Commonwealth University.

Strong, S. R., Hills, H. I., Kilmartin, C. T., DeVries, H., Lanier, K., Nelson, B. N., Strickland, D., & Meyer, C. W., III (1988). The dynamic relations among interpersonal behaviors: A test of complementarity and anticomplementarity. *Journal of Personality and Social Psychology, 54*, 798–810.

Strupp, H., & Binder, J. (1984). *Psychotherapy in a new key: Time-limited dynamic psychotherapy*. New York: Basic Books.

Sullivan, H. S. (1953). *The interpersonal theory of psychiatry*. New York: Norton.

Sullivan, H. S. (1956). *Clinical studies in psychiatry*. New York: Norton.

Summers, F. (1994). *Object relations theories and psychopathology: A comprehensive text*. Hillsdale, NJ: Analytic Press.

Suomi, S. J. (1987). Genetic and maternal contributions to individual differences in rhesus monkey biobehavioral development. In N. A. Krasnagor, E. M. Blass, M. A. Hofer, & W. P. Smotherman (Eds.), *Perinatal development: A psychobiological perspective* (pp. 397–420). New York: Academic Press.

Suomi, S. J. (1999). Attachment in rhesus monkeys. In J. Cassidy & P. R. Shaver (Eds.), *Handbook of attachment: Theory, research and clinical applications* (pp. 181–197). New York: Guilford.

Suomi, S. J. (2000). A biobehavioral perspective on developmental psychopathology: Excessive aggression and serotonergic dysfunction in monkeys. In A. J. Sameroff & M. Lewis (Eds.), *Handbook of developmental psychopathology* (2nd ed., pp. 237–256). New York: Kluwer Academic Plenum.

Swann, W. B., Jr. (1996). *Self-traps: The elusive quest for higher self-esteem*. New York: W. H. Freeman.

Sylvester, D. (1992). *Magritte: The silence of the world*. New York: H. N. Abrams.

Tafarodi, R. W., & Milne, A. B. (2002). Decomposing global self-esteem. *Journal of Personality, 70*, 443–483.

Tafarodi, R. W., & Swann, W. B., Jr. (1995). Self-liking and self-competence as dimensions of global self-esteem: Initial validation of a measure. *Journal of Personality Assessment, 65*, 322–342.

Talavera, J. A., Saiz-Ruiz, J., & Garcia-Toro, M. (1994). Quantitative measurement of depression through speech analysis. *European Psychiatry, 9*, 185–193.

Talbot, M. (1957). Panic in school phobias. *American Journal of Orthopsychiatry, 27*, 286–295.

Tannen, D. (1990). *You just don't understand: Women and men in conversation*. New York: Ballantine Books.

Tausig, M. (1982). Measuring life events. *Journal of Health and Social Behavior, 23*, 52–64.

Taylor, M., & Hort, B. (1990). Can children be trained in making the distinction between appearance and reality? *Cognitive Development, 5*, 89–99.

Taylor, S., & Goritsas, E. (1994). Dimensions of identity diffusion. *Journal of Personality Disorders, 8*, 229–239.

Taylor, S. E., & Aspinwall, L. G. (1996). Mediating and moderating processes in psychosocial stress: Appraisal, coping, resistance, and vulnerability. In H. B. Kaplan (Ed.), *Psychosocial stress: Perspectives on structure, theory, life course, and methods* (pp. 71–110). San Diego, CA: Academic Press.

Taylor, S. E., & Brown, J. D. (1988). Illusion and well-being: Social psychological perspective on mental health. *Psychological Bulletin, 103*, 193–210.

Taylor, S. E., Lichtman, R. R., & Wood, J. V. (1984). Attributions, beliefs about control, and adjustment to breast cancer. *Journal of Personality and Social Psychology, 46*, 489–502.

Tennen, H., & Affleck, G. (1990). Blaming others for threatening events. *Psychological Bulletin, 108*, 209–232.

Thoits, P. A. (1982). Conceptual, methodological, and theoretical problems in studying social support as a buffer against life stress. *Journal of Health and Social Behavior, 23*, 145–159.

Thompson, R. A. (1999). Early attachment and later development. In J. Cassidy & P. R. Shaver (Eds.), *Handbook of attachment: Theory, research and clinical applications* (pp. 265–286). New York: Guilford.

Thompson, R. A., & Zuroff, D. C. (1999). Development of self-criticism in adolescent girls: Roles of maternal dissatisfaction, maternal coldness, and insecure attachment. *Journal of Youth and Adolescence, 28,* 197–210.

Tiedens, L. Z., & Fragale, A. R. (2003). Power moves: Complementarity in dominant and submissive nonverbal behavior. *Journal of Personality and Social Psychology, 84,* 558–568.

Tomasello, M. (1995). Joint attention as social cognition. In C. Moore & P. J. Dunham (Eds.), *Joint attention: Its origins and role in development* (pp. 103–130). Hillsdale, NJ: Erlbaum.

Tomasello, M. (1999). The human adaptation for culture. *Annual Review of Anthropology, 28,* 509–529.

Tomasello, M., & Barton, M. (1994). Learning words in nonostensive contexts. *Developmental Psychology, 30,* 639–650.

Tracey, T. J. (1994). An examination of complementarity of interpersonal behavior. *Journal of Personality and Social Psychology, 67,* 864–878.

Tracy, R. L., & Ainsworth, M. D. S. (1981). Maternal affectionate behavior and infant–mother attachment patterns. *Child Development, 52,* 1341–1343.

Trobst, K. K. (1999). Social support as an interpersonal construct. *European Journal of Psychological Assessement, 15,* 246–255.

Troisi, A., & Moles, A. (1999). Gender differences in depression: An ethological study of nonverbal behavior during interviews. *Journal of Psychiatric Research, 33,* 243–250.

Tronick, E. (1989). Emotions and emotional communication in infants. *American Psychologist, 44,* 112–119.

Tronick, E., & Gianino, A. (1986). Interaction mismatch and repair: Challenges to the coping infant. *Zero to Three, 6,* 1–5.

Troy, M., & Sroufe, L. A. (1987). Victimization among preschoolers: Role of attachment relationship history. *Journal of the American Academy of Child and Adolescent Psychiatry, 26,* 166–172.

Trull, T. J., Useda, D., Conforti, K., & Doan, B. T. (1997). Borderline personality disorder features in nonclinical young adults: 2. Two-year outcome. *Journal of Abnormal Psychology, 106,* 307–314.

Tsai, G. E., Condie, D., Wu, M. T., & Chang, I. W. (1999). Functional magnetic resonance imaging of personality switches in a woman with dissociative identity disorder. *Harvard Review of Psychiatry, 7,* 119–122.

Turkat, I. D., & Maisto, S. (1983). Functions of and differences between psychiatric diagnosis and case formulation. *The Behavior Therapist, 6,* 184–185.

Turner, R. M., Steketee, G. S., & Foa, E. B. (1979). Fear of criticism in washers, checkers and phobics. *Behaviour Research and Therapy, 17,* 79–81.

Umberson, D. (1987). Family status and health behaviors: Social control as a dimension of social integration. *Journal of Health and Social Behavior, 28,* 306–319.

Urban, J., Carlson, E., Egeland, B., & Sroufe, L. A. (1991). Patterns of individual adaptation across childhood. *Development and Psychopathology, 3,* 445–460.

Urdan, T. C., Midgley, C., & Anderman, E. (1998). The role of classroom goal structure in students' use of self-handicapping strategies. *American Educational Research Journal, 35*, 101–122.

Vallacher, R. R. (1980). An introduction to self-theory. In D. M. Wegner & R. R. Vallacher (Eds.), *The self in social psychology* (pp. 3–30). New York: Oxford University Press.

Van den Boom, D. C. (1989). Neonatal irritability and the development of attachment. In G. Kohnstamm, J. Bates, & M. Rothbart (Eds.), *Temperament in childhood* (pp. 299–318). New York: Wiley.

Van den Boom, D. (1994). The influence of temperament and mothering on attachment and exploration: An experimental manipulation of sensitive responsiveness among lower-class mothers with irritable infants. *Child Development, 65*, 1457–1477.

Van den Boom, D. (1995). Do first-year intervention effects endure? Follow-up during toddlerhood of a sample of Dutch irritable infants. *Child Development, 66*, 1798–1816.

Van Ijzendoorn, M. H., & Sagi, A. (1999). Cross-cultural patterns of attachment. In J. Cassidy & P. R. Shaver (Eds.), *Handbook of attachment: Theory, research, and clinical applications* (pp. 713–734). New York: Guilford.

Vanger, P., Summerfield, A. B., Rosen, B. K., & Watson, J. P. (1992). Effects of communication content on speech behavior of depressives. *Comprehensive Psychiatry, 33*, 39–41.

Vaughn, B., Egeland, B., Sroufe, L. A., & Waters, E. (1979). Individual differences in infant–mother attachment at twelve and eighteen months: Stability and change in families under stress. *Child Development, 50*, 971–975.

Vaughn, C. E., & Leff, J. P. (1981). Patterns of emotional response in relatives of schizophrenic patients. *Schizophrenia Bulletin, 7*, 43–44.

Velligan, D. I., Miller, A. L., Eckert, S. L., Funderburg, L. G., True, J. E., Mahurin, R. K., Diamond, P., & Hazelton, B. C. (1996). The relationship between parental communication deviance and relapse in schizophrenia patients in the 1-year period after hospital discharge. *Journal of Nervous and Mental Disease, 184*, 490–496.

Vitkus, J., & Horowitz, L. M. (1987). Poor social performance of lonely people: Lacking a skill or adopting a role? *Journal of Personality and Social Psychology, 52*, 1266–1273.

Von Domarus, E. (1944). The specific laws of logic in schizophrenia. In J. S. Kasanin (Ed.), *Language and thought in schizophrenia: Collected papers* (pp. 104–114). Berkeley: University of California Press.

Vondra, J., Barnett, D., & Cicchetti, D. (1989). Perceived and actual competence among maltreated and comparison school children. *Development and Psychopathology, 1*, 237–255.

Wagner, A. W., & Linehan, M. M. (1999). Facial expression recognition ability among women with borderline personality disorder: Implications for emotion regulation? *Journal of Personality Disorders, 13*, 329–344.

Wagner, C. C., Kiesler, D. J., & Schmidt, J. A. (1995). Assessing the interpersonal transaction cycle: Convergence of action and reaction interpersonal circumplex measures. *Journal of Personality and Social Psychology, 69*, 938–949.

Wagner, C. C., Riley, W. T., Schmidt, J. A., McCormick, M. G. F., & Butler, S. F. (1999). Personality disorder styles and reciprocal interpersonal impacts during outpatient intake interviews. *Psychotherapy Research, 9*, 216–231.

Wahlberg, K. E., Wynne, L. C., Oja, H., Keskitalo, P., Pykalainen, L., Lahti, I., et al. (1997). Gene–environment interaction in vulnerability to schizophrenia: Findings from the Finnish adoption family study. *American Journal of Psychiatry, 154*, 355–362.

Waldinger, R. J., Seidman, E. L., Gerber, A. J., Liem, J. H., Allen, J. P., & Hauser, S. T. (2003). Attachment and core relationship themes: Wishes for autonomy and closeness in the narratives of securely and insecurely attached adults. *Psychotherapy Research, 13*, 77–98.

Waldron, I., Weiss, C. C., & Hughes, M. E. (1997). Marital status effects on health: Are there differences between never married women and divorced and separated women? *Social Science and Medicine, 45*, 1387–1397.

Ward, A., & Mann, T. (2000). Don't mind if I do: Disinhibited eating under cognitive load. *Journal of Personality and Social Psychology, 78*, 753–763.

Ward, S. E., Leventhal, H., & Love, B. (1988). Repression revisited: Tactics used in coping with a severe health threat. *Personality and Social Psychology Bulletin, 14*, 735–746.

Waring, M., & Ricks, D. (1965). Family patterns of children who became adult schizophrenics. *Journal of Nervous and Mental Disease, 140*, 351–364.

Watson, D. C., & Sinha, B. K. (1998). Comorbidity of *DSM–IV* personality disorders in a nonclinical sample. *Journal of Clinical Psychology, 54*, 773–780.

Watson, J. B. (1919). *Psychology from the standpoint of a behaviorist.* Philadelphia: Lippincott.

Watzlawick, P., Weakland, J., & Fisch, R. (1974). *Change: Principles of problem formation and problem resolution.* New York: Norton.

Waxer, P. (1974). Nonverbal cues for depression. *Journal of Abnormal Psychology, 83*, 319–322.

Weary, G., & Edwards, J. A. (1994). Individual differences in causal uncertainty. *Journal of Personality and Social Psychology, 67*, 308–318.

Wegner, D. M. (1994). Ironic processes of mental control. *Psychological Review, 101*, 34–52.

Wegner, D. M., Schneider, D. J., Carter, S. I., & White, L. (1987). Paradoxical effects of thought suppression. *Journal of Personality and Social Psychology, 53*, 5–13.

Weiner, B., & Graham, S. (1999). Attribution in personality psychology. In L. A. Pervin & O. P. John (Eds.), *Handbook of personality: Theory and research* (2nd ed., pp. 605–628). New York: Guilford.

Weinfield, N. S., Sroufe, L. A., Egeland, B., & Carlson, E. A. (1999). The nature of individual differences in infant–caregiver attachment. In J. Cassidy & P. R. Shaver (Eds.), *Handbook of attachment: Theory, research, and clinical applications* (pp. 68–88). New York: Guilford.

Weiss, J., & Sampson, H. (1986). *The psychoanalytic process: Theory, clinical observation, and empirical research.* New York: Guilford.

Weiss, R. S. (1973). *Loneliness: The experience of emotional and social isolation.* Cambridge, MA: MIT Press.

Weiss, R. S. (1975). *Marital separation: Coping with the end of a marriage and the transition to being single again.* New York: Basic Books.

Weiss, R. S. (1982). Attachment in adult life. In C. M. Parkes & J. Stevenson-Hinde (Eds.), *The place of attachment in human behavior* (pp. 171–184). New York: Basic Books.

Weiss, R. S. (1991). The attachment bond in childhood and adulthood. In C. M. Parkes, P. Marris, & J. Stevenson-Hinde (Eds.), *Attachment across the life cycle* (pp. 66–76). London: Routledge.

Weissman, A. (2000). Dysfunctional attitude scale (DAS). In K. Corcoran & J. Fischer (Eds.), *Measures for clinical practice: A sourcebook* (vol. 2, 3rd ed.; pp. 263–266). New York: Free Press.

Wenzlaff, R. M., & Beevers, C. G. (1998). Depression and interpersonal responses to others' moods: The solicitation of negative information about happy people. *Personality and Social Psychology Bulletin, 24,* 386–398.

West, D. J., & Farrington, D. P. (1977). *The delinquent way of life: Third report of the Cambridge study in delinquent development.* London: Heinemann Educational Books.

West, M., Keller, A., Links, P., & Patrick, J. (1993). Borderline disorder and attachment pathology. *Canadian Journal of Psychiatry, 38,* 1–6.

Westen, D. (1991). Cognitive–behavioral interventions in the psychoanalytic psychotherapy of borderline personality disorders. *Clinical Psychology Review, 11,* 211–230.

Whiffen, V. E., & Sasseville, T. M. (1991). Dependency, self-criticism, and recollections of parenting: Sex differences and the role of depressive affect. *Journal of Social and Clinical Psychology, 10,* 121–133.

Whitlock, F. A. (1967). The etiology of hysteria. *Acta Psychiatrica Scandinavica, 43,* 144–162.

Widiger, T. A. (1989). The categorical distinction between personality and affective disorders. *Journal of Personality Disorders, 3,* 77–91.

Widiger, T. A., Sanderson, C., & Warner, L. (1986). The MMPI, prototypal typology, and borderline personality disorder. *Journal of Personality Assessment, 50,* 540–553.

Wiggins, J. S. (1979). A psychological taxonomy of trait-descriptive terms: The interpersonal domain. *Journal of Personality and Social Psychology, 37,* 395–412.

Wiggins, J. S. (1982). Circumplex models of interpersonal behavior in clinical psychology. In P. C. Kendall & J. N. Butcher (Eds.), *Handbook of research methods in clinical psychology* (pp. 183–221). New York: Wiley.

Wiggins, J. S., & Trobst, K. K. (1997). When is a circumplex an "interpersonal circumplex"? The case of supportive actions. In R. Plutchik & H. R. Conte (Eds.), *Circumplex models of personality and emotions* (pp. 57–80). Washington, DC: American Psychological Association.

Wild, C. M., Shapiro, L. N., & Goldenberg, L. (1975). Transactional communication disturbances in families of male schizophrenics. *Family Process, 14,* 131–160.

Wilkinson-Ryan, T., & Westen, D. (2000). Identity disturbance in borderline personality disorder: An empirical investigation. *American Journal of Psychiatry, 157,* 528–541.

Williams, A. W., Ware, J. E., Jr., & Donald, C. A. (1981). A model of mental health life events and social supports applicable to general populations. *Journal of Health and Social Behavior, 22,* 324–336.

Williams, T. (1947). *A streetcar named desire.* New York: New American Library.

Williamson, S., Harpur, T. J., & Hare, R. D. (1991). Abnormal processing of affective words by psychopaths. *Psychophysiology, 28,* 260–273.

Wilson, G. T., & Fairburn, C. G. (1998). Treatment for eating disorders. In P. E. Nathan & J. M. Gorman (Eds.), *A guide to treatments that work* (pp. 501–530). New York: Oxford University Press.

Winer, D. L., Bonner, T. O., Blaney, P. H., & Murray, E. J. (1981). Depression and social attraction. *Motivation and Emotion, 5,* 153–166.

Winston, B., Winston, A., Samstag, L. W., & Muran, J. C. (1994). Patient defense/therapist interventions. *Psychotherapy, 31,* 478–491.

Wiseman, H., Barber, J. P., Raz, A., Yam, I., Foltz, C., & Livne-Snir, S. (2002). Parental communication of Holocaust experiences and interpersonal patterns in offspring of Holocaust survivors. *International Journal of Behavioral Development, 26,* 371–381.

Wolfe, D. A. (1985). Child abusive parents: An empirical review and analysis. *Psychological Bulletin, 97,* 461–482.

Wolfe, R. N. (1993). A commonsense approach to personality measurement. In K. H. Craik, R. Hogan, & R. N. Wolfe (Eds.), *Fifty years of personality psychology* (pp. 269–290). New York: Plenum.

Wolpe, J. (1958). *Psychotherapy by reciprocal inhibition.* Stanford, CA: Stanford University Press.

Wood, N., & Cowan, H. (1995). The cocktail party phenomenon revisited: How frequent are attention shifts to one's name in an irrelevant auditory channel? *Journal of Experimental Psychology: Learning, Memory, and Cognition, 21,* 255–260.

Wynne, L. C. (1977). Schizophrenics and their families: Research on parental communication. In J. M. Tanner (Ed.), *Developments in psychiatric research* (pp. 254–286). London: Hodder and Stoughton.

Young, M., Benjamin, B., & Wallis, C. (1963). Mortality of widowers. *Lancet, 2,* 454–456.

Youngren, M. A., & Lewinsohn, P. M. (1980). The functional relation between depression and problematic interpersonal behavior. *Journal of Abnormal Psychology, 89,* 333–341.

Zanarini, M. C., & Frankenburg, F. R. (1997). Pathways to the development of borderline personality disorder. *Journal of Personality Disorders, 11,* 93–104.

Zubek, J. P., Bayer, L., & Shephard, J. M. (1969). Relative effects of prolonged social isolation and confinement: Behavioral and EEG changes. *Journal of Abnormal Psychology, 74,* 625–631.

Zuckerman, M. (1979). Attribution of success and failure revisited, or: The motivational bias is alive and well in attribution theory. *Journal of Personality, 47,* 245–287.

Zuroff, D. C., & Duncan, H. (1999). Self-criticism and conflict resolution in romantic couples. *Canadian Journal of Behavioural Science, 31*, 137–149.

Zuroff, D. C., & Mongrain, M. (1987). Dependency and self-criticism: Vulnerability factors for depressive affective states. *Journal of Abnormal Psychology, 96*, 14–22.

Author Index

Subject Index

About the Author

Leonard M. Horowitz, PhD, is professor of psychology at Stanford University. He received his PhD from the Johns Hopkins University, where he was a Woodrow Wilson Fellow and a Social Science Research Council Fellow. He was also a Fulbright Fellow at University College, University of London. He received his clinical training at the Mt. Zion Psychiatric Clinic as a Special Fellow of the National Institute of Mental Health and received a James McKeen Cattell Award in 1986–1987. He has been a panelist of the National Science Foundation and served on a number of ad hoc committees for the National Institute of Mental Health as well as on advisory boards of numerous journals. Together with Hans Strupp and Michael Lambert, he directed an American Psychological Association (APA) task force on creating a core battery of standardized tests for evaluating the outcome of psychotherapy. That work resulted in the book *Measuring Patient Changes in Mood, Anxiety, and Personality Disorders: Toward a Core Battery* (APA, 1997). His test, the *Inventory of Interpersonal Problems*, was published in 2000 by the Psychological Corporation. He was president of the Society for Psychotherapy Research from 1992 to 1993 and president of the Society for Interpersonal Theory and Research from 1999 to 2000.